The People's House

Governor's Mansions of Kentucky

THOMAS D. CLARK
AND
MARGARET A. LANE

THE UNIVERSITY PRESS OF KENTUCKY

Publication of this volume was made possible in part by a grant from the National Endowment for the Humanities.

 *kentucky*
humanities
council

Scholarly publisher for the Commonwealth,
serving Bellarmine University, Berea College, Centre
College of Kentucky, Eastern Kentucky University,
The Filson Historical Society, Georgetown College,
Kentucky Historical Society, Kentucky State University,
Morehead State University, Murray State University,
Northern Kentucky University, Transylvania University,
University of Kentucky, University of Louisville,
and Western Kentucky University.
All rights reserved.

Editorial and Sales Offices: The University Press of Kentucky
663 South Limestone Street, Lexington, Kentucky 40508–4008

06 05 04 03 02   5 4 3 2 1

Library of Congress Cataloging-in-Publication Data available
from the Library of Congress

ISBN 0-8131-2253-8

♾ This book is printed on acid-free paper meeting
the requirements of the American National Standard
for Permanence of Paper for Printed Library Materials.

Printed and bound in Hong Kong

*Facing page: The formal gardens in front of the mansion
feature red tulips. (FCS)*

Published in cooperation with
Kentucky Division of Historic Properties
and with the generous support
of the Historic Properties Endowment Fund

To Loretta Gilliam Clark

and

Fred D. Lane

Contents

Part I: The Palace

Part II: The New Mansion

Part III: A Symbol of Dignity

Preface

When the Kentucky General Assembly enacted legislation on December 21, 1795, requiring the governor, the auditor, the treasurer, and the secretary of state to live in Frankfort, it placed the responsibility of housing the governor with the commonwealth. The General Assembly's mandate led to construction from 1796 through 1798 of the state's first governor's residence at the corner of Clinton and High Streets. More than one hundred years later, a much-needed new governor's mansion was built atop the Kentucky River palisades. Always in proximity to the capitol, the executive mansion has ever served the dual capacity of domestic residence for governors and their families and quasi-political nerve center. As such, the role of the executive mansion in Kentucky's history and in the Kentucky political process has been cardinal. Rendering precise that role, however, is difficult. One can read the published histories of Kentucky, including my own, and be left oblivious to the fact that a governor's mansion has existed in Kentucky since 1798 and is said to be among the oldest in the nation.

Documentary sources relating to the history of the Kentucky governor's mansions are as scattered as dandelion seeds in the wind. The public archival agencies hold voluminous official records, but those dealing precisely with the mansions are enmeshed in scores of irrelevant files. Information for this volume was culled partly from treasurers' and auditors' reports, the occasional public properties inventory, and minutes of committees related directly to the maintenance of the mansions. Periodically, governors included sections in their messages to the General Assembly describing the conditions of the residences. In turn, legislative committees biennially marched over to the governor's grounds to inspect the mansion and its outbuildings and returned to the legislative chambers to report needs. Occasionally a conscientious committee chairman reported on the most minor details in the house's structural status and the household furnishings.

Of course, to fully appreciate any house is to have an understanding of life inside its bricks and mortar. What are the accomplishments and failures of the people who have lived there? What influences have been exerted by those visiting the home? What ideas have been hatched inside its walls? What conversations have been whispered in its halls? Basically the governor's mansion is a family home. The arrival before its portal every four years of a new governor and his or her spouse and children marks the opening of an era of some degree of change. There has come a veritable kaleidoscopic mixture of gubernatorial and family personalities. In many respects, the houses have sheltered a microcosm of Kentucky domestic life. Children have been born; governors and their wives have died. Relatives have come for extended visits; weddings have been celebrated; and, on occasion, young couples have moved in to live with their parents. There have been fires and other tragedies, and even moments of tension with neighbors.

Of course, the governor's residence is not just another Kentucky domicile. The list of celebrated guests at the mansions includes presidents, writers, artists, foreign dignitaries, governors of other states, and an endless procession of national and Kentucky politicians. There have arrived at the mansions' doors outriders bearing news of pending military engagements, defeats, the commission of crimes, and the results of elections. Depending upon the inclinations of governors and their wives, there have been teas, levees, dinners, receptions, and balls. How much "political arm twisting" has occurred out of view and earshot of political opponents or a prying public press? How many times have the gubernatorial pillows been wallowed flat in anxiety over the demands of the office? Major decisions involving Kentucky troops in war, the overheated Old Court–New Court fiasco of the 1820s, the chronic problem of raising enough revenue to operate a state government on the slenderest budget possible, and other unrelenting issues have taken up residence in the mansions.

Few recorded sources give an intimate insight into life in the mansions or into the gubernatorial families' participation in Frankfort society. Although the governor's office was located in the governor's residence for three-quarters of a century, even executive journals of the governors contain little more than brief glimpses of state-related affairs in the mansions. Moreover, most of the earlier governors took away their collected papers when they left office. Kentucky newspaper files contain occasional golden grains of information, but usually reporters paid little attention to the governor's residence and its daily affairs. They seemed, rightly perhaps, to have regarded it as a private family home and pointed most of their stories away from its direction.

The lack of written records surely stems, at least partially, from the historically informal attitude toward the mansions. In true Jeffersonian democratic tradition, the governor's residence always has been regarded as "the people's house," and, in fact, some governors emphasized this status. From the outset, the people of Frankfort and the rest of the state have seemed to regard the mansion as just another hospitable and neighborly home where they can visit without observing much formality or gubernatorial protocol. Until more recent decades, there were no security guards. Visitors were met at the door by a butler or a member of the governor's family and invited in or turned away. Over the years there appeared before the door of the mansion political, military, and other seekers of commissions or gubernatorial favors. Today, the formal first floor lies largely within the public domain and, under some guidelines, is open to special assemblies and programs. Of late years it has become a center for historical, official, and cultural gatherings.

Obviously the houses in which nearly sixty Kentucky governors and their families have lived generate curiosity. This book undoubtedly will answer many often-asked questions and provoke many new ones. It is a web of information about the stages in the evolution of the executive mansions, the governors themselves—their personalities and the overall tenor of each one's administration, gubernatorial families, history, and politics. The locating and examining of the diffuse collection of materials pertaining to this ostensibly family institution is at once a tedious and arduous task. Where possible, the text is documented in order to give factual substantiation to the history of the two mansions. As would be the case with the history of any home, however, the history of Kentucky's governor's mansions must be an extrapolation of documented facts, first-hand accounts, educated guesswork, legend, and lore.

Acknowledgments

The documentary sources relating to the history of the Kentucky governor's mansions are almost as diffuse as the straws in a haystack. The public archival agencies hold voluminous official records, but those dealing precisely with the mansions are enmeshed in scores of almost irrelevant files.

It all but defies belief that no governor, governor's wife, or members of their families are known to have kept private journals, personal diaries, or packets of informative letters describing day-to-day life in the governor's mansions. There was one exception. Stephen Collins, son of Governor Martha Layne Collins, gathered historical information involving the two houses.

Unfortunately, most of the earlier governors took away from their office their collected papers. Those left behind give ample evidence they were left as innocuous. There are still miscellaneous collections of papers that have not as yet been classified. There are treasurer's and auditor's reports, and occasionally public properties inventories. For an official and detailed history of the conception and construction of the new mansion in this instance, the minutes of the Sinking Fund Committee are indispensable.

Kentucky newspaper files contain occasional golden grains of information, but usually reporters paid little attention to the governor's mansion. They seemed, rightly perhaps, to have regarded it as a private family home and pointed most of their stories away from that direction.

Some published secondary materials, much of them falling into the fugitive category, contain references to the governor's mansion. Most of this material, however, is tinctured with a dreamy-eyed conception of an imperial governorship housed in a Scottish mountainside castle. Only one of Kentucky's fifty-six governors

seems to have become entangled in the hedgerow of authorship. Wallace Glenn Wilkinson published a post-administrative book almost immediately after leaving office. Many parts of this book, detailing personal and official history, seem to be a hedge against history and his public detractors.

As a normal matter of fact the use of archival sources invokes the generous assistance of many people. Due to the very nebulosity of personal and public documentary sources, the authors have laid themselves under deep indebtedness to many generously obliging persons and institutions. None could have been more helpful than the members of the Kentucky Department for Libraries and Archives staff. Richard Belding, Barbara Teague, Diana Moses, Tim Tingle, Bill Richardson, Mark Stone, James Prichard, and Rick Arterburn of the Archives Records Management staff were most efficient in finding sources in the mountainous file of public records. Kandie Adkinson, curator of Public Lands and Official Papers Division of the Secretary of State's Office, went well beyond the call of duty in making available documents from the more recent gubernatorial journals.

No one could or should attempt to write comprehensively about Kentucky without enlisting the services of Claire McCann of the Special Collections department in the Margaret I. King Library at the University of Kentucky. This holds true for William J. Marshall, Terry Warth, James Birchfield, Frank Stanger, Jeff Suchanek, and Terry Birdwhistell. Bryan Houck of the Micrographics Division of the William T. Young Library was generous in rendering technological service.

J. Kevin Graffagnino, Melba Hay, Mary Winter, Nathan Prichard, Charlene Smith and the Research and Publications staff at the Kentucky Historical Society provided expert assistance and made available the Society's rich documentary and library collections. The Kentucky Oral History Commission and Kim Smith also rendered valuable support. Obviously the production of a history of two important Kentucky public properties would necessitate the support and cooperation of the Historic Properties Advisory Commission and the Division of Historic Properties.

We are honored to have James Archambeault's artistry gracing the cover of this volume. Gary Robinson and his staff of expert photographers at the Finance Cabinet's Division of Photography provided monumental assistance in locating and reproducing historic and modern photographs, including the official governors' portraits. The original portraits can be viewed at the Kentucky History Center's Hall of Governors. The modern photography on these pages can be attributed to Steve Mitchell and John Perkins, unless otherwise noted.

Both Margaret Lane and I are indebted to Professors James C. Klotter, Lowell Harrison, and Wade Hall, who read the manuscript and made invaluable suggestions to improve its quality. Too, Professor Tom Appleton kept a watchful eye out for obscure bits of information pertaining to the mansions and their peripatetic tenants. Jo Fisher of Midway also contributed valuable assistance to the project. We were honored in 2000 as this project joined a select group of national projects receiving America's Treasures designation by the White House Millennium Council.

Margaret Lane, co-author, had spent twelve years in executive mansion administration and served as Executive Director in the both the old and new mansions. She conceived the idea of producing as objective a history of the two houses as possible, and something of the lives of the people who occupied them in four-year intervals. With this background experience she had the insight to conduct revealing oral interviews not only with living former governors and their wives but with individuals who had direct association with the operation of the governor's mansions, those who advised, served, and protected the chief executives. She made diligent searches for both major sources and the fugitive ones. In addition, she performed the nagging task of keying drafts of the manuscript text into the computer.

Jointly we have incurred heavy indebtedness to a relatively large number of individuals and institutions.

We are indebted to Helen Evans, Director of the old governor's mansion during Julian Carroll's administration, for her foresight in compiling a notebook of old mansion history, and to the Kentucky Division of Historic Properties for preserving that history. At the outset, Edward Breathitt, Libby Jones, Peggy Silhanek, Barbara Hulette, Martha Gregory, Charles Stewart, and Philip Ardery rendered diligent and helpful yeoman service in support of the project.

We offer special appreciation to Virginia Smith and the Kentucky Humanities Council, who stepped up early in this project and offered enthusiastic support and their services of fiscal management. We are deeply obligated to Martin Schmidt, Nana Lampton, and John Speed of Louisville; C. Michael Davenport of Frankfort; Joe and Anne Duncan; Lucille Little, James Gray, and the Lexington Newcomers Club for appreciable financial support. The Kentucky Historic Properties Endowment Fund provided major support for the publication process.

No one has been more directly involved in the production of this book than Loretta Gilliam Clark, an author in her own right. With a keen eye for form and style, she offered many constructive suggestions. Indeed, Fred D. Lane has also been deeply involved, and generous and co-operative, tolerating the inevitable disruptions caused by the research, writing, and publication of a book of this nature.

Finally I, Tom Clark, and I alone, must accept full responsibility for the writing, interpretations, and historical quality of the text. In the text I have made a serious effort to be as objective as possible in dealing with such a complex human history where individuals have been so fully exposed to public view. From beginning to end I have skated along the all but invisible line that separates each governor's domestic life in the public mansion from his or her official role as the chief administrative officer of the commonwealth.

The history of the house cannot be treated separately from the fortunes of the commonwealth itself, as the governors and their families nearly always reflected the flow of the political and social history of the times. This is not a history of Kentucky, yet the history of the governor's mansions has been inextricably interwoven with that of the everyday commonwealth for over two hundred years.

Thomas D. Clark

PART I

The Palace

CHAPTER 1

A Good and Convenient Dwelling House

D uring the exhilarating and frenzied days, weeks, and months when the people of Kentucky engaged in the steps necessary to make their home a state, the thought of where the governor might live weighed heavily on no one's mind. While the process of separating from Virginia and entering statehood required nearly a decade of interminable discussion, heated debate about whether or not to remain in the Union at all, interruptions to fight Indians, and exasperating bureaucracy, a state constitution was written in a mere thirteen days. Six weeks later, voters had chosen electors who, in turn, had named a governor and eleven state senators; Kentucky officially had become the fifteenth state; the governor had been inaugurated; and the legislature had convened. Two weeks passed, and, in one day, a complicated procedure produced the committee that would select the state capital. Committee members set about examining and reviewing sites, and, during the next meeting of the legislature, they announced their choice. The succeeding legislative session was held in Frankfort, Kentucky's new, if tenuous, seat of government. It was a whirlwind of profound constitutional and public responsibilities, with little respect given to the polite notion of comfortably sheltering the new governor and his family.

Ultimately, of course, establishing a home for Kentucky's chief executives began with the aforementioned process of designating a seat of government for the newly formed state. The formation of state government in Kentucky, including tapping the site from which that government would be administered, had a decided aura of romance. In the concluding session of the ten Danville conventions—the series of conventions held to discuss Kentucky's separation from

Governor Isaac Shelby, 1792–1796. (Kentucky Historical Society [KHS])

Virginia and admission into the Union as a state—the committee that drafted Kentucky's first constitution revealed an awareness of the sectional sensitivities of the people. Section X of the 1792 constitution prescribed an intricate mode of selecting an acceptable committee to locate the governmental seat.[1] In 1792,

A drawing of the 1792 inauguration of Governor Shelby in Lexington. (From Elizabeth Shelby Kinkead's *A History of Kentucky*, 1913)

the Kentucky River virtually formed a political rift line between the populations north and south of its banks. Whichever section gained the permanent seat of government stood to gain economic, political, social, and cultural advantages, and, more especially, the exercise of political power. The formula outlined in Section X of the constitution mandated that a pool of twenty-one names of individuals, divided between the two sections (except for one name), be chosen. Then representatives from Fayette County, north of the river, and Mercer County, south of the river, would strike names alternately until only five were left. The five remaining persons constituted a Site Selection Committee with rather broad powers of decision. The five commissioners thus chosen were Robert Todd of Fayette County, Thomas Kennedy of Madison, Henry Lee of Mason,

and John Allen and John Edwards of the future Franklin area (then Bourbon County).[2]

Almost by foreordination, Isaac Shelby (1750–1826)— hero of the Revolutionary War conflict at King's Mountain, defender of the Kentucky frontier, and chairman of major statehood convention committees— was to be made Kentucky's first governor. By conscientious doubt or feigned modesty, Shelby expressed a fear of his capabilities in assuming the office of governor. Nevertheless, he received the election committee and accepted their offer with good grace.[3] On June 3, 1792, Shelby mounted a favorite horse and bade good-bye to his wife, Susannah, who was on the verge of giving birth to their eleventh child. He departed Traveler's Rest, his dignified stone home in Lincoln County, and set forth to Lexington by way of Danville. Shelby was warmly welcomed in Danville, scene of the statehood conventions, and was accompanied partway to Lexington by an honor guard. On the morning of June 4, the governor-elect reached the Fayette County boundary, where he was greeted by the county lieutenant and a company of militiamen who escorted him in triumphant entry to Lexington.[4]

Assembled in a log building, perhaps the public market house, near the corner of Main Street and Broadway, the governor-elect took the oath of office.[5] There was a highly sobering aspect to Isaac Shelby's gubernatorial inauguration. Kentuckians, after all, were in the process of conceiving a state government. Hubbard Taylor, a shrewd political observer, wrote to his cousin James Madison about the occasion, saying, "I must confess I feel some uneasiness on this head . . . not so much on account of a disposition not contrary to the interest of the community, as for the real capacity to do so in a regular, proper & equitable manner." This statement no doubt was tinged with a bit of cynicism, but many ominous issues confronted Governor Shelby and the unskilled legislators on June 4.[6]

Three days following his inauguration, Isaac Shelby, being guided by Washingtonian protocol, met with legislators on the upper floor of the same log house. He was ceremonially escorted to a seat to the right of the president of the senate. Assembled were eleven senators and forty representatives. In his brief address, the governor uttered a few pleasant greetings and then got down to the business of commencing the governing process. He told the legislators that they should immediately nominate two United States senators, look to the speedy administration of justice, create a legal procedure for adjudicating land disputes and counter claims, and hasten the location of a permanent seat of government. Responding to the governor, Robert Breckinridge, speaker of the House of Representatives, gave assurance that the admonitions would be promptly heeded. Breckinridge said, "Early and particularly attended to, we feel sensibly the force that they ought to have on those whose only object will be the prosperity of the state."[7] Thus finished with his official duties, Isaac Shelby again mounted his horse and rode away to Traveler's Rest, possibly to greet a new addition to his family. The domestic way of life at Traveler's Rest was no doubt an active and full experience of proper rural-agrarian adequacy for Isaac and Susannah Hart Shelby. The legislators saw no immediate need for a governor's domicile.[8]

The Site Selection Committee responded promptly to Governor Shelby's plea for haste. They commenced their inspection of possible capital sites on August 4, 1792, and visited Lexington, DeLaney's Ferry, Lees Town, Ledgerwood Bend, Danville, Petersburg, and Louisville at the Falls of the Ohio.[9] After a final meeting at the Love and Brent's Tavern in Lexington, the committee submitted a report on December 5 that they had chosen Frankfort "as the most proper place for the seat of Government."[10] A group of prominent Frankfort residents, which included wealthy businessman Andrew Holmes and Federal District Judge Harry Innes, had made a citizens' proposal in behalf of the tiny flatboat landing village on the Kentucky River. For the times, the Frankfort bid was exceedingly generous. The village promoters promised the use of a house owned by Holmes, eight lots of public grounds along with the cession of fifty more acres of land if needed, use of a warehouse rent free for seven years, ten boxes of ten-by-twelve-inch window glass panes, fifteen hundred pounds of nails, $166 worth of locks and hinges, fifteen hundred perches of stone, the use of a sawmill, a carriage and wagon along with two horses, and the privilege of cutting logs in James Wilkinson's woods. In addition to these substantial enticements, Judge Innes, Nat Sanders, Bennet Pemberton, Benjamin Craig, Jere Craig, William Hayden, Daniel James, and Giles Samuel subscribed $3,000 to be paid in silver or gold, guaranteed, in the form of a promissory note.[11]

Aside from the land and materials listed as contributions by the citizens of tiny Frankfort, additional and perhaps greater compelling reasons for locating the state capital on the banks of the Kentucky River existed, in spite of the fact that the area was directly within the flood plain. By 1792, the growing of field crops and raising of livestock in central Kentucky was impressive, and Frankfort was strategically located adjacent to a considerable area of highly fertile Elkhorn inner bluegrass farmland just then coming into a profitable state of production. Frankfort also was an important staging place on the Kentucky River, which was floating a large volume of agricultural products downstream to the faraway market in Spanish-held New Orleans. Revealing a sensitivity to the prevailing sectional tensions, Humphrey Marshall, a contemporary viewer of the Kentucky scene, wrote, "The situation of Frankfort, immediately on the northward bank of the river, which separated the parties; in a bottom, common to both—if the expression may be allowed—but largest, on the south side, whence in time the town might be extended; should have silenced, if anything could all opposition,

Reported to be Kentucky's first governor's mansion, this house opposite the Capitol Hotel was rented for the governors before 1798. (*Louisville Courier-Journal*, KHS)

and complaint."[12] What Humphrey Marshall called the "bottom" was a sloping plain, east and west of the Kentucky River, wide enough to permit future expansion of Kentucky's public governmental buildings alongside an expanding commercial area.[13]

Whether or not all opposition and complaint was silenced, the Site Selection Committee had concluded its task, and the Kentucky General Assembly held its first session of 1793 "in the house of Andrew Holmes, at Frankfort on the Kentucky River." During the first four years of Kentucky's elevation to statehood, however, its constitutional officials did not remain constantly in Frankfort. The state's first permanent capitol was constructed in 1793–1794, and Weisiger's Tavern, the town social and bedroom center, was said to have housed at times from 1792 to 1800 the entire legislative body in a large common room. Governor Shelby, who stayed possibly in a rented log house by the Kentucky River when his presence was required in Frankfort, was involved immediately in dealing with a

multiplicity of diplomatic, military, and domestic problems which arose in Kentucky and the western country. It is doubtful that any other Kentucky governor has had a more direct association with a president of the United States than Isaac Shelby had with George Washington.[14] There were the complex issues of protection of the frontier against British-Indian threats, negotiations to open the Mississippi River to free access, the so-called French Conspiracy, the failures of Generals Josiah Harmar and Arthur St. Clair in their campaigns against the Miami Indian villages, the raising of revenue to finance the state government, and the opening of a wagon road from the Kentucky River to the Cumberland Gap. Too, there was the state political charge of setting in motion the various divisions of state government. Some of the old problems of reconciling the differences between the state and national governments, and between Kentucky and Virginia, lingered as well. In somewhat reduced fashion, Isaac Shelby exercised a similar patience in dealing with

Governor James Garrard, 1796–1804. (KHS)

public affairs as did George Washington with national ones. For his patient services Shelby received an annual salary of 500 pounds, or approximately $1,900, not enough in low late-eighteenth-century prices to sustain a wife and eleven children, to say nothing of an executive mansion in frontier Frankfort.[15]

In spite of the fact that all the states in existence prior to 1792, with the exception of Vermont, furnished some kind of governor abode, the Kentucky General Assembly first indicated an awareness of the domestic needs of the governor on December 21, 1795—three-and-a-half years into Isaac Shelby's four-year term. When on that day it enacted legislation requiring the governor, the auditor, the treasurer, and the secretary of state to reside in Frankfort,[16] it placed the responsibility of housing the governor with the commonwealth. The act required the commissioners of public buildings to rent a suitable house and garden for five years and then to buy or build an executive man-

sion. The parsimonious lawmakers appropriated 100 pounds to finance the rent.[17] In 1796, a house owned by Major James Love was rented for the incoming governor, James Garrard (1749–1822), and his numerous brood. Neither a description of the house and grounds nor its exact address is available.[18] It is said to have been located across the street from a lot that in later years was occupied by the Capitol Hotel.[19]

James Garrard was a man of many aspects. He was a native of Stafford County, Virginia, and had fought with the Virginia militia in the American Revolution, rising to the rank of colonel. After moving to the District of Kentucky, he served in five of the separation conventions and helped prepare the constitution. A Jeffersonian Republican and a Baptist minister in the frontier tradition of that faith, Garrard had the proper political credentials.[20] However, his 1796 gubernatorial election was the first—but not the last—to require two rounds of voting. In the first round the electors gave Benjamin Logan a plurality, but, due to a lack of constitutional specificity as to whether a plurality or a majority was required, electors chose to take a second vote on the top two candidates. Garrard won round two.

Both James Garrard and his wife, Elizabeth Mountjoy Garrard, had a Virginian sense of society and ceremony, if not of pomp. It was said that James brought Elizabeth across the mountains in far greater comfort than had been the common lot of most immigrant women.[21] The way of life at the Garrards' Bourbon County homestead, Lebanon, may well have had its great moments of family enjoyment and comfort. Certainly the prospect for social refinement was brighter there than seemed possible in the physical surroundings in Frankfort in 1796. When the governor and his family descended into Frankfort—in their carriage drawn by four black horses, a somewhat sharp departure from simple backwoods Jeffersonian style and the usual mode of travel—the town was just beginning to grow up to its status as the capital of the commonwealth. In his crusty style, Humphrey Marshall wrote, "anybody who can find Frankfort, can find where the governor lives." This facetious remark by the old Federalist curmudgeon sharply contrasted his earlier commendation of the Site Selection Committee's choice of the place for the capitol.[22] A reminiscent article in an 1873 edition of the *Frankfort Tri-Weekly Yeoman* noted that in 1800 "every house in the town [was] of wood—mostly of hewed or unhewed logs—excepting only the State House and Weisiger's Tavern, which were of stone." Moreover, not a foot of street pavement existed in the town. Rains left the streets quagmires. On one occasion, legislators held a ball in the statehouse preceded by a dinner in Weisiger's Tavern. Such a heavy rain fell that legislators formed two-by-two human sedans and transported the ladies across the mud and water to the capitol door.[23]

In their experience of locating a house for rent that would be large enough to accommodate Governor Garrard and his numerous family members, the commissioners of public buildings concluded that it would be cheaper to build a governor's residence than to continue to rent one for five years. In 1796, a bill to that effect was introduced in the General Assembly.[24] Legislators responded favorably. On December 4, 1796, the General Assembly appropriated 1,200 pounds, with authorization to the commissioners, Bennet Pemberton, Daniel Weisiger, and William Trigg, to obtain "a good and convenient dwelling house, together with such necessary outhouses as will be sufficient for the accommodation of the governor."[25] They were further instructed to furnish the house with a sufficient number of chairs, tables, cupboards, and bedsteads; a commodious desk; a sideboard; a bookcase; and a chest of drawers. In addition, the legislators told the commissioners to plot a two-acre area to be enclosed behind a neat fence to be used as the gubernatorial vegetable garden. Governor Garrard signed the bill authorizing construction of the governor's palace, as it was called.[26]

The commissioners of public buildings took immediate action. From Thomas Todd, they purchased a lot bounded by Clinton, Ann, and High Streets upon which to construct the residence. One can only speculate on how much planning of the house occurred. Records are clear, however, that in 1798 a house was built. Another fact—this one fixed hard and fast in brick—is that the original governor's mansion, which today houses Kentucky's lieutenant governors, was too small and family oriented to be called a palace by either the whimsical humorist or the incurable romanticist. At the time that legislation regarding a governor's residence was passed, the thought was that the house would be of modest design and construction and in keeping with the conception of a plain democratic governorship rather than an imperial one. In plain words, it was to be on a level with a moderately imposing central Kentucky farm home but shy of the affluent Frankfort homes being built in the exclusive corner of land created by the curvature of the Kentucky River. Indeed, the structure is characteristic of the bastard Georgian style of houses prevalent on many early

Bluegrass farms and in the surrounding towns. The house is essentially four stories in height, including a basement and a cramped attic. The walls of the two main stories are perforated by a generous number of windows, and four chimneys thrust up on the ends of the building. The house's foundation was elevated above the Frankfort floodwater plain, and some pasturage for cows and horses along with a vegetable garden surrounded the residence.[27] A detached southern-style kitchen was connected to the house by a dogtrot or walkway. A legend persists that there was a tunnel leading out from the house, but this was not so. It was not until the last reconstruction of the sagging residence in the 1970s that a tunnel was dug to connect the kitchen with the mansion basement.[28] In simple analysis, the building symbolized a rising Kentucky agrarianism.

The construction of the governor's residence gave rise to an interesting bit of ironic history, if not pure legend. If the tales, which have been repeated often, have any basis in fact, then what surely must have been the most precocious bricklayer in North American history and an equally precocious stonemason were to become Kentucky governors. The tales assert that Robert P. Letcher laid brick in some of the palace walls while Thomas Metcalfe laid the building's stone foundation. During the construction of the residence, they would have been lads of ten and eighteen, respectively. In future years, each lived in the house as governor.[29]

Though the documentary records are clear as to the legal background and much of the construction history of the governor's residence, they do not reveal whether or not a portion of the building, the library, was specifically designed to be the governor's office. Three pieces of evidence, however, compellingly give that impression and make it impossible to ignore the significance of the mansion in Kentucky's political history. Embodied in the act pertaining to the governor's dwelling, almost as an afterthought, was a provision that the commissioners would furnish two tables for committee rooms. These tables were to be four feet wide and sixteen feet long and topped with green baize, and there was to be included a number of benches sufficient to seat twenty-four persons. The law is unclear in its intent, but this part of the act seems to imply that the governor's office was to be located in the residence and that legislative committees, at least, would hold sessions in the governor's executive quarters.[30] Furthermore, no rooms in the capitol building were assigned to the governor. The governor's mansion was built on the square east of the capitol, and the proximity, undoubtedly, was purposeful. Finally, the floor plan of the mansion clearly indicates the thought that the governor's palace would be a combination of residence, executive chambers, and center for local social intercourse. Thus, the already vague, thin lines between family domesticity and political activities inherent in any gubernatorial abode became invisible at times.

Stripped of legend and legalistic vacuities, indisputable facts relate to the numerous public issues facing the first occupant of the palace—issues enough to make the walls of the executive residence crackle with both excitement and concern. At the close of the eighteenth century, the commonwealth of Kentucky was still in a highly formative stage. Although most all the Indian aggression from the north was ended by the success of General Anthony Wayne's army at the battle of Fallen Timbers and the subsequent Treaty of Greenville, the Cherokees remained a threat to the south along the great emigrant road from the Cumberland Gap.[31] There was the rousing issue of the Alien and Sedition Acts that gave the president special power against foreign-born residents and those who attempted to incite resistance against the government—and the Kentucky Resolutions, which protested the Alien and Sedition Acts. Other issues which arose during Garrard's two terms as governor were the Louisiana Purchase and the opening of the Mississippi River to free trade, the creation of new counties, and the ever nagging land ownership disputes.[32]

One issue faced by the lately formed state government was not as lofty as the rights of foreign-born residents and provisions for economic growth but every bit as compelling. By no means were all eighteenth-century Kentuckians upright yeoman citizens who cherished the new constitution or the institutions it shielded. Certain free-spirited souls obeyed neither the laws of God nor the laws of man. The General Assembly acknowledged this fact on December 20, 1794, when it provided for the construction of a state penitentiary.[33] An appropriation of $333 was made, and the commissioners of public buildings were instructed to locate a site and begin construction. Judge Harry Innes contributed an acre of land across High Street from the gubernatorial residence, where a modest jailhouse was to be constructed and concealed behind a wall. Thus, during James Garrard's term, the palace acquired new neighbors. Governor Garrard could look across the street from his library windows and note the progress of the builders, a fact he reported to the legislature, saying that "the penitentiary house is in considerable forwardness."[34] The house was in enough of a state of "forwardness" in September 1800 to receive its first guest. John Turner of Madison County was to achieve a modest footnote in Kentucky history by being the first prisoner consigned to the penitentiary. Judge John Coburn of the Fayette County district circuit court sentenced Turner to a two-year term in the new jail for horse stealing. The judge ordered that Turner would subsist on a coarse diet and spend a twentieth of his time in solitary confinement. The last condition was not difficult to administer since Turner, for a time, was the lone prisoner.[35]

Throughout his incumbency, James Garrard took to heart the declaration in the constitution that the governor represented the supreme power of the commonwealth. As a prosperous Bourbon County farmer, Garrard was keenly attuned to the economic realities of the times. He operated a mill and still, owned slaves, and dealt in land transfers. For his times, Garrard was the agrarian businessman in politics. He was to prove himself quite capable of nudging a laggard General Assembly into action, as revealed in his messages and the acts and journals of the General Assembly.[36]

The details of how well the Garrard family made the transition from its Bourbon County landed barony to the "town of wood" are skimpy. The architectural style of the palace and its surrounding setting of conventional farm buildings, some pasturage, and even a place to grow Elizabeth's herbs would not have been wholly unlike that of the Garrard home back in Paris.[37] However, the governor, despite his Baptist ministry, exhibited a degree of Adamesque pomposity rather than a plainer form of Jeffersonian backwoods republicanism.[38] He was listed in the tax rolls as possessing six slaves, several horses, two carriages, and at least one wagon; in fact, his wagon was the only one of record in the capital.[39] Elizabeth, too, made her presence felt. Back at Mt. Lebanon, Elizabeth had gathered herbs and ground and compounded them into folk pharmaceuticals. It was said that she operated a miniature still, which sat on a mantel, for the distillation of alcohol to be used in the concoction of her folk remedies. She continued the practice in the mansion.

The social and economic worlds of Kentucky when James and Elizabeth Garrard drove down the long slope into Frankfort and later moved their belongings and their family into the newly constructed governor's palace were rapidly emerging ones in which the gover-

Com'r Governors house

1797	To the Treasury for Warrant N°			
Jan'y 21	ued to James Black as p° Journ	154	75	0	0
"	Ditto Tho. Todd Ditto	"	50	0	0
Feb'y 2	Ditto G. Letcher Ditto	"	120	0	0
5	Ditto Harry Innis Ditto	155	150	0	0
"	Ditto P. G. Voorhies Ditto	"	12	1	3
"	Ditto C. Cammock Ditto	"	53	0	8
22	Ditto P. G. Voorhies Ditto	159	18	0	0
May 16	Ditto Rouck and Anderson	166	113	19	4
Aug 25	Ditto Letcher and Voorhies	171	124	10	0
Sept 15	Ditto W. Trigg	173	50	0	0
28	Ditto P. G. Voorhies	174	17	0	0
"	Ditto C. Cammock	174	18	0	0
Oct 19	Ditto E. Craig	177	3	13	4
Nov 23	Ditto Christopher Cammock	179	19	4	5
"	Ditto Will Trigg	180	3	0	0
Dec 3	Christopher Cammock	184	16	2	3
7	Com'r Krieger and Trigg	186	18	0	0
16	Letcher and Riddle	188	126	0	0
			988	9	3
	1798				
Jan'y 23	Ditto Peter G. Voorhies	202	1	10	0
Feb'y 6	Ditto Ja. Adams	205	6	0	0
10	Ditto Christopher Cammock	208	12	0	0
13	Ditto Peter G. Voorhies	213	1	8	6
21	Ditto C. Cammock & others	214	165	5	11
	Carried back to F. 78.				

The auditor of public accounts' general ledger no. 1, 1793–1798, showing expenses of building the old governor's mansion. (Kentucky Department for Libraries and Archives [KDLA])

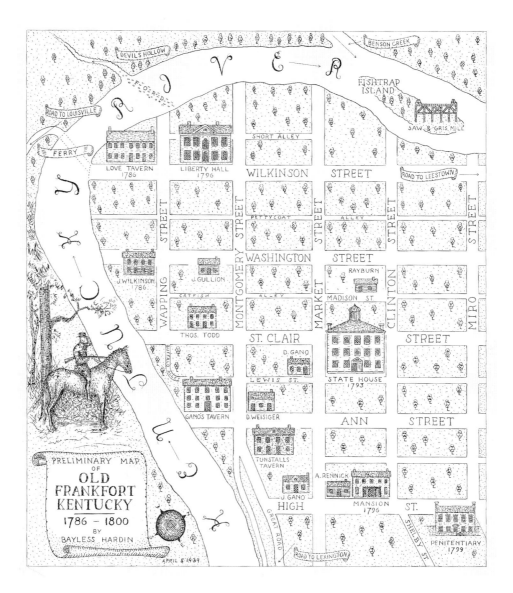

A preliminary map of old Frankfort, 1786–1800, drawn by Bayless Hardin in 1939.
(KHS)

nor had golden opportunities to set several official and social precedents.[40] Contemporary Frankfort was not exactly a metropolitan center where the arts and manners of high society flourished. Outside the pale of politics and everyday Kentucky domesticity, the Garrards created several sensations among local social circles.

As a minor example of the Garrards' impact on Frankfort society, the amusing history of pianos and carpets causing commotions in the governor's mansion began with the home's first occupants. In 1799 or 1800, the governor commissioned local craftsman John Goodman to build a piano to be used by one of the Garrard daughters. Decades later, Kentucky-born drama critic John Mason Brown noted that John Goodman's instrument set a precedent in the state's cultural history: "Until this day there was not in the Commonwealth a musical instrument less portable than the wicked violin or the pocket flute. . . . and its first exhibition was an event in the town."[41] Indeed, a guest attending a Christmas levee in the palace commented that "Miss Garrard's forte-piano, made here by Mr. Goodman, is now at home, and is as pretty a piece of furniture as I ever saw. I think it will be well toned when it is better seasoned. The tones are now sweet but weak. It cost two hundred dollars."[42] The Garrards created an even greater sensation when they carpeted the palace floors.

People, it was said, flocked into the house to inspect this unheard of wonder. A contemporary observer called the floor covering "the envy and pride of the community."[43]

Overall, the nation and Kentucky enjoyed a distinct vibrancy during the era of James Garrard. Dispensing a kind of Virginia–Bourbon County hospitality, the Garrards held an annual levee, the first in Frankfort. Guests came to listen to the sweet but weak tones of the forte-piano, to trample the carpets, and to feast.[44] The guest who critiqued Goodman's piano also described the celebration dinner that took place at the Christmas levee: "We had a good substantial dinner at the Governor's—two large turkeys, two pieces of beef of about twenty-five pounds each, and bacon and ducks. The dessert was tolerable, but being placed on the table, by the direction of his excellency, it was not disposed to the greater advantage. We had very fine peach wine of Mrs. Garrard's own make."[45] Farmer and agricultural lobbyist Robert Wilmot Scott later gave some sense of how a Frankfort levee compared with one in the Jacksonian White House. In his *Memoranda Itenris* he wrote, "I left the ball and reached home about one o'clock well tired and better satisfied that fashionable society was no where superior to that of Frankfort Ky., though it is true that the belles had more accomplishments, that is immodest airs and fancy millinery, about them in Washington than in Ky. and what is more my suspicions were confirmed that the ladies of Washington were not the most pure in soul and chaste in deed of all the Fair which I had seen. P.S. several of the most fashionable young ladies wore short dresses and pantalets."[46] Pantalets were not worn in Frankfort.

When the Garrard family packed up and went home to their estate in Paris in 1804, they left behind a mansion which had been well lived in—a centerpiece home in the Frankfort community.[47] From 1798 to 1914, for thirty-five governors and their families, the house was both a residence and a veritable political center. Many of the governors and their wives even operated on-site miniature farms with horses, cows,

chickens, and sheep. There were stables, a carriage house, and a garden plot, and in at least one case the governor was permitted to graze his herd on the nearby capitol grounds. Only the concept of the palace made it a centerpiece, however; the structure itself did not deserve the designation. Three indelible facts are associated with the original governor's residence: it was hurriedly and cheaply constructed, it was meagerly and plainly furnished, and it was not spacious enough to house the numerous children of the early governors or to accommodate appreciable political and social gatherings. Even by late-eighteenth-century standards it lacked many of the amenities to make it a comfortable home. Moreover, almost from the moment James Garrard moved his family into the palace, it needed some kind of repairs.

Contributing to the mansion's constant state of distress was the possibility of removal of Kentucky's capital to a larger urban center—a threat that hovered over Frankfort for most of a century. After all, Frankfort was little more than a traditional and provincial small town. At the time it contained no college or university, no medical center, and no significant manufacturing industry except for that operated by the Kentucky penitentiary and an early sawmill on the Kentucky River. On a visit to the statehouse in 1807, Fortescue Cuming, an Irishman who wrote about his travels through Kentucky, climbed up into the cupola and counted "exactly" ninety houses. "The public buildings here," Cuming wrote, "are a statehouse, a courthouse, a jail, a market house, the state penitentiary, and government house. . . ."[48] An abundance of the news published in the local newspapers was generated solely by politics and state government. The General Assembly used the uncertainty of the permanency of the capital location to underfund the maintenance and renovation of public buildings. Paltry amounts of money continuously thrown at the mansion were never sufficient to solve the home's indigenous problems and produce long-lasting results. Nearly from day one, then, Kentucky's beloved governor's palace was rarely in fully livable condition and was often unsafe for occupancy.

CHAPTER 2

Sheltering Kentucky's Warrior Governors

During the first quarter of the nineteenth century, years that encompassed lingering British-Indian threats on the western frontier and then the War of 1812, Kentucky voters favored gubernatorial candidates who possessed significant military backgrounds. For most of this time, the condition of Kentucky's governor's residence was eclipsed by oppressive events and controversies that faced the young commonwealth. Over and again, the General Assembly enacted legislation designed to make the governor's palace a structure of "decent appearance" that provided "comfort and conveniency" to the families it harbored, yet the body never allowed adequate appropriations with which to do so. With each administration of the early 1800s, the commonwealth of Kentucky confronted new challenges as the governor's mansion fell further into disrepair.

Virginian Christopher Greenup (1750–1818) served as Kentucky's governor from 1804 to 1808. Before his election, Greenup had seen service with the Virginia militia in the American Revolution and on the Indian frontier and had served two terms in the United States Congress after 1792.[1] Christopher Greenup and his wife, Mary Catherine Pope Greenup, came to the palace with less fanfare than their predecessors, the Garrards—an indicator, perhaps, of distinct differences in life styles and in the turns of gubernatorial minds. Irish traveler Fortescue Cuming, who met Kentucky's third governor during his visit in 1807, later wrote, "[Governor Greenup] saluted us with much familiarity. He is a plain, respectable looking elderly man, much esteemed throughout the state."[2] Christopher Greenup was a meticulous executive who examined the record of every person put forward for public office. One can imagine him sitting day after day in the library-office of the governor's house interviewing candidates for public

Governor Christopher Greenup, 1804–1808. (KHS)

jobs or examining plans for a state bank or contemplating the restoration of Judge George Muter's pension, which a penurious legislature had disallowed. One wonders: did he take time out on June 16, 1806, to go out on Clinton Street to view the full eclipse of the sun?[3]

There was no lack of excitement in Frankfort during the Greenup years, for, whether or not the executive couple held levees at the mansion, a nearly constant round of social affairs transpired in the town's four taverns.[4] Two such affairs centered on the acquittal of Aaron Burr, the former vice president of the United States who had been accused twice of ulterior political motives. Burr appeared in Kentucky apparently to enlist support for a separatist movement in the Louisiana area. The Frankfort editors of the *Argus of Western America*, Joseph Street and John Wood, stirred the issue to fever heat. When Burr finally was acquitted, he was honored with a banquet and ball held in a local tavern. The prosecuting attorney, Joseph Hamilton Daveiss, was honored at another one. No doubt Christopher and Mary Greenup attended the latter; the parlor of the palace was not opened to the ex-vice president.[5]

In the closing year of the Greenup administration, Mary died in the palace. Christopher Greenup was left to finish his term and to retire to his nearby Frankfort home alone. Every public house must acquire a ghost, and Mary Greenup apparently fulfilled this dictum at the palace. Folklore has it that Mary's ghost appeared either in the face of a clock or in a mirror, no doubt proper places for a ghost to stir imaginations about a historic home.

General Charles Scott (1739–1813) was a one-of-a-kind Kentuckian who balanced his life between being a military hero and a non-politician and found himself elected governor in 1808. When the general crossed through the Cumberland Gap in 1785 with his wife, Frances Sweeny Scott, and six of their seven children to lay claim to generous tracts of military bounty lands in Fayette and Bourbon Counties, he brought along an impressive record of military services. During the American Revolution, he was present at Valley Forge, Monmouth, Trenton, and Germantown. Late in the war he was taken a prisoner by the British at Charleston, South Carolina, but was later paroled to fight again.[6] The Scotts settled near the Kentucky River in present-day Woodford County; developed Petersburg, a petitioner in 1792 for the location of the seat of the Kentucky government; and began administering 21,035 acres of land claims. Locating Fayette and Bourbon Counties' land boundaries in 1785–1792 was almost as daunting as wintering at Valley Forge with George Washington's hard-pressed troops.[7]

Ever the soldier, General Scott had hardly built his home at Petersburg before President Washington appointed him, along with Isaac Shelby, Harry Innes, and John Brown, to be a member of the strategic special defense committee for the western country. For the immediate defense of the West, an army of volunteers

Governor Charles Scott, 1808–1812. (KHS)

was called into service to attack and destroy the Indian villages above the Ohio. General Scott was appointed to command this force. In time he became involved in the western campaigns on the Wabash and in the abortive ones of Harmar and St. Clair. The grand finale of General Scott's active field command career came at Fallen Timbers, when he led Kentucky volunteers in General Wayne's assault on the northwestern tribes.[8]

Fourteen years later, General Scott—who did not personally seek the office of Kentucky's governor and on occasion even spoke highly in favor of his opponent John Allen—was the people's choice at the polls by an impressive majority. Frances Scott had died in 1804, and three years later General Scott had married Judith Carey Bell Gist. Judith's son-in-law Judge Jesse Bledsoe was the general's vigorous campaigner. Once in office, the old governor continued to lean heavily upon the willing shoulders of his stepson-in-law: Secretary of State Jesse Bledsoe was the major source of energy for the Scott administration.[9]

During his tenure, few issues converted Charles Scott into a wise, precedent-setting statesman, or excited a historian. The period that was sandwiched between the Aaron Burr conspiracy and the onset of the War of 1812 was one of great national debates over diplomatic and commercial issues but of relative calm for the governor in Frankfort. He seems not to have been agitated by the comic opera duel between Henry Clay and Humphrey Marshall or all the oratory uttered in the Kentucky General Assembly against Britain and its infamous Orders in Council—he had his own ideas about who was to blame for the mess in which the nations found themselves. The majority of Scott's administration may have been calm, but the governor and state legislators certainly were not always on friendly terms. Scott is said to have been masterful in using salty language to express himself, and the walls of the palace's office-library surely rang with his angry expressions of disregard for the Kentucky General Assembly.[10] Contentious topics included the persistent and complex banking issue, the rising flood of paper currency and a dearth of collateral security, and inadequate state revenues to support rising militia demands.

Until the prelude to the War of 1812, minor annoyances usurped much of the governor's time. On one occasion, so it was said, a flickering military and political light challenged the old soldier-governor to a duel. This sensitive "statesman" had been injured, he imagined, by some statement General Scott had made, and sent a challenge. Scott ignored the challenge. Further incensed, the challenger appeared at the governor's office to make some personal inquiries. In the governor's office, there followed a somewhat ridiculous conversation in which the challenger said that if Governor Scott did not reply to his challenge he would have to post him a coward. Scott was said to have replied with a smirk, "Post and be damned; but if you do, you will only post yourself a damned liar, and everybody else will say so."[11]

In other moments, Governor Scott must have sat in his palace library wondering if the sovereign commonwealth was populated by rational human beings or Neanderthal tribesmen. There came up from Ohio County in November 1810 a six-page legal-size communication. The document covered in detail a dispute between Andrew and William Campbell over what was called a "passel" of hogs. Some of the hogs were marked, and some were unmarked, and for a year they had wandered about the neighborhood to wherever they could find something to eat. Essentially Governor Scott was called upon to exercise the wisdom of a modern Solomon and determine ownership of the hogs. More serious than two brothers in Ohio County wrangling

over stray hogs was a letter that James White, apparently a Kentucky merchant, wrote to Governor Scott on April 14, 1809. He wrote from Philadelphia to inform the governor that Kentucky's character was below par in that city. He said there was a rumor that the "Old Prince" (James Garrard) had misappropriated funds collected to pay for Frankfort's first fire engine. White lamented, "I am really ashamed of such conduct & for the *Honor* of Kentucky, send engine maker his money & clear the account; I have been so much mortified & bor'd in different company that I cannot come to Philad with a good grace that not only me but all the rest of the Kentuckians must shift their quarters."[12]

One continual annoyance with which Governor Scott was beset was the condition of his quarters. On the occasion of the twelfth anniversary of the governor's house, the blunt old soldier minced no words in his message to Kentucky legislators:

> I beg leave to call attention of the house and premises set apart for the use of the governor of the state. When I was first about taking possession of them, I found the ruinous state in which they were, that it was impossible to occupy them with any tolerable degree of comfort or convenience, without having some repairs effected. These I have in part had done, relying upon the liberality of the legislature to make the necessary appropriations; and I have also procured some chairs, etc. which were absolutely necessary having in view the same reliance. The situation of the house at present appears to me, in the way of looks particularly, to require some further repairs, and some are actually indispensable to the enclosures. I am far from wishing the public money to be lavished for my accommodation; but I feel an assurance, that is was the wish and intention of the state in providing for their governor to make his situation at least comfortable.

While Governor Scott swore oaths in his library-office, Judith Scott prevailed over the remainder of the residence, which held only limited attraction for the grizzled old veteran of numerous Revolutionary battles and Indian fights. In fact, judging by the mansion's condition in 1812, the Scotts apparently had been unable to make necessary repairs of the palace or to make it safe and livable, and doubtless spent much of their time at their former home, Canewood in Clark County.[13] No other governor's wife had quite the social and personal history of Judith Scott. Like her predecessor Elizabeth Garrard, she came to Frankfort from a far more impressive household than the one on High and Clinton Streets.[14] Descendant of a prominent Virginia colonial family and mistress of legendary Canewood, she had the background and presence to be a wife of a famous warrior and governor of the commonwealth. Judith was the granddaughter of Archibald Carey, a member of the committee that devised the Virginia Bill of Rights, and the widow of Colonel Nathaniel Gist. The Gists had had seven children—four daughters who made notable marriages, one daughter who remained single, and two sons who drifted into anonymity. At times Judith must have had serious thoughts about her marriage to Colonel Gist, the reputed father of the famous Cherokee scholar and grammarian, Sequoya. Whatever her innermost thoughts were on the subject, she was "to the manor born" and kept them quiet. At Canewood, she lived in the heart of Nathaniel Gist's claim to six thousand or seven thousand acres of military bounty land.

Governor Scott's residential office became a veritable beehive of activities and excitement prior to the onset of the War of 1812. In November 1811, a posthaste messenger brought the governor news of the consequential battle of Burnet's Creek and Tippecanoe between the combined Indiana-Kentucky militiamen, under the command of territorial governor General William Henry Harrison, and the Shawnee Indians, led by Chief Tecumseh's half-brother, the Prophet.[15] In that battle Joseph Hamilton Daveiss, a former Kentucky attorney general, fell mortally wounded when he led troops afoot and was struck by a Shawnee bullet.[16] Six months later, on May 18, 1812, John Bradford, editor of the *Kentucky Gazette*, boasted that there soon would be ten thousand Kentucky volunteers on the march to the various points of military need in the northwest British-Indian frontier.[17]

Indeed, within a month of Bradford's forecast, President James Madison had been vigorously nudged by the militant war hawks—a group of which Henry Clay was a dominant leader—into declaring war,[18] and, with the formal declaration of war, the time had arrived for both the nation and Kentucky to make good Clay's rash boast that a contingent of Kentucky volunteers could take and hold Montreal.[19] In one of his final acts, Governor Scott commissioned William Henry Harrison major-general in command of the Kentucky militia in a ceremony at the executive residence. Harrison had come to Frankfort as a guest of the governor's to discuss the impending drive against the British and Indians in the Northwest.[20]

His four-year term at its end, Charles Scott and his famous wife went back to Canewood to weather the storm of the war and to live out their lives in peace, well away from the turmoil of Kentucky politics, quarreling, hog-owning brothers, and James Garrard's defections in Philadelphia. The general, however, carried with him a painful token of his time in Frankfort. Early in his occupancy of the palace, Scott had slipped on a patch of ice on the front steps and broken a hip, an injury that put him on crutches for life. He undoubtedly paid his respects to that patch of ice and the palace's difficult steps in barracks expletives.

In the election of August 1812, Isaac Shelby was returned to the office of governor for a second term. This time he had faced opposition—Virginia-born Gabriel Slaughter. Slaughter, however, was without the usual Revolutionary and Indian wars military background that commended a candidate to the frontier voters of Kentucky, particularly when their state was in the throes of war.[21] The change of administrators in that time of military excitement was somewhat like changing leading and experienced actors in the midst of a dramatic theatrical performance. In the areas of raising militia forces and trying to meet the national pro rata requests, there was a remarkably smooth transition from Governor Scott to Governor Shelby,[22] assuredly eased by ample discussion of the crisis in the governor's office at the executive residence. In fact, Isaac Shelby's return to Frankfort in the fall of 1812 was no more dramatic than his arrival twenty years earlier. Frankfort in that year, however, was a changed town. Its population had increased, its society was more established and sophisticated, and its residents bubbled with excitement over the onset of the war.[23]

Enthusiasm notwithstanding, the commonwealth of Kentucky was caught wholly unprepared fiscally to equip and pay even half the number of volunteers requested of it for the war effort. President Madison had requisitioned Kentucky immediately to place in the field fifteen hundred militiamen, to report to General William Henry Harrison at Detroit.[24] To divert attention from Harrison's expedition, Governor Shelby sent a contingent of volunteer troops to raid tribes in Indiana and Illinois. In October 1812, the revered and aging General Samuel Hopkins, a veteran of the Battle of Monmouth and other major Revolutionary War engagements, was in command of these two thousand raw, undisciplined, under-armed, and underfed Kentucky volunteers. This unruly army assembled in Louisville and marched off to the Wabash to

A view of early, primitive Frankfort in 1813. A British army officer incarcerated in the Frankfort penitentiary due to the war of 1812 painted this watercolor from Arsenal Hill overlooking the penitentiary. Unfortunately, the old mansion is behind the large tree (center left) or outside the left edge of the watercolor. (KHS)

destroy the Peoria and Kickapoo Shawnees.[25] Never did a Kentucky volunteer troop give such a disgraceful performance. The volunteers complained, rebelled, and ran. The Indians set the prairie on fire and most of the Kentuckians fled all the way back to Louisville. General Hopkins undertook to control the troops, but to no avail.[26] He remained in the field with five hundred dependable militiamen. One can imagine the consternation that news of Hopkins's fleeing volunteers created in the governor's house. Shelby was infuriated over this colossal act of cowardice.

By winter 1812, the Great Lakes front was ablaze with war.[27] Traumatic news of a calamity at Frenchtown on the frozen River Raisin refuted Henry Clay's boast about Kentucky troops taking and holding Canada. This stream flowed across the peninsula tip of Michigan Territory into Lake Erie. In biting cold on January 22, 1813, Kentucky militiamen were trapped and defeated in battle. Prisoners taken were brutally slaughtered by the Shawnees, who were uncontrolled by the British officers.[28]

In the face of military crises along the Wabash and about Lake Erie, the General Assembly requested that Governor Shelby personally take command of Kentucky troops and gave him legislative permission to leave the state.[29] In his stead, Lieutenant Governor Richard Hickman performed the duties of governor. Four thousand volunteers and militiamen gathered at Maysville ready to march to Michigan. This large contingent of troops arrived on the lakefront just in time to participate in the Battle of the Thames on October 5, 1813. When the British had been defeated, Chief Tecumseh had been killed, and most of the lost ground had been reclaimed, General-Governor Shelby and his command marched back to Kentucky. Some of the command stopped at Frenchtown on the River Raisin long enough to give dignified burial to the bleaching skeletons of sixty-five fellow soldiers who had fallen in battle and in ambush on that grisly day and night of January 22.[30]

A mist of pride created by the victory at the Thames still hung in Frankfort's supercharged air when on

16

November 25, 1813, the state capitol building was destroyed by fire.[31] The General Assembly approved its reconstruction, and John Brown, Daniel Weisiger, Richard Taylor, William Hunter, and Joseph Dudley were appointed commissioners to oversee the planning and construction of a capitol building that would accommodate various agencies of the state government. The commissioners were told to plan a building that would "combine, as far as practical, that taste of design and execution, with that utility in the disposition of its various parts, which the present state, as well as the future increasing population and prosperity of the commonwealth requires."[32] A plan was approved. The new structure was to be of brick, with provisions to house the General Assembly, the register for lands, the state auditor, the state treasurer, and the secretary of state. The legislators made no mention of provisions for a governor's office in the new structure. Citizens of Kentucky were solicited for building funds but were not promised that the seat of government of the commonwealth would remain permanently in Frankfort. Thus, the risk of removal of the capitol was left to hover over the town for years to come.

By December 7, 1813, Governor Shelby was back in the governor's palace, which now overlooked the charred remains of the statehouse. He reported to the General Assembly in an extraordinarily cheerful manner that "the [Great Lakes] campaign, under the guidance of a gracious and over-ruling Providence, terminated to our arms. To say nothing of the destruction of public property, and the immense stores of arms and munitions of war taken by our army from the enemy. It had added to the United States an extent of territory of great value; which, if not surrendered to the enemy upon a general peace, will forever put to silence our savage foes, that have so long infested the western country; they being completely severed from British influence."[33] Sitting in the office in the governor's residence, Isaac Shelby figuratively drew the historical curtain on an extended portion of Kentucky's frontier past.

No doubt the Shelby family celebrated Christmas 1813 in the palace with considerable joy, if not in comfort. The governor's mansion had been in sore need of repair from the moment the Shelbys moved into it. The home certainly was not nearly up to the standard of Isaac and Susannah's pleasant residence, Traveler's Rest. At the outset of the Shelby administration, members of the General Assembly expressed some concern for all the public grounds and buildings but, with legislative penuriousness, approved only an appropriation

of twelve dollars to pay for digging stumps out of the capitol lawn and an additional forty-five dollars to pay for a communal capitol grounds water pump and a smaller one for the governor's residence.[34] Apparently palace residents depended on a well as a source of water, which no doubt was polluted by the presence of outdoor privies and stabled animals.[35] Certainly, however, stumps and water pumps were the farthest thing from Isaac Shelby's mind in late 1812, with the swirling storm of war raging throughout the western country and pressure bearing down upon him to recruit far more volunteer troops than the commonwealth could arm and subsist.

Regardless of its ongoing dilapidation, the earlier Kentucky governor's mansion on High and Clinton Streets had never experienced a moment in its history more exciting than the period from late 1811 through 1814, when both Governor Charles Scott and Governor Isaac Shelby were besieged by the exigencies of war. Numerous Kentuckians tramped into the governor's house seeking commissions as officers to command volunteer units of local and state origins. The governors' papers of the War of 1812 consist almost overwhelmingly of requests for officer commissions and of other military concerns. In these years, news poured into the governor's study with disturbing regularity. The palace was the point of destination of express riders who brought news from the Wabash and Detroit fronts with almost weekly regularity. There came word of the Battle of Tippecanoe, of the actions of Congress and the final declaration of war, of the approach of General William Hull to Detroit and then of his capitulation, of the Hopkins debacle on the Wabash, of the massacres at Frenchtown on the River Raisin, and finally of victories in the Battle of the Thames and the Battle of New Orleans. These were heady years for Kentucky and Governors Scott and Shelby. Once again the old warriors were involved in the business they knew best, making war on the western frontier.

After the last hurrah of war was shouted and just before ground had been broken for construction of a new capitol, the General Assembly finally turned its attention back to the governor's residence. The body enacted legislation on February 5, 1815, authorizing Governor Shelby to make repairs to the palace as he deemed necessary "for the preservation of the building, and the decent appearance of the house—and also such other repairs as he may deem necessary for the comfort and conveniency of the family residing in it."[36] The General Assembly granted Governor Shelby almost free

Governor George Madison, 1816. (KHS)

Governor Gabriel Slaughter, 1816–1820. (KHS)

rein to reconstruct the building and its out structures.[37] When Isaac and Susannah Shelby departed Frankfort in autumn 1816, they left behind a governor's house that was still in desperate need of restoration and repair but at least in somewhat better condition than when they came to it. Moreover, a new state capitol was rising phoenix-like from the ashes of the disastrous fire.[38]

George Madison (1763–1816), a brother of President James Madison, had been an officer in the battle on the River Raisin. Two years after his return from Quebec, George Madison was elected governor, but he died not long after he took office and never occupied the governor's house.[39] Instead, in late 1816, it was Madison's lieutenant governor, Gabriel Slaughter (1767–1830), and his wife, Elizabeth Thomson Rodes, who moved into the house that Isaac and Susannah Shelby must have at times looked forward to escaping. By no stretch of the imagination was the place a romantic setting for Kentucky's chief magistrate, and in no way was it comparable to former United States Senator John Brown's elegant and spacious nearby Liberty Hall.

That year, the General Assembly appointed a special committee, under the chairmanship of John Lancaster, to make a survey of the governor's house, its grounds and outbuildings, and its furnishings.[40] Lancaster reported for the group: "Your committee find the dwelling house, kitchen, stables, carriage house, and a considerable part of the fence that encloses the lot, are very much out of repair." Roofs were old and decayed. Chimney pieces were shattered. Shutters were not in place on the windows, and glass panes were broken or missing. The home's steps, front and back, were sunken below the lines of the passage floors. Inside, room interiors were gloomy, plaster was peeling off the walls, there were no locks and keys for the closets, and floors had sunk. Much of the fence enclosing the executive demesne was missing, and a considerable hump marred the High Street front entrance to the house. The outbuildings were badly decayed, and the stables could accommodate only four horses.[41] The furniture, which included a corner cupboard with glass shutters, eleven chairs, ten tables, a sideboard, a desk, a bookcase, a screen, a set of shelves, and two pairs of andirons with brass knobs (though a knob was missing from one of them), was described by Lancaster as old, "the most of it clumsy, a great part of it shattered and unfit for use."

The committee suggested that all the furniture should be junked or sold and that the state should finance a general refurbishing of the palace by purchasing $2,638 worth of new materials, including those for laying a new roof. They listed a need to procure new shutters for the windows, new hearths, better locks, a sideboard, a cupboard, ten new bedsteads, a settee, chairs and tables, andirons, hearth shovels, and fire tongs. Even this list was insufficient to equip the house with proper "conveniency" for the governors' families and to present a proper image to important guests of the state. No mention was made of even cooking utensils, let alone china, silverware, curtains, carpets, or fabrics. All the latter may have been outside the taste and aesthetic imagination of the rural male legislators. Lancaster and his colleagues further recommended that a new carriage house should replace the old one, new stables should be built to care for eight horses, a stone wall should be raised across the front of the residential grounds, and a brick walk should be laid about the property. They emphasized that all the property should be painted and put in decent repair.[42] In fact, the committee came close to suggesting that a whole new house and outbuildings should be constructed.

The General Assembly responded to the Lancaster report by appropriating its traditional two thousand dollars to pay for repairs to the house, the purchase of new furnishings, and work on the stables. Legislators were quick to specify in the law the repairs that could be publicly financed and the furnishings which should be supplied.[43] In 1816–1817, still an age of low prices, two thousand dollars was an insufficient sum to restore the house and outbuildings, even using cheap carpentry and brickwork and buying cheap household furnishings. In fact, the appropriation was little more than a gesture of support.

The General Assembly's appropriation for repairs to the gubernatorial residence might be the only gesture of support Gabriel Slaughter witnessed during his time at the palace, as the succession of Slaughter to the office of governor after George Madison's death created a somewhat bizarre political situation. Immediately there arose the issue of whether or not he was in fact governor. The constitution of 1799, which provided for the office of lieutenant governor, was vague, if not ambivalent, on the matter of succession. The arguments put forward, and the treatment of Slaughter's

title, constituted an unseemly incident in Kentucky political history. Consistently in the formal printed legislative sources, and in most of the correspondence with Slaughter, he was addressed as "acting governor." In many respects, Gabriel Slaughter was one of the brightest and most progressive governors for this period to hold the office. His addresses to the General Assembly reveal a comprehension of the main issues in Kentucky in 1816 and beyond, yet legislators several times rebuffed him and virtually snarled at him the title "acting governor."[44]

From 1816 to 1820, the gubernatorial head (acting or otherwise) had many moments when it rested uneasily in the governor's house. In general, the people of the commonwealth were drifting on a veritable tide of fiscal disaster at the time of Isaac Shelby's departure because of the inflationary condition caused by the War of 1812. Speculation in land and business, especially banking, ran rife, and the General Assembly all but threw fiscal reason to the wind.[45] With reckless abandon the body chartered banks right and left, including forty-six on one day alone. In 1818 the state collected only $180,710 in revenue,[46] and the Panic of 1819 reduced even this amount. The new statehouse, which was said to be one of the finest in the western country, was completed in 1820 at a cost of $40,032, of which the citizens of Franklin County and a few others had contributed $20,899. Politically, Kentucky was still paying off military debts to its Revolutionary War heroes and was honoring the new ones generated in the late war.

When once again time came to install a new head of state in the palace, the legislature was called upon anew to authorize refurbishing the mansion in such a manner as the incoming governor might "deem necessary for the appearance of the house" and "building a brick stable and carriage house on said lot." In addition, the household furniture was to be repaired "for the comfort and conveniency of the family residing therein."[47] The immediate family to reside therein was that of John and Katherine Palmer Adair of Mercer County.

Late in the year 1820, a tumultuous time of economic and constitutional crisis, John Adair (1757–1840) became governor. Adair had managed to support his wife—who by 1820 was retiring and ill—and their brood of twelve children partly from farm income and partly from political service income. For an extended period, he was speaker of the Kentucky House of Representatives, and he served a brief interim term as a United States senator. He, like most of the preceding

In a later photograph, the old mansion's brick stable can still be seen at left. (KHS)

governors, was a Revolutionary War veteran. Adair's immediate claim to political favor, however, stemmed from the fact that he had served as an aide to General-Governor Isaac Shelby in the famous march to Canada in 1813 and participated in the decisive Battle of the Thames. He then commanded the Kentucky volunteers in the Battle of New Orleans in January 1815. When the tempestuous Andrew Jackson denounced as cowards the retreating and virtually unarmed Kentuckians who were shunted aside to defend the west bank of the Mississippi River, Adair took up a thorny cudgel in their defense.[48] In a published retort that later would become an interesting political campaign document, he fired back at the Hero of New Orleans with vigorous anger.[49]

John Adair served Kentucky on a salary of two thousand dollars annually during one of the most stressful

times in Kentucky history. All of the banks recklessly chartered by the General Assembly during Gabriel Slaughter's term had been permitted to issue paper notes that during the Adair administration became worthless. The Panic of 1819 came near bankrupting Kentucky. A fiscal era ensued in which the sanctity of contracts was sorely threatened by heedless legislation.[50] In that troubled era, which extended beyond Adair's tenure, the governor's residential office surely was an enclave of activity if not downright anxiety. The General Assembly trampled the Kentucky constitution underfoot in the creation of a new and sycophantic Court of Appeals to supplant the constitutionally established one. In the same era the United States Supreme Court rendered a landmark decision in *Green* v *Biddle* when it declared the Kentucky "occupant claimant law" unconstitutional

Governor John Adair, 1820–1824. (KHS)

Governor Joseph Desha, 1824–1828. (KHS)

based upon the premise that the Virginia Compact was an organic part of the Kentucky Constitution and was binding in a contractual sense.[51]

If the devastating effect of the biting financial Panic of 1819, the adverse court decision in *Green v Biddle*, and the shrieking cry of anguish which went up from the mass of Kentucky debtors were not bitter enough to dampen the gubernatorial pillow, there were issues of unsettled boundaries, none more so than the one which separated Kentucky and Tennessee. Thomas Walker's survey, in 1779–1780, only created confusion. Perennially the boundary between the states was a matter of major concern. In 1820, Kentucky and Tennessee signed an "Articles of Stipulation" that authorized a joint states commission to establish a fixed permanent boundary. This agreement had cardinal importance because it divided the area of the Jackson Purchase between the states. It also clarified the southern border-line for new counties that were being created in the purchase region.[52]

The skimpy collection of Adair's domestic papers gives no hint as to whether any of his twelve children resided in the governor's house. Because of their various ages, most of them surely lived away from the central family. Nevertheless, by the close of the Adair years, ten new bedsteads had been purchased for the palace. On the other hand, floors and furniture—not to mention gubernatorial patience—had been worn thin by that endless army of Kentuckians who came to boost the causes of replevy on the payment of common notes and to seek the firing of Judge James Clark for handing down the adverse decision in the *Blair v Williams* case, which upheld the right of contract.[53] There still came those ambitious constituents seeking military commissions to boost their egos. The farmstead in Mercer County was a far quieter and more secure haven than the dwelling on Clinton Street in Frankfort.

John Adair's successor, Joseph Desha (1768–1842), also embraced the relief crusade, but he was a far different personality than Adair. In his campaign for election to the office, Desha made rash promises to relieve the horde of bankrupt voters . . . promises on which he had to deliver.[54] If John Adair served as governor in a stormy political-economic moment in Kentucky's history, Joseph Desha came to the office in 1824 in a veritable financial-political hailstorm. Moreover, he was beleaguered by public and private calamities. It would be difficult for a historian to describe the emotions and tensions that laced through the activities in the governor's mansion during most years of the Desha administration. Surely no great joy prevailed at the palace for Joseph and Margaret Bledsoe Desha.

Governor Desha and his large family had hardly unloaded their carriage at the governor's palace before the ill winds of disturbing news swept about them. For them, there was neither time for getting adjusted to the house nor for relaxation: tragedies were to occur back-to-back. On November 4, 1824, there rang out in the streets the horrifying cry of FIRE! A blaze was thrusting its angry tongue up through the summit of the new capitol building. Within an hour's time, the fire had weakened the superstructure and charred timbers pitched into the rooms below. The firefighters who arrived with their little fire engine were unable to check the flames, and the heat became too intense for the bucket brigade to get near the building.[55] Some records and furnishings were saved, but the capitol building—just four years old—was a total loss.

Almost at the precise moment when fire crumpled the new statehouse into a smoldering mass of cinders, a messenger came posthaste to Frankfort to inform Governor Desha that his son Isaac was being charged in Fleming County with having committed murder. His alleged victim was a handsome young stranger, Francis Baker of Natchez, Mississippi. Baker had come up the Natchez Trace and over the Nashville and Maysville road across Kentucky astride a fine gray mare with saddle and saddlebag accoutrement of impressive quality. On the surface at least, he gave the impression of being wealthy.[56] Baker stopped to eat breakfast at Doggett's Tavern near Mayslick, where he inquired of a group of local men the directions to Captain John Beckley's residence. Isaac Desha promptly volunteered to ride with the stranger to Beckley's place. Along the way, young Baker seemed to have disappeared. A local man caught the unmounted mare as she ran down the road, but there was no sign of her rider. Later Baker's body, with its throat cut and evidence of other injuries, was found in a ditch and under cover of a tree limb.

Isaac Desha's murder trial became sensationalized and, in time, involved both political and constitutional issues.[57] For more than two years, the case was embroiled in legal technicalities and legislative and gubernatorial interference. A jury in Fleming County found Desha

guilty of murder and instructed that he be hanged. By the exercise of a generous amount of influence, Governor Desha was able to prevail upon the "relief" legislative partisans to enact a law ordering the Fleming County court to transfer records and witnesses in the case to the Harrison County court for retrial.[58] This placed the case well away from the scene of the murder and in Governor Desha's home county, where he wielded strong political influence. Isaac's fate rested with a new jury, if one could be empaneled. In the second trial, Isaac Desha again was found guilty with the jury asking that he be hanged. A third trial was instituted, and for two years and three months Isaac Desha was brought into court by the Harrison County sheriff only to learn that no jury could be empaneled. This difficulty was caused partly by the influence of the governor and partly by the fact that the case had received so much publicity that prospective jurymen shied away from serving.[59] In jail and awaiting what seemed almost a certain and third conviction and hanging penalty, Isaac Desha attempted suicide by slashing his throat.[60] When a jury at last was organized and ready to hear the evidence, and with the defendant sitting at the bar of the court in a highly emaciated condition, Governor Desha stood up in the courtroom and granted his son a pardon, bearing the date June 18, 1827.[61] As in ancient Hebraic terms, the scene in the Cynthiana courthouse was reminiscent of that moment when Father Abraham held another Isaac being threatened with execution. An angry public outcry followed.

In a much more complex spectrum of public affairs, the Old Court–New Court controversy raged on in the commonwealth. Even had Joseph Desha been confronted by no other issue, that notorious contest over relief laws raised emotions and tensions enough to mar or even wreak havoc on an administration.[62] There were, however, other issues and deep-seated political conflicts. The Kentucky fiscal and banking systems were in shambles, and the general economy of the state itself was at a low ebb despite the fact that Kentucky farmers enjoyed seasons of some relatively high production.[63] During the latter half of the 1820s, some grassroots agitation for the creation of a system of public common schools occurred. At a higher level, a conflict developed between Governor Desha and Horace Holley, president of Transylvania University in Lexington—a conflict that led to Holley's departure and the smothering of the torch of intellectual progress in Kentucky for a century-and-a-half to come.[64] A student orator at Transylvania had delivered an oration critical of the handling of the Isaac Desha murder case and of the governor for issuing a pardon under unusual personal circumstances. Governor Desha maintained that because Horace Holley had sat on the speakers' platform and not silenced the orator, he was culpable of tolerating disrespectful criticism of Kentucky's chief executive. Holley defended the student's right of free speech. Holley left the Transylvania presidency December 23, 1825 (final in 1827), citing as reasons the implacability of Governor Desha and the animosity of "relief" legislators.[65]

Virtually the moment Horace Holley appeared in Frankfort to discuss the oratorical issue with Governor Desha there occurred a second murder which was to have recurring repercussions far into the future. On the night of November 6, 1825, Jereboam Beauchamp knocked at the door of Solomon P. Sharp's house, which was just across the public capital grounds from the governor's house.[66] He murdered Sharp, then a member of the General Assembly, with a knife.

Beauchamp claimed that Sharp, a strong relief supporter in the General Assembly, had made defamatory remarks about his wife, Ann Cooke. This murder, Beauchamp's emotional trial, and his hanging attracted nation-wide attention. A spectacular aspect of this incident was the Romeo and Juliet–like love pledge made by Beauchamp and Cooke, who waited in jail while Jereboam was being executed. Simultaneous with the hanging, Ann Cooke committed suicide. The Beauchamp-Cooke deaths and burial in a common grave and under a joined inscribed marble tablet in the Bloomfield Cemetery has captivated the imagintion of American writers for almost two centuries.[67]

The high point during Desha's stint as governor might have been the appearance of the revered General Lafayette in Frankfort. The announcement in Washington that Lafayette would visit the nation excited both Governor Desha and members of the General Assembly. In a typical burst of Deshaen oratory, the governor proposed to the legislators that the commonwealth extend a praiseworthy invitation to the French soldier and statesman. The members of the General Assembly responded in kind. In an eloquent but wordy resolution, they instructed Governor Desha to extend the state's formal invitation to Lafayette and to draw on the state treasury "for any sum which shall be necessary for that purpose."[68] Clearly visible was a hint that somehow Kentucky might be slighted by the general's national tour.

Lafayette set out from Washington on February 23, 1825,[69] to visit all of the southern states. He reached Louisville on May 11 and on May 13 set out for Frankfort by way of Shelbyville. After an appreciable delay, General Lafayette and his party, accompanied by a host of private citizens and militiamen, arrived in Frankfort at four o'clock on a rainy afternoon.[70] Never before had the town been scrubbed so clean to receive such a distinguished visitor. The streets had been scraped, and the old bridge across the Kentucky River was festooned with a profusion of United States flags. Even an unsightly public well curbing was covered. The line of procession paused at a pavilion covered in fine Irish linen. From the hills, cannons boomed. Apparently every member of the town's population turned out to shout patriotic greetings.[71]

Governor Desha awaited the arrival of the "guest of the Republic" at Weisiger's Tavern, on this occasion dignified by the name "house." General Lafayette proceeded to meet the governor while being showered with rose petals cast by a select group of young women. In welcoming General Lafayette, Governor Desha was highly voluble if not eloquent. In fact his speech was too long to be published in the *Western Argus*.[72] A. Levasseur, General Lafayette's secretary, no doubt had become satiated on welcoming addresses by governors who had exhausted the stock of adjectives praising the great Frenchman. He wrote that Governor Desha had "advanced in the midst of a profoundly attentive crowd, and delivered an eloquent and appreciative address. This discourse was loudly applauded by the multitude, and I heard it asserted everywhere around me that it was impossible to express the sentiments of the people of Kentucky with greater exactness."[73]

At a banquet, the general and his staff were served a bounteous Kentucky meal that had little in common with French cuisine, and a succession of thirteen distinguished Kentuckians arose in turns to toast the guest and to praise him for his great service in the American Revolution. Unarranged and unexpected there rose up other patriots who launched into speeches.[74] A grand ball followed the banquet, the toasts, and the interminable speeches. The young daughter of General Samuel Smith, the Kentucky state treasurer, had been chosen to dance with General Lafayette.[75] Unhappily, the general was suffering from a painful backache and danced only a step or two. Later a historian of the moment wrote, "Many are the traditions about the ball, as with others in honor of Lafayette. Nearly every family will tell you that a member was the first, or the only one to dance with the General."[76]

A more awkward moment for a visitor of so great an eminence to visit Frankfort could not have existed. The statehouse lay in ashes, and the governor's house was too small, and maybe too shabby, a place in which to entertain him.[77] Perhaps the Lafayette party simply was too pressed for time to visit the governor's palace. Levasseur wrote, "Notwithstanding his desire to avoid transgressing any of the established customs of the United States, the general was obliged to travel on Sunday, for his time was rigorously appropriated until arrival at Boston where he was obliged to be on the 17th of June."[78]

By 1828 the relief fever had run its political and constitutional courses, and some degree of legislative rationality had begun to emerge. Joseph Desha's place in Kentucky history, however, was fixed. He had practically wrecked Transylvania University and had overlooked the opportunity to create an effective system of common schools. The great crusade to deliver relief to the people from their financial follies was a gross failure, and the last vestiges of the fly-by-night state banking system had vanished with the Kentucky River fog. Desha also had failed to initiate an effective network of internal improvements. Many mercurial twists and turns of Kentucky partisan politics had occurred. Long debates over relief of indigent debtors had raged, the conflict between the court and the General Assembly had blazed, and the banking crises had produced economically blighting effects. All of these issues were charged with senseless infighting which was counterproductive; in fact, it was historically devastating.[79] The governor's own papers, along with records of other state officials and the published legislative records, document a deeply troubled and misguided executive-legislative era in which the commonwealth was led down a thorny political path to disaster.[80] Invisible though it was in 1828, a bold chapter of shattered Kentucky political history was to be spread on pages of the state's chronicles many times over in the future. But in the face of tragedy, gubernatorial stubbornness, and administrative shortcomings, there was a gracious moment. When Joseph Desha sat at his desk in the palace and drafted his executive journal valedictory, he produced an eloquent recapitulation of his years in Frankfort and extended a welcoming and felicitous hand to his successor.[81] He must have realized, however,

that the judgment of Clio might be harsh and that Kentucky in 1828 was actually no better off than it had been two decades earlier.

Despite the formal nicety of the final entry in his executive journal, Governor Desha raised a technical issue regarding the constitutional question of exactly when the governor was required to vacate the chief executive seat. Desha maintained that he was not being allowed to fill out his full term as governor, that incoming Governor Thomas Metcalfe wished to jump the gun.[82] There would be an eight-day overlap between the constitutional end of his term and the beginning of that of Governor Metcalfe; thus, for that interval Kentucky would have in power two governors. This debacle occurred in an age when Kentuckians were wont to be intensely disputatious. There are legendary implications that Metcalfe and a band of ruffian Clay-Whig partisans went from a Frankfort tavern after being well fortified with liquid courage to dispossess the Deshas. Too, there is the implication that Joseph Desha snobbishly did not want to see a "commoner" occupy the governor's house.

On September 17, 1828, Joseph Desha resolved the succession issue by departing Frankfort with his family. Twenty-five "gentlemen horsemen" were said to have accompanied the retiring governor on his way to have dinner with William T. Barry in Georgetown. A second party of Desha partisans met the cavalcade at the Scott County line.[83] In their departure, the Deshas might well have halted on the hill above Frankfort and meditated on the events and emotions of the previous four years. Joseph Desha bore a considerable burden of historical baggage. He had been willful, at times shortsighted, perhaps arrogant, and beset with issues he could not solve. Margaret Bledsoe Desha and her daughter, Eleanor Desha Pickett, carried away with them the brightest token of the administration. They were said to be model Kentucky housekeepers, and Margaret had been active in public celebrations.[84] On High and Clinton Streets, Joseph Desha and his family had experienced soul-shattering incidents of anxiety and grief coupled with calmer ones of joy. They could even recall that fleeting golden moment when General Lafayette stopped briefly in Frankfort, albeit not at the governor's house, on his tour of the nation as a "guest of the Republic."[85]

CHAPTER 3

A Mansion in the Maelstrom
of Politics and Tragedy

In 1828 a new day was dawning in Kentucky, and the elevation of Thomas Metcalfe (1780–1855) to the governorship marked a distinct watershed in public affairs. When Governor-elect Metcalfe went to Frankfort under the new banner of Clay-Whig partisanship, the Jacksonian "relief–anti relief, old court–new court" barrier had been temporarily breached. In the wide scope of the nation itself this was an era of social, economic, and political fermentation and change. Well beyond the borders of Kentucky, forces were at work that would have a profound impact on the state.[1]

Election of Thomas Metcalfe to the Kentucky governorship represented departures from the past in several significant ways. The governor-elect arrived in Frankfort bearing the common-man sobriquet of "Stonehammer" and profited, perhaps, from the legend that he had laid the stone foundation of the house he was to occupy as governor of the commonwealth. This legend all but overshadowed the fact that Metcalfe was a seasoned politician and well-schooled in the vagaries of Frankfort. In his youth he may have been skillful in spreading a thin line of mortar, but somewhere along the way he cultivated the more sophisticated art of expressing ideas in forceful English. No legislator, unlettered though he might be, could have failed to comprehend the governor's messages.[2]

Like some of his predecessors, Thomas Metcalfe possessed a high military title. He had been denied his moment of military glory when he undertook to organize a militia regiment to force Spain to release the newly purchased Louisiana Territory,[3] but he later won the prestigious title of "General" on the Great Lakes–

Governor Thomas Metcalfe, 1828–1832. (KHS)

Canadian frontier during the War of 1812.[4]

As a politician Thomas Metcalfe had been elected to two terms in the Kentucky General Assembly, and three terms in the United States Congress. In the latter body he gained some notoriety by facing up to the fiery

South Carolina nullifier, George McDuffie. In the heat of debate McDuffie challenged Metcalfe to a duel. "Stonehammer" accepted the challenge, exercising his right to select weapons. He chose "hog" rifles at close range.[5] This bit of congressional buffoonery inspired Bob Short to write the whimsical doggerel:

> McDuffie, you were surely tight
> For deeming it but a trifle
> To let the fierce Kentuckian fight
> with his infernal rifle.[6]

Governor-elect Metcalfe lost no time in going to Frankfort. Setting out from his home, "Forest Retreat," in the company of enthusiastic Whig supporters, he rode horseback over the famous road from Maysville to Lexington. It was hoped that Congress would soon appropriate funds to make it a link in a great national highway. At the Fayette County line the cavalcade was joined by more whooping and cheering Whigs, who rode on to Frankfort with the conquering "Stonehammer." When they reached the crest of the Frankfort hill, they found a third band of Whigs had gathered to accompany their hero down to the Methodist church.[7] There, standing before the altar, Thomas Metcalfe was administered the oath of office by a local justice of the peace. Governor Desha was not present; perhaps he was sitting in the palace office gnashing his teeth because he was being succeeded by a Henry Clay Whig.[8]

Contrary to legend, the Metcalfe inauguration seems to have been a relatively quiet affair up until the gathering left the church door. Their dignity dissolved into a state of hilarity, if not rowdyism. The party trooped into Weisiger's Tavern to gorge themselves on a "log rolling" meal and to raise their glasses in frequent toasts to the new governor, to the republic, to Henry Clay, and to almost everybody else except Joseph Desha.[9]

Nancy Mason Metcalfe was not to be part of her husband's masculine swearing-in ceremony and the "big" dinner. She came to Frankfort later, and in a much more subdued manner. However, Governor Metcalfe brought to the palace a valuable human asset in his stalwart wife. Nancy was in every way a match for her husband. Virginia-born, the daughter of Burgess and Jane Lee Mason, she stood not on ceremony. Both at "Forest Retreat" in Nicholas County and in Frankfort, she was a lady of compassion, decision, and courage. At "Forest Retreat" she diligently ran a household and looked after a farm.[10]

Surviving the Metcalfe years in Frankfort is an anec-

dote which reveals Nancy Metcalfe to be a woman of both compassion and independence. Once, so it is said, she was told that a man lay ill almost at the door of the palace on Clinton Street. She went out and had the stranger brought into the governor's house where she could care for him. The man grew progressively worse and a doctor was called to diagnose the disease. To the horror of the governor's family, he pronounced it small-pox and said the man should be moved out of the palace, advice Nancy refused to follow. She ministered to the stranger until he miraculously recovered. Fortunately, not one of the four Metcalfe children, nor any member of the palace family, contracted smallpox.[11]

It was with a touch of rural Kentucky glory that Thomas Metcalfe had journeyed from Nicholas County to become governor. Practical man that he was, and as occupant of the palace, he no doubt examined the structure to determine how well it had survived the elements and usage of almost a half century. If, in truth, he had laid its stone foundation, or as a young apprentice craftsman had spread only enough mortar to cinch the vote-getting "man of the people" tag, "Stonehammer" surely took pride in the fact that he had returned to live in the house as governor of the commonwealth. He found a structure in need of major refurbishing, with the outside service buildings in an even poorer state of repair. Thomas and Nancy Metcalfe moved into a house that was in decrepit condition.[12]

No dwelling of traditional domestic construction could have withstood the almost incessant pounding of constituents' feet, the wear inflicted by the continuing stream of casual visitors, and the hard use by the large families of the various governors. The executive journals contain listings of visitors to the palace who came seeking military commissions, of lawyers and convicts' family members who came pleading for pardon of kinsmen, and of those who came for no other purpose than to see how well the governors and their families lived.[13] Floors, carpets, furniture, and even the grounds of the house were worn and rutted by hordes of Jacksonian Democrats and Henry Clay Whigs who trod this hall of democracy. It was the price extracted by a rugged physical democracy in action at a feverish moment in Kentucky history.

At his desk in the palace library-office, Governor Metcalfe took stock of the social travails and financial condition of the commonwealth. Much of the population remained isolated because rugged land barriers had not been breached. A traveler entering Kentucky that year would have found existing roads rutted, all but impassable in winter, pock-marked with stifling dust holes in summer, and frequently obstructed by farmers' gates. Streams were unbridged, and in the eastern segment of the state most of the population was entrapped in a thralldom of geography, a "contemporary ancestral bind." The western region was still being formed into counties, engrossed in the settlement of a population and in gaining a foothold in the mainstream of Kentucky culture and economy. Sectionally, Kentuckians nurtured their particular regional culture, folkways, politics, commerce, and even regard for laws. Three-fourths of Kentucky's children were growing up illiterate.[14] The politically stormy decade of 1819–1828 had opened angry scars of antagonism in the fields of internal improvements, education, banking, and even in the management of the medieval penitentiary. In 1828, measured by objective criteria, Kentucky teetered on the brink of bankruptcy.[15] "Stonehammer" Metcalfe faced a commonwealth languishing in a condition of near despair; the central question was which problem to attack first.

In his first message to the General Assembly, a document which was drafted in the palace, Governor Metcalfe told the legislators that the commonwealth had been ill-served, actually harassed and injured by years of raucous debating and heedless controversy, by inept attempts to solve economic and constitutional issues, and by embittered in-fighting among self-serving interest groups.[16] No one in Kentucky at the time could have had more information than Thomas Metcalfe about the divisive forces stirring within Kentucky; there flowed across the desk of this accessible governor a veritable encyclopedic stream of information and political gossip.

In 1830, two years into his administration, beset with demands for internal improvements and lacking the fiscal resources to finance them, the governor and legislators mounted a vigorous campaign to persuade Congress to enact the so-called Maysville Road Bill. This bill would finance the improvement of the historic road from Maysville to Lexington, making it a link in a national highway system. Congress passed the bill,[17] but President Andrew Jackson vetoed it on the grounds that the road lay entirely within a single state. The walls of the palace office-library surely reverberated with agitated cries of frustration and disappointment over the loss. Fading public documents echo the stifling blow dealt by the presidential veto.[18] Even so, the General Assembly mustered the resolve to initiate some improvements in the state's road system.

By 1830, the dependability of the steamboat as a vehicle of commerce had become attractive to Kentucky. The state boasted that it had more miles of potentially navigable streams than any member of the Union. None of these streams, however, with the exception of the Ohio, was even reasonably clear of blockages by sandbars, overhanging trees, driftwood, and treacherous narrows. Yet, the label "internal improvements" captivated the legislators and prodded them to obligate an inordinate portion of the commonwealth's income and credit to opening the streams to efficient use.[19] Unfortunately, this occurred at the dawn of the railway age in America. When in 1830 a Lexington consortium of promoters secured a charter for the Lexington and Ohio Railroad, the merest gesture had been made by the General Assembly toward initiating railway organization and construction.[20]

It can be seen that impulses to social and economic change stirred Kentucky in the 1830s. The state was in dire need of a common school system; most of its children were growing up illiterate. In his message to the General Assembly, Governor Metcalfe goaded legislators with the statement that "Kentucky is in the rear of a majority of her sister states, and even Scotland and Sweden, on the great and vital subject of common education. Is not this a reproach? Does this not rebuke us for our unprofitable and wasteful party strifes and struggles?" In one of the gloomiest observations on Kentucky's educational history, Thomas Metcalfe, in his forthright manner, informed the legislators that the "lands thus assigned to the interest of education have been generally lost through neglect, wasted to temporary projects, or are lying useless to those institutions and to the people. The system of county academies has been almost an entire abortion, attended with the loss of an immense fund to the state."[21] The governor, perhaps too optimistically, told the legislators that it was within their power to reverse this shameful neglect and create and maintain an effective system of common schools. Responding to this admonition and some public pressure, in 1830 the General Assembly enacted a public school law, a statute more distinguished for its eloquent expression of good intentions than for its mode of practical application.[22] Nevertheless, it was a pivotal step forward.

Hardly less pressing was the problem of the Kentucky penitentiary. In no other state was the governor's residence and office situated literally across the street from the penitentiary's front door. The prison yard was piled high with flammable hempen dross which was regularly exposed to sparks from the blacksmith shop and to the maliciousness of convict laborers. Added to the constant threat of fire was the fact that many convicts suffered from chronic diseases, and dysentery was a commonplace affliction. When Governor Metcalfe appealed to the General Assembly for reforms of the prison management, he and his family had more at stake than mere bureaucratic efficiency.[23]

When South Carolina proposed to negate the federal tariff to be levied on imported goods, a shrill hue and cry of opposition was heard in both the house on Clinton Street and from the nearby state house during the Metcalfe administration. In self-interest, Kentucky joined the Union in vigorously opposing the effort. Even so, in 1832 South Carolina passed the nullification ordinance, but later repealed it.[24]

Meanwhile, like Banquo's ghost, the dark shadow of slavery haunted the commonwealth. The interstate slave trade had become a scarlet letter of guilt, damaging the image of Kentucky. In 1828 Willis Green, master of a Rough River barony, introduced in the House of Representatives a bill to curb importation of slaves into Kentucky for resale south. This issue was debated until 1833, when it was enacted as the famous "Anti-Importation Law."[25]

During his time in the palace, Governor Metcalfe became aware of the growing concern of many Kentuckians over the treatment of slave criminals, which was both medieval and downright sinful in the sight of God and the constitution of the commonwealth. Running throughout the treasurers' reports, like a crimson thread, were entries paying executioners who, under the law, dispatched slave criminals beyond the pale of human and legal appeal.[26] The early Kentucky slave code made no provision for the incarceration of convicted slaves in the penitentiary; their punishment was both harsh and murderous. The General Assembly recognized this fact during the Metcalfe administration and softened the statute. It placed in the hands of the governor and on his conscience the responsibility for ameliorating slave sentences.[27]

Most governors were slaveholders and doubtless brought slaves to Frankfort as household and stable-grounds help. Perhaps, too, there were convict servants. Social gatherings and dinings went unrecorded, though it is a safe assumption that most of the governors set ample dining tables.

The Metcalfe governorship was among the most exciting times in Kentucky's history. The state was caught up in a surging era of cultural and economic renaissance, and the palace on High and Clinton Streets was more or less a storm center of change. Both Thomas and Nancy Metcalfe added a new chapter to Kentucky politics and gubernatorial legend. They left behind in August 1832 a palace which had a bold smearing of domestic patina that made it more than ever "the house of the people."

CHAPTER 4

A House Grown Weary with
Usage and Change

Kentucky voters in 1832 once again demonstrated their boundless political inconsistency. Only four years earlier they had sent a Clay Whig–Jacksonian Democratic combination governor and lieutenant governor to Frankfort. In this year they reversed the field, electing John Breathitt (1786–1834), a Jacksonian Democrat, governor, and Joseph Turner Morehead, a Clay Whig, as lieutenant governor. John Breathitt, among the last of the Virginians to be made chief executive, was the first to be elected from the western region of the state, winning by the small margin of 1,224 votes.[1]

John Breathitt accomplished little during his short term as governor, though there was promise of some excitement when he put Kentucky in a strong Union position on the South Carolina nullification issue.[2] The governor showed little interest in public education in a time when there was a growing public awareness of its plight.[3] Indeed, frequent entries in the Breathitt executive journal reveal that conditions in the penitentiary received more attention than the cause of common schools. The words "remitted" and "pardoned" were recorded with staccato-like repetition. Governor Breathitt, like his predecessors, pardoned horse thieves, murderers, felons, and counterfeiters with a generous hand. Interspersed with the pardons were the remittances of petty fines and magisterial sentences, and the tide of military commission seekers never ebbed. Would-be colonels came in full phalanxes to seek the title.[4]

Tragedy and sorrow marked the era. In 1832–1833 a horrifying outbreak of Asiatic cholera, as forewarned by Thomas Metcalfe in his executive journal, cast a

Governor John Breathitt, 1832–1834. (KHS)

heavy pall of death over Central Kentucky. As the deadly plague spread, it penetrated the walls of the state penitentiary. There, across the street from the governor's palace, Joel Scott, keeper of the penitentiary, personally nursed convict victims of the cholera until he, too,

Governor James T. Morehead, 1834–1836. (KHS)

Governor James Clark, 1836–1839. (KHS)

contracted the disease and Governor Breathitt ordered him to retreat to his farm in Scott County to recover.[5]

Fortune, however, frowned on Governor Breathitt. Within six months of their arrival in Frankfort, his seriously ailing wife, Susan Harris Breathitt, died in the governor's house. Upon her death John Breathitt invited his widowed sister, Elizabeth Harwood, to become hostess of the palace.[6] Her stay was cut short. Two years into his administration, the governor, himself, suffering from tuberculosis, fell victim to his disease and died on February 21, 1834. At his passing the palace was draped in twenty-two yards of mourning tape, at a cost to the commonwealth of $18.75. The General Assembly also appropriated $500 to pay his funeral expenses. He was the first governor to die in the palace.[7]

Following the death of John Breathitt, Lieutenant Governor James Turner Morehead (1797–1854) succeeded to the office of governor. He was married to Susan A. Roberts and they had two sons.[8] Like all of the preceding governors, Morehead was besieged by constituents seeking favors ranging from divorces to the appointments of sheriffs and magistrates. Fortunately for

his peace of mind, the new governor had a marked capacity to live above the crowd, and was little more than a caretaker executive. He gathered in the mansion a good collection of books and often took refuge in the annals of history. In fact, a notable claim to lasting fame was his generation and delivery of "An Address in Commemoration of the First Settlement of Kentucky" at Boonesboro. Though chronologically in error, it was an eloquent bit of historically slanted oratory. James Turner Morehead's most lasting monument is the highland village of Morehead, which is named for him.[9]

A shaking of the Kentucky kaleidoscope in 1836 produced a new political alignment. The state had become a Clay fiefdom, a fact established when the Whig candidates overwhelmed the Van Buren Democrats in the election of a governor and members of the General Assembly. That year James Clark, of Clark County, the famous judge who had rendered the momentous decision in the 1823 *Blair v Williams* case, which invalidated the state's debt relief law, was elected governor.[10] Clark's stout defense of this decision on sound constitutional grounds when challenged by the General Assembly had gained him a permanent niche in Kentucky and national judicial history.[11] An erudite lawyer and a Virginian by birth and legal training, James Clark was, perhaps, one of the ablest men to be elected governor. He brought to the palace mature experience as a member of the Kentucky Court of Appeals, as a circuit judge, and as a former congressman.[12]

James Clark (1779–1839) was married to widow Margaret Buckner Thornton, whose first husband had been a grand nephew of George Washington.[13] She had one daughter, and Clark had four children by his first wife. In Winchester the Clark family was housed in a stately residence which in many ways was superior to the governor's palace in Frankfort.[14] Sadly, Margaret Buckner, Clark's second wife, died two weeks before her husband was to depart for the capitol to take the oath of office, leaving Clark's daughter Judith Clark to become his hostess in Frankfort.[15]

On August 3, 1836, Judge Clark set out for Frankfort on horseback, traveling from Winchester to Lexington, where he was joined by Lieutenant Governor–elect Charles A. Wickliffe. In Lexington the two men, accompanied by supporters, boarded a Lexington and Ohio Railroad train. In Midway they were joined by Colonel Dudley, commander of the Frankfort Light Infantry, and his troops. Traveling over the shaky little flat-iron railroad, the party passed the spot at which a wreck had occurred just two days before. The train halted at the crest of the Frankfort summit and the passengers descended into town by way of an inclined plane.[16] In town, Clark and Wickliffe were loaded into a carriage and, accompanied by a noisy welcoming throng, driven to the new Gideon Shryock-designed Greek revival capitol building. There, in the house chamber, Magistrate Wingate administered the oath of office. In turn, James Clark delivered his gubernatorial address, following which he, in company with Governor James T. Morehead, walked across the way to the palace.[17] Clark and Wickliffe had set a precedent; they were the first gubernatorial officials to travel to the capitol by train.

Preceding Governor Clark to the palace was his faithful servant, Daniel Clark, who in time would become a man of official note. He had been purchased by a slave trader and shipped to Charleston, South Carolina, by way of the "middle passage." Ultimately, he was bought by James Clark. During the next thirty-six years, from 1836 to 1872, Daniel Clark became as much a permanent fixture in the palace as its front door, outliving nearly every governor he served. During the last year of Clark's life, the General Assembly had before it a bill to grant the faithful old servant a lifetime pension of $12.50 a month, but he died while the proposal was being debated. Both the house and senate penuriously concluded the matter by posthumously awarding the "middle passage" slave the title "Ancient Governor." Legislators resolved that the "Ancient Governor" had been a man of well-defined ethical principles and unshakable integrity. Their resolution proclaimed Daniel Clark to be "deserving of both public and private recognition in this fidelity to duty no matter for whom performed: and whereas the said deceased body servant of early governors of this commonwealth gave, in his lifetime, a notable example to all men, white and black, of industry, sobriety, courtesy, according to his station, and integrity in office."[18]

Once settled in the palace, Governor Clark quickly discovered that life on High Street could have its rare moments. On the morning of October 5, 1830, he went for a pre-breakfast stroll. Hardly had he reached the street before a wiry backwoodsman accosted him, asking where he might find the governor. The man said his name was Larkin Lisle, and that he had walked from Vanceburg in Lewis County to "go to the penitentiary." He was to meet Bud Parker, he said, the high sheriff of the county, who was coming by stagecoach, but had not arrived. Larkin explained to the governor that he had been sentenced to the penitentiary because he had gotten into a fight with Edward Campbell and had bitten off Campbell's lip. Though Larkin did not protest the sentence, he did loathe being taken to Frankfort in shackles, aboard a stagecoach. With the high sheriff's permission, he had been allowed to make the trip afoot after saying goodbye to his folks.

Governor Clark was so taken aback by Larkin Lisle's story that he invited the man into the palace for breakfast and to await the arrival of the tardy high sheriff. The two waited ten hours for Sheriff Bud Parker to come and corroborate Larkin Lisle's fantastic story. By the time Parker did arrive, the governor had had enough of the Lisle case, and he pardoned the hapless fellow on the spot. Larkin Lisle was sent home afoot, no doubt to fight another day.[19]

In contrast to his predecessor, Governor James Clark highlighted the biting need in Kentucky for the organization of a system of common schools. Sitting at his desk in the office-library section of the governor's palace, he contemplated both Kentucky intellectual and pecuniary plights. There he inserted in his message to the General Assembly a basically practical reason

Governor Charles Wickliffe, 1839–1840. (KHS)

Governor Robert P. Letcher, 1840–1844. (KHS)

why Kentucky should shake off the shackles of its dark age, and give both the state's youth and the country a new course to the future.

Clark raised the question of the intellectual environment in Kentucky. At the moment, broad support for common schools was little more than a gleam in the eye of a small band of crusaders. In his message to the General Assembly, he told legislators that "The expediency of establishing a system of common schools without delay may be made also apparent, solely in a pecuniary point of view, as tending to diminish in a very considerable extent, one of the channels that serve as outlets to the wealth and pecuniary resources of this state. The condition of learning is such in Kentucky, that our young men are drawn abroad in search of education, and the amount thus drawn annually from the country would fall very little short of, if any, the sums sufficient to defray the ordinary expenses of our State Government." Thus there emanated from the governor's palace office the most powerful challenge to date for the establishment of a common school system in Kentucky.[20]

In the wake of the panic of 1837, the palace walls surely echoed with discussions of the state's strained financial condition. Kentucky was $800,000 in debt, and its revenue plan was murky at best. The earlier ill-conceived and ill-executed plan of internal improvements had been a fiscal and political blunder. Almost all state services were affected by the monetary stringency, including the maintenance of the governor's house, outbuildings, and grounds, and legislators followed Clark's advice to give the Sinking Fund Commission more leeway to bring order out of the chaotic situation.

Governor Clark's death in the palace on August 27, 1839, cut short his promising administration.[21] He was the second governor to die in the house. His successor, Lieutenant Governor Charles A. Wickliffe (1788–1869), brought to the governor's house little of the legal and intellectual brilliance of his predecessor. Charles and Margaret Cripps Wickliffe were the parents of eight children.[22]

A lively figure who occupied the governor's house in 1840 was Virginia-born "Black Bob" Letcher (1788–1861), the son of a Mercer County bricklayer who sought to make a tradesman of his son. A legend persists that Robert Letcher laid brick in the construction of the governor's palace. If so, he was a precocious ten-year-old craftsman. There is a further flaw in the story; Stephen and Betsy Giles Letcher did not move to Kentucky with their twelve children until 1800.[23]

Whatever the precise date of the Letcher emigration, Robert P. Letcher arrived in Kentucky during the state's formative years, and he garnered the political asset of having been engaged in the War of 1812 when he went to serve as the judge advocate in James Allen's command of Mounted Kentucky Volunteers. Having read law under the tutelage of Kentucky's famous curmudgeon and historian, Humphrey Marshall, he opened a law office in Lancaster, only to find himself ill-fitted by temperament to pore over legal papers.

"Black Bob" Letcher was of Welsh extraction, by way of Ireland. Rotund of body, with short arms and a thick neck, he possessed a robust wit and pleasing personality. Never a profound statesman, he relied heavily on his ready and playful wit, and on his shrewd sagacity. At twenty-five he was elected to the Kentucky House of Representatives, where he served four terms. He served in Congress from 1822 to 1835 and there merited political laurels by his actions as good will communicator between Henry Clay and John Quincy Adams in the great political "compromise of 1824."[24]

After returning to Kentucky, Robert Letcher was again elected to the House of Representatives. In 1838 he became involved in a balloting endurance contest for speaker of the House, which he won by a slim margin, and two years later he was elected governor.

Robert P. and Charlotte Robertson Letcher were the first childless couple to occupy the palace. However, Charlotte's ninety-year-old mother, Margaret Robinson-Robertson-Johnson, more than made up for the missing gaggle of children. Margaret was of Colerain Irish extraction and was amply endowed with indomitable ancestral genes, bounteous courage, and indefatigable energy. At eighteen years of age, she had married Alexander Robertson, a professional Indian fighter. One day, Alexander took to the war path and did not promptly return. Margaret waited weeks, then months, and finally years. After what she considered a proper waiting time, she consented to marry a circuit-riding Methodist preacher. The wedding date was set, the feast prepared. The marriage ceremony was about to begin when the crack of a rifle shot shattered the calm. Margaret cried out, "That's my husband!" and left the bewildered circuit-rider standing at the altar.

Many years later, while the widowed Margaret Robertson was living with her daughter and Robert Letcher in the governor's palace, she demonstrated again the impulsiveness which had characterized her youth. The Letchers returned home after attending a Fourth of July picnic to find that Margaret had eloped with the once-jilted circuit-rider, Johnson. The new Mrs. Johnson explained to her daughter and the governor that she decided it was high time she "got religion." It was in the middle bedroom of the governor's palace that Margaret, donned in a lace nightcap, sat in the middle of her bed and told her stories of the old pioneers and of her own life to the historian Lewis Collins.[25]

Mother-in-law Margaret was no doubt a match for her extrovert son-in-law governor. She added spice to life in the palace. During the Letcher years on High Street, proceedings were never cast in a formal mode. Charlotte, the "Queen" as she was called, never knew whether, how many, or whom the governor would invite to dinner, to eat what he called "good Kentucky produced viands." He felt the "fancy dishes" were far too extravagant for the slender gubernatorial purse.

During the Letcher administration a precise inventory was made of the public property in the governor's house. The report listed a miscellaneous assortment of fifty-six chairs, two mahogany sofas, and two parlor lounges, one dining table and several smaller ones, a piano and stool, a mantel clock, six looking glasses, three chandeliers, a bureau and bookcase, a sideboard, eight bedsteads, and a child's trundle bed. The inventory stated that the floors and stair treads were covered with well-worn Brussels carpeting. The report made no mention of any private furnishings, nor of linens, tableware, or kitchen utensils, which must have been supplied by the governors themselves. The inventory describes neither style nor quality of the furnishings and reflects nothing that would approach a royal mode of gubernatorial living. Inventories of John Brown's nearby Liberty Hall, Orlando Brown's mansion, Robert Wilmot Scott's Locust Hill, or certain houses in other parts of the state would have revealed more elegance and style.[26]

In 1844, as the Letcher governorship came to an end, Kentucky's political partisanship reached a boiling point. William Owsley, a solid Whig, farmer, and judge, was pitted against the popular William O. Butler, one of the last Kentucky Jacksonian Democrats. Owsley was too young to have been around at the time of the American Revolution, or the War of 1812, and every biographer refers to his "unsocialness" and portrays him as indifferent to both social affairs and to people, a dis-

Frankfort in 1841. (KHS)

position somewhat ameliorated by his wife. His background did include service as a deputy sheriff, a legislator, and a stern circuit and appeals court judge. And his political experience and practice of law in Frankfort had exposed him to and schooled him in the political vagaries and mores of the place. Owsley was the last Virginian to be elected governor.[27]

When Governor William Owsley (1782–1862) and his wife, Elizabeth Gill Owsley, left behind five grown and married children in 1844 and moved from their stable home environment in Boyle County to the High Street palace in Frankfort, they were met upon arrival with the acrid stench of smoldering timbers. On August 30, 1844, a disastrous fire had gutted the penitentiary workshops across the street, quickly reducing buildings, tools, and large stockpiles of unprocessed hemp to ashes. The cells were spared, though for a tense moment it looked as if the prisoners might be roasted alive. In the melee, a guard shot and killed one inmate, and another prisoner escaped, never to be captured. Though it remained unproven, a convict apparently started the blaze in a remote corner of the stockade

as a device to create pandemonium and allow an easy escape, an occurrence Senator Hobbs had already warned against. Officials were still raking the ashes and searching for incriminating clues when the Owsleys arrived at the palace.[28]

Documents relating to the governor's house during Owsley's term do not indicate whether livestock still grazed the public grounds. Yet, in 1845, the General Assembly approved a somewhat strange agreement with the Frankfort trustees, assigning them responsibility for the capitol grounds. The trustees were to establish walkways, plant trees and shrubbery, and fence the area, including that surrounding the governor's palace; the grounds were to be protected against roaming livestock and other intrusions. This legislation seemed to imply that the Frankfort environs were still a quasi-country village where farm animals roamed at large. Two years later, the editor of the *Frankfort Yeoman* scolded the General Assembly, asserting that it had been a blunder to turn over the grounds' maintenance to the Frankfort trustees, who, he lamented, had done nothing. Cows still wandered around the capitol build-

Governor William Owsley, 1844–1848. (KHS)

ing. Writing in September 1847, the editor expressed the opinion that "If the trustees are willing that the place should be made a cow pasture, it might be well for them to rent it out for that purpose, as they could no doubt secure a small addition to their revenue by so doing, and the property would be equally as well cared for as at present." The editor decried the shabby, run-down condition of the town and capitol grounds, and chided: "It has always been an eyesore to see public grounds surrounded by a rickety and decaying fence, which during our recollection, has probably cost the state very nearly as much to keep in repair as it would have cost at that time to have built a substantial stone wall eighteen inches to two feet high."[29]

Running through the state auditors' accounts for the years of the Owsley administration are frequent notations of materials purchased for the governor's house. Minor sums were paid out for lumber, sundries, and personal services. Daniel Clark, the resident houseman, was paid $37.50 every three months for his services. Newton Craig and William Henry, keepers of the penitentiary, supplied pieces of furniture from time to time;

for instance, on November 16, 1846, the establishment furnished a chair for the governor's office at a cost of $18.00.[30]

William Owsley and his wife, Elizabeth, spent four years in the palace, and they undertook to make it livable and presentable. The governor had a mantelpiece made to enclose the fireplace in the main parlor, and when his term ended in 1848 he had the mantel taken out to be carried to Lancaster. Today it is built into the home of Owsley Brown Frazier in Louisville. There appears no record in the Crittenden papers as to how the fireplace was enclosed in a new mantel.[31]

In early 1845, barely six months into his administration, Governor Owsley encountered a situation for which Kentucky had no precedent. Delia Ann Webster, a twenty-six-year-old schoolteacher, had been sentenced to two years in the penitentiary for assisting Calvin Fairbanks in transporting a slave family to freedom. No woman of such stature and notoriety had been received in the prison before. A small, one-room, frame structure was built in the middle of the yard to house her, and Newton Craig, the warden, read to her the rules of the institution, including the one against conversation with outsiders, and asked if she objected to anything about them. She replied that she desired no partiality, whereupon Craig told her that he would sooner spill his blood than allow any ill treatment of her while she was under his care. Indeed, her treatment was remarkable. Delia Webster was not required to wear prison garb, and she was furnished a fine library. The warden's wife often visited Delia and invited her to walk out with her, presumably through the streets of Frankfort, and she made sure the food was, as described by Delia, "of the most delicious quality, and prepared with neatness and elegance." On Sunday afternoons local ministers came calling. Soon all Frankfort society was beating a path to Miss Webster's door. The governor, after retreating from an earlier decision to pardon Delia Webster, visited her several times in an effort to extract a promise that, if pardoned, she would leave Kentucky, never to return. His attempts failed, but after some wrangling Governor Owsley issued Delia Ann Webster a pardon.[32]

No doubt William Owsley was thoroughly familiar with the challenge that his predecessor James Clark had presented to the Kentucky General Assembly. Following the same line of reasoning, he speculated on two points: why had Kentucky not made more educational progress, and were the abolitionist charges true that slavery had deterred intellectual progress in

Kentucky? He told legislators that in contrast, "The young state of Michigan, just starting as it were in life, was spending annually about $90,000 for school purposes. Her schools are flourishing and no complaint is heard. Kentucky spends about $7,000 on common schools. Our schools are languishing and the whole state murmurs at the inefficiency of the system." This lament may well be considered a basic refrain in Kentucky history. It would be repeated almost without end. The commonwealth faced multiple problems in the 1840s. The burden of a $4,000,000 debt against a $400,000 annual revenue income weighed heavily on Owsley's mind.[33] Yet, sitting at his desk in the palace, the governor penned a message to the legislators in which he stated that no demand or cause they might address in the 1847 session could be more worthy of advancement than education, no duty more important than that of educating Kentucky's youth. Owsley averred, "Nothing but money will do it and it is left to . . . the legislature . . . to determine the expediency or inexpediency of raising it." The governor was a personal force behind enactment of legislation consolidating the miscellaneous school laws into a cohesive statute. Decrying that "a law on the statute books is a far cry from opening the school house doors," William Owsley's fervent but shaming plea would echo through two centuries of Kentucky history.[34]

The conclusion of William Owsley's administration brought to an end a half-century of occupation of the governor's palace. In its warpings and wearings, the building reflected the sinuous course of Kentucky politics of the era. Posthaste messengers had dashed up to the High Street portal with tidings of wars, national congressional actions, family tragedies, and more cheer-ful moments in Kentucky history. The quality of men who had passed through that door to become the commonwealth's chief executive was mixed. Among them were both statesmen and time servers. Presidents James Madison, Andrew Jackson, James Monroe, and William H. Harrison, numerous senators, and several congressmen had crossed the house's threshold as visitors; so did military figures of all ranks. But the truest of the visitors were the Kentucky common people who came to speak with their governor.

Behind the front portal and the window blinds, governor's wives and children had snatched as much privacy as possible. They had come to the governor's house to live out four constitutional years and then go home to more private environments. In keeping with the times, most wives were insulated from the rough and tumble of Kentucky partisan politics. Some were active in Frankfort social affairs, but few created public lives for themselves.

With the elapse of a half-century, the governor's house became haven to fact and myth in almost equal measure, reflecting life in the commonwealth. Physically, the house had been in disrepair from the day it was first occupied by Governor James Garrard and his family.[35] Although the foundation and walls were cracked and crumbled, the outhouses needed shoring-up, the fences needed mending, and the legislature remained penurious in financing its care, the palace had endured the passage of time and the ravages of the environment with the fortitude of an aging Kentucky pioneer matriarch. In spite of it all, the wide front door opening on to High Street stood sphinx-like, smiling enigmatically on visitors, keeping its political and family secrets and legends locked within.

CHAPTER 5

"A Straggling Old Fashioned House"

The stalwart Whig king-maker, John Jordan Crittenden (1786–1863), brought to the Kentucky governorship in the seminal year 1848 a strong political and social verve. He had just defeated Democrat Lazarus Powell by a majority of 9,463 votes.[1]

Crittenden arrived in the governor's office in the midst of change. No Kentucky governor was better qualified by wide-ranging experiences than was he. Born in Woodford County, the son of John and Judith Harris Crittenden, John Jordan returned to his parents' home state of Virginia to attend Washington College (Washington and Lee), and then the College of William and Mary. He was licensed to practice law in Kentucky, and because of the competitiveness of the Lexington–Central Kentucky bar, he moved west to Russellville in Logan County.[2]

Like his predecessors, John Jordan Crittenden profited politically from a military record. He served as an officer in General Samuel Hopkins' abortive raid against the Wabash-Illinois Shawnees, and as an officer of the Green River volunteers on Governor Isaac Shelby's march to the Great Lakes. He served as an aide to Governor Shelby along with William T. Barry and John Adair. He received certain political sanctifications not only by these personal associations but also by having been present at the Battle of the Thames. Later Crittenden attained political notice as one of the commissioners in adjudicating the evergreen issue of the boundary between Kentucky and Tennessee.[3]

In his private life John Jordan Crittenden was first married to Sarah Lee of Woodford County, May 27, 1811, and she died in 1824. Two years later he married the widow Maria Innis Todd.[4]

On succession to the governorship, both John Jordan and Maria Crittenden were already well rooted in the

Governor John J. Crittenden, 1848–1850. (KHS)

Frankfort community and its famous alcove of social relationships. Their comfortable home, at the corner of Main and Washington Streets, stood in sharp contrast to the governor's house on High and Clinton. Mrs. Chapman Coleman, a Crittenden daughter, described the latter as "a straggling old fashioned house."[5] Maria Crittenden no doubt made the move to the governor's house with some considerable reservation. Whatever her hesitations, she planned to make some changes in the public residence. First, she disliked the popular local designation of the house as a palace. She preferred the simpler yeoman designation the "governor's house," and so it became. In stark reality this was a more precise name. Toward the start of the new administration, the "ladies of Frankfort" made the Crittendens a house-warming gift of a handsome one-of-a-kind chair, designed and made under the supervision of Mr. A. Throckmorton of Louisville.[6] In response to their generosity, Governor Crittenden wrote in stilted antebellum social hyperbole that "the chair is a most beautiful one, and emblematical as the nursery of my early character." As for the chair's housewarming qualities, however, there is a question of how completely the Crittendens moved into the house.

During January and early February 1849, Kentuckians prepared to honor the return of one of their own, now a conquering hero of the Mexican War, on his way to the nation's presidency. To welcome General Zachary Taylor, the General Assembly appointed five senators and ten representatives to brave the icy currents of the Kentucky and Ohio Rivers to go to Louisville and escort him to Frankfort.

General Taylor arrived in Frankfort on a cold and soggy February 13, 1849. On hand were the welcoming legislators dressed in plug hats and frocktail coats ready to wade down the muddy bank of the Kentucky River to greet the general. The general, however, was not in a frock-tailed mood. On the Ohio boat he had stumbled over a trunk on deck and had bruised himself, and on the Kentucky the little steamer *Sea Gull* had been rocked and tossed by chunks of ice floating downstream. He no doubt was in a less than jubilant frame of mind to respond to the greetings of veterans of the Mexican War who were on hand to wave their tattered campaign flag, or to respond to the roar of welcome that went up from the tightly packed multitude staring down from the bridge over the river. Albert Gallatin Hodges, editor of the *Frankfort Commonwealth,* wrote, "It is impossible to describe the sensation which this [the battle flag] produced on the great crowd. Shout after shout hailed the Old General as he passed through the ranks of his brave comrades at arms, and ascended the steps of the carriage hard by over which that powder scorched flag was drooping."[7]

The editor of the *Kentucky Yeoman* viewed the occasion from a different social and political perspective. He said he did not mingle with the crowd, but from the noise it made he assumed everything went off well. Later he said

he was mortified to learn that things had been badly handled, a reflection on Kentucky hospitality. The legislature, he said, had failed to make proper arrangements. He deemed the flag-draped carriage supplied an unsuitable conveyance. After General Taylor's drive to the state capitol to be welcomed by Governor Crittenden, he was then driven about Frankfort "in a miserable old hack of a concern drawn by spavined unmatched horses, to the Mansion House, where a room was suitably prepared for himself, but none for his suite." The *Yeoman's* editor said the members of the general's suite were left to shift for themselves. They were bedded down on the steamboat, and were not invited to the dinner in the evening. He fired a closing shot at the legislators by saying, "If ever another eminent citizen is invited to Frankfort, of either party by the Legislature, or by the citizens, we venture to say the people of Frankfort will not allow the reproach to go abroad that he was received in a shabby manner."[8]

The editor of the *Yeoman* may, in part, have misfired. The "Gallant Old Don," as George Prentice of the *Louisville Daily Journal,* called him, was warmly received by the ladies of that town. He was said to have received many a sweet kiss from his fair admirers and "That instead of kissing as a mere matter of form, the old man kissed with a very decided appetite."[9]

But General Taylor had not come to Frankfort to listen to a lot of puffery welcoming oratory or to kiss all the women. He came on a far more serious mission. He needed advice and help from Governor John Jordan Crittenden. He and the governor sat in the governor's house study well into the night discussing the problems General Taylor would face as president of the United States. The general had come to Frankfort with the hope that he could persuade Crittenden to accept appointment as his secretary of state. The governor turned down the offer on the grounds that to accept the appointment would subject both of them to a possible charge of "bargain and corruption," a virus which had tinctured the Adams-Clay relationship.[10] General Taylor left Frankfort with little to show for his visit but a specially bound copy of the Constitution of the United States, a Bible, the ring of oratory in his ears, and the pain of John Jordan Crittenden's refusal.

It is unclear whether General Taylor was actually housed in the governor's house or in a public house called the "Mansion House." Apparently he did not stay in the Crittenden residence at Main and Washington Streets, though it is likely that John J. and Maria Crittenden occupied both houses simultaneously

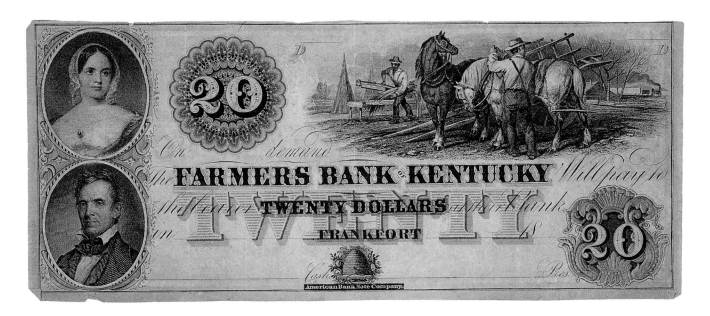

A twenty-dollar bank note issued by the Farmers Bank in Frankfort in 1850 featuring the likeness of Governor John J. Crittenden and his wife, Maria Todd Crittenden. (KHS)

(Maria was an ardent Presbyterian who devoted a generous amount of time and energy to church affairs, and the church was near their private residence). Certainly he was present in the governor's house.[11]

The era in which John Jordan Crittenden occupied the Kentucky governor's office was, measured by many standards, a colorful one in the history of the commonwealth. In the preceding half-century, 1800–1850, significant divisions of state government had gotten out of adjustment with the needs of the age. Voters in 1847 had favored the calling of a constitutional convention, ostensibly to re-invent state government. On October 1, 1849, a hundred delegates, representing 103 counties, arrived in Frankfort to indulge in a vigorous constitutional debate. The work of the convention was finished just in time for the delegates to go home for Christmas. The town and the governor's house had been enlivened during the three months of the convention.[12]

Events well away from Frankfort had a profound bearing on John Jordan Crittenden's political career when President Zachary Taylor died on July 9, 1850, leaving an administration in a near state of chaos and a nation on the brink of political disaster. At Taylor's funeral in Louisville, Crittenden delivered an eloquent and gracious oration, and went home to resign the governorship.[13] The death of Taylor freed him from the possible taint of "bargain and corruption" which had plagued Henry Clay, and Crittenden was tolled away

from Frankfort by Millard Fillmore, who offered him a cabinet appointment as United States attorney general.[14]

John Jordan Crittenden no doubt had found the daily routine of the governorship somewhat unexciting as documented by the pedestrian entries in his executive journal. The terms "remittance," "respite," "pardoned," and "granted" had long been part of the Kentucky gubernatorial lexicon.[15] Too, the Crittenden family had found it difficult to sustain its lifestyle on the governor's minimum wage salary.

The decade that followed, 1850–1860, saw the governor's house on High and Clinton sink deeper into a state of decrepitude, a fact eloquently revealed by Margaret Leavy Morehead. In this era not even the dreamiest-eyed Frankfort romanticist could have spread a gossamer of splendor over the palace.[16]

Reflective of the tenor of the gubernatorial way of life in Kentucky in mid-nineteenth century are the day-to-day recordings in the Helm (1802–1867), Powell (1812–1867), and Morehead (1802–1868) administrations' journals. These more closely resemble the entries in a local magistrate's order book than those of the chief executives of the commonwealth. Keeping well within the groove of executive tradition, these governors whiled away much of their time remitting ridiculously petty fines, reviewing jail sentences, granting pardons and commissions, and, paradoxically, writing glowing statements of the condition of the common-

Governor John L. Helm, 1850–1851. (KHS)

Governor Lazarus Powell, 1851–1855. (KHS)

wealth while bemoaning its fiscal, social, and cultural shortcomings. The brightest spot in Lazarus Powell's administration, for instance, was the educational awakening under the stubborn realist state superintendent of education, Robert Jefferson Breckinridge.[17]

Several highly sobering social issues intruded themselves upon the Powell administration. There occurred in Louisville in 1855 the soul-scaring election-day riots of "Bloody Monday,"[18] and three years earlier Harriet Beecher Stowe had stirred the already bubbling cauldron of anxiety over Kentucky slavery with the publication of her *Uncle Tom's Cabin, or Life Among the Lowly*.[19]

Hostesses of the governor's house during the Helm and Powell administrations seemed to have remained distinctly behind the scenes. Lucinda Hardin Helm had from birth been extensively exposed to politics, but as the mother of twelve children she had little time for anything but her family.[20] Later Jennie Morton wrote of this daughter of "Kitchen Knife" Ben Hardin that she was a woman of diligence and well adapted to the daily routine of running a noisy, busy household. There is no record of how many of the numerous Helm

brood lived in the governor's house, nor of what role Lucinda played in provincial Frankfort society. She may have been limited not only by her numerous family but also by her husband's modest salary of $2,500 a year.[21]

Lazarus Powell, a widower, no doubt found the governor's house in need of care. He sought to persuade his daughter, Mary Drake Metcalfe, wife of his secretary of state, James Metcalfe, to be his hostess. The Metcalfes lived in the Capitol Hotel and were reluctant to move. Governor Powell clinched his plan by having his daughter's property moved from the hotel to the palace during the Metcalfes' absence from Frankfort. Socially there seems to be little or no documentation of unforgettable moments of festive gatherings in the Powell years.[22]

When Charles and Margaret Leavy Morehead moved into the governor's house in 1855 they came determined to indulge their love of music, the arts, and social gatherings. Already established socially in Frankfort, they too lived in the Main-Washington Streets area.

Local gossip had it that Charles Morehead was a pompous, vain man, who on occasion made the journey from Main and Washington Streets to High Street

Governor Charles Morehead, 1855–1859. (KHS)

Governor Beriah Magoffin, 1859–1862. (KHS)

riding in an open carriage followed by a brass band, and along the way, so it was said, admiring constituents cheered the governor. The history of the Morehead administration is a mixed one. Perhaps it could best be characterized by a leisurely stroll to the office with a few handshakes on the way. He did get the county seat of the 104th Kentucky county named for his grandfather, James Morehead.[23]

While Margaret Leavy Morehead busied herself with restoring the house,[24] her husband labored in the library-office solving such problems as finding enough teachers for the public schools, segregating the sexes in the penitentiary, lowering the rate of violence, staving off the inroads made by the abolitionists, and dealing with Louisville's "Bloody Monday" tragedy. On top of these problems, the sands of both local and national politics were shifting.

At least one issue was settled during the Morehead occupancy of the governor's house. The governor and legislators had grown weary of financing the drunken militia muster orgies and declared the historic militia system archaic. This action halted the traditional pro-

cessions of commission seekers who grooved the house floors with their incessant visitations.[25]

Amidst the constant stir of political affairs, Margaret Leavy Morehead continued to deal with the problems of readying the house for the approaching wedding of her stepdaughter, Margaret, to Charles Walker. This was to be the first wedding reception celebrated in the mansion. Preparations for the event magnified the shabbiness of the house and furnishings. Apparently they were well below the standards of the Morehead mansion on Washington Street.[26] A report of the state auditor revealed that Margaret Levy had actually accomplished little more than make the palace presentable for the wedding. The task of enacting significant improvements would have to await the arrival of Governor Beriah Magoffin (1815–1885) and his wife, Anna Nelson Shelby Magoffin.

When the new first family, the Magoffins, rode into town by way of Lawrenceburg, they did so in high executive style. Beriah's inauguration on August 30, 1859, was an impressive affair. The regional newspaper said Frankfort had never been so decorated for a gubernatorial inauguration. The Magoffin carriage was met at the outskirts of the town, where Beriah was transferred to a ceremonial vehicle drawn by four matched white horses. Apparently Anna was politely shielded from the political ardors of the occasion and was left to ride into Frankfort alone.[27]

Present that morning were many militia companies, which gave the capital the appearance of an approaching war rather than the inauguration of a governor. Sam Goin's artillery company fired four ten-pounder brass cannons in a thunderous salute. Captain John Hunt Morgan, dressed in a fancy self-designed uniform, was there with his Lexington Rifles. Down the hill, and before the capitol, a speaker's stand stood in place, and the square literally fluttered with brightly colored streamers. There were banners, flags, and floral arrangements everywhere. Militiamen and brass bands along the way hailed the new governor, and the outdoor extravaganza was followed by a fancy ball at the Capitol Hotel. The high style arrival in Frankfort by the Magoffins somewhat resembled that of Anna's grandfather, Isaac Shelby, in Lexington in June 1792, and later in Frankfort in 1812.[28]

Like many of the preceding gubernatorial couples, Beriah and Anna Magoffin had a considerable number of children, eleven of them. The governor's mansion could not possibly have housed so large a family, but the record is silent as to how many of the Magoffin offspring actually came to live with their parents.

Governor Magoffin insisted that the General Assembly authorize a major overhauling of the governor's house, outbuildings, and household furnishing. Despite the efforts of Margaret Leavy, the Moreheads had left the house still in a poor state of repair. In fact some legislators believed it would be better to tear the house down and build a new one.[29]

Reflective of the repairs to the buildings and the furnishings needed was an extensive auditor's report on the subject, for March 1, 1860. Listed in detail were purchases of items and materials, and payments for personal services. For the first time in sixty-two years, the auditor's listing of repairs and materials actually indicated something of the Kentucky gubernatorial lifestyle.

The 1859–1860 repairs and purchases included twenty-three new window frames and glass, finished inside and out, plastering of several rooms, and the installation of pipes and guttering, and other structural work. Workers whitewashed the kitchen and washhouse, and they renewed the roofs on the house, icehouse, and stables—a task that required the purchase of 13,999

riven shingles. Penitentiary convicts were used in making repairs, refinishing, and varnishing furniture. Around the house the pavement and curbing on the west side were renewed.

Inside the house the aged piano, battered and out-of-tune, perhaps fifty years old, was sold for $100 and a new one purchased in Louisville for $400 plus $4 in freight charges.[30]

The invoices indicate that every piece of fabric in the house was too worn and tattered for future use. "Two Ladies" went to Louisville on a two-day shopping adventure to purchase new furniture, fabrics, and silver tableware to refurnish the mansion. Working furiously, these agents made numerous and diverse purchases, accumulating two-day costs for lodging and subsistence of $10, plus $4 for unitemized "contingent expenses." The Louisville to Frankfort Railroad scalped the pair, charging them a $15 fare.[31]

After the ladies' shopping foray, the Louisville purchases began arriving—dozens of cups and saucers, tea plates, breakfast plates, cut-glass tumblers, a full set of ivory-handled knives and forks, and other tableware. The invoice included four fancy French china spittoons, one cuspidor handsomely trimmed in green and gold design, and an assortment of "night" toilet sets of both fancy and plain design.

On December 28, 1859, Page, Gaines, and Page of Frankfort rendered their bill for six dozen dinner plates, three dozen champagne goblets, three dozen German silvered nutcrackers, and five dozen wine glasses. The inventory also included two ice cream freezers with sufficient capacity to serve a well-attended public reception or formal soirée.[32]

Beriah and Anna Magoffin seemed eager to make the governor's house a Kentucky-Frankfort social magnet. In fact Anna seems to have had an imperial notion of the ambience of the executive residence. At this late date, a historian can only surmise the reactions of legislators—especially the rural ones—to the raising of the environmental and social standards of the governor's palace.

Costs no doubt would have been much greater for the improvements of the governor's house had it not been for generous use of convict labor. Illiterate though most of the convicts were, some could at least heave an axe or hatchet, make a wheelbarrow or stepladder, install windows, and repair and refinish furniture. Their services were rich rewards to the penitentiary superintendent in both money and political favor.[33]

In a modern sense it seems a far-out semantic adventure to think of the state librarian being placed in charge

The governor's mansion, circa 1860. One of Governor Magoffin's free-ranging cows can be seen grazing alongside the mansion's entry. (KHS)

of the restoration work on the governor's office-residence. A.W. Vallandingham and his assistant, James W. ("Honest Dick") Tate supervised the purchases of materials, and the hiring and paying of workers and craftsmen. Vallandingham's wife supervised the work of seamstresses and other female domestics. She oversaw the selection of furniture and silverware and managed the laundering. All of this was a form of patronage which a politically minded governor and legislator could cherish. A.W. Vallandingham had been appointed Kentucky State Librarian without the slightest hint that he was even literate or had any qualifications for the job of handling books. His name was presented in the General Assembly by Joseph T. White, a representative from Ballard and McCracken Counties, and he was elected by a unanimous voice vote. Little could legislators have imagined the future escapades of Vallandingham's assistant, James W. Tate. Later he was

to make his negative mark in Kentucky history as "Honest Dick," who absconded to no one has ever known where with the commonwealth's funds.[34]

While the governor's house was being restructured and refurbished, Governor Magoffin sought permission of the General Assembly to use the public grounds as a pastoral demesne. In March 1860, that body concurred in a resolution to "Allow the Governor to use the State-House yard for grazing, provided it shall not be injured thereby."[35]

Earlier, in February 1860, John K. Goodloe, chairman of the committee of propositions and grievances, reported to the General Assembly a proposition that a committee comprised of Dr. Hugh Rodman, A.J. James, A.W. Bailey, J.W. South, and G. Swiggert be authorized to choose a new location and have constructed "A suitable residence for the Governor of this Commonwealth." This proposal came on the heels of the major overhauling of the aging governor's house on High Street. Only seventeen legislators favored the proposal.[36]

The first two years of the Magoffin administration was a stirring time in Frankfort. In February 1860, the Louisville mayor and city council appeared before the General Assembly to lobby for the capitol to be removed to the city. They came in vain. At the moment there were weightier political decisions to be made.[37]

The glitter and extravagance of greeting which welcomed Beriah and Anna Magoffin to Frankfort in the fall of 1859 almost immediately died away. Incidents and their accompanying forces mitigated against the governor and his family's enjoying four years of peace in the house. There drifted through the front portal a stream of unsettling domestic and national news. Hardly had the Magoffins moved into the house and begun its refurbishing before political winds began blowing.

There was little time to enjoy the fact that the kitchen, stable, and carriage houses were nestled under new roofs and freshly whitewashed walls. No rational Kentuckian could have predicted in the fall of 1859 that so soon thereafter the politics and Kentucky way of life would be so deeply eroded by threats of war and strife.[38]

As usual, there passed onto the desk of the governor's library-office the traditional supplications for gubernatorial favors, great and small in nature. Locally the most sensational were the requests that Governor Magoffin do something to stem the ravages of hog cholera in the state. There, however, came late in 1859 three letters of a startling nature. One was a cowering note addressed apparently directly to the governor, and signed anonymously by "A. Traveler." The second was an impassioned pleading by Mary Homer to her husband begging him to come home and forget John Brown's harebrained schemes.[39] And the third was a lengthy report from Lawrence Thatcher regarding his trip through the South.

Thatcher's letter was addressed to, "Capt. J. Brown, Genl' Com. in Chief of Provisional Government, U.S.A. (at Harper's Ferry)." He wrote from Memphis, Tennessee, and entrusted his highly confidential communication to William Homer for delivery. In his journey north Homer boarded a train in Philadelphia for a way station in Pennsylvania. When he prepared to leave the train a passenger seated behind him saw that something fell out of the man's overcoat pocket. This passenger discovered it was a letter. Writing later from New York, he described how he came by the letter and signed his own letter, "A. Traveler."

The author of the dropped letter, Lawrence Thatcher,

was an agent of John Brown's who came south to sound out sentiment among slaves and some slave owners in Tennessee, Arkansas, and Mississippi as to the possibility of organizing a massive slave flight to freedom. He told John Brown, "Our October Strike" would be carried out under the direction of a Dr. Palmer of Memphis, an angered and cuckolded husband and former slaveholder who seemed to be eager to strike back at his enemies.

Thatcher wrote that he was departing Memphis to go by Clarksville, Tennessee, to the Mammoth Cave area of Kentucky, where he would spend some time, "Before anything comes off there. William Homer has just arrived from New Orleans on his way to join you at Harper's Ferry. Nothing could have happened better for me. I guess I must be in a streak of good luck. I feared to write you by mail, for the dangers of interception. As but William [Homer] is here, I write you in full, and trust it to his care. He swears to me that he will deliver it to you in person, 'or die trying.'"[40]

There is no documentary revelation as to what if any influence these letters might have had on Governor Magoffin. It may be assumed, however, that they were among the most sensational ever to arrive on the governor's desk in the library-office of the governor's house.

By late summer of 1861, a phenomenal, irreparable rift had developed between Governor Magoffin and a majority of the members of the Kentucky General Assembly, a rift created by distinct divisions of opinions on many complex issues of a border state in the great national conflict. Kentucky's position of neutrality in the Civil War had been violated frequently by both Confederate and Union forces. The federal government had even violated the state's constitutional and legal rights.[41]

By mid-August 1861, the moment had arrived to resolve the differences between the governor and legislators as to Kentucky's position in war. The governor and the General Assembly were hopelessly deadlocked. The walls of the governor's house must have echoed with the anguish of their embattled, Confederate-minded tenant. Moving toward a resolution of the issue, the General Assembly on August 14, 1861, removed control of the Kentucky State Guard from the governor and placed it under a military board. Governor Magoffin vetoed a bill to have Confederate forces removed from the Jackson Purchase Area. He contended that all military forces should be driven out of Kentucky.

The nub of the controversy was the fact that a majority of the members of the General Assembly were of the opinion that if the state guard were left in the

Governor James F. Robinson, 1862–1863. (KHS)

hands of the governor, he would commit it to the service of the Confederacy. On what surely must be a misdated entry (October 1, 1862) in the *Journal* of the House of Representatives, that body requested the governor's resignation, saying, "The Governor of our State of Kentucky does not, and will not, carry out the will of the people of Kentucky." This resolution was approved by a majority of the representatives.

On September 16, 1862, Governor Magoffin responded to both houses of the General Assembly in a lengthy letter declaring that he had acted within constitutional bounds. He bemoaned the fact that he had been stripped of funds and the military authority necessary to protect the rights of the citizens. But the governor was no longer in a tenable position, and in a behind-the-scenes political trade Magoffin was allowed to pick his successor in return for his resignation.[42]

The gubernatorial succession was complicated by the fact that Lieutenant Governor Linn Boyd had died. The president of the Senate, John F. Fitch, was unacceptable

to Magoffin, so it was arranged that Fitch would resign, and James P. Robinson would be elected in his place. Robinson was acceptable to Magoffin, and so was chosen to be "acting" governor with Magoffin's blessing.[43]

At 10:00 A.M., August 18, 1862, by pre-arrangement Governor Magoffin met James P. Robinson and the two were escorted onto the floor of the House of Representatives, where Magoffin's resignation was accepted and Robinson took the oath of office. There perhaps had never been an interval in Kentucky history in which so many sweeping cross and contrary currents clouded the political scene.

Surely behind the portals of the governor's house on High and Clinton Streets there had been days, even weeks, of bitter anguish. There bright dreams of the flamboyant inauguration had been erased by stinging controversy, and finally by resignation of office. The letter of resignation, composed at the desk in the mansion, was carefully and passionately written. Now all the fine chinaware, cuspidors, champagne goblets, the new piano, the carpeted floors, and the freshly papered walls became symbols of a state of rejection.

In 1861 and 1862, there was little time or spirit for joyful assemblages in the governor's house. The kitchen no longer bubbled with the essence of Anna Magoffin's prized pickled hog's head. It was said the former hostess took special pride in preparing and serving this somewhat bizarre delicacy. There is no record as to what the Magoffin family did with the rest of the hog.

The new governor, James F. Robinson (1800–1882) of Georgetown, was a wealthy man and no doubt well adapted to a "manorial" way of life. At the time he was elevated to the Kentucky governorship he was thrice widowed and the father of twelve children. He chose his widowed daughter Emily Robinson Downey to be his hostess. Emily has been described as a dazzling beauty who drew army officers and Kentucky statesmen about her with magnetic compulsion. She adopted, for the Kentucky of the day, a lavish lifestyle. She was said to have entertained in grand continental style. A surviving note says, "The mansion, like an old woman in black and spectacles, looked askance over her glasses at the pretty creature flitting about like a fairy with a wand; but one touch with her exquisite white hand, a dazzling smile, and winning repartee for reproach, and the old mansion smiled at the transformation."[44]

Emily surely lifted many Kentucky eyebrows by her leisurely daily schedule for dining. Breakfast was served at 11:00 A.M., luncheon at 3:00 P.M., and dinner anywhere from 9:00 P.M. to midnight. A commentator

Emily Robinson Downey, daughter of
Governor James Robinson, famous for her
"frenchy" events at the mansion. (*Louisville
Courier-Journal*)

rightly observed that the governor's house had never
seen anything like that before.[45]

Maybe it was fortunate that Emily Robinson Downey
was hostess in the mansion for only the brief span of a
year. Her style of entertaining and dining was certainly
not in rhythm with that of the rest of Kentucky. She
was not of the pickled hog's head groove of cuisine.

During the weeks of late summer and early autumn
of 1862, Kentucky found itself in the midst of a military maelstrom when Union and Confederate armies
converged on the central region. So troubled had the
situation become that Governor Robinson went to
Washington to seek a clarification of the Lincoln administration's intent as to Kentucky. Prevailing sentiment
in Frankfort was no doubt unionist. On September 3,
1862, only a few weeks after Robinson took over the
reins of government, Colonel John S. Scott, a subordi-

nate to General Edmund Kirby Smith, led a force of
Confederate troops into the town, resulting in considerable chaos. According to William Wallace's report in
the *Frankfort Tri-Weekly Commonwealth,* both officers
and enlisted soldiers plastered the place with Confederate currency of undetermined validity.[46]

The main object for Confederate occupancy of
Frankfort was to inaugurate a Confederate governor.
The choice was Virginia-born Richard Hawes, then of
Bourbon and Clark Counties. He had all the early
standard qualifications for the office, except he was not
a Revolutionary War veteran. Hawes was a graduate of
Transylvania University, a lawyer, a state legislator, a
congressman, and an astute businessman. He was not,
however, a choice of the people.

The Confederate presence in Frankfort forced Governor Robinson and members of the General Assembly
to seek safe haven in unionist Louisville. In all the
excitement no one seems to have recorded an account
of what was happening to the governor's house at the
moment. It no doubt was left in the charge of servants,
with the "Ancient Governor," Daniel Clark, overseeing
its care.

William Wallace Harney, the local newspaper editor,
joined the stampede to Louisville but not until he had
listened to Richard Hawes's inaugural address and
watched soldiers hoist a yellow Confederate flag atop
the capitol. Hawes was eloquent and full of promises in
his speech. He told the assembled crowd that the Confederacy would maintain control of Kentucky at all
cost. This was perhaps the most completely broken
political promise in all Kentucky history, as the appearance of Union troops along the Louisville Road west of
Frankfort caused a hasty Confederate retreat. A month
later, when William Wallace Harney returned to
Frankfort, in a vein of anger-humor he labeled the
Confederate retreat "The Great Skedaddle."

Richard Hawes may have hastily visited the governor's house, but if he did he did not linger long enough
to partake of a sample of Anna Magoffin's pickled hog's
head or one of Emily Robinson Downey's leisurely
"frenchy" midnight suppers.[47]

A virtual prisoner of war in the governor's mansion,
James F. Robinson was an official fraught with anxiety
because of the vacuities of national policy toward
Kentucky in the freeing of slaves, the enlisting of black
troops, and a bankrupted treasury. Both Confederate
and Union armies had marched into the state, and at
least three bloody battles littered virgin fields with
corpses and burdens of constitutional guilt. Lawless

brigands, called guerrillas, were unloosed on helpless communities and folk to pillage and kill at will.

The front portal of what observers increasingly called the governor's mansion was an open conduit for the in-flow of disturbing news. Much of the record of the moment is gapped by a shrinking supply of news-print, and by military interference that halted newspaper publication for several weeks.[48] Amazingly, no one in Frankfort seems to have kept a diary or preserved descriptive letters during the dark moments of war. The governor's mansion seems to have been largely an island of neglect.

CHAPTER 6

Adopting a New Lifestyle in the Palace

Constitutional government and civil life in the Kentucky governor's mansion in 1863 were caught up in the maelstrom swirl of civil war and the trampling of the state's neutral stand. The years 1863–1867 were surely some of the darkest in state history. At intervals, all pretenses of respecting the sanctities of Kentucky's neutral position were blasted by the harsh storms of battle, and divisive politics. Just prior to 1863, Kentucky's soil had been swathed in the blood of battles at Wildcat Mountain, Mill Springs, Richmond, and Perryville, to say nothing of internal raiding and property destruction.[1] There hovered over the dilapidated mansion on High and Clinton Streets grave uncertainty as to how Kentucky's future might unfurl.

The gubernatorial election of 1863 was won by a stout-minded Union Democrat, Thomas E. Bramlette (1817–1875) of Cumberland (now Clinton) County. He was largely a self-taught lawyer who brought to office a strong will, generously endowed with native intelligence and a full dollop of common sense. Behind a heavy, black, Lincolnesque beard lurked one of Kentucky's better governors.[2]

Thomas E. Bramlette brought up from the Kentucky-Tennessee borderland his wife, Sallie Travis, and their two children to live in the governor's mansion. He also brought along his experience as a commonwealth attorney, a legislator, and a circuit judge. At the beginning of the Civil War he had organized a union regiment and served as its commanding officer until he found it judicious to resign because of the Kentucky position of declared neutrality.[3]

Social life of any variety was hardly a matter of primary concern in the governor's mansion between 1863 and 1867. No one, including newspaper writers, left an appreciable record of such affairs. Surrounding the his-

Governor Thomas Bramlette, 1863–1867. (KHS)

tory of the mansion in those years were the peals of that ancient refrain, a dilapidated house and outbuildings to say nothing of internal furnishings. Certainly the Thomas E. Bramlette family could hardly have been described as occupants of anything more than a rundown Kentucky back road farmhouse.

Either by fact or fancy, the perennial and nagging threat of removal of the capital from Frankfort continued.

Uncertainties raised by this question left the state's public structures suspended in doubt.[4] On February 16, 1864, the war-weary and penurious General Assembly had a moment of generosity and authorized purchases of furnishings for the governor's mansion.[5] They ordered the superintendent of public properties to supply the house with fuel, lights, water, and ice. No mention was made of telegraphic connections, despite the fact this service had been available in Frankfort since 1848, or that in the same year a small gas plant had been installed on the public square.[6] On the same date the Kentucky Senate, with House of Representatives concurrence, appointed a committee to investigate the feasibility of locating the capital in another town. Its members were admonished to "visit such localities as they deem advisable" and were told not to rely on correspondence with town petitioners.[7] But Frankfort continued to hold the seat of government at war's end.

In the presidential campaign of 1860, Thomas E. Bramlette had been a Lincoln partisan, but by 1864 he had turned against the president because of the enlistment of black soldiers, and the invasions of state and individual constitutional rights.[8] There also arose the bitter controversy with the egocentric General Stephen Gano Burbridge, commanding general of the central Kentucky District, and with the thoroughly corrupt General A.A. Paine of the Paducah District.

General A.A. Paine was a character directly out of a school for scandal and rascality. He exhibited not one shred of honesty or human decency. He ran roughshod over private citizens' constitutional rights, imprisoned some of them on no stated charges, declared a tariff on the trade in hogs, and embargoed commerce of any sort across the Ohio River. He "shook down" bankers and farmers with equal zeal, and he couched his address to citizens in expletives of the most profane and obscene manner.

In 1864 it was imperative that Governor Bramlette intercede with President Lincoln and Generals Grant and Sherman to curb both Burbridge's and Paine's high-handed actions. A special commission, consisting of General Speed S. Fry, of Zollicoffer killing fame, and Colonel John Brown was appointed to investigate General Paine's brigandage in Western Kentucky. Speed and Brown reported to Governor Bramlette that their findings surpassed belief. For instance, Colonel H.W. Barry, commanding the 8th United States Colored Artillery, had bullied a banker to pay $150 in gold to a local prostitute who had generously extended the colonel domestic hospitality. The commissioners said

that General Paine, in his usual profane manner, had a Dr. Milan arrested on no stated charges and incarcerated for fifty-one days and then released without a stated reason. The commissioners also discovered that the general had raised $95,000 from some of his embargoes, including a hog tariff.[9] General Paine vanished from the Paducah scene, leaving no forwarding address. He left behind only a few carelessly made and filed records, and certainly few if any friends among the populace.

Stephen Gano Burbridge had come to the central Kentucky command with the service record of having been involved in battle at Shiloh, Vicksburg, and Port Gibson. He conceived his mission in Kentucky to be the stern application of martial law to private citizens. His injudicious acts were numerous, but none more so than his swindling farmers of the sales of their hogs. At the outset, Burbridge found himself involved in cross wills, with a direct actionist governor.[10]

The correspondence between Governor Bramlette and President Lincoln, and ultimately with Grant and Sherman, resulted in Burbridge's withdrawal from command. Kentucky, however, gained little in the appointment of General John M. Palmer of Illinois as Burbridge's successor. In 1864–1865 he acted precipitately in freeing Kentucky slaves who, technically, were not free until the adoption of the Thirteenth Amendment to the federal constitution. Palmer recruited considerable numbers of black troops as a way to grant them freedom, and issued to others his famous passes permitting them to move across the Ohio River and out of slavery.[11]

The combined collection of Bramlette correspondence, the voluminous file of pardon records, and his executive journal reveal the trauma of a neutral border state caught in the vice of civil war. There does not, however, appear in the massive collection of papers of the governor, or in the journals and acts of the General Assembly, 1864–1867, a sliver of information pertaining to domestic and social family life of the Bramlettes in the mansion.[12]

Personally Thomas E. Bramlette was, as he wrote General Burbridge, truly, "A plain, blunt spoken man," a fact discernible in the letters, messages, reports, and proclamations he drafted in his mansion office. Be it said, he had much to be plain spoken and blunt about during his four-year occupancy of the mansion. He spoke directly and clearly when writing President Lincoln, Secretary Stanton, and other federal officials in opposition to the federal government's invasion of Kentucky's constitutional rights, and the mistreatment of its citizens. Nevertheless, Thomas E. Bramlette remained loyal to the Union. He and the people of Kentucky faced a difficult and complex moment in the history of their state in war and then radical reconstruction. The high-handed guerillas had to be curbed, military invasions of citizens' rights had to be called to account, plus the chronic internal political partisan divisions required constant attention. The whole question of the status of slavery was muddled in 1864–1865, and then there arose at the end of the war a flush of plaintiffs seeking adjustments of complaints and payments for damages caused by military operations. Nowhere are these facts more clearly revealed than in the voluminous collection of pardon records included in the Bramlette papers at the Kentucky Department for Libraries and Archives.[13]

When the ticking clock of historical chronology signaled the time of departure from the office of governor, and from the mansion, Thomas and Sallie Travis Bramlette, no doubt, looked back on their past four years with strong mixed emotions. They carried away with them no bright memories of late morning breakfasts or past bedtime dinners. If they were hosts to fancy formal levees they left no record of the fact. Like so many of their predecessors they left an aged mansion standing on the corner of High and Clinton Streets like a tottering monument to the perilous times of a recent past.

As emphasized *ad finitum* in special committee reports, governors' messages, and auditors' notations, the governor's mansion in its six score age stood worn and torn by heavy family and executive usage. Domestically, the mansion household staff underwent a radical change when the traditional household slaves took leave by way of Palmer's passes, or by the Thirteenth Amendment path. Both the Bramlettes, in the latter months of their occupancy of the mansion, and the incoming John Stevensons had to employ "free" servants. Apparently only the faithful and honorable Daniel Clark remained on the staff.[14]

John White Stevenson (1812–1886) was the last Virginian elevated to the office of Kentucky governor. He perhaps brought to that office one of the most sophisticated educational and socially experienced backgrounds of any governor. An Andrew Johnson supporter, a former member of the United States House of Representatives, and a delegate to the Philadelphia National Union Convention in 1865, he had been elected lieutenant governor on the pro-Andrew Johnson ticket with Governor-elect John L. Helm, but Helm died before taking office and Stevenson succeeded him. In

the following September 1867 election Stevenson himself was chosen governor.[15]

In one of the most bitter and trying moments in Kentucky history, John and Sibella Winston Stevenson settled into the mansion, after the death of Governor-elect John Helm. They were socially and hospitably active in the entertainment of guests at breakfasts, dinners, and formal balls. They implied at least that they realized they stood astride a social and historical divide in the history of the commonwealth.[16]

In 1867 the governor's mansion and its furnishings were dilapidated, even ravaged by neglect, and maimed by fiscal penury. Kentucky's revenue system was beset by every problem imaginable, and no structural refurbishing could be undertaken. The gloomy shade of depression which hovered over the mansion's doorway arose from a mixture of the ill fortunes of war and continued doubt as to the future location of the capital.[17]

Soon after war's end, Governor Stevenson, in his first formal message, admonished legislators to settle the issue of the capital's location. No matter whether it was to be in Louisville, Lexington, or remain in Frankfort, the veil of uncertainty must be removed. Whatever decision was to be made, there would be urgent need for office space to accommodate the governor and the other constitutional officers.[18] At present all of them except the treasurer and auditor were barred from the capitol building for lack of space. The plan for an office building was to have a definite impact on the mansion.[19] Governor Stevenson was pointed in his message to the General Assembly in 1868, stating that "The present buildings are wholly insufficient for the transaction of the public business, they [including the governor's mansion] are rapidly decaying, and are utterly insecure. Many of them are absolutely unsafe. None of the public offices belonging to the state are [*sic*] fireproof."[20] A fire, he said, could wipe the commonwealth out of business so far as its essential records were concerned.

In this first message Governor Stevenson revealed that he had a sophisticated view of the functional feature of architecture, and that he leaned toward keeping the capital in Frankfort. He thought that additional ground could be purchased on which to enlarge the present classical temple. Wings, east and west, could be added. He also suggested that a site on the knoll west of the Kentucky River, opposite the Frankfort Cemetery and the Daniel Boone Monument, should be purchased for the future location of the capitol. This would remove the government offices from the Kentucky River flood basin.[21]

Governor John Stevenson, 1867–1871. (KHS)

Governor Preston Leslie, 1871–1875. (KHS)

Wherever the capitol building might be located, the governor wrote that it should be an impressive structure. "The character and dignity of the Commonwealth," he said, "requires a statehouse becoming not only its present importance, but also its future prosperity and grandeur." He said, "No narrow lines should confine its significance, no unsightly contiguities should mar its beauty. The statehouse of Kentucky should be an ornament to the Commonwealth, a gem to the Union, a trophy of architectural skill and science."[22]

Governor Stevenson was prophetic of things to come. In time, Kentucky was to erect a federal-romanesque capitol on his suggested site. The 1867 General Assembly, however, dreamed in a more limited fashion. After extensive discussion it was decided to construct a three-story executive office building of dull gray Kentuckyesque lines, and separate from the classic Shryock temple.[23] For the first time, the governor would be able to maintain his office apart from the family residence and gain more room in the mansion for entertainment.

After considerable nudging, the General Assembly at the war's end also finally approved major reconstruc-

tion and refurnishing of the governor's house. Reflective of the depth of this action, the Kentucky state auditor, in 1868, filled sixteen printed documentary-sized pages with details of purchases for the house and documentation of the cost. Appearing throughout the detailed listing of materials and furnishings for the mansion are many semi-luxuriant items. Ceilings of the parlors and hall were adorned with French chandeliers fitted with gas burners.[24] China cabinets were filled with dozens of breakfast, tea, and dinner plates, and with almost enough common teacups and saucers to serve members of the British Parliament. The executive family purchased six "fine" chairs for the dining room, and thirty "common" ones on which to seat less important guests. In addition, two oriental window chairs and bedrooms refurnished with new bedsteads and mattresses added to the sense of newness.

Surely the inclusion in the inventory of two dozen tumblers and an equal number of champagne glasses promised moments of scintillating joy, as did the four sets of fine waiters, two dozen demitasse coffee cups and saucers, and dozens of gilt china teacups. The audi-

51

tor's report listed an assortment of gilt, green, pink, and flowered chamber pots, an assortment of blue and red spittoons, four dozen especially engraved tumblers bearing the governor's seal, and a generous number of gravy boats, soup tureens, and meat dishes of assorted sizes.

The mansion's kitchen was completely re-equipped with a new patented stove, two modern ice cream freezers, six smoothing irons, a half dozen pie tins, a gravy strainer, a patented churn, and virtually every other kind of hand utensil listed in the wholesale catalog.[25]

Workers repapered, carpeted, and fitted the mansion with gas pipes for lighting. Fabrics of every sort were purchased for every room in the house. The installation of thirteen double swing brackets indicated the placing of flowerpots in the parlors and hall. A full-sized zinc bathtub for the governor's personal use was a bit of modernization, but the restoration of the mansion's privy was not.[26]

The auditor's report listed an amazing amount of lumber, nails, paint, and other construction materials. Of a more domestic nature was the purchase of a fly brush, rat and mouse traps, numerous mosquito nets, clothes brushes, boxes of matches, candles, a hatchet, and a box of tacks. No item was too small to be listed.

In the newly restored mansion, Governor and Sibella Stevenson could loll away time in the new bathtub, pour spirited drinks from one of the fancy new decanters, eat their meals off one of the lacy tablecloths, wipe their chins with one of more than a hundred napkins, and be profligate in the use of towels. Finally, they could tuck themselves into a new bed, underneath a pair of the two-dozen fresh sheets, and pull up a handsome "Marseilles" quilt. During the night, they were secure from the ravenous Kentucky river bottom mosquitoes under a mosquito net, and were assured that no mouse or rat gnawed its way to the pantry. The ice house was filled with two loads of sawdust and an equal measure of straw to insulate enough ice to cool a generous quantity of bourbon whiskey. More than two hundred bushels of coal were scuttled into the bin, the outside privy had been rebuilt, and a stout new clothesline was stretched across the back yard, in keeping with Kentucky farmhouse tradition.[27]

Despite a lingering sense of security in the restored mansion, times were changing in Frankfort. On Monday night, September 2, 1870, a burglar climbed into a mansion bedroom and attempted to remove a pair of diamond earrings from a sleeping maiden. When the girl awakened and screamed, the thief departed so

hurriedly that he left the purloined governor's watch and chain dangling on a nail. The incident resulted in the employment of a watchman to stand guard nightly, at a cost of $1.50 per watch.[28]

When the tap of the hammer and the whine of the saw died away, twelve loads of rubbish and eleven of dirt were left behind on the mansion grounds. "Pole cat" gas had been piped into the house as early as 1848 from a tiny state-owned generator, but in the refurbishing, new and more efficient chandeliers were installed. These gave the mansion a brighter nighttime glow. Earlier, people in Frankfort had howled protests over the foul odor of gas, but this complaint seems not to have extended to the tenants of the mansion. Overall, the improvements cost the commonwealth $16,276.50.[29]

Before the restoration bill was paid, ambition swept John White Stevenson out of the governor's chair. Early in September 1871 the General Assembly appointed him a United States senator. Maybe it was with some relief, if not joy, that he and Sibella went away to Washington, leaving behind the newly restored house, and the army of remittance seekers. They were returning to a political scene that the new senator had known in his youth.[30]

In 1871 the governorship passed to Preston Hopkins Leslie (1819–1907). A native of Wayne (later Clinton) County, he had striven up from a modest rural farm background to become a man of the people. True to the Kentucky political tradition, Leslie had served an apprenticeship in various public offices. During the Civil War he had revealed a distinct southern partisanship as a state senator.[31]

Governor Leslie brought his wife, Mary Kuykendall, to live in the mansion, and in sharp contrast between the way of life of the Stevensons and their own, the Leslies retired the decanters, whiskey tumblers, and champagne glasses to the sideboard, to serve as glittering ornaments or historical artifacts. The ice packed away under straw and sawdust was cracked and placed in tea glasses or the ice cream freezer—a practice which gained the governor the sobriquet "Cold Water Preston"—and the pall of temperance was draped in heavy folds over the house on High and Clinton.[32]

By mid-nineteenth century the demands of Kentucky state government far exceeded the available building space in Frankfort, and the town was poorly prepared to stave off threats of removal. At the same time the state's tax base, if such it could be called, was inadequate to meet the crushing demands of the disturbed and violent post-war era.[33] A movement had started in 1867 to

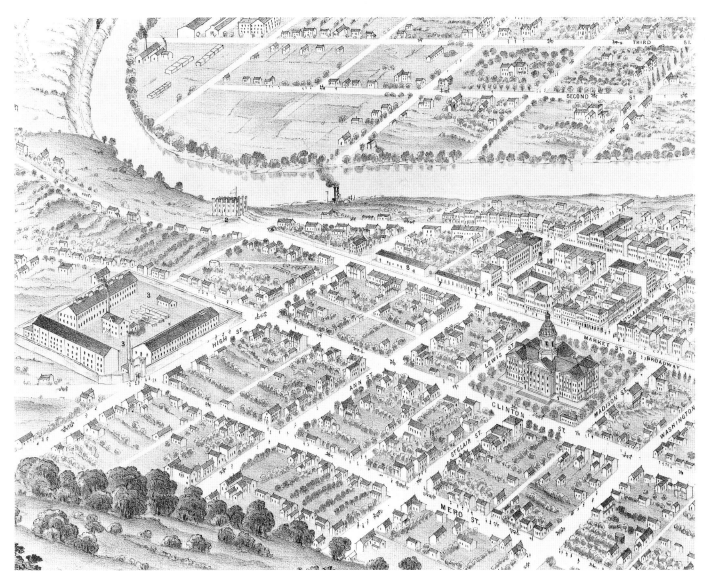

A detail from an 1871 bird's-eye view of Frankfort. The old mansion is seen at the intersection of High and Clinton Streets, and is bordered at the back of the lot by Ann Street. The print shows a planned capitol, but it was only partially built. (KHS)

bring about the construction of a fireproof building, and the new building was to be located southeast of the capitol, but the contractor was delayed by his own dilatoriness and by foul weather. As a result, Preston and Mary Leslie were caught in the period between the crush of official visitors to the mansion and the removal of the governor's office to the new building.[34]

Like Maria Crittenden before her, Mary Leslie was a good Kentucky hostess and passionately involved in her work with the church, in this case Frankfort Baptist. While she was at church, her governor-husband labored diligently with problems of guerrillas and violence, the penitentiary, education, and the re-establishment of relations with the federal government. One of his crown-

ing achievements was the organization of a geological survey to explore and assess Kentucky's mineral wealth.[35]

For the first time, a Kentucky governor and his family had moved into a house that was reasonably livable. The major overhauling of the house in 1868, however, was not enough to convert it into a respectable governor's mansion. Although the Leslies entertained moderately, it was said that Mary Kuykendall Leslie was a gracious, conservative hostess—despite her husband, the ardent temperance crusader.

Preston Leslie exercised his gubernatorial powers in the social area by vetoing, on April 21, 1873, a Senate bill, in which the house had concurred, that would have permitted saloon keepers in Covington to sell liquor to

Mary K. Leslie, wife of Preston Leslie, shared with her husband the principle of strict "dryness" for the governor's mansion. She enjoyed the high esteem of the Woman's Christian Temperance Union. (Montana Historical Society and Myrtle Bates Webb family collection)

minors. He said the state had as much interest in the children of Covington as in the rest of Kentucky. The veto was upheld overwhelmingly.[36] The strangely named Bourbon Lodge of Good Templars resolved, "Hailing with joy the noble act of Gov. Preston H. Leslie, in excluding all intoxicating liquors from his sideboard, at a recent reception."[37]

Not only was the sideboard in the Leslie years a Sahara of liquid cheer, so was the rest of the house. The mansion in those years was in fact a haven of rural–small town Kentucky domesticity. The governor and Mrs. Leslie made only modest demands of the state and the mansion, even though the house was dilapidated, and in need of basic rebuilding to make it a dignified and safe abode for Kentucky's chief political executive. Historically this fact was emphasized on March 26, 1871, when an unnamed legislator submitted a bill in the House of Representatives, "To provide a residence for the Governor of Kentucky." This bill sank into

oblivion in the bog of parliamentary obfuscation.[38] The problem, however, remained.

Seven years later Joseph B. Read, chairman of a ten-man legislative committee, again considered the matter of a suitable gubernatorial mansion. The committee reported that after many years of wear, tear, and patchwork repairs, the mansion remained dilapidated and unsafe.[39] The building was too shoddy, said the committee, for the use of the governor. The committee also expressed the belief that the state should respond to an offer from Captain H.L. Todd to trade his rather palatial house at the corner of Wapping and Washington Streets for the one at High and Clinton, plus $15,000.[40] The Todd residence contained nineteen rooms, five water closets, adequate gas and water piping, and a spacious linen storage room. The roof was slate covered, and a sturdy perimeter brick wall enclosed a kitchen, stables, carriage house, large ice house, and two oversized cisterns. By every architectural criterion of the times, the Todd residence gave promise to be a proper abode for Kentucky's governors and families for several generations to come.[41]

Simultaneous with the committee's report, there appeared another by an unidentified critic. The writer described the old house on High and Clinton Streets as containing ten rooms, four each on the first and second floors, and two in the attic. All were described as being inadequately lighted and ventilated, with no modern conveniences. During one of the previous repairs, carpenters had lowered the ground floor; later it had to be propped up with heavy timbers, a fact to be mentioned many times in the future. Overhead the shingled roof was said to be in an advanced state of disrepair and leaking.[42]

The special legislative committee also said that the "front entrance was up a steep flight of steps, particularly inconvenient and probably dangerous in winter season."[43] Nevertheless, by that date the mansion had accumulated a patina of vari-colored social and political Kentucky history. It, however, stood at the moment naked and shabby in contrast to the Todd residence. The record is vague as to why the exchange with Captain Todd was never consummated. Perhaps the state lacked the $15,000, and assuredly there was some element of politics involved.[44]

By the 1875 election, the much-discussed new building by the capitol was only partially complete, but enough so to permit removal of the governor's office from the mansion and thus relieve that house from its historical tramplings and public invasions. James Bennett McCreary (1838–1918), a Madison County Democrat and Confederate veteran, won the election and joined the ranks of the "Confederate Brigadiers," having served as a major of cavalry in the Confederate Army. McCreary was married to Katherine (Kate) Hughes of Lexington and Boyle County. She was, to date, the youngest hostess to live in the governor's mansion.[45]

James B. McCreary was inaugurated in high style on August 15, 1875. A welcoming committee from Lexington escorted the couple to the capital by train. Frankfort Mayor (Colonel) E.H. Taylor Jr. met the governor-elect, who was then driven in a carriage drawn by four "spanking good" horses to the statehouse square, where Governor Preston H. Leslie welcomed the entourage. McCreary took the oath of office and then rode with ex-Governor Leslie to the governor's office in the mansion. There, seated behind the executive desk, McCreary received the executive journal and the Great Seal of the Commonwealth.[46] This may have been the last official act to be performed in the library-office.

Newspaper reports of the McCreary inauguration seem to indicate that no women attended the swearing-in ceremony, not even Kate. The ladies, however, were conspicuous at the inaugural ball. Throngs of constituents crowded into Frankfort, coming by special trains from all points to be a part of the great festival. The Western Star Band boomed out reassuring notes that a new day was dawning, and Captain Trausnicht's German Fusiliers made a great clatter in their precision drills. A *Louisville Courier-Journal* reporter wrote that an exciting feature of the day was Captain John Hefner's flight in his forty-foot-high paper balloon. It soared into the air several hundred feet before bursting into flame and perishing. No doubt there was some kind of reminiscent gesture when Captain Sam Goin placed new oak casks filled with ice water about the capital grounds. Surely this brought cheer to the Good Templars and the departing "dry" Preston Leslie.[47]

The years 1875 to 1879 were stirring ones in the history of the governor's mansion. Kate McCreary arranged a succession of lavish parties, suppers, levees, and balls, with the public at large being invited to attend many of the functions.[48]

The governor's papers do seem to indicate that a part of the executive office functions may have been removed from the mansion in 1875, but the removal must have taken place before what became the Executive Building was completely finished. Three years later Governor McCreary noted in his 1878 message to the General Assembly that the walls of the new building were up and the roof was in place, but work on the structure had to be halted because of a lack of funds. He wrote, "I know no good reason why it should remain in its present condition. The necessity of the building being manifest, and its construction commenced, it should be finished without delay."[49] Certainly the transfer of the executive office from the governor's mansion had a distinct bearing on family life.

When Governor and Kate McCreary departed Frankfort in 1879, and Governor Luke (1816–1887) and Julia Churchill Blackburn, his second wife, moved into the mansion there occurred an almost diametrical change in the social tenor of the house. If one is to place full faith in the sources of historical information, and in the sound presentations of Nancy Disher Baird in *Luke Pryor Blackburn: Physician, Governor, Reformer*, and Edward Steers Jr., author of *Blood on the Moon: The Assassination of Abraham Lincoln*, Governor Luke P. Blackburn's name must be burnished into the annals of American history as belonging to the author of one of

Katherine Hughes McCreary and Governor James B. McCreary, 1875–1879. James McCreary's second term was 1911–1915. (KHS)

the most diabolical schemes in American history. He surely lugged into the governor's mansion in Frankfort one of the heaviest burdens of sin against humanity. In the records of Confederate activities in Canada is the account of Dr. Blackburn's attempt to institute a wave of germ warfare. Paradoxically, Dr. Blackburn had a reputation of heroic proportions in the combating of the scourge of yellow fever in the Lower Mississippi River Basin South. Now, a century and a half later, his name is darkened by his attempt to infect northern communities with the fever germ. His effort involved shipping tightly packed trunks of infected clothing to Halifax in Nova Scotia, where they would then be sent on to northern communities of the United States. One package of infected shirts was even to be sent directly to President Lincoln.

If the charge of raising the "Black Flag" is irrefutable, then Luke P. Blackburn took up residence at High and

Clinton Streets with the most mixed professional reputation of any Kentucky governor. The shadow of attempted germ warfare all but negates Governor Blackburn's great humanitarian effort to erase the ghastly social scar of the evil hellhole that was the Kentucky penitentiary.

In 1879, cautious Julia Blackburn made an immediate inventory of the contents in the mansion's ground floor rooms. This listing showed the entry hall contained four floor mats, carpeting, four chairs, two cuspidors, and a portrait of John C. Calhoun. Four sofas lined the walls of the drawing room. There were also a piano and a music stand, a clock, a large mirror, a marble top table, and two china cuspidors. Portraits of Henry Clay and Daniel Webster hung on the walls. The dining room included many things purchased in 1867, but only one goblet or whiskey tumbler seems to have remained. There were nine coffee and teapots, a molasses pitcher,

Governor Luke Blackburn, 1879–1883. (KHS)

a revolving butter dish, a fly brush, a cuspidor, a plate warmer, a coal hod, and other small items.[50]

Life during the years when Luke P. and Julia Blackburn occupied the mansion seemed to have been cast on two levels. There were some public levees, the comings and goings of numerous visitors, guests, and politicians. There also came the reformers who sought to persuade the governor to bring an end to the leasing of convicts to private and inhumane industrial interests. Both the governor and his wife became well aware of the conditions that prevailed in the close-by medieval chamber of horrors, the Kentucky penitentiary, just across High Street.[51] Governor Blackburn knew that the keeper was a shrewd political manipulator and an ardently self-interested man.[52]

By no means could the governor's head lie easily in the mansion in 1880, nor could there be conscience-free levees and balls. Disease, prison overcrowding, human abuses and derelictions, and violence out in the state generated a moral stink which permeated the mansion. Both the Blackburns became deeply involved

in alleviating the evil fleshpot of human degradation at the mansion's front door.

Across High Street and squarely in the Blackburns' faces, nearly a thousand human bodies were crammed into three-by-six coffin-shaped cells.[53] Even more daunting, the fate of so many human souls rested largely in the hands of a venal political hack. The keeper of the penitentiary, Jerry South, is believed to have committed outrages against prisoners and the commonwealth of greater severity than had many of the inmates.[54]

Governor Blackburn told the General Assembly, "I almost feel the blush of shame when I think of the accumulated horrors to be witnessed in our state prison." He said there were 189 more prisoners confined in the penitentiary just out his office window than there were cells to accommodate them. He warned, "The terrible state of affairs required as a necessity, that three hundred and seventy eight of these wretched men should be thrust into cramped and filthy cells." He reported that seventy-four prisoners had died within the past three months.[55]

Julia Churchill Blackburn was equally concerned. A frail woman physically, she was strong of will and spirit. She taught Sunday school classes in the prison and on one occasion had a hardened criminal brought in fetters and chains, then stood beside him while they sang "Where He Leads Me I Will Follow."[56]

Governor Blackburn resorted to an unsettling tactic to gain legislative action. He began pardoning convicts with the threat to depopulate the pit of shame. In an executive message Governor Blackburn noted the fact that he was aware of Jerry South's mismanagement of the institution. He pardoned fourteen bed-ridden and terminally ill convicts, who in turn requested that they be hauled to the mansion so they could express their thanks to him in person.[57]

While Luke P. Blackburn raised public and political hackles over free-handed pardoning of convicts from the hellhole penitentiary, Julia Churchill provoked a stir in provincial Frankfort society. She sent out from the mansion invitations to a "german." These, said a *Louisville Courier-Journal* reporter, "Became the all-absorbing topic. On the street, in the hotel, at the table in the parlor, and even during the most interesting debate in the legislative halls, the question was heard 'Are you going to see the "german"?'" None was more puzzled by the term than a legislator whom the reporter described as "A long, lank, grizzly mountaineer member, in a faded brown velveteen jacket and corduroy pantaloons stuffed in his muddy rawhide boots,

The east section of a 1925 Blanche panoramic photograph of Frankfort. The penitentiary is situated along High Street, and a glimpse of the governor's mansion is at far right center. (KHS)

[who] suspended for a moment the expectoration of copious streams of tobacco juice fired over the heads of other members at a spittoon four seats removed from him, and stood listening intently to a conversation in the lobby about the debt of gratitude society owed to Mrs. Blackburn in introducing the german here. Old mossback couldn't stand it any longer, and just as there chanced to come a lull in the proceedings of the House, he blurted out to the gentleman speaking, "Say you, sir! tell me who that gol darned Dutchman is that everybody is excited about and wants ter see at the palace down 'round the corner?" At news filing time, the "Dutchman" had not been spotted on the streets of Frankfort.[58]

In no place or institution in Kentucky could evidence of demand for change be more clearly defined than the relocation of the state capital and the governor's mansion. In 1880, Luke P. and Julia Churchill Blackburn had literally the stench and human degradation of the Kentucky Penitentiary at their door. This fact was recognized by the Kentucky Senate on March 10, 1880,

when it enacted a bill to have the mansion and its surrounding grounds sold at public auction. The palace and plots of ground were to be sold separately to the highest bidder. In turn a new mansion was to be located well beyond the blighting environment of the penitentiary. The Senate authorized an appropriation of $15,000 in addition to the money raised in the auctions. The House of Representatives defeated the bill on the same day as the Senate action. The House's action was influenced by the fact it would have to appropriate the additional sum to finance the purchase or construction of a new mansion. Thus the ancient house was once again propped up and patched for future governors and their families to tolerate.

Between the administrations of John White Stevenson and James Bennett McCreary there occurred some visible changes and transitions in the general nature of rural-agrarian domestic family life in Kentucky. This was an era in which the pressures of the times brought changes in the economy, insistent social demands, and

Governor J. Proctor Knott, 1883–1887. (KHS)

A porcelain punch bowl embellished with grapes and flowers that is used in the new mansion today. The record is silent about its history, but it bears a striking resemblance to the descriptions of Governor Proctor Knott's roman punch bowl. (Kentucky Finance Cabinet, Division of Creative Services and Photography [FCS])

the reassessing of the structure of state government itself.

Social life in the governor's mansion was patterned after the individual ways of life of its ever-changing tenants, and perhaps the most exciting things that happened and concerned the tone of life in the mansion were settling the issue of the permanent seat of the capital, the removal of the governor's office to the new executive building, and the growing press awareness of social events and family affairs associated with the governor's house.[59] The transitions of governors in flamboyant inaugural festivals brought new personalities to the mansion, and bright new promises to the commonwealth. Such was the occasion when J. Proctor (1830–1911) and Sarah Rosannah McElroy Knott arrived on Clinton Street. They were childless but had frequent visitations by nephews and nieces.[60] Like Julia Blackburn, Sarah Knott was a frail woman, but not too frail to be aware of social demands. She, like several preceding hostesses, had a quasi-political background. She was able to rely upon her cousin Charles Wickliffe and his wife to assist her in the gatherings in the mansion.[61]

There was nothing frail about Governor Knott; he had a robust Kentuckian's love of life, politics, and vittles. Unlike the austere Leslie, his sideboard bubbled with the roseate "Spirit of Kentucky." The man from Marion County was a hardy trencherman, who served food and drink with a generous hand, especially to male company. He poured bounteous helpings of hot roman punch from his favorite antique china bowl. Governor Knott was even said to have served a gathering of stag companions a robust banquet featuring a table burdened with lavish helpings of opossum, roast pigs' heads with ears of corn in their mouths, goblets of stout cider, and generous wedges of pumpkin pie. A full corporal's guard of Frankfort maidens, dressed in Dolly Varden frocks, bore, "Maid Marian" style, generously ladened panniers to the table.[62]

When the possum, pig's heads, and pumpkin pie had been washed down with cider, the table was cleared and a brass band struck up a waltz tune and the guests danced until well beyond the hour which many Frankfort citizens considered a decent bed time. No doubt present that evening was that jovial and benevolent public servant James W. "Honest Dick" Tate, who at the very moment was directing the flow of public funds into oblique channels.[63]

By no means did all of life in the mansion during the Knott years reflect so robust a nature and taste. Much of Kentucky was in social, economic, and political turmoil, acts of violence were repeatedly sullying the Kentucky image, and Kentucky's treasury cupboard was too bare to permit even the purchase of a fancy cuspidor for the mansion.[64]

The gubernatorial election of 1887 brought to the governor's office the noblest of the "Brigadiers," Simon Bolivar Buckner (1823–1914). Kentucky to date had elected few, if any, abler men to the office of chief executive. General Buckner had a colorful history as a Confederate general, a real estate speculator, a farmer, and a friend of his West Point contemporary Ulysses S. Grant. Beyond his military and business record, General Buckner took to Frankfort one of the youngest and most attractive of the governor's wives. He had met and wooed Delia Claiborne at White Sulphur Springs in West Virginia. General Buckner married her on June 10, 1885, in Richmond, Virginia, and brought her to live at his farm, Glen Lily, in Hart County.[65]

Delia Claiborne was twenty-eight years of age, while General Buckner was sixty-two. Born to the couple on July 15, 1886, was Simon Bolivar Buckner Jr., who was taken as a year-old infant to live in the governor's mansion in Frankfort. General Buckner had been nominated to be governor by the Democrats, and to oppose William O. Bradley, a Republican from Garrard County. For the campaign that year the Democrats had adopted the alliterative battle cry "Bolivar, Betty, and the Baby," though Delia was not named Betty. Delia was said to be an invalid when the Buckners moved to Frankfort, and in the elaborate inaugural ceremonies she sat by her husband, too feeble to participate in the more taxing social activities of the inaugural festival.[66]

Delia Buckner was said to have been seated and elegantly attired on "an impromptu throne" for the early receptions in the mansion. She sat couched upon magnificent cushions that lined her elevated chair of state. It was said she wore a gown of bewitching splendor, while behind and around her stood the staff officers of the Governor's Guards dressed in their "full official uniforms." Clustered about the ballroom were battalions of young women who had received special invitations to act as hostesses. These belles of Frankfort were described as being robed "to the nines" in silks, laces, and jewels.[67]

Governor Simon Bolivar Buckner, 1887–1891. (KHS)

On the evening of October 10, 1890, Governor Buckner gave a reception for the delegates to the fourth constitutional convention. In that assembly of guests several "country men" came to see how the famous Confederate general-governor lived in the one-time palace. One such guest was George C. Harris of Simpson County, who made close observations of the surrounding happenings of the evening. The following day he wrote his daughter, Stella, a rather detailed account of his visit to the mansion. He observed the hostess, the food, and drink. He told Stella there was a broad porch across the front of the house that was enclosed for the evening behind a tarpaulin, "or something of the kind." A brass band was seated there and played until late in the evening. When Harris entered the front door he was ushered upstairs to shed his hat, and then he came down and entered the parlor, where he saw Governor Buckner standing beside his wife. He was told that Delia was unable to stand, but to Delegate

George Harris was ushered up the mansion's stairs in 1890 when he arrived at Governor Buckner's party. At left, the old staircase still stands in the abandoned mansion, circa 1945. (Department of Public Information) And at right, after the restoration, Shirley Ford is escorted down the old mansion stairs by her father, Lieutenant Governor Wendell Ford, on June 26, 1971. (Ford family collection)

Harris she seemed to be the picture of health. He wrote that Delia wore "a very fine dress with long train held up in folds around some way." After he had been greeted by the Governor and Delia, Harris was free to greet the other guests, "and enjoy yourself as best you could."

In making the circuit, the observant Harris wandered into the dining room, where he saw the tables arranged "hotel style." There he said he was free to eat at any time he chose. He wrote, "I had for supper or lunch whatever it might be called, sparrow on toast, at least I took it to be either sparrow or canary. It was so small I could not tell. Oysters, or oyster in some light roll, salad, crackling beat biscuits, about the size of a quarter, buttered inside. I think coffee, candies, goodies, ice cream, sliut [sic], and punch. The salad was in some kind green leaf." This was the kind of fare that a hardy western Kentucky statesman hardly expected to find on General Buckner's dining table. Harris was somewhat overwhelmed that all the feminine guests were elegant-

ly dressed, but, he told his daughter, "But you know I could never tell how anyone was dressed."[68]

In a less formal way than a state reception, the Buckners hosted a number of distinguished visitors. There came in their grand tour of the states to gather information Lord James and Mrs. Bryce. James Bryce was engaged in research for his monumental two-volume classic, *The American Commonwealth, 1888*. On another occasion Delia Buckner's cousin, Thomas Nelson Page, arrived from Virginia. This budding author stood before a fireplace in the reception room parlor and read his to-be-famous *Marse Chan* (1884). Theodore Roosevelt made his way from Louisville to Frankfort and the mansion to do research in preparation for his multi-volume *Winning of the West*. Charles Dudley Warner, the popular observer of the American scene, visited Frankfort in 1887 and was a guest in the governor's mansion. Warner had been commissioned by *Harper's Monthly Magazine* to revisit the postwar

South to observe the social and economic changes that had come to the region.[69]

Thus the four years of Simon Bolivar Buckner's administration as governor of Kentucky were years of some glory, but they were also fraught with frustrations and excitement. By that date the governor's office had been permanently located in the "fireproof" executive office building. During the four years he was in Frankfort, Governor Buckner was plagued by Kentucky's unsettling internal problems. Comparable to an outbreak of the plague, the state was being morally and fiscally stifled by violence and official rascality. Coupled with this was a chronic shortage of public funds. The defalcation and abscondence of the state treasurer, "Honest Dick" Tate, set the state back for some time to come.[70]

Feuds were responsible for much of the commonwealth's rampant violence. The Kentucky–West Virginia border seethed with the Hatfield-McCoy feud. Whatever the cause for this outbreak of murder and general lawlessness, when graphic accounts of the Tug River troubles reached the governor's office, they demanded emergency executive action. For instance, there is lodged in the Buckner papers a pencil-inscribed confession made by Ellison Mounts. This document presented a vivid first-hand testimonial of the heartless murders of the adolescent McCoys.[71]

Perhaps no governor to date had spent so much time at the desk writing messages and communications as did Governor Buckner. He was said to have been an indifferent speaker, and much preferred communicating through the written word. Both the Buckner papers and the executive journal bear this out.[72]

The terminal date of the Buckner occupation of the mansion came on the morning of September 3, 1891. A *Louisville Courier-Journal* reporter noted that this event brought to an end the rule of the "Brigadier Governors" and proclaimed the departing Buckner "a good man." An editorialist wrote that Buckner had "displayed in the exercise of his high office the qualities the people admire." He was said to have done so with staunch dignity as "a sterling Democrat." Though General Buckner had brought about some important governmental reforms, his meager $5,000 contingency fund, even in terms of 1890 dollars, hardly supported a lavish imperial way of life. No doubt Simon Bolivar and Delia were ready to pack up and be off. "Bolivar, Betty, and the Baby" moved back to Glen Lily and a less stressful environment in Hart County. Behind them they left a mansion in peril.[73]

The *Courier-Journal* ran a drawing of the mansion at the time of the inauguration of John Young Brown Jr. (1835–1904). A reporter for the paper said the drawing "is too flattering to be exact, it is rickety-rackety and its dilapidated condition is too well known to need comment." He thought adoption of the new constitution might pave the way for the commonwealth to undertake the relocation and construction of a new mansion.[74]

Those were hard times, politically and financially. John Young Brown, of Elizabethtown-Henderson, arrived in Frankfort on inauguration day boasting that he had spent less than a thousand dollars on his campaign.[75] The new governor was accompanied to Frankfort by his wife, Rebecca Dixon Brown, their three teenage daughters, and a son, Archibald Dixon. Of all the new governors who had clamored down the Kentucky River Palisades into Frankfort to take the oath of office, none received a more bizarre welcome than did John Brown. General Simon and Delia Buckner had invited them to come directly to the mansion, but due to a bumbling mix-up, the new governor and his family arrived by train and there was no one to meet them. They boarded the rickety old public horse-drawn omnibus, driven by a jehu whom the *Lexington Leader* described as not having been "endowed with too much sense." He drove the Browns around South Frankfort and then finally reached the governor's mansion. The Lexington reporter wrote that the "escort committee, whose duty it was to have carriages at the depot, are catching Hail Columbia on all sides for this gross carelessness."[76]

Frankfort more or less made up for the blunder. When Governor Buckner and governor-elect Brown were ready for the inaugural ceremony they were escorted to the statehouse by an also belated military unit and by a brass band that made the Frankfort pan-bowl ring with the emotion-stirring refrains of "Dixie."

There wandered through the throng of people that day some of what were said to be the "hungriest" office-seekers ever to trample the political turf of those grounds. Towering above the crowd was the famous Kentucky giant, Smith Cook, who wooed the power brokers to be made a legislative door-keeper. In all the excitement of the day the new governor lamented that he had at his disposal "Only fifteen openings to which I could apportion only twenty of the 141,000 expectant men" who claimed to have voted for him.[77]

Through it all, the old mansion stood sphinx-like. The Buckners had left it in as good condition as the stingy legislators who provided funds to repair and furnish it would allow, and at the outset the Brown occupancy promised an air of sociality. The three daughters, Birdie, Susan, and Evelyn, brought youthfulness to the place. Too, Archibald Dixon Brown and his wife, Virginia Marshall, were there as part of the family circle.[78]

The promise of gaiety, however, was never fully realized. Susan died of tuberculosis on October 30, 1894, and soon after there was a second death. On May 1, 1895, there occurred an incident that shattered Governor Brown's future political ambition. His son and secretary, Archibald Dixon Brown, was murdered in a house of assignation on Madison Street in Louisville.[79]

On several occasions Arch had taken Mrs. Fulton (Nellie Bush) Gordon to Lucy Smith's house of ill fame. Some never-to-be-identified person in Frankfort sent Fulton Gordon word, in Louisville, that his wife was possibly having a clandestine affair. Following up on the message, he tracked his wife to the Smith house. It was a dramatic encounter when he found her nude in bed with Arch Dixon Brown. A scuffle ensued, and Gordon shot and killed both his wife and Brown.[80]

The case of Fulton Gordon being charged with the murder of Governor Brown's son and secretary received a sensational amount of publicity, and Governor Brown employed the fiery lawyer James Andrew Scott to participate in the trial. Governor Brown seems to have been as much concerned with who in Frankfort sent the anonymous note as with the murder of his son.[81]

Those pistol shots in the Louisville house of assignation cut short Governor Brown's political ambitions to become a United States senator. He wrote Cassius M. Clay Jr., the former president of the fourth Kentucky Constitutional Convention, that, "I shall not be a candidate for the Senate. The calamities of my children, which have recently befallen, have utterly unfitted me for the contest. My grief is so severe that, like a black vampire of the night, it seems to have sucked dry the very arteries and veins of my hope and ambition."[82]

If there has ever been a ghostly presence in the governor's mansion on High and Clinton Street, it is surely that of Archibald Dixon Brown. Just a few months earlier he had divorced Virginia Marshall Brown, at a time when the Brown family still mourned the death of his sister Susan. When the Brown family left the mansion in 1895 it may well have resembled that gloomy day in 1891 when they arrived in Frankfort.[83] The miscarried plans on that occasion when they had been hauled over the town in a shabby old horse-drawn omnibus surely must have been an omen of sadness to come. Added to the Brown family's grief was the haunting

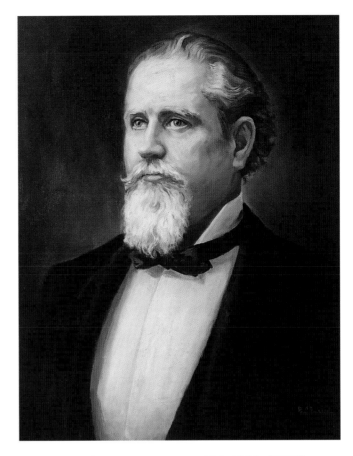

Governor John Young Brown, 1891–1895. (KHS)

historical fact that the governor left behind an administration of a sorely mixed reputation of ineffectiveness. However, they at least left some mark of their presence in the mansion. Before they vacated the house to William O. and Margaret Duncan Bradley, they had had the hall and some of the rooms recarpeted. They also had added some pieces of furniture, made some temporary repairs of the building, washed the curtains, and run up a water bill of $75.[84] The ancient and crumbling building, which the *Louisville Courier-Journal* had labeled a "rickety-rackety" structure, was no better off than it had been four years before.[85]

One of the aftershocks of the 1890s depression may have been the faint dawning of new political and economic promise under the new constitution, and some perceptive improvement in the Kentucky economy. A better governor's mansion might be purchased or constructed. Whatever the fates offered, the crumbling house on High and Clinton Streets was doomed.[86]

CHAPTER 7

Mansion Tenants of a Fading Era

By December 1895, local and national issues had divided Democrats into two sharply dissenting groups, and during the same era the Republicans had grown more numerous and self assured—none more so than William O. Bradley (1847–1914) of Lancaster, a native son. In the moment of Democratic discord, he was elected governor, the first Republican to hold the office.[1] Bradley, a master campaigner, had defeated Democratic P. Wat Hardin, and token Populist Thomas S. Pettit.[2]

Retiring Governor John Young Brown Jr., in departing Frankfort, left behind a mixed administrative record. His successes and failures surely summed up the tenor of Kentucky politics and politicians. In a letter to Cassius M. Clay Jr., he labeled his fellow Democrats, and the silverites among them especially, as being guilty of "hypocrisy, ingratitude, lies, and treachery."[3] In bold, tangible terms Governor Brown left a governor's mansion as profoundly in need of repair and refurbishing as were the Democrats. For four years the mansion had stood in need of legislative attention.

In the moment of gubernatorial transition, a *Western Argus* reporter wrote that nearly all the money spent on the governor's mansion had been wasted. Each of the past thirty-one governors had made repairs to satisfy his needs and fancies. Perhaps the most distinguishing feature of the house in 1895 was the brag that it was one of the oldest in Frankfort. The *Argus* reporter reiterated the often lamented fact that "the amount of money expended on it in its lifetime would have made for Kentucky's governors a marble Mansion."[4]

Marble mansion or not, Governor Bradley and his wife, Margaret Robertson Duncan, and their daughter Christine, traveled from Lancaster to Richmond to board a Louisville and Nashville Railroad train drawn

Governor William O. Bradley, 1895–1899. (KHS)

by a "special locomotive," headed for Frankfort. Passing through Lexington they were welcomed by a "whooping, hollering, hat-tossing" throng of Republicans.[5] A good number of them went on to Frankfort to demonstrate their loyalty on inauguration day. In Frankfort the Bradleys were met at the train by Colonel L.P. Larkin and were hustled away to his country home, "Fleetwood."[6]

On the morning of the inauguration, Governor-elect Bradley was driven to Second Street, where Governor John Young Brown Jr. greeted him and then drove him to the capitol in a carriage drawn by four white horses. Reporters did not describe what became of Mrs. Bradley and Christine. That day in Frankfort, said a Lexington news reporter, was one of "jubili-jubalo" for the Republicans. Men whooped hosannas and threw their hats into the air. "The scene," said the reporter, "as Bradley mounted the stand beggers description."[7]

The inaugural occasion for the Bradleys may have been somewhat temporized by the fact that they were still in mourning, after two years, over the death of their son George Robertson. Too, they left behind in Lancaster a nineteenth-century, Victorian-style cottage that was in much better condition than the governor's mansion in Frankfort. Among the personal belongings the family brought with them were portraits of the departed son and of Governor Bradley's father, Robert McAfee Bradley.[8]

At the outset of his administration Governor Bradley corroborated the *Argus* reporter's description of the mansion. In his first message to the General Assembly he warned that all the public buildings were in a poor state of repair and were unsafe for the state employees who worked in them. "The Executive Mansion," he wrote, "is old, out of repair and uncomfortable, and the lower floors are sustained by props to prevent them from falling. Enough has been expended in repairing it to have built several edifices. Its site is by no means eligible and its surroundings is [sic] everything but cheerful and agreeable."[9]

In his second message Governor Bradley again warned the Democratically controlled legislature to initiate action to alleviate the inadequacies and threatening dangers in the public buildings. "As to the Executive Mansion," he wrote, "for years its floors have been propped up to prevent them from falling, and it required more than seven hundred feet of weather strips to make it comfortable in the winter [1895–1896]. The present site is disagreeable, the view from one side overlooks the walls of the penitentiary, and from the other the smokestack of a large flouring mill nearby."[10]

Gathered up in the malevolent political maelstrom which sucked all political and economic issues into its vortex of partisanship, there was no real hope for improvement of the mansion. Certainly the governor's mansion provided only limited space and financial support for any glittering entertainment or pageantry. Further complicating life in the house was the petty

action of a "ripper minded" General Assembly which smarted under the loss of the governorship. Democrat legislators undertook to snatch control of the mansion from the governor and place it under the supervision of the Kentucky Court of Appeals and authorize the employment of a $1,200-a-year custodian. Governor Bradley had such disdain for the law that he refused to sign or return it to the House of Representatives.[11]

Despite the factional political infighting and other woes, the Bradley family occupied the mansion with some degree of social conviviality. Their feastings and entertainments were strictly "cold water" affairs, with both the governor and Mrs. Bradley confirmed teetotalers. By nature a quiet and retiring woman, Mrs. Bradley had only a limited taste for entertaining. Her daughter Christine, however, reveled in the excitement of parties and receptions. For a little more than three years the decrepit old mansion reverberated with some kind of social excitement.[12]

William O. Bradley, himself, was a gregarious man who enjoyed the stimulus of masses of people. A master raconteur, an eloquent debater, a vigorous campaigner, and a master of the indigenous Kentucky anecdote,[13] he knew well that the Republican party had for the first time a political and social foothold in Frankfort. He also knew that he was a target for paranoid legislative snipping at his office.[14]

Christine Bradley, in Republican eyes, was the fairest maid in Kentucky. She made her social debut in the mansion, the first ever such occasion, and even became slightly interwoven in the fabric of Kentucky literary history. During the winter of 1895–1896, John Fox Jr. was in Frankfort. He, along with the poet Robert Burns Wilson, had rooms in Miss Ludie Ware's boardinghouse. On that visit Fox was inspired to write *The Kentuckians*, and he was said to have included Christine in his forthcoming *Little Shepherd of Kingdom Come*, as the character Miss Annie Bruce.[15]

Christine Bradley was sent to school in Washington during the year 1897–1898. While she was away Governor Bradley received word from the United States Department of the Navy that the battleship *Kentucky* was ready to be christened. The Navy suggested that a member of the governor's family should be chosen, and the governor chose Christine. In the meantime the governor did some research and discovered that the famous old *Ironsides* had been christened by having a bottle of water broken over its bow. Being a teetotaler, he sent a bottle of water from the Lincoln Spring in Hodgenville.[16] Soon after the christening ceremony there appeared at the mansion a delegation from the Woman's Christian Temperance Union, led by the indomitable Frances Beauchamp. The nemesis of the Kentucky saloon keepers, she came to present a gift and a commendation. The gift consisted of an inscribed silver tray, a water pitcher, and two goblets. The inscription read, "Kentucky Christian Temperance Union to Miss Christine Bradley, as a tribute to her loyalty to conviction in the christening of the Battleship *Kentucky* with water. March 10, 1898."[17]

Nearly one year later, on the morning of February 10, 1899, Mrs. Bradley and Christine went across the way to board a train for Lexington, accompanied by the pompous General Wilbur Smith of Lexington business school fame. Christine was to appear that intensely cold day in a Lexington Terpsichore tableau of "The Republic." A messenger brought news that the governor's mansion was ablaze. At that moment the thermometer in Frankfort registered 20 degrees below zero. Mrs. Bradley returned to the mansion, leaving her daughter and General Smith to go on to Lexington. By the time she reached the house the second floor bedroom was fully engulfed in flame.[18]

When the Frankfort fire fighters arrived at the mansion, they had difficulty pumping water through the rapidly freezing hoses. In the meantime Governor Bradley and other state officials arrived and joined in the fight. The governor was anxious to rescue the portraits of his son and father, saying these were the only likenesses he had of them. In spite of the cold and frozen equipment, firemen finally extinguished the fire, or so they thought. In a short time a second fire flared up. This time the fire hoses were too frozen to be useful, and the firemen resorted to the use of buckets.

Executive papers, most of the furniture, and the two portraits were saved, but the fire concluded temporarily the Bradleys' occupation of the mansion. The fact that executive records were in the house seems to indicate that much of the governor's activities still were performed in the residence.[19] It was later discovered that the fires had started around a defective flue in the governor's bedroom.[20] Despite some vagueness in the record, it is almost certain that Mrs. Bradley and Christine eventually returned to their home in Lancaster. Immediately after the fire Governor Bradley and his family stayed with a neighbor on High Street, Miss Jennie Gaines. Later Governor Bradley said he would take up residence in the Capitol Hotel until the end of his term.[21]

The commonwealth suffered no loss from the fire. The house was adequately insured, and an immediate evaluation of the property indicated it was worth $9,500. No doubt a *Courier-Journal* reporter expressed a consensus when he wrote, "There was but little regret shown today while the old structure was being devoured. By the flames, many of the onlookers expressing their desires, 'That while there is no authority to rebuild, the burned mansion may be repaired,' notwithstanding this means building outright."[22]

As the *Courier-Journal* reporter indicated, the fire did considerable damage to the "patched-up-propped-up" mansion, enough in fact that in a more rational moment it would have seemed sensible either to demolish the old structure and build a new and more fitting mansion, or simply to buy one of the more palatial Frankfort homes.[23] Democratic legislators, however, were hardly in a mood to accommodate a Republican governor. Once again the building was "patched up" and made ready for gubernatorial occupancy.[24] The rebuilding had cost the commonwealth a modest amount, as internal changes were made, such as replacing the old gas lighting pipes and fixtures with electrical wiring to usher the mansion into the age of electricity, with current supplied by a small generator located on the public grounds.[25]

Governor Bradley and his wife and daughter may have moved back into the mansion during the remaining five months of his term. Of greater importance, however, was the fact that the fire surely must have portended the violent political eruption of the following year when the commonwealth would be thrown into a near state of anarchy.[26] The intensity of the growing political rivalry was reflected in the extraordinary number of laws passed by Democrat legislators, only to be vetoed by Governor Bradley.

In another area, the executive journals and the public press document eloquently the fact that Kentucky in this era was plagued by a wave of rising bloody crimes.[27] Outbreaks of guerrilla raiding prevailed in Louisville, Frankfort, and elsewhere. The press chronicled the murderous activities of the earlier Tolliver-Martin conflict and the chronic flouting of civility and the law in the "blood feuds" of Appalachian Kentucky.[28]

The raucous gubernatorial election of 1899 heightened existing tensions. At the center of the political upheaval stood a cold, calculating man, William Goebel (1856–1900). In juxtaposition was an all-powerful corporation, the Louisville and Nashville Railroad.[29] Add in a mixture of all but irreconcilable forces resulting from the national issues of the currency-populist crusade,[30] and Kentucky's public temper was greatly agitated.

By 1895, William Goebel had already masterminded

The calculating William Goebel. (KDLA)

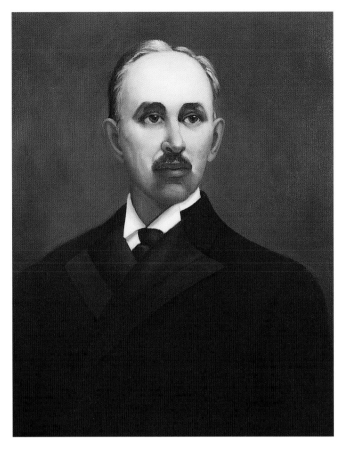

Governor William S. Taylor, 1899–1900. (KHS)

enactment of an insidious election regulatory law, a modification of the McChord Railway Law, and projected a school textbook bill.[31] The textbook bill failed passage because of textbook company lobbying pressure, despite Governor Bradley's sanctioning such a law. He told legislators, "It is said that Kentucky pays twice as much for school books as states north of us."[32] Kentucky, in fact, was a virtual fiefdom of the American Book Company.

The tragic conflict that followed the gubernatorial election sullied Kentucky's image for decades to come. William Goebel and John Young Brown became embroiled in a divisive intra-Democrat rivalry; at the same time the Republicans put forth the current attorney general as candidate for governor. In the general election William S. Taylor (1853–1928) received an announced vote of 193,714, and William Goebel 191,381.[33] On the basis of this vote count, Taylor was inaugurated governor on December 12, 1899. He came to the office completely from outside the pale of the traditional political matrix. He was a resident of isolated rural Butler County, and was married to Sara Belle

Tanner. They were the parents of nine children, seven of whom had come to Frankfort to live with their parents when Taylor was elected attorney general.[34] When Governor Taylor took the oath of office on December 12, 1899, there hovered over Frankfort a heavy political mist of election frauds. The fog of political intrigue and conflict was thickened by the assassination of William Goebel on January 30, 1900.[35]

The Taylor inaugural ceremony was of the traditional type, with a fairly large crowd milling around inside the fenced-in area in front of the capitol. Almost immediately following the inauguration, Democrats in the General Assembly challenged the accuracy of the vote count, and for almost sixty days the Frankfort scene was disturbed by bitter controversy. The Taylor family occupied the mansion for approximately fifty days, during which no levees, lavish parties, or other forms of public entertainment took place. Because of the vote challenges, the mansion became a virtual armed fortress.[36]

Enraged Republicans from several Eastern Kentucky counties went to Frankfort to protect the integrity of

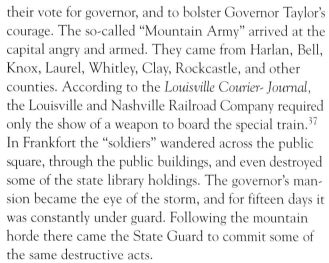

GOVERNOR GOEBEL

Governor William Goebel taking the oath of office on his deathbed at the Capitol Hotel. (*Cincinnati Enquirer,* February 3, 1900)

Governor William Goebel, 1900. (KHS)

their vote for governor, and to bolster Governor Taylor's courage. The so-called "Mountain Army" arrived at the capital angry and armed. They came from Harlan, Bell, Knox, Laurel, Whitley, Clay, Rockcastle, and other counties. According to the *Louisville Courier-Journal,* the Louisville and Nashville Railroad Company required only the show of a weapon to board the special train.[37] In Frankfort the "soldiers" wandered across the public square, through the public buildings, and even destroyed some of the state library holdings. The governor's mansion became the eye of the storm, and for fifteen days it was constantly under guard. Following the mountain horde there came the State Guard to commit some of the same destructive acts.

Among the latter troops was S.P. Embry of Louisville who, a half-century later, billed the commonwealth for $19.50, which he claimed was due him as back pay. He submitted his bill on August 15, 1953, saying that he had belonged to Company C of the State Guard, that, "We really suffered standing guard on Governor Taylor's Mansion." Despite the fact he had moved to West Virginia, Embry expressed deep affection for Kentucky

even if it had been in debt to him a half century. He, however, would be much prouder of the state if it would pay its debt. In 1900, Guardsman Embry said, he could have bought a steer with the money, but in 1953 he could only buy two T-bone steaks.[38] The record is silent as to whether Embry was paid.

A dark cloud of bitter political discord, if not murder, hovered over Kentucky during January of 1900, and the Taylor family, all but barricaded within the governor's mansion, surely faced uncertainty, frustration, and possibly harm. Neither the governor nor members of his family could have had peace of mind enough to think of refurbishing the house and entertaining in its rooms.[39]

By May, their occupancy of the mansion rested in the hands of the United States Supreme Court.[40] In the feverish moment, Governor Taylor and his family went to Louisville to await the Court's decision. When a 5–4 decision in favor of the Democrats was rendered, the Taylors boarded a Monon Railway train and went across the Ohio River to a haven of safety at French Lick, Indiana. Friends had advised Governor Taylor

A sterling silver sugar spoon used in the old governor's mansion during the Taylor administration (1899–1900), and displayed in the house today. (KHS)

Governor J.C.W. Beckham, 1900–1907. (KHS)

that if he remained in Kentucky he most assuredly would be arrested on trumped-up charges of conspiracy, if not as an accomplice to murder.[41] On that May afternoon, the Taylors left behind in Frankfort a house in the same poor condition in which they had found it the past December.

During the ides of the political calendar in Kentucky, the wheel of fate turned on a warped spindle. The Supreme Court decision brought to office young John Crepps Wickliffe Beckham (1869–1940) of Bardstown. The youthful lieutenant governor–new governor had been a schoolteacher, a practicing attorney, and a member of the Kentucky House of Representatives. Politically, and most important of all, he was heir apparent to the Nelson County–Bardstown Democratic enclave.[42]

With an appreciable degree of reservation, William Goebel had accepted Beckham as his running mate in 1899. He certainly could not have had any notion that the lieutenant governor would actually become governor. In his ascendancy, the thirty-one-year-old J.C.W.

Beckham became the youngest man in Kentucky history to hold the governorship.[43] He also was the first bachelor to occupy the mansion, Breathitt having been a widower.

On May 21, 1900, the governor's mansion stood in chronic need of repair. There remained the soot and stains of the fires, and an indeterminate amount of damage from occupancy by the "Mountain Army" and the State Guard had been suffered. Nevertheless, it stood a scarred and creaky symbol of the power of the governorship itself.[44]

Julia Tevis Wickliffe Beckham, a stalwart social and political veteran, came to Frankfort to be her son's hostess. A graduate of the Science Hill Academy in Shelbyville, she bore the name of its founder, Julia Tevis. She was the daughter of former Governor Charles Wickliffe, and the sister of Governor Robert Wickliffe of Louisiana. An anonymous author wrote in 1913 of Julia Tevis Wickliffe, "She was a woman of noble presence and queenly bearing, intelligent, genial and

Governor Beckham and his Bardstown family outside the governor's mansion, prior to his marriage to Jean Raphael Fuqua in 1900. (KHS)

gracious mannered—a true type of southern matron, born to command, direct, and in control of her own and the destinies of others committed to her care."[45] Mrs. Beckham faced a grim task in the ordering of her son's household in emotionally drained Frankfort. Her reign as hostess, however, was brief. The governor was in love.

No one attending the notorious Musical Hall Convention in Louisville in 1899 could have predicted that the handsome, young bachelor from Bardstown would be more than a stand-in official in Frankfort.[46] But in 1900 he ran for election to fill the rest of Goebel's term. Somewhere, perhaps during that fall campaign, he met Jean Raphael Fuqua of Owensboro, and apparently conducted a joint political-romantic

campaign. As profuse as the report of their marriage is, there is no hint of their courtship.[47]

Annie Chambers Czapskl, a *Louisville Courier-Journal* social reporter, interviewed Jean Fuqua on the eve of her marriage. She described "a tall, slight girl, very pretty, very young, with modest unassuming deportment, self-possessed and gracious in manner." The governor's approaching marriage was perhaps the only bright and romantic interlude in Kentucky's bitter history at the turn of the century.[48]

The wedding of J.C.W. Beckham and Jean Raphael Fuqua occurred in the First Presbyterian Church of Owensboro on November 22, 1900. In the words of a newspaper society reporter, it was "the most brilliant

The governor's mansion at the time of the Goebel assassination in 1900. It was here that J.C.W. Beckham brought Jean Raphael Fuqua Beckham, his bride and the hostess of the mansion. (KHS)

function ever held in this little town. At the Presbyterian Church guests were crowded into every seat, and as many were left standing on the outside."[49]

In many respects Governor Beckham's marriage to a young, unsophisticated bride was for the commonwealth a romantic antidote to that era of public trauma. Annie Chambers Czapskl subtly raised the question of how adequately the sheltered Jean Fuqua would fill the role of hostess of the governor's mansion. She had attended the Owensboro schools, and had studied French and music in the Mary Baldwin Junior College in Staunton, Virginia. At home she played the piano and sang in church gatherings, but she responded with a resounding "NO" when asked if she had an interest in philosophy and psychology. A friend said Jean would not miss church or Wednesday night prayer meeting for anything. She did not play cards, and disapproved of drinking, but left in doubt whether or not she would approve serving wine at official mansion dinner parties.[50]

Not only was the Owensboro Presbyterian Church

overwhelmed by the Beckham wedding, the city's creaky public conveyances were paralyzed at the outset. Private citizens were asked to step in with their carriages and accommodate visitors. Commercial conveyances were also brought in from Evansville, Indiana.[51]

The overcrowded church proved not to be a safe sanctuary, as pickpockets got into the sanctum and garnered a rich harvest. A *Louisville Courier-Journal* reporter wrote that Kentucky State Treasurer S.W. Hager was relieved of $65, the Reverend Lewis Tallifero was robbed of $8 or $10, and a distinguished guest lost a diamond-mounted shirt stud worth $150. Other persons discovered that they too had made contributions against their will.

Jean Beckham, following her wedding, surely must have been somewhat surprised at some of the great number of wedding gifts. A Louisville delegation came bearing twelve each of claret and champagne glasses, along with an ample punch bowl. In all, the couple received a dozen or more punch bowls.[52]

71

Jean Raphael Fuqua became the wife of Governor John Crepps Wickliffe Beckham on November 22, 1900, in Owensboro. (*Louisville Courier-Journal*, KHS)

Events moved at a fast pace for the newlywed couple. At midnight in Owensboro, they boarded Jean's brother-in-law W.B. Nickern's private railway car for Chicago. Their honeymoon in the city, however, was cut short by the fact that Governor Beckham had to return to Frankfort to prepare for his inauguration on December 11.[53] The bride was literally thrust into the responsibility of being the governor's mansion hostess without time to unpack her trousseau. Crowds gathered in Frankfort, and at the inaugural reception Jean Fuqua stood for hours, again dressed in her wedding gown shaking hands with the citizenry. Such a crush of people came to the reception that it was necessary to control the crowd by closing the doors of the room to permit one wave of well wishers to pass out a side door before a new one was allowed into the hall.

The grand reception following the inauguration was the beginning of a seven-year occupation by the Beckhams.

During those years they set several precedents. J.C.W. Beckham was the youngest man to become governor in Kentucky history, and Jean was the youngest hostess.[54] The couple arrived at High and Clinton Streets well endowed with wedding gifts, many of them bearing the labels of Tiffany, Gorham, and Wedgewood, even of the glassmasters of Ireland.

Among the throng gathered about the wedding bower in Owensboro had been ardent Goebel-Beckham Democrats bearing gifts,[55] but, as always, expectant of future favors. The ardent Goebel-Beckhamites, in fact, had come bearing so many gifts that a reporter speculated that their weight would place a burden on the tottering foundation of the mansion.[56]

No doubt the treasure trove of wedding presents lent grace and style to the furnishings of the mansion. Three quarters of a century later, Eleanor Beckham, their daughter, had some of the objects appraised when she gave them to the commonwealth during a sentimental journey back to Kentucky. The objects were appraised at nearly $5,000.[57]

Unlike her predecessor hostesses, Jean Fuqua Beckham was little more than a stripling girl. On the afternoon of August 14 she went up the Frankfort Hill to visit with the wife of the newly appointed superintendent of the Kentucky State Mental Institution. When labor pains set in she was rushed back to the mansion to spend a night in labor.[58] She gave birth to a daughter, Eleanor Raphael Beckham, who was born at 6:15 A.M., August 15, 1901. While the governor was in Owensboro inspecting a unit of the State Guard, Eleanor became the first child born in the mansion to gubernatorial parents.[59]

Eleanor Beckham spent her early and formative years in the governor's mansion. Aside from her birth in the house, there were other incidents to break the tedium of life. Actually, the routine there differed little if any from that in most Frankfort households. There were still the horses and carriages housed on the grounds. Too, there was the ever-faithful cook, whose presence was daily in evidence. Her husband, a handyman, died in the servants' quarters and she refused to have him buried until he became too "ripe" to be tolerated.[60]

The environmental surroundings of the mansion grew ever more bleak, even more so than William O. Bradley had said they were. Buildings in the public governmental square were often described as dilapidated and overcrowded. The only building on the square of any real distinction was the Gideon Shryock-designed Temple of Athens, the classic Kentucky capitol.[61]

A collage of Mistresses of the Executive Mansion from the March 24, 1901, *Louisville Courier-Journal* features Kentucky's first ladies from 1798 to 1901.

Despite the stormy events that brought J.C.W. Beckham into office, he conducted for a little more than seven years a remarkably sober administration. Seldom did he wave the "bloody shirt" of Goebelism. He brought about a modification of the Goebel Election Law, effected a settlement of the Civil War claims against the United States Treasury, and initiated a somewhat tepid movement to improve public education, to stop mountain feuding, and to curb violence all across the state.[62] No doubt two of the most important achievements of the Beckham years were the enactment (at the prodding of the superintendent) of major educational laws and an appropriation to build a modern state capitol. All of these things had, in some way,

an association with the governor's mansion. Obviously, in time, the ancient house on Clinton Street would have to be replaced by a new mansion, largely because of the stifling environment surrounding the time-worn and battered veteran of 1798.[63]

Governor J.C.W. and Jean Fuqua Beckham lived in the house longer than any of their predecessors except James and Elizabeth Mountjoy Garrard. Their tenancy was a mixture of political and routine domestic incidents. An impressive amount of "off the record" political discussions and decisions were made beneath the mansion's roof.[64]

The rhythm of life in the Beckham household was set in large measure by the retiring and gentle-mannered

Breaking ground for the new capitol, May 20, 1905. Holding the spade is Governor J.C.W. Beckham. To his left is Colonel E.H. Taylor Jr., who fought so hard to keep the capital in Frankfort. (KDLA)

hostess. Jean Beckham was indeed a dedicated church-goer and worker, and a devoted mother to two young children. The home was made somewhat more somber by the Beckhams' attitude toward serving liquor. As a result, social affairs in the mansion were marked by a degree of irony. While Kentucky's legendary image was rooted in the fact the state's name and bourbon whiskey were all but synonymous, only a limited amount, if any, of the amber fluid found its way to the governor's sideboard.[65]

Governor Beckham's executive journal and public papers reveal graphically the flow of major political events during his extended term in office. Obviously much of the political supplications and political "arm twistings" went unrecorded. Much of this took place in the mansion. Scores of the pages of the executive journal reveal constant political favor-seeking, the scramble for titles and appointments, beseeching of pardons, and

appointments of myriads of justices-of-the peace. The record shows only the final decision, however, not the seeking. Surely Governor Beckham's days were filled with conversations with Democratic constituents, or with the eternal pleadings of families and friends for pardons of convicted members, and for the remission of petty fines and penalties. During the post-Goebel years, almost constant litigation appeared regarding the assassination.[66]

Paradoxically, the Beckham years might well have been considered in some areas seminal ones. There, however, had to be a balancing of positive facts against deeply traumatic negative ones. Blood feuds still occurred in parts of Eastern Kentucky, while a state of anarchy prevailed in the dark tobacco belt of the western counties. All across the commonwealth the toll road scheme of road maintenance proved a failure, and in some instances tollgates were destroyed and toll keep-

The silver plate attached to a grandfather clock presented to J.C.W. Beckham upon his retirement. (KHS)

The silver tea service presented to Governor J.C.W. Beckham by the people of Frankfort at the conclusion of his administration is displayed in today's old mansion under the governor's portrait. (KHS)

Governor Augustus E. Willson, 1907–1911. (KHS)

inadequate to furnish proper halls, offices, and places of businesses, to enable the General Assembly and the state officials to properly and efficiently discharge the duties of their offices." A sinking fund was created and a board of commissioners appointed with the mandate to have plans drawn, select a site, and oversee the construction of a new statehouse.[71]

Aside from providing for the location and construction of a new seat of government, the law had far-reaching historical implications. Once and for all, the issue of the permanent location of Kentucky's capital was settled; it would remain in Frankfort.[72] Too, the law revealed how shabby the Kentucky public buildings were, and especially the condition of the governor's mansion.

Records pertaining to the acquisition of the site, the construction, and the decoration of the capitol are full and revealing. The building commission selected F.M. Andrews of Dayton and New York as the architect, and a number of special contractors, among them the General Supply and Construction Company, Balke and Zehner Company, and Joseph Williams and Company.[73] In many respects this moment in Kentucky history marked an advance onto a new plane of state pride. For the Beckham administration and the Democrats, the collection of the federal funds and the construction of a new capitol were their most notable accomplishments since 1891 and the adoption of a new constitution.

Political fortunes changed in the gubernatorial election of 1907. For the third time a Republican was chosen governor. In that campaign the Democrats were sharply divided by that ever-haunting ghost, local option in the sale of liquor, and over issues that had arisen within the Beckham administration.

The new master and hostess who came to the governor's mansion in December 1907 were in many ways an untraditional couple. Augustus Everett Willson (1846–1931) was born in Kentucky, to parents of a distinctive New England background. He was born in Maysville, lived briefly in Covington, and then in New Albany, Indiana. Most of his formative youthful years, however, were spent in New York City, and Cambridge, Massachusetts. In the latter city he became socially acquainted with many of the New England literati, including Ralph Waldo Emerson, Henry Wadsworth Longfellow, and James Russell Lowell.[74] Willson graduated from Harvard University in law.

Augustus E. Willson returned to Kentucky and established a law practice in Louisville. Five times he sought election to public office without success. In an astonishing upset in 1907 he defeated the Democratic

ers were abused.[67] In a far more positive vein a highly motivated and energized superintendent of public instruction mounted a crusade to lift Kentuckians and their legislators out of the slough of illiteracy that had so long stymied public economy and culture. John Grant Crabbe set out to create an entirely new and more valid school system.[68]

In the fiscal area of Kentucky public affairs, the state successfully brought to a settlement its lingering claim against the federal government for costs and damages arising out of the Civil War, with the state receiving $1,323,999.35.[69] Governor Beckham announced this windfall to the General Assembly on January 5, 1904, and in February that body enacted a law appropriating $1 million to finance the construction of a new capitol building.[70]

The preamble to the act of appropriation declared that the existing public buildings were "notoriously

Kentucky's new state capitol was under construction from 1901 until 1910. The task was performed by man and mule. (KHS)

state treasurer, Samuel W. Hager, for the governor's chair. Augustus Willson was no doubt one of the most highly educated of the Kentucky governors, a fact reflected in his public papers.[75]

Augustus E. and Mary Elizabeth Elkin Willson were the parents of only one child, and this one died in infancy.[76] Their arrival in Frankfort was once again an occasion for a Republican stampede in the town. They came en masse on December 9, 1907, wearing Willson hats, and swinging Willson canes. They came "local option" sober, and "free market" tipsy, all in a jubilant mood. Governor and Mrs. Willson came the afternoon before the inauguration by train from Louisville. In Frankfort they were hastened off to spend a quiet evening away from the admiring mob as guests of Colonel L.P. Tarlton and his family.[77]

At 10 A.M. on inauguration day, precedent was set when Governor-elect Willson was driven into Frankfort in an automobile, ending the long tradition of an inaugural carriage drawn by four white horses. The record is

unclear as to whether or not the new governor owned an automobile, but it is certain there was less use for a carriage house and stables in connection with the mansion. Aside from uttering the usual felicities at the inaugural ceremonies, Governor Beckham left on the executive desk the challenges of ending the mountain feuds, devising a new public roads program, ending the Black Patch tobacco war, reorganizing the public school system, and completing the new state capitol.

Governor Beckham also left behind a shabby governor's mansion. In his first message to the General Assembly, Governor Willson informed the legislators that "The old time honored mansion is worn out, dilapidated and untenable in its present condition, and location undesirable and will still be more when the public offices are moved to the new capitol, across the river." Governor Willson said it would cost several thousand dollars to repair the structure and it still would be "an old house." He said, "I cannot live in the old house in its present condition, not without several thousand dollars worth of repairs, and it will be very inconvenient to the members to have the Executive residence in the old place after the new Capitol shall be occupied."[78] There are two implications in this statement: first, the Willsons may not have spent all of the administration in residency in the mansion, and second, there is the strong implication that the mansion was a center of administrative activity.

That December inauguration day morning in 1907 was more than a moment of gubernatorial succession. Across the Kentucky River the skeleton of a new and impressive capitol building, like a giant mushroom, was pushing up out of the ground. The new building represented a monument of pride for Democrats, but offered a moment of glory for the people of Frankfort and the Republican administration. For the people of Frankfort the great fog of doubt about the permanency of the location of Kentucky's capital was burned away. A *Lexington Leader* reporter wrote, "It was a proud day for the people of Frankfort, for it was the formal ending of a fight of over a hundred years to retain the seat of government here, and they have been on the anxious bench all that time until the million dollar appropriation was made in 1904 for a new Statehouse to be erected in Frankfort."[79]

The great educational crusade was in full pitch that December as petitioners came with their pleas, endorsed by hundreds of signers. Caleb Powers, a staunch Republican, faced a fourth time in court on a charge of complicity in the assassination of William Goebel, Jim Howard and Henry Youtsey were in prison on charges of committing the murder.[80] And the Black Patch War was winding down. Kentucky was in a historic moment of change, a moment which was to be stamped deep in public consciousness with the dedication of the new capitol building. Already a cry was heard throughout the land that the "Democrats built the Capitol, and the Republicans would dedicate it." There came that delicate moment on June 2, 1910, when a Republican governor would preside over the dedicatory celebration, and a Republican United States senator would make "the speech of his life" in dedicating it.[81]

Governor Willson exhibited the utmost tact and consideration for the Democrats, giving ex-Governor Beckham full credit for his service. Underneath the swirl of partisan politics and the pageantry of dedicating the new building, however, there brewed a rippet among the citizens of Frankfort when a complaint was voiced that a group of "Frankfort sycophants were on hand to grab all the glory."

Present in the throng that day were Gilbert White and his wife. White had painted the famous lunettes which shone down upon both the Senate and House of Representatives chambers.[82] The large Louisville delegation, among them W.B. Haldeman, Judge W.G. Dearing, and Dr. William Bailey, was also present for the moment when the Louisville dream to remove the Kentucky capital to that city ended forever.[83] The ceremonial moment that June day made heavier demands of hospitality than the governor's mansion could possibly serve. For it, that moment was one of fading glory.

Events came fast in Frankfort during the Willson administration. In November 1910, twenty-three state governors descended upon the town, among them governor-elect Woodrow Wilson and John Franklin Fort, both of New Jersey, Frank W. Weeks of Connecticut, Eben S. Draper of Massachusetts, Joseph M. Brown of Georgia, Judson Harmon of Ohio, and that ancient relic of Victorian fancy, Governor Edmund F. (Granny) Noel of Mississippi.[84]

The gathering of so many distinguished guests made heavy demands on the governor's mansion, and upon the town of Frankfort. To meet the needs for dignified transportation of the governors and their wives to see the local sights, the Phoenix Motor Car Company of Lexington sent six automobiles and chauffeurs to Frankfort.[85] Both Democrats and Republicans were on hand to greet the governors. When Governor Judson Harmon of Ohio arrived in the town at the Frankfort and Cincinnati Railway Station, he was mobbed by a throng of hand-shaking, hat-tossing Democrats, and he responded by shaking hands with most of them. Even when Governor Harmon was seated in an automobile to be driven to the new capitol he had to stop and shake more Democrat hands along the way.[86]

Visitation of the governors was a scintillating moment in Kentucky social and political history, but a grim one for the governor's mansion. The previous January Governor Willson had once again reminded the General Assembly that "the Executive Mansion was untenable." He asked if the legislators preferred to rent, build a new mansion, or have the governor make extensive repairs on the present one? No immediate action was taken. He wrote, "The Governor under the power always exercised to repair the old mansion and make it tenable, the expense for my term will be less than it would have cost to rent another mansion, and it is now so late that it would not benefit me to have a new mansion built." He advised the General Assembly that a new mansion should be built near enough the new

A 1945 photo of a third floor bedroom in the abandoned old mansion, where not even a gubernatorial ghost could find a respectable place to hide. (Department of Public Information)

statehouse to share the light, heating, and sewer facilities. The sewage, he said, could be emptied directly into the Kentucky River along with that from the capitol.[87]

Governor Willson advised the General Assembly that a new mansion should not be constructed so elaborately as to be beyond the capabilities of future governors to maintain it. The furnishings, he said, should be the best obtainable, but should be suited to the "life styles of the men who are usually elected governors of Kentucky." He was specific in his declaration that he and his wife would not be in Frankfort long enough to live in a new mansion.[88]

In a somewhat strange communication to the General Assembly in January 1910, Governor Willson confessed that he had been charged by the press as saying

Democrats were guilty of graft in the construction of the new capitol. He said that after three years in office he could declare the charge baseless. He wrote, "I had no proof that there was graft and I did not charge it, I have paid this tribute to my predecessor [Governor Beckham] and those of the opposition party who have deserved well of the State for their work on the new Capitol because it is the nature of a true man and worthy of Kentucky."[89]

Governor Willson wrote that the Democrats, "have done well, and it was for this that he took pride and pleasure of pitching an oratorical bouquet over the garden wall of partisan politics."[90] The brightest sprig in that bouquet was the governor's saccharine declaration that "The delightful and interesting Democrat Party of

The sad requiem of a parlor which once had been the scene of gaiety and sadness. Old mansion parlor in 1945. (Department of Public Information)

Kentucky, and while I hope to be spared to dwell upon this theme to a ripe old age, this Capital never has been and never will be held up by me to the people as anything but an honor and a credit to the party, from the time it was begun, to the time when it was turned over to the present commission."[91] It would have been an ingrate Democrat who could have revealed even a trace of an abused feeling. The temple was built and dedicated, and its rising dome pointed the way to the next election.

The Republicans may have dedicated the new capitol, but the Democrats were to have their moment of glory. In December 1911, they paraded for the first time a governor-elect up the newly opened strand from the Kentucky River to the capitol pediment. There for the second time James Bennett McCreary (1838–1918) took the oath of office, and on February 7, 1912, he signed the appropriation bill of $75,000 to build a new governor's mansion on the capital grounds.[92]

In a preamble to their bill, legislators laid one more stripe of shame when they declared, "The Governor's Mansion at the capital is notoriously inadequate to furnish a proper home for the Governor of Kentucky; it is now old and dilapidated and much out of repair." It was said the house "did not comport with the dignity and wealth of the State."[93]

Governor McCreary moved his household into the new mansion in 1914. He was a widower during his second term. His granddaughter, Harriet Newberry McCreary, a student at Wellesley College, served as mansion hostess during the summers. Governor McCreary's housekeeper, Miss Jennie Shaw, orchestrated the details of mansion life for the chief executive in both the old and new mansions. In January that year the Sinking Fund Commission reported to the General Assembly that the new mansion had been erected and furnished at a cost of $94,902.40.[94] The commission hoped "the legislators would be pleased with the

The old mansion's photo gallery of Kentucky lieutenant governors who have resided in the house from 1955 to the present. From left to right, Harry Lee Waterfield (1955–1959, 1963–1967), Wilson Wyatt (1959-1963), Wendell Ford (1967–1971), Julian Carroll (1971–1974), Kentucky's first woman lieutenant governor, Thelma Stovall (1975–1979), Martha Layne Collins (1979-1983), Steve Beshear (1983–1987), Brereton Jones (1987–1991), Paul Patton (1991–1995), and Dr. Steve Henry (1995–1999, 1999–). (KHS)

Mansion that has been erected, which will, for more than a hundred years, be the home of the various Governors of the State of Kentucky."[95] One thing was certain, it pleased Governor McCreary. He sent a formal invitation on March 10, 1914, inviting legislators and all other public officials to a formal reception and public viewing of the new mansion.[96]

Back across the Kentucky River the old mansion stood abandoned, its shade-drawn windows staring vacantly upon the dreary scene of the penitentiary, the flour mill, and the ragged slope of the palisades. Gone were the governors and their families, the favor seekers, and levees. Like Governor Charles Scott of old, it

stood a shamble waiting to learn its fate. Both its rooms and its crumbling exterior walls were sealed beneath the patina of more than a century of layering during the formative years of the commonwealth itself.

After James McCreary moved to the new mansion in January 1914, the Sinking Fund granted permission for the custodian of public buildings, Samuel Lykins, to rent the old house and garden for $25 per month. On February 27, 1914, a second fire resulted in damages that required $683 to repair.[97]

Believing that the old property was of no good use to the state, Governor McCreary authorized an auction on September 12, 1914. The old mansion was offered

The parlor of the old mansion as it is enjoyed today. Top center is the grandfather clock given to retiring Governor J.C.W. Beckham in 1907. (FCS)

The old mansion's dining room today. Twin fireplaces remain in the room that from 1798 until the mid nineteenth century was divided into the governor's office (top of photo) and a dining room. (FCS)

The lieutenant governor's gardens. (FCS)

The restored old governor's mansion. (FCS)

in lots, and the final bid was $13,600, which the commissioners rejected as an unfair price.[98] The old house remained rental property for the next decade.

In an interview, Billie Whitaker related to Margaret Lane that she lived in the old governor's mansion from 1927 until 1931. Her father, William T. Short, a Richmond lawyer, was Governor Flem Sampson's commissioner of the Workers' Compensation Board. The family lived upstairs and the Workers' Compensation office, with seventeen to eighteen secretaries, operated downstairs. Mrs. Whitaker had fond memories of swinging on a front porch decorated with ornate wrought iron and covered with morning glories. The family's second-floor residence was complete with three bedrooms, a large dining room, a kitchen, and a living room with a piano.[99]

In January 1937, Frankfort's great flood drove two thousand people from their homes, swirled to the door of the old mansion, and rose several feet into the prison yard across the street.[100] That same year, the roof of the porch fell and destroyed the grillwork as the building was being repaired for occupancy as headquarters for the state highway patrol, forerunner of today's state police. "Trout's Trotline," a column in the *Louisville Courier-Journal*, indicated that despite the elaborate latticework of wrought iron supports, the porch roof fell and required extensive restoration of the front of the mansion, as well as relandscaping of the front grounds. The highway patrol used the facility until 1941.[101]

Although the footprint of the house occupied the corner of High and Clinton Streets, the old mansion lot originally extended to Ann Street. A 1940 Sanborn map identifies a massive state highway patrol building extending from the back yard of the residence to Clinton and Ann Streets.[102]

As for the house itself, after the highway patrol vacated the property in 1941, Howard Henderson wrote, "To the vandalism of its tenants has been added the work of later vandals who have torn away even the plumbing fixtures from the walls.

"In disuse, it is littered with loose paper and scrap lumber, fallen plaster and sagging timbers. Its wrought iron grill porch has been torn away. Its iron fence is gone. Vines bar the way to the front entrance, which is unsafe, anyway, because of rotting timber."[103]

There was "talk—just talk—during the Willis administration of tearing the old building down and erecting on the lot a new office for the Unemployment Compensation Commission."[104]

According to a *Louisville Courier-Journal* reporter of the day, "The edifice has been down at the heels most of the time since Governor James B. McCreary moved out to the new mansion on the Capitol grounds in 1914. But somehow the moldering old pile never lost its fascination for the public-at-large, and the State never found the heart to relinquish ownership of it."

After public outcry to maintain and restore the old building or demolish it, after hearing a local citizens' committee report, and bowing to the interests of his preservationist wife, Governor Simeon Willis signed an order on March 23, 1946, providing for restoration and "use as State Museum of Old Governor's Mansion, under the control of the Kentucky Historical Society." The legislature appropriated $30,000 for the project, $22,000 of which was spent on exterior stabilization. Governor Wetherby, during his 1950–1955 administration, began renovation of the interior of the old mansion, but found only two original doors and one window intact. The remainder would have to be reproduced.

Governor Albert Chandler in 1955 had another plan in mind. Governor Chandler spent $90,000 to finish the house and lure Harry Waterfield to move to Frankfort. Lieutenant Governor Waterfield and his family resided on the third floor of the new mansion as guests of the Chandlers until the renovation of the old mansion was complete. In April of 1956, Harry Lee Waterfield and his family moved into the mansion, the first of Kentucky's lieutenant governors to make the "palace" their home.[105] From that era to the present, the old governor's mansion has been inhabited by ten lieutenant governors, whose private and official residence has served as gathering place for social and political guests.

In 1971 the old mansion was added to the National Register of Historic Places. Various renovations and additions have been made to make the official house/residence more convenient for families and more accessible to the public. In 1973, a small garden in the mansion's side yard was enclosed, immediately adjacent to Governor's Alley, the pathway traveled by ancient governors and their couriers to and from the old capitol. The dirt paths and vegetable-herb gardens of old have given way to brick walkways and rose-filled parterres, complete with fountains and modern amenities.

Today, the house is entered via the same flight of steps that General Scott blamed for his injuries, and visitors bid entrance through a simple doorway, the large veranda and wrought iron porch railing now only memories of another era. Antique and reproduction furniture, along with portraits of many former governors, decorate a central hall and parlor to the left. The nineteenth-century governor's office/library and sitting room to the right of the central hall have been combined into the house's large dining room, a unique space containing two fireplaces. A smaller family dining room occupies space long since enclosed from the old kitchen's dogtrot. The kitchen, many times renovated and modernized, serves as center of the lieutenant governor's hospitality, as do porches on both sides of the house, which have been enclosed to add to the livability of the house. Bedrooms and sitting rooms make up the second floor, and the old cook's apartment over the kitchen houses the mansion's office. Several lieutenant governors' children have been at home in a third floor garret space, modernized to include two bedrooms. The old basement provides a utility area and meeting/recreation room, with ancient oak beams and the stone foundation still in evidence.

Having celebrated its two hundredth birthday in 1998, the old mansion remains steadfastly anchored on High and Clinton Streets and reportedly is the oldest official residence still in use in the United States today. Backdrop for much of Kentucky's political and social history, exemplifying undeniable tenacity by surviving fire, plague, neglect, misuse, abandonment, and the myriad lifestyles of its residents, this enduring edifice represents the indomitable spirit of the people of Kentucky. Now surrounded by the Kentucky History Center, the old mansion today remains one of the finest examples of the Commonwealth's cultural heritage.

PART II

The New Mansion

CHAPTER 8

A Mansion to Match a Capitol

Near the end of his administration in 1911, Governor Augustus E. Willson assumed that now that Kentucky had a new capitol building, the General Assembly would at last approve the construction of a new governor's mansion. He advised the legislators that realistically the new mansion should be in keeping with the lifestyles of the men usually elected governors of the commonwealth. Too, Willson added, the mansion should be located well outside the pale of deteriorating High and Clinton Streets.[1] Earlier John White Stevenson had expressed the notion that the governor's mansion might ideally be located on the knoll nestled atop the first shoulder of the palisade west of the Kentucky River.[2]

In 1912 the legislators were just recovering from the fiscal shock caused by the whopping cost overrun of the new capitol. It took fully two years for them to gain enough courage to authorize the building of a new executive mansion. Finally, responding to executive and public pressures, the General Assembly enacted the necessary legislation to build a mansion. On February 7, 1912, it approved an appropriation of $75,000 to finance the purchase of land and to pay for a building. This was done with little or no previous planning or even with any realistic concept of what a suitable executive mansion might cost.[3]

At the outset the price of as yet unlocated land was unknown. The appropriation act contained an emergency clause mandating immediate action. This necessitated early consultation with an architect to have some kind of a preliminary proposal for a suitable residential-executive structure.

Having approved the construction of a mansion, legislators turned over to the Sinking Fund Commission full responsibility for its planning and construction.[4]

Governor James B. McCreary, 1911–1915. (KHS)

First was the matter of purchasing a site. The Sinking Fund Commission members were James B. McCreary, governor; C.F. Crecellius, secretary of state; Thomas S. Rhea, treasurer; H.M. Bosworth, auditor; and James Garrett, attorney general.[5] It hardly required formal documentation to know that the dominant voice on the commission was James B. McCreary, a man who was said to have had "aristocratic bearings and notions."[6] He no doubt conceived of a mansion of classic form and style.

The Sinking Fund Commission lost no time in responding to the legislative mandate to locate a site near the new capitol, and to have a mansion built on it. One can detect in the commission minutes an element of gubernatorial excitement about the task at hand. The first meeting of the commission occurred on February 22, 1912.[7] Doubtless at that moment none of the members had any concept of the style of a mansion beyond that of general spatial dimensions. In the same vein, no member truly envisioned the complexities of designing and constructing a classical style building. The legislators had made a blind estimate that a suitable mansion of proper domestic proportions could be built for less that $75,000. They assuredly agreed with former Governor John White Stevenson that a solid democratic type structure should be created that would be in harmony with the lifestyles of future governors.

The Sinking Fund Commission made an early appeal to F.M. Andrews of the architectural firm that had designed and overseen the construction of the new capitol. Andrews came to Frankfort to meet with the commissioners and on February 28, 1912, discussed in general terms a type of executive mansion that might be built with the amount of money appropriated. He emphasized the immediate necessity to locate and acquire a site before true plans could be drafted for the building. He did agree to prepare a preliminary projection of a building and have it in the hands of the Commission by March 7.[8] The commissioners were anxious to have such a sketch before beginning the search for an architect. Apparently Mr. Andrews' firm had no interest in making a bid, or the commissioners wished to hire an architect from within the state.

On his return to New York, F.M. Andrews became ill and was unable to prepare and forward the promised sketch in time to meet the commission's deadline. He was sent a prickly telegraphic message stating that March 7 was positively the last day on which the sketch of the new mansion would be received.[9]

Four Kentucky architectural firms submitted bids to design and oversee the construction of the mansion. They sent sketches that the members of the commission took a week to review. By week's end they were ready to make their choice of an architect. At that date the location and acquisition of a building site became imperative. In every case the architects submitted plans without knowing precisely where the building might be located. Despite this lapse, the commission chose the Weber Architectural Firm of Fort Thomas, a firm with both professional and political ties to Kentucky.[10]

C.C. Weber headed the Fort Thomas firm, and supervised plans and their execution. The Webers employed a good number of architects and draftsmen, and often assigned work to outside specialists. In conjunction with this practice, a vague question remains as to how much personal contribution the Webers made in the actual generation and drafting of the plans for the new governor's mansion. There seems to be sustainable evidence that much of the design for the building was created by John Scudder Adkins of Cincinnati. By 1912, Adkins already had an extensive background in public capitol construction in Kentucky, having been associated with F.M. Andrews in the construction of the new capitol. In fact, Adkins was said to be the designer of the new governor's mansion.[11]

Once the Weber architects were chosen, the members of the Sinking Fund Commission turned their attention to locating a building site near the capitol grounds on which to build the new mansion. The proximity of the two buildings was stipulated in the legislative act, but there was no place on the capitol grounds for the mansion. The most suitable nearby site was on lands owned by L. Frank Johnson, Louise Sargent, and Carrie Nowell. Their properties fronted on Logan Street in front and on the Kentucky River bluff in the rear. Negotiations were begun with Johnson, who readily agreed to sell his property for $9,500. He owned a residence and five tenant houses on the land and agreed to remove them promptly. In addition, L. Frank Johnson agreed to intercede with Louise Sargent to sell her lot and house to the state. This she agreed to do for $4,000, provided she could be given time to locate another residence. Carrie Nowell also agreed to sell her house and lot.[12]

In the meantime a question arose in the commission's discussions as to the political conflict of interest of members of the Weber firm. E.A. Weber, a former legislator, appeared before the commission to respond to an enquiry about a possible financial interest in the firm of Senator L.A. Arnett. He assured the commissioners that Senator Arnett was his company's attorney, not a partner. The legislative act had been both specific and emphatic about conflicts of interest.[13]

The consummation of the purchase of the Johnson property was effected promptly, a warranty deed being filed on March 26, 1912, in the office of the Franklin County Clerk.[14] Johnson honored his commitment to assist in the purchase of the Sargent house and lot. Thus the necessary land on which to build the new

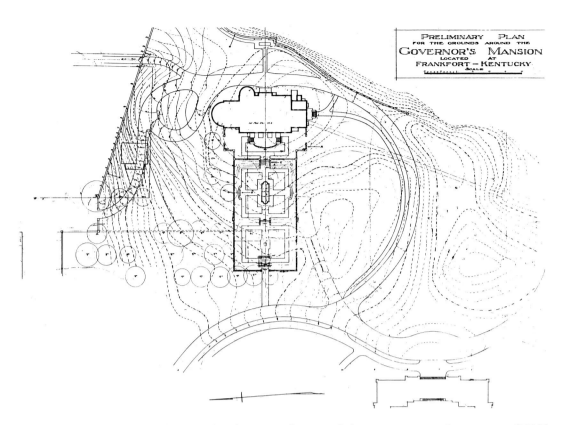

A preliminary plan, dated 1913, for the grounds around the new governor's mansion. (FCS)

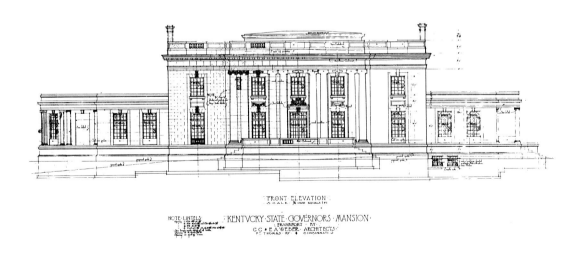

Preliminary plans for the front elevation of the governor's mansion, 1913. C.C. & E.A. Weber, architects. (FCS, Engineering Department)

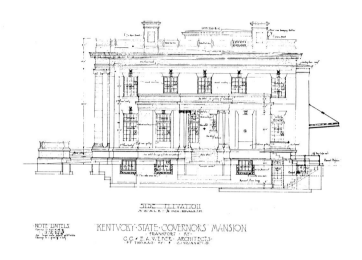

Preliminary plans for the south side elevation of the governor's mansion, 1913. (FCS, Engineering Department)

Preliminary plans for the rear elevation of the governor's mansion, 1913. (FCS, Engineering Department)

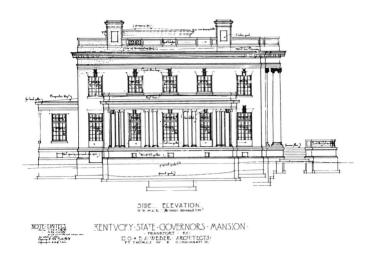

Preliminary plans for the north side elevation of the governor's mansion, 1913. (FCS, Engineering Department)

mansion was acquired and the way was cleared for the commission to proceed with planning and constructing the building.

The Webers presented their final drawings for the new mansion on April 21, 1912, and after the commission gave them an extensive viewing they approved them and directed that an advertisement should be published in the principal Kentucky newspapers soliciting bids from local building contractors.[15] The commission on May 7th employed Samuel Price of Richmond as an assistant superintendent of construction. In this instance there seems to be a strong implication of McCreary political patronage.[16] At the same time, the Webers were requested to make a significant change by replacing the planned conservatory with a large ballroom. The architects were instructed to inform the bidders of this change, which would involve additional costs. Clearly the addition of the ballroom was a matter near and dear to Governor McCreary's social heart.[17]

By June 1, 1912, contractor bids were in the hands of the Sinking Fund Commissioners, and every one of them was higher than the amount appropriated for the

project. The bids ranged from $76,000 to $93,000, and none included the cost of preparing the building site, utility connections, and what the commission called "special branches."[18]

The high construction bids necessitated a major re-examination of the plans. New bids were opened on June 1, 1912, and this time they ranged from $59,000 to $61,219.[19] After adjustments, the Capital Lumber and Manufacturing Company of Frankfort submitted the lowest acceptable bid of $60,879. The record is blurred as to what modifications were made in the overall design of the building, but apparently some concerned the quality and type of stone to be used. There may even have been some changes in the internal features of the building. The Sinking Fund Commission authorized a switch from stone produced by the Victoria Quarries to Bowling Green stone, in keeping with the legislative act of February 7, 1912, which specified that the new mansion should be "constructed, trimmed and finished with native stone produced from quarries in Kentucky."[20]

No doubt the chairman of the Sinking Fund

The nearly completed mansion in 1913. The photograph was made from the dome of the four-year-old capitol building. (FCS, Dawson family collection)

Commission, Governor McCreary, exerted a strong personal influence in the overall design and many of the internal features of the building. He was said to have had an "aristocratic taste" for buildings, glittering social entertainment, Democratic politics, all facts eloquently revealed in his administrative record. Pages of his executive journal literally crackle with recordings of appointments, granting of pardons, and listings of other favors.[21]

In the final list of contractor bids for construction of the new mansion, the Capital Lumber and Manufacturing Company had an aggressive manager in the person of Edward H. Elliott. For some inexplicable reason the sum of his company's bid was listed as $62,945 as compared with the Combs Lumber Company bid of $63,641. The construction contract was drafted and signed on June 29, 1912,[22] but it appears that the contractor was already moving material onto the Johnson land. There quickly arose a controversy between supervisor of public properties, Wiard, and the Capital Lumber Company over use of Capitol Drive, as wagon wheels were slashing deep ruts in the drive and leaving muddy quagmires. As arbiter of the dispute, the newly appointed highway engineer, Robert G. Terrill, was asked to devise a roadway use plan. An agreement was reached that the contractor could use the driveway, but his wagons were to be equipped with tires no narrower than three inches, and no load was to exceed five thousand pounds. In addition, the road was not to be used when wet.[23]

Ground was broken on July 25, 1912, with the only refreshment being "cool limestone water ladled from a whiskey barrel in tin cups."[24] Once construction was begun, one problem after another arose. At the outset there was the major one of connecting the mansion's water and sewage systems to those serving the capitol building. The Webers suggested that a tunnel be bored to connect the mansion's sewage system with that of the capitol, and that both of them empty into the Kentucky River.[25]

"Changes" became the monotonous refrain throughout the 1912–1914 construction of the mansion. There were many departures from the original plans. One such change involved the use of stone instead of wood in some of the interior walls to make the building more fireproof.[26] Unexpected delays in the delivery of Bowling Green stone caused a moment of concern as to whether or not the commission should return to the Victoria Quarries instead.[27]

With the building in an advanced state of construc-

tion, there arose the question of landscaping the grounds jointly with those surrounding the capitol. One proposal advocated the encirclement of the grounds with a row of one hundred and twenty trees, one each for the hundred and twenty counties.[28] Samuel Wiard was asked to supervise the tree planting project. The aesthetic question was raised as to whether the trees should be planted in a circular row or be grouped in clusters. The Sinking Fund Commissioners expressed the view that whatever pattern was used, the panoramic view from the capitol and mansion should not be obscured. They agreed, though, that there was one spot where a cluster of trees should be placed, to "screen out the exceedingly objectionable outlook just west of the Capitol Building."[29]

Samuel Wiard prescribed no varieties of trees to be planted, leaving the choices up to the individual counties. To facilitate the tree project, Kentucky's pioneer forester J.E. Barton was asked to place stakes indicating where each "county" tree would be planted. For his part, Governor McCreary was asked to choose a state tree to be planted on the new "Automobile Road."[30] The tree-planting project stirred enthusiasm of Kentucky Arbor Day observers, and that year the annual event was celebrated with a bit of pomp and ceremony when the commonwealth paid out thirty dollars to have John Bandy's Brass Band give musical overtone to the occasion.[31] But even this tiny fee placed a strain on the Kentucky treasury. That year the commonwealth spent $400,000 more than it collected in revenue. This impoverished condition limited Kentucky's credit rating and put an appreciable limitation on the amount of money available to be spent on the new mansion.[32]

Despite changes in the plans, the failure of the stone quarry to deliver on time, and other delays, the contractor had advanced construction of the building. The time had arrived to select doors, windows, and hardware; meanwhile, architects drafted plans for wiring, heating, and ventilating the building. Distinctive new built-in housekeeping equipment, such as a central vacuuming system, was to be installed, possibly the earliest one placed in a Kentucky public structure.[33]

Anticipating a fairly early occupation of the mansion, discussions of internal decor and furnishings soon began. Because of a financial stringency there were fairly extended discussions of what furnishings could be removed from the old mansion. It was decided to move much of the furniture, the kitchen range, cooking utensils, and bed furnishings. To keep moving costs as low as possible, the Sinking Fund Commission mem-

Construction workers before the mansion in 1913. (KHS)

bers authorized William Wiard to purchase a one-horse wagon on which to transfer the furnishings from one house to the other.[34]

By mid January 1914, the new mansion was sufficiently finished to permit Governor McCreary to move in, despite the fact that the grounds were bare and muddy. On January 10, 1914, William Wiard had driven the one-horse wagon back and forth between the two buildings to empty one and fill the other. He submitted a bill of $94.50 to the Sinking Fund Commission for work around the new mansion, and a second bill for $17.50 for clearing internal and external debris from the old.[35] At the same time, Hammond and Company submitted a bill for $462.50 for the cost of

the governor's backyard stable and carriage shed.[36]

The new mansion was virtually complete. Nevertheless, there remained scores of minor but unfinished areas in the house. Thomas R. Wiard, superintendent of construction, submitted a detailed report to the Sinking Fund Commission in which he recommended that the numerous contractors be paid and released from their bonds. Some contractors who submitted bids for specialty work were warned beforehand that they would have to await redemption of state warrants until the commonwealth could collect sufficient revenue to pay its debts.[37]

Governor McCreary, in a figurative shout of joy, sent the General Assembly a message saying, "I believe

James Bennett McCreary's coach in 1914. It was the last horse-drawn vehicle to be used by a Kentucky governor. (KHS)

the members of the General Assembly will be pleased with the mansion which has been erected, and which will be occupied for more than a hundred years by the governors of Kentucky."[38] This oratorical outpouring no doubt was inspired by the architectural beauty of the new building. Also, it may have been aimed at softening the fact that, to date, the cost was $94,902.40, an overrun of $19,002.40.[39] And that sum did not include furnishings, subsequent additions to the heating facility, additional lighting, and sanitary facilities. Actually the building itself was not completely constructed.

Exhibiting the pride they had in their handiwork, the Sinking Fund commissioners approved having tablets bearing photographic likenesses of the individual members attached to the building.[40] In addition, the commission ordered another plaque to bear the names and likenesses of prominent Kentuckians. Those so honored were W.C.P. Breckinridge, W.N. Haldeman, John C. Breckinridge, John L. Helm, Ephraim McDowell, John C. Young, John G. Carlisle,

William Preston, John J. Crittenden, and J.C.C. Mayo.[41] These names represented a distinctive Confederate favoritism plus a nod to the Kentucky newspaper press. Significantly, the names of Isaac Shelby, Henry Clay, James Guthrie, and Simon Bolivar Buckner were not included.

Later, on April 16, 1915, the commissioners of the Sinking Fund, in an eloquent outpouring of praise, thanked Robert Wiard for his conscientious and effective services in overseeing the construction of the mansion. In this connection no mention was made of the services of Governor McCreary's political appointee, Samuel Price.

With the paint fumes subsiding, and the furniture moved in from the old mansion, the caterers and confectioners came to work their magic. They created a lavish collection of saccharine flora and prepared a reception menu which must have been one of the most sophisticated ever served at a Kentucky formal reception. While maids and other household staff busily starched and ironed their fancy new domestic uniforms,

The unveiling of the dedicatory plaques marking the completion of the mansion. Present are members of the Kentucky General Assembly and other state officials. (KHS)

The Sinking Fund plaque. (FCS)

A Lexington automobile dealer demonstrating to Governor McCreary a new Overland car outside the newly finished mansion in January 1913. (KHS)

the governor's secretaries sent hundreds of invitations to selected citizens to come to Frankfort to view what the governor euphemistically called "the people's gift" to the executive branch of Kentucky state government.[42]

Perhaps no prior governor in Kentucky history was more involved in so lavish a social event as was Governor James Bennett McCreary in January 1914. He had spent almost seven years in the old mansion, and had tolerated its deficiencies. Surely he must have looked back on the decrepit old house on High and Clinton Streets with mixed sentiments. In contrast the new mansion stood out as a veritable Greek temple, dropped down from the heavens by the gods. It was a regal match, qualitatively and architecturally, to the new capitol building. Raw and barren though the grounds were, the new mansion stood as a bold declaration of Kentucky pride. Both the new buildings made a clear and tangible declaration that the capital of Kentucky was in Frankfort to stay.

In a symbolic gesture, Governor McCreary was ushering out one age in Kentucky and welcoming a new

one. The age also marked the end of the horse and carriage era and the opening of that of the automobile. He largely documented this fact when he was photographed in front of the new mansion seated in an automobile, dressed in his dignified gubernatorial garb of a full skirted coat reaching to his knees, and opening wide enough at the chest to reveal a white shirt and a ruggedly chained gold watch, and all this topped off with a box-shaped derby hat. No longer was there a primary need for the hastily constructed stable and carriage house out back.

By the close of the McCreary administration, Kentucky governors would come to have greater use for a garage. This fact was graphically illustrated on January 21, 1913, when Governor McCreary was portrayed sitting in another new car, this time a Willys-Overland car, no doubt on a dealer demonstration drive. He filled the rear seat of the little vehicle, and in the front seat was an unnamed chauffeur and S.E. Drake, the Lexington Overland dealer. The car, equipped with a self starter, sold for $1,075.[43] The new mansion is shown in the background amidst barren

Governor James McCreary enjoying the new parlor of the 1914 mansion, resplendent with damask wall coverings, brass sconces, and a handsome Victrola. (KHS)

Governor James B. McCreary and his housekeeper,
Miss Jennie Shaw, in 1914. (FCS)

Harriet McCreary, granddaughter of Governor James B. McCreary, served as the official hostess of the new mansion during her summers home from school. (FCS)

modest ones. The first and grandest affair occurred on the evening of January 20, 1914.[44] The invitations which went out of the governor's office bore clear implications that the affair would be a brilliant fashion extravaganza, the like of which Kentucky had not seen since Sally Ward's marriage to Bigelow Lawrence in Louisville in 1848. Not only were feminine guests suddenly turned into fashion "plates," their masculine counterparts came dressed "to the nines." Governor McCreary's staff of colonels appeared in full dress uniforms. Colonel Bennett H. Young and Colonel W.A. Milton, by imperial command, were present wearing their Confederate uniforms,[45] largely to inflate the nostalgic vanity of Major McCreary (C.S.A.), veteran of the Battle of Richmond, the march on Cumberland Gap, and John Hunt Morgan's abortive raid on Indiana and Ohio, and then as a prisoner of war at Johnson Island.[46]

Thus the stage was set for showing off the new mansion behind a gossamer frame of artificial flowers, and beneath the brilliance of the newly installed chandeliers. Fortunately the temperature on the night of January 20 was mild for that time of year.[47] On hand and in line to greet guests at 8:00 P.M. were the governor flanked by his brigade of colonels, Lieutenant Governor Edward J. McDermott, Mrs. Elmer Black, a New York grande dame, Miss Jennie Shaw, the mansion's hostess, Miss Norma Von Schiller of New York City, State Auditor and Mrs. Henry Bosworth, Attorney General and Mrs. James Garrett, State Treasurer Thomas Rhea, and the speaker of the House. As the all but endless line of guests drifted through the reception hall, Governor McCreary, one of Kentucky's all time masters at political hand-shaking and patter, was put to the test in his boast that he could greet every individual by calling his or her name.[48]

That January night in 1914 Frankfort was the scene of a historical and fashion orgy of sorts. Never had so many elegantly dressed women gathered on the banks of the Kentucky River. The display of modern fashion provided a lavish moment fitting for the social dedication for such a fine building. The display of diamonds and other precious jewels rivaled the brilliance of the drawing room chandeliers.[49]

In an outburst of effusive rhetoric, a *State Journal* reporter said, "Fashions were displayed in an unscrupolous [sic] variety last evening in the reception by Governor McCreary to mark the opening of the new Governors Mansion, and the affair aside from the artistic beauty, was notable for bringing together from

grounds, but in a full architectural projection. In the designing of the new mansion and in the creation of its decor, no one seemed to have taken seriously Governor Augustus Willson's observation that the Kentucky executive mansion should reflect in its lines and decor the traditional lifestyles of future governors. Both members of the Sinking Fund Commission and the architects were caught up in the great American trance of the Beaux Arts. Certainly Governor McCreary and his administrative colleagues seemed not to have been too deeply concerned with Kentucky's fiscal shortfalls.

In Governor McCreary's mind and actions, the opening of the new mansion was a moment in Kentucky history that must not be slighted. It called for one grand reception, to be followed by several more near and far a brilliant assemblage of women in full regalia of gorgeous gowns and handsome jewelry."[50]

The reporters reviewed and reported on a fabulous number of costumes, male and female. The *Louisville Courier-Journal* reporter wrote of the affair, "No more brilliant spectacle ever was witnessed in the Capital City than the first reception in the new executive mansion given by Gov. McCreary tonight from 8 to 12 o'clock. Beauty, garbed costly gowns, the Governor's staff in full uniforms, society men and leaders of the bench, bar, and politics from all over the State were there."[51]

The high fashion echelon of Kentucky society descended on Frankfort for the reception. Women came draped in extravagantly fancy imported fabrics and laces, and in embroidered brocades. Some of them paraded around the halls and parlors flashing a veritable spectrum of blues, whites, pinks, yellows, and gold. Few shoulders were bared, but most of the women were wrapped in furs, and their fingers flashed the flame of diamonds and other precious stones. Collectively the assemblage created the simulation of a rainbow. Some of the dresses were so heavily ornamented with sequins, brilliants, laces, and reflective silks that many of them appeared as virtual pillars of light. There were gowns fitted in revealing contours of iridescent silks, brilliant brocades, embossed chenilles, and "blue crepe metour trimmed with lace, and charmeuse trimmed in lace." The local society reporter observed that "The brocades, however, predominating, and draped and clinging effects much in evidence."

Many of the women had their hair coiffured in the high style mode, with some of them wearing sparkling bandeaux of diamonds and pearls. The more adventuresome maidens among them had their curls pulled back so as to expose the full face. For some the rapidly vanishing nineteenth-century "puff rats" and highback gutta percha combs were but a lingering memory.[52]

Selected members of the bluegrass, Frankfort, and Louisville social and political set were on hand to give the opening of the new mansion a proper christening, but the women, perhaps, were there more to show off their gowns. One newspaper reporter performed the meticulous and delicate task of describing in even the most minute detail what many of the feminine guests wore. Matilda and Norma Van Schiller of New York, special guests of Governor McCreary, were robed in high style. Matilda wore a black charmeuse with a lace overdress trimmed in jet black. Mrs. Samuel J. Shackleford set the party aglow in her gown of black

charmeuse with a bodice made entirely of lace, and all her garments trimmed with brilliants and beads overlaid with white butterfly bows. To enliven the feminine rivalry, Mrs. Graham Van Vreland greeted the governor robed in an imported model of lavender velvet overlaid with tulle, silver lace, and embroidery. This striking dress was set off with a "trim" of diamonds. Surely Mrs. Elmer Black of New York, who assisted Governor McCreary in the receiving line, was the belle of the evening. She appeared in a Worth gown of emerald green charmeuse with V-shaped cut bodice, highly sprinkled with crystal beads. She wore a diamond and pearl coronet set in platinum. This was the identical dress she had worn when she had been presented recently at the Court of St. James.[53]

The society reporters of the *Louisville Courier-Journal* and the *State Journal* surely must have been briefed on the costumes worn that evening, that or they lined up the women to gather details of their dresses. There was not among the thousand plus guests a woman attired in anything approaching the Madison County Sunday dress of gingham and calico.

There was more than a hint of Governor McCreary's view on a prevailing socio-political issue of the moment. There does not appear in the published list the name of a single feminist rights crusader. This was even more remarkable because suffrage leaders were assembled in Frankfort to lobby the General Assembly. Among them were Madeline McDowell Breckinridge, Laura Clay, and Miss Anne Martin, a militant crusader from Arizona. The collective Kentucky political mind assembled that night was upon women dressed out in fancy imported gowns, not in voting booths.[54]

That night the new mansion literally glistened like the heavens above. It not only shed an aura of newness but of elegance compounded. The fresh textile fragrance of newly laid carpets and rugs was that of modernity itself. The tentacles of grand chandeliers rivaled the mid-day sun. The twin parlors were trimmed in white and gold wainscoting which reached well up the walls. The north parlor had entries to both the grand dining room and the thirteen hundred-square-foot "McCreary" ballroom.[55]

The spacious banquet room stood in sharp contrast to the cramped dining and dancing space in the historic old mansion. This room was trimmed in red and gave off a simulated heat. The great table was flanked with regal chairs, giving it the appearance of one in a French or English manor house. On that night of the grand reception, the room and table resembled a floral

Public visitors at the new mansion in 1914. (FCS)

shop display. Tall candle stands adorned each end of the table, and in the middle stood a three-foot-high "French" candy basket filled with confections. "Scattered about the table holding the bonbons, glaceed fruits, maroons [sic], etc., had the Bohemian glass effect." All of this was nestled inside clusters of four-dozen confectioner-concocted American Beauty roses and candy chrysanthemums. The flowers appeared so real, said a reporter, "to put the real thing to blush." In like measure the decorator used a lavish hand in the private dining room. The table was adorned with tall red taper candles surrounded by confection narcissuses. Adding to the aesthetics of the evening, an orchestra played until midnight in what surely was an endurance feat.[56]

John Klein, a Louisville caterer, came to Frankfort with a boxcar load of party food and a small army of helpers. The mansion servants were robed in bright colored uniforms and, along with the Klein staff, served sweetbread patties, Benedictine sandwiches, chocolate and cheese straws, individual ices, nesselrode pudding, bisque glace, Coup St. Jacque, and fancy cakes.[57] One

can imagine a backcountry Kentucky legislator trying to figure out the nature of this gourmet collection. In all the history of the Kentucky governor's mansion, nothing like that menu had been served up on the bank of the Kentucky River. Governor McCreary and John Klein were not through with their fine dining. Klein and a part of his staff remained in Frankfort to serve the next evening a ten-course dinner to the governor and his guests just prior to a grand ball. The names of Louis XV and Louis XVI were mentioned in descriptions of the mansion's furnishings and parties as casually as if they had just driven over from Paris, Versailles, or Louisville.

Now for the first time in more than a century, Kentucky governors could be housed in a palace worthy of the name. However, despite the fact that the mansion bore some resemblance to the Petit Trianon in Versailles, France, it was in fact more of the Cincinnati-Kentucky Beaux Arts style of mixed architectural ancestry. It is not the purpose here to trace all the influences and sources of architectural design which

Governor McCreary had a hand in designing the mansion's double staircase, shown here in 1983. (FCS)

were blended into the new mansion. Certainly there are discernable traces in Frankfort of the impact of the great Chicago Exposition of 1893, and that of St. Louis in 1904. This fact was to be documented in the construction of both public and private buildings all across America.[58] No doubt the Webers and John Scudder Adkins were influenced not only by the architectural trends exhibited in the two national exhibitions but also by the fabulous million-dollar Newport, Rhode Island, home of Peter G. Thompson. Thompson, the founder of the Champion Paper Company and a fine printing innovator, was a prime example of what Thorstein Veblen labeled a "conspicuous consumer."[59] His fabulous home and its surrounding grounds were shining examples of the newly rich's taste. This house must have impressed the architects of the Kentucky governor's mansion. Whatever the mansion's architectural antecedents may have been in the classical sense, there was just as impressive a one in the state's fiscal limitations. The minutes of the Sinking Fund Commission contain a consistent reminder of the state's fiscal stringencies, and the statutory limitations as to contractors and materials.

On dazzling display in January 1914 was the dance-drawing room on one end of the mansion and the governor's private study-political office on the other, both symbols of Kentuckian affections, dancing and politics. The governor's mansion office was an impressive men's club type enclave. It was furnished with a desk, said to be a copy of the melodeon in Washington's Mount Vernon. Sturdy chairs and a table accommodated the traditional procession of supplicants who besieged the McCreary administration with requests for every sort of favor, from being pardoned for hog stealing to being commissioned a Kentucky Colonel.[60] The petitioners could await a visit with the governor in an anteroom furnished with chairs which were upholstered in what was described as "Mary Tudor tapestry." This was no replica of the library-office in the old mansion, a time-worn and battered chamber where the "unwashed" could feel comfortable.[61]

The impressive staircase, which Governor McCreary took a hand in designing, bore a close kinship with those designed by F.M. Andrews for the new capitol, and behind it lay the governor's private domain. The arrangement of living quarters resembled somewhat that of many of Kentucky's more elaborate country farmhouses. The governor's master bedroom was lined with "antique mottle" of a silver blue caste, and rugs the color of the walls covered the floor. An adjoining

elaborate, modern bathroom provided the governor choice of a tub, shower, or "needle spray" bath. He could then drape himself in a woolly robe and sit by a fake marble fireplace and pore over constituent petitions, or work up a sweat over the state auditor's gloomy report.[62]

Governor McCreary's claim in the annals of Kentucky history rests somewhat on his attempts to modernize the state's revenue system. In 1914 the state was spending almost half again the amount of money it was collecting in revenues. At the moment of the grand reception, however, the governor seemed to be free of fiscal concerns.

Along the hallway was the mansion hostess's bedroom, which was similarly decorated. It had candle holders of antebellum style, which were fitted with electrical connections. Nevertheless, the room had a hint of "moonlight and roses." Other rooms of the private quarters were furnished in comparable style.[63]

Outside, plans for the development of a formal garden had to be delayed because of a lack of funds. A straight utilitarian walkway led down from the front portico of the mansion to the capitol driveway. A curving "macadamized" automobile driveway led around the mansion from its rear basement entry. Samuel Wiard had leveled the grounds but had not yet sodded them with grass or planted trees and shrubbery. Never again would the mansion stand out in such a condition of stark boldness as in January 1914.

Though the fabulous first public reception occurred with verve and style, the mansion at that date was still not fully finished. When the legislative reception was held in March, this was still true. In that month Governor McCreary held a special reception for the General Assembly. He sent messages to both bodies that he would receive them on March 11. The invitation was directed to "Senators, representatives, state officials, subordinates, and all other persons who will honor me with their presence."[64] This second reception rivaled the first. A *Louisville Courier-Journal* reporter wrote that "The Governor's reception Wednesday evening at the Executive Mansion was the last of the series he has been giving for the members of the General Assembly and was one of the most brilliant functions ever given here. Again the mansion sparkled from cellar to upstairs with electric lights, baskets of spun candy flowers, and jonquils. This time the banquet table was abloom with candy and natural flowers. A huge epergne in the center was filled with early blooming jonquils."[65]

Miss Jennie Shaw at a center table in the mansion's state dining room just prior to a meeting of the Daughters of the American Revolution in 1915. (KHS)

With a sense of time and history, James B. McCreary anticipated that the opening of the governor's mansion would take place on the eve of the end of his administration. He was determined to leave office in a blaze of glory, partly because he had his heart set on being elected to the United States Senate. He was meticulous in presiding over the Sinking Fund Commission, communication with the architects, the contractors, and the numerous suppliers of fabrics, rugs, and general furnishings. The mark he would leave behind was the classical governor's mansion, an elegant physical monument that would both outshine and outlast his record as governor of the commonwealth. McCreary's history as a two-term governor is vividly reflected in his executive journal, the minutes of the Sinking Fund

Commission, the annals of Kentucky public education, and in the reports of the superintendent of public education and the commissioner of highways.

As a new political era dawned in Kentucky, the world at-large was disrupted by the outbreak of World War I. In a burst of emotion, Governor McCreary declared the new governor's mansion would serve a succession of future governors with comfort and dignity for at least the next seventy years. Even so, it is doubtful that the great house would ever again recapture such jubilancy in a social event as the night of the first reception, or the next evening when an elaborate ten-course dinner was served to a select party of Kentuckians and few out-of-state guests.

CHAPTER 9

Riding a Mule into the Mansion

J ames Bennett McCreary had occupied the new
mansion long enough by December 1915 to cor-
rect some of its shortcomings and make the house
livable. There lingered, however, problems of
connecting the mansion to the water, sewerage, ice
making, and electrical facilities of the capitol's power
plant at the foot of the bluff on the Lawrenceburg
Road.[1] On the whole, though, the mansion lived up
to its brightest promises.

Outside, the public grounds remained rutted and
scarred by construction activities and awaited landscaping and planting of trees. The ledge at the rear of
the mansion was narrow and hazardous, with a steep
drop down to the Kentucky River. The photograph of
Governor McCreary in a dealer's automobile reflects
the virtual absence of a roadway. No plan had been
made to curb the rim of the cliff, but fortunately there
was a little room for the construction of crude outbuildings such as a stable and a carriage shed.[2]

When the moment of James McCreary's vacating
the mansion arrived in December 1915, he packed
away his last frock coat and drove back to Richmond
with the dream that his next political triumph would
be election to the United States Senate. To realize this
ambition, however, he had to vanquish the Democratic
icon J.C.W. Beckham, a dream that was fraught with
failure from the outset.[3] For the old Confederate veteran the political climate in Kentucky changed, and the
governor had become almost as archaic as his little
one-horse carriage, stable, and buggy shed. In Frankfort
his fiscal policies had been undefined, and he left
behind a government in financial disarray.[4]

The troublesome clouds of war in Europe were already
casting a shadow in Kentucky in 1915. On the local
political scene, two new and untraditional candidates

Governor Augustus O. Stanley, 1915–1919. (KHS)

sought election to the governorship, stirring partisan
spirits in county courthouse squares all across the state.
Augustus Owsley Stanley, Democrat, and Edwin Porch
Morrow, Republican, laden the annals of Kentucky history with antics, legends, and pungent repartee.[5]

Owsley Stanley (1867–1958) was politically bred
and born in Kentucky, the son of a Disciples of Christ

minister. In the course of his life he had been a farmer, schoolteacher, lawyer, and in 1914 a member of the United States House of Representatives.[6] Edwin Morrow, a nephew of Governor William O. Bradley, grew up in Somerset, heartland of the Kentucky Republican party. He was a graduate of Cumberland College and had studied law at the University of Cincinnati. He mounted the political ladder one rung at a time, as city councilman, then as federal district attorney. In 1912 he had unsuccessfully sought election to the United States Senate.[7]

A plethora of vital issues screamed for discussion and resolution in 1915, issues which neither candidate had a zeal to discuss. In the Democratic primary campaign the issue of prohibition was central. "Dry" forces nominated the eloquent but conservative superintendent of public instruction, Harry V. McChesney of Frankfort. He had the support of a strong battery of ministers, temperance crusaders, and perhaps a hefty but silent squadron of moonshiners and bootleggers.[8] The "wet" Democrats chose Owsley Stanley as their candidate, and during the summer of 1915 the issue of prohibition was debated and beaten to a pulp. Personally Congressman Stanley was, by self admission, a walking, breathing persona of "wetness."[9]

Paradoxically, Kentucky's image bore the sharp glow of bourbon. The state's distilleries had spread the name of Kentucky far and near on their labels. The state also spawned a hefty and militant brigade of temperance crusaders advocating absolute prohibition of the distillation and drinking of whiskey. In the Democratic primary Stanley fended off the prohibitionists and was nominated Democratic candidate for governor.[10] Stanley came into the fall campaign in 1915 as a seasoned debater and master of political repartee. Already he had nurtured a grass roots rural Kentucky constituency. As a congressman he had been attentive to constituent requests. He had sent out a lavish number of improved garden and field seeds, and had performed myriad other errands on their behalf. As a candidate he promised Kentuckians he would pare the state employment rolls, modernize the revenue system, and (responding to voter mandate) advocate educational reform.[11] He faced a formidable opponent in Edwin Porch Morrow, the Republican nominee.[12] That summer both candidates were primed to conduct a vaudevillian "one-upsman" campaign for the governorship, and the right to live in the new mansion. They generated enough legend, myth, and political folklore to leaven Kentucky political history for a century to come.

As a commitment to Eastern Kentucky Republicans who were true to the cause, Edwin P. Morrow avowed he would see to the repealing of the state's dog tax. In certain areas of Kentucky this was an issue as sacred as motherhood. The proposition of every good Republican highlander owning a free dog was an unwritten codicil to the Bill of Rights itself.[13]

Edwin Morrow shouted in every eastern courthouse square he could reach that all citizens had an all but God-ordained right to own a tax-free dog. Thus his campaign was dubbed by Democrats as the one to save "Old Dog Ring." A.O. Stanley said on occasions his opponent literally wrung tears from the eyes of his supporters. He even made Stanley seem to be a dog-hater. The gubernatorial campaign that year had many of the aspects of a traveling sideshow rather than a serious one for the Kentucky governorship. On one occasion Stanley became nauseated and vomited on the platform, an act repulsive enough to turn every voter present against him. He, however, humbly begged the audience's forgiveness, saying that every time he heard Edwin Morrow speak it made him sick at the stomach.[14]

In many areas of Kentucky in 1915, the population was barricaded behind a great land barrier, making it difficult for state-wide candidates for office to travel. This was especially true in the eastern highlands where Morrow had his greatest political strength. He rode a Chesapeake and Ohio passenger train to Wayland, but out of personal fear refused to ride a mule into the more rugged reaches of the mountains. Stanley, no less fearful, seized the opportunity and rented a mule and rode across the ridge to Knott County. Everywhere he spoke he told his listeners that Edwin Morrow was too proud to ride a mule to visit them. He said Morrow would not and could not ride a mule. "He doesn't want to see you as badly as I do. He thinks he has got you in a bag. He didn't think I'd come over here on a mule either. But here I am. Where's Ed? He's only speaking where he can ride a train."[15] In the election Stanley won, but only by a slim majority. Edwin Morrow observed that "Owsley has gone into the Governor's Mansion on a mule."[16]

Quickly there were to be reverberations of Stanley's mountain adventure. On his visitation to the region he had been hospitably entertained, spending nights in mountain cabins while bragging on the "old woman's" cooking sowbelly, turnip greens, sweet potatoes, and corn pone. He had invited his hosts, who had greeted him so warmly with the legendary Appalachian salutation of hospitality, to "Light, hitch, and come on and

Sue Stanley, her children, and the family dog seated on the mansion lawn in 1915. (FCS, Dawson family collection)

One of the Stanley boys at the mansion steps. (FCS)

set," to come to Frankfort for a visit. He had told his listeners, Democrat and Republican, that he was certain to be elected governor, and, "When I get to Frankfort I want you all to come and see me and my old woman and bring the younguns." He had avowed the doors of the mansion would be flung open to welcome them. Come they did, bearing petitions begging the governor to pardon sons and relatives who had been "unfairly" incarcerated in the penitentiary and county jails.[17]

Stanley's "old woman," as he described her to the mountaineers, was the youthful and handsome former Sue Soaper, daughter of a prominent Henderson family. She was much younger than the governor, and, as he said, much handsomer. She was the mother of three boys, the youngest four years old. They were the first children to live in the new mansion. There on the mansion and capitol grounds the boys had space to romp at will, sometimes accompanied by their mother.[18]

On one occasion a lean and lanky mountaineer came up with a sack slung over his shoulder. He told Sue he had spent two days trying to get in to see the governor. He had brought him some presents and wanted to talk to Stanley. He was a hill man who Stanley had met on his mule ride, and who the governor called "Bum." Sue had difficulty convincing Bum that she was the governor's "old woman" and not his daughter. She called the governor and told him Bum was there to visit with him, and sent him back to the capitol lugging his sack of "taters." Bum was in a reciprocating mood. Besides the sack of potatoes, sassafras roots, and other mountain delicacies, he produced a petition signed by an appreciable number of Knott County citizens declaring his son was an innocent victim of miscarried justice and should be pardoned. He had been convicted for fatally shooting a neighbor, which Bum declared his son had not done. Stanley reviewed the court record, which alleged the boy had used a pistol, but the boy and Bum declared he did not own a pistol. Stanley had the boy brought to his office and pardoned him.[19]

Bum returned to the hills and spread the good news. A few weeks later he was back in Frankfort accompanied by seven or eight neighbors. They came laden with jars of wild honey, turnip greens, sassafras, and other good things plus petitions seeking pardons for sons and kinfolk who had been, so they said, unjustly packed off to the penitentiary. The notations, so liberally inscribed in Stanley's executive journal, reveal him to have been a compassionate governor, if not an astute politician.[20]

On the face of the extensive formal documentary executive record, Governor Stanley surely spent an inordinate amount of his time reading petitions and granting pardons and remissions of fines. He also filled the state's official roster with an army of petty officer commissions. Occasionally there passed over his desk a petition that proved more fascinating than those accompanied by reams of citizen signatures. One such petition described the plight of Willie Patrick, a Morgan County yeoman farmer. Willie had landed in the penitentiary on a shaky conviction of having committed rape on a female farm hand. He and the woman, named Dora Bell Grace, were working alongside one another in a field when they opened a conversation on the subject which the Morgan County court euphemistically called "domestic felicity," or in Dora's case, a lack of it. She, however, expressed the idea that an open cornfield was not the most propitious place to improve domestic relations. She invited Willie to visit her at her house at nightfall.

Willie Patrick, being weak of flesh, and carnally inclined, responded to Dora's invitation, and under cover of darkness appeared at her door. She greeted him in what the court described as "night clothes." She was said to have uttered sweet words of welcome and seated Willie on a narrow chest beside her. She gave him food, but at that point Willie saw the shadowy figure of a man prowling around outside the house. The ghostly figure turned out to be Dora's husband, there to entrap Willie in a compromising act with his wife. A few days later, on a complaint from the Graces, Willie Patrick was hauled into court on a charge of committing rape. In the meantime Dora Grace had sought to blackmail him by making him pay a sum of "hush" money. A Morgan County jury found Patrick guilty as charged, and the judge sentenced him to a term of years in the penitentiary at Frankfort.

On January 21, 1919, eight of the jurors and a host of citizens had a stroke of conscience and recanted their precipitated action by signing a petition requesting that Governor Stanley send Willie Patrick home a free man. The governor used more than two pages of his executive journal detailing Willie Patrick's plight and explaining his grant of clemency. He signed a pardon and sent Willie back to his cornfield in Morgan County to be a farmer, not a specialist in the sociological matter of "domestic infelicity."[21]

Governor Stanley then turned his attention to the Morgan County Circuit Court and jurors, observing that, "It is almost inconceivable that the twelve jurors believing such a state of facts would have convicted this man. However they did convict him when they believed him to be guilty of no other offense than visiting this woman for an improper purpose with her full consent, and having signed a statement they are convinced the verdict is unjust?"[22]

Indeed Governor Stanley must have sat in the mansion office staring at the Mary Tudor tapestry and pondering the fact that in many of Kentucky's "little kingdom" counties justice—or the lack of it—dangled at the end of a slender thread. He also spent a lot of time preparing and issuing requisitions for his fellow governors to send home to Kentucky many of its wayward sons who had wandered beyond the state's borders after committing high crimes and misdemeanors. He reciprocated by honoring requisitions by other governors who sought the return of their own fugitives, some from as far away as California. In monotonous succession, Stanley's executive journal entries were prefaced with "The Governor this day granted. . . ."[23]

Owsley and Sue Stanley made the mansion their full-time home, and Sue found living in Frankfort a friendly and pleasing experience. Despite all the glittering fanfare in the opening reception in the mansion, there was the cold reality that the commonwealth lacked the necessary funds to make it fully and comfortably livable. This difficulty was compounded by the scarcity of many of the materials needed to finish the building during World War I.[24]

The Stanley family was also the first to live in the mansion in the full-blown age of the automobile. On July 19, 1916, the Sinking Fund Commissioners approved an expenditure of $2,259 to construct a garage on the narrow ledge area in the rear of the mansion. In the same meeting the commissioners instructed the supervisor of public properties to accept a bid of $125 to have Governor McCreary's buggy shed and stable removed.[25]

Earlier, the Sinking Fund Commission had approved the building of a fence extending from Logan Street to the Old Lawrenceburg Road, separating the mansion's grounds from the property of Mrs. Sargent. They also instructed the supervisor to lay a "granitoid" walk from the capitol driveway up to the front entrance of the mansion. They should have also authorized the construction of a safety barrier around the rim of the precipitous bluff immediately behind the mansion. This need was dramatically revealed on a Sunday morning when Governor Stanley and his family were dressed and ready to attend church. Two houseboy "trusties" cranked up the governor's brand new black sedan and drove it to the rear basement entry of the residence.

Mansion servants horsing around in 1918. (FCS, Dawson family collection)

One of the trusties remembered he should get something from the house and left the other one in the running car. When the second trusty went into the basement, the unattended car rolled backward and over the cliff and was smashed. Staring down at the wrecked car, Governor Stanley turned to the cringing trusties and said, "There's another $1,500 gone to hell."[26]

For the governor at that date there was more than a car gone to hell. In the great pack of earlier congratulatory letters he found two that created for him a political Scylla and Charybdis. In the first, Frances Beauchamp, president of the Kentucky Women's Christian Temperance Union, wrote in her imperious manner that she wanted to confer with him at the earliest possible moment to discuss a matter of vital importance to the state. Governor Stanley did not have to ask what the urgent matter was. The second letter came from N. Millen of the Eminence Distilling Company of Louisville, thanking him for his "beneficial services to 'our industry.'"[27]

Kentucky in 1916 found itself in a highly ambivalent social and economic dilemma. Almost from that natal moment when the first pioneer settler hacked a corn patch from the forest, whiskey making was virtually synonymous with hog killings, spinning, carving and weaving, and drying fruits. There had come to reside in the governor's mansion in 1915 a well publicized patron of the industry, but who, figuratively at least, claimed to have boarded "the wagon" during the most intense years of the world war. Frances Beauchamp, at the head of her militant temperance crusaders, all but demanded that Governor Stanley cry out in fervency for a "dry" Kentucky. The distillers wanted him to keep it "moist." In the middle, Stanley proclaimed that he was "the wettest governor in a dry state."[28] This issue flowed into the mansion's cellar itself.

A more pressing issue for Governor Stanley even than prohibition was the complete revision of Kentucky's revenue system that he had promised during his election campaign. No doubt many conferences were held in the mansion's downstairs "war room." In addition there was the necessity to curb the flagrant activities of the Ku Klux Klan, rein in lynch mobs, and promote with severely limited fiscal resource the burgeoning good roads movement. And of course the never-ending demands by constituents for pardons, remission of fines, and appointments to petty offices continued.

Owsley Stanley, a thoroughly political animal, was also a hard-working governor. He perhaps never derived much joy from the office. Long after he departed Frankfort he told a group of ex-Kentucky governors assembled in Washington that there were two things he had no desire to have again—"the governorship of Kentucky and gonorrhea."[29] He no doubt had used the governorship as a stepping stone into the United States Senate. The way was opened for him when Senator Ollie James died on August 28, 1918, and after the election in November Stanley succeeded him in the Senate.[30]

After the Stanleys moved out, there followed a period of an interesting succession of gubernatorial tenants. Lieutenant Governor James Dixon Black had spent only brief periods of time in Frankfort. Perhaps the family had lived in Frankfort when Black was an assistant attorney general in 1912. He had been there for two sessions of the General Assembly, and on two or three brief occasions when he presided over the Senate

Governor James D. Black, 1919. (KHS)

and acted as governor in the absence of Stanley from the state.[31] But apparently Black was seldom if ever privy to any of the gubernatorial actions until that hour when he met in privacy with Owsley Stanley just prior to Stanley's leaving office. Stanley seems actually to have ordered Governor Black to retain all his appointees on the state payroll. After his conference with Stanley, the new governor walked down a capitol corridor to visit the state treasurer, where he learned that the commonwealth teetered on the brink of bankruptcy.[32]

On that gloomy day Governor Black (1849–1938) told a *Louisville Courier-Journal* reporter that he was going home to Barbourville to discuss with his wife, Jeanette (Nettie) Pitzer Black, the move into the governor's mansion, a move which involved family decisions. He said Nettie would come to Frankfort to make arrangements. As it turned out, the Blacks and their three children were little more than temporary tenants from May 1919 to December 1919.[33] The family left little record behind of their being in Frankfort. It appears that nothing of a social nature took place at the man-

Governor and Mrs. Black standing at the south side entrance of the governor's mansion. In the foreground stands the wire-wheeled executive limousine. (FCS)

sion, and the family lived from day to day tolerating the irritations caused by the deficiencies of the facilities.

Politically Kentucky's post–World War I years were murky. The Black administration, if it could be called such, accomplished no major changes. In fact it became entangled from the outset with the sticky issue of settling the tax dispute in the collection of the Kentucky inheritance tax from the estate of the late Mrs. Robert Worth (Flagler) Bingham. Mrs. Bingham was the wealthy widow of Henry Flagler of Florida East Coast railway and real estate fame, and a member of the North Carolina Kenan textile family. For Governor Black and the Commonwealth of Kentucky, the more pertinent fact was that her wealth was subject to Kentucky state taxation. In the state's effort to collect the tax it was necessary for Governor Black to appoint special legal counsel. In performing this duty he incurred the wrath of Judge Bingham and his new newspaper, both of which were critical of his administration.[34]

The new governor also confronted another politically sensitive matter in coming to grips with the longtime festering issue of awarding contracts for school textbooks, and the appointing of a special commission to oversee their selection and purchase. Governor Stanley had served as chairman of the textbook commission that had substantially over-ordered books from the politically astute American Book Company of Cincinnati. In binding himself not to remove the Stanley appointees, Black almost automatically became involved in near—if not outright—scandalous activities on the part of entrenched officials. Thus the seven months of the Black administration were fraught with the controversy in which the seeds of his electoral defeat were sown. No doubt for the "accidental Governor" the nights and days in the mansion were sore and troubled ones.

In his campaign for election to the governorship, Black was handicapped, but his opponent Edwin Porch Morrow was benefited. Black was in no way Stanley's equal as a campaigner. Morrow elevated the temperature of the summer of 1919 by charging from the stump that both Stanley and Black were guilty of gross political corruption, and that he would enter the governor's mansion an avenging servant of the people wielding the gubernatorial sword of power to lop off the public roll their unworthy appointees. If voters took Morrow's charges seriously, Stanley and Black were guilty of textbook fraud and of unloosing on the public a host of felons.[35] Cast in the traditional mode of Kentucky political campaigning, Edwin Morrow promised to keep the medieval Kentucky penitentiary crowded with the convicted criminals, to build good roads past every voter's door, and to improve the status of public education.[36]

This time around Morrow chose to let "Old Dog Ring" slumber away undisturbed by taxation or charges of sheep killing. He had the Republican faithful well in hand, and expected to snare a generous flock of alienated Democrats. In the end Morrow won a clear voter mandate to move into the governor's mansion. The Morrows rode into Frankfort in December 1919, with the new governor bent on sending the Stanley-Black rascals scurrying up the bluffs of the Kentucky River Palisades. He would set Kentucky on a new political bearing.[37]

James Dixon and Nettie Pitzer Black gathered up their belongings and drove down the winding old Wilderness Road to Barbourville to lick political wounds inflicted by prohibition, labor unrest, and the Armstrong purchase debacle. He performed one last official act in leaving office; he pardoned Henry Youtsey, who had served extensive prison time for his involvement in the assassination of William Goebel.[38] In the annals of Kentucky political history the Black gubernatorial administration was little more than a historical blip. Nettie Black, however, left behind tangible evidence that she had lived in the mansion by planting trees on the grounds.[39]

Since that day in 1804 when James Garrard completed his second consecutive term as governor, Kentuckians for almost two centuries adhered to the archaic policy of limiting their governors to a single term. Thus every four years the governor's mansion received new tenants, and every one of them made some kind of modification of the house to suit the needs of the incoming family.[40]

If one were gullible enough to give credence to Kentucky gubernatorial campaign bombast and felonious accusations, the courts might have prudently locked the front door to keep the newly elected rascal out, and locked the back door to keep the incumbent one from escaping. The charades of campaigns aside, one fact is irrefutable. Carpets were trampled threadbare, furniture was scratched and broken, china and glassware was cracked and destroyed, and even the floors and walls were stained by the passage of time and the citizenry. From the first occupancy of the old mansion in 1798 to the present, Kentuckians have all but asserted an inalienable privilege of visiting the mansion, and many governors have encouraged the idea by declaring the mansion the people's house.

Governor Edwin Porch Morrow, 1919–1923. (KHS)

Katherine Waddle Morrow was first lady from 1919 through 1923. (FCS)

Only spasmodically have incoming governors and their wives had inventories made of the furnishings of the mansion or made documentary listings designating private and public properties. No matter, the cost of maintenance of the mansion for every administration virtually since 1804 has exceeded—sometimes by three or four times—the governor's salary. There were in the twentieth century, at least, the hidden costs of pilferage. Some visitors to the mansion purloined "souvenirs."[41] This has been especially true, so it is said, since the opening of the new mansion.

The privilege of public access to the mansion was tradition at the moment Edwin Porch Morrow (1877–1935) went by the office of the secretary of state to file the certificate of his election as governor on December 9, 1919.[42] He and his wife, Katherine Hale Waddle Morrow, then drove up to the door of the mansion in style. They arrived seated in an automobile, not on mule back as Morrow said Stanley had done. This was a day of Republican jubilee.

A noisy horde of patronage-hungry Republicans swarmed into Frankfort in Morrow's wake. They came to throng the inaugural parade route, to shout for their Ed, to see him take the oath of office, and to congratulate him with their right hands while presenting their requests with their left. The raucous Morrow-Stanley campaign in 1915 had whetted their partisan fangs. From the campaign stump in the summer of 1919 Morrow had charged the Stanley-Black appointees with being corrupt.

When the Morrows moved into the governor's mansion with their two teenagers, they immediately heightened the social tempo of the place. They entertained with long lines of velvet- and taffeta-draped women and their more soberly attired male escorts. There came to the mansion troops of Kentucky and national Republicans to plan political strategies. The basement "war room" became a haven for legislators and others out to thwart the unyielding Democrats who controlled the Senate. For Governor Morrow this mansion retreat

Governor Edwin Porch Morrow, surrounded by a delegation of the Kentucky suffragettes in his office at the state capitol, signing the legislative act—the Anthony Amendment—granting women the right to vote, circa 1919. (KHS)

was the place where he came to understand that there was a sharp difference between campaign rhetoric of reform, and the day-to-day struggle to effect it.

The era of the immediate post–World War I years was a time of appreciable social and economic turbulence in Kentucky. As a candidate, Edwin Morrow had promised to divest the commonwealth of many of its archaic legislative and administrative practices. He advocated equal political rights for women, paring state employment rolls, halting mob violence and lynchings, new educational reforms, and the building of "good" roads. Kentucky was cringing under a cloud of human disgrace. The lynchings of Will Lockett in Fayette, and Richard James in Woodford were horrendous incidents in Kentucky human history.[43] These incidents occurred at the moment the state was pitching headlong into an

economic depression. Burley tobacco farmers were in a crisis of over-production and worn-out methods of marketing. These events cast long shadows across the commonwealth and into the governor's mansion.[44]

No changes, however, were of more far-reaching consequence than the changed political status of women after 1920. When laggard Tennessee cast the thirty-sixth and confirming vote for adoption of the Nineteenth Amendment, the act had reverberations in the Kentucky governor's mansion, as the first ladies and other female officials commanded a stronger presence.

For the four years of Morrow's administration his executive journal reflects the fragility of Kentucky's social and economic conditions. Prohibition and enforcement of the Eighteenth Amendment to the United States Constitution turned Kentucky into a

A 1920s house party at the mansion hosted by Governor Morrow's daughter, Edwina (#7 in the photograph). (FCS)

near state of anarchy, and in his second message to the General Assembly, Governor Morrow wrote, "The violation of the Prohibition Law challenges the sovereignty and authority of Kentucky. From one end of the State to the other this law is being openly, persistently and contemptuously violated. The moon shiners and the bootleggers defy courts and juries, judges and sheriffs, and boldly proclaim themselves above the law of the land. Outlawed whiskey has and is rapidly becoming sinister and powerful, expressing itself in armed resistance of officers of the law, corruption of public officials, and the disturbance of church and school, and the intimidation of those who oppose it."[45] This was a doleful executive comment on a Kentucky caught in the clutches of the lawless.

Moonshining, bootlegging, and gun toting went hand in hand. The governor told the General Assembly

that "The habit of carrying concealed deadly weapons can be charged [with] eighty-five percent of all homicides committed in the Commonwealth. Nearly every wound inflicted by a bullet; every death caused, or life endangered from a revolver shot, has been fired from a weapon concealed in violation of the law."[46] Three-fourths of the pages in the governor's portfolio volume executive journal pertain to lawlessness in some way. They are filled with petitions for pardons, the remissions of fines, and requisitions to other state governors for the return of Kentucky miscreants who had skipped beyond the state's borders to escape their day in court.[47]

No doubt Governor Morrow had moments of discomfort from the fact he had derived a major portion of his political support from one of the regions where moonshining, bootlegging, and carrying concealed weapons flourished. Dockets of both state and federal courts were burdened with whiskey cases. Ironically, much of the vote which sent Edwin Morrow to live in the Frankfort mansion also proved his nemesis. He was faced with the enemy-making charge of enforcing the laws in a time and a state run rampant with lawlessness.[48]

Just across the driveway from the mansion, Governor Morrow was confronted by a more immediate opposing force, the Kentucky Senate.[49] In his message to the General Assembly in 1922 he asked legislators to let campaign scurrility be bygone and to become Kentuckians in spirit and devote their attention to the state's public institutions, which were suffering from lack of state support. Morrow asserted that Kentucky's rural schools were in a deplorable condition. Students were huddled in shabby buildings. Some counties were unable to employ teachers because salaries ranged from $210 to $420 a year.[50] Surely, in the face of such dire conditions Governor Morrow's days in the mansion were clouded with anxiety and a feeling of helplessness in the face of the bitter partisanship of the times.

The framers of Kentucky's four constitutions revealed a lack of confidence in the man elected governor, obstinately holding to a term of four years and out. For the mansion this meant that every four years adjustments had to be made in the building and its furnishings to accommodate the lifestyle of incoming families. This was once again the situation as Edwin P. Morrow granted his last pardon and signed his last commission for a petty office.

On December 9, 1923, the highland Republican surrendered the Great Seal of the Commonwealth to another hill countryman, a Democrat. William Jason Fields, the self-denominated "Honest Bill of Olive Hill," had followed a circuitous route to arrive as master of the mansion. The first graduate of the University of Kentucky to become governor, for several years he had traveled Eastern Kentucky's mud-dusty back roads as a drummer for a meatpacking house. He escaped the back country to become a member of the United States House of Representatives. In Congress "Honest Bill" advanced up the ladder of limited fame to become a member of the Military Affairs Committee during World War I.[51]

William Jason Fields (1874–1954) may well be considered in Kentucky political history a truly "accidental governor." When Alben Barkley, on the death of J. Campbell Cantril, refused the nomination to be the Democrat candidate, the party committee turned to the Eastern Kentucky congressman. The time for decision-making was short.[52]

Governor William Jason Fields, 1923–1927. (KHS)

The Republicans had chosen onetime Democrat Charles I. Dawson of Louisville as their candidate. In the campaign that September the newspapers carried frequent stories of revenue officers razing moonshine stills and arresting bootleggers. Kentucky was embroiled over the issues of prohibition of the making and selling of liquor, the need for major internal improvements, and the legality of horse racing and pari-mutuel betting. True to electoral tradition, both candidates skillfully sidestepped the essential issues and engaged in puerile personal attacks. Charles I. Dawson was labeled by Democrats as "Changing Charlie," and Judge Dawson retorted by saying his opponent was "dodging Bill from Olive Hill who answers no questions and never will."[53] Fields at least answered one question, for he won the election by a substantial majority.

The gubernatorial election in 1923 placed an extraordinary family in the mansion. Governor Fields was a fundamentalist Methodist, and a proclaimed prohibitionist. He mandated, almost before he reached the second floor of the mansion, that there would be no

Dora McDavid Fields, first lady of Kentucky from 1923 through 1927. (FCS)

liquor, no dancing, and a curfew on telephone calls and other activities after 9:00 P.M. He plastered the mansion walls with prohibitionists placards, and adorned his desk with "dry" prohibitionist "souvenirs."[54] Up the Kentucky River and its headstreams back country, however, moonshiners and bootleggers drove a thriving business from Golden Pond in the "Tween Rivers" safe haven to the Forks of Beaver on the eastern mountain rim.

In her own fashion Dora McDavid Fields, whom William had married in 1893, was one of the most colorful hostesses ever to occupy the mansion. A living personification of the plain Kentucky mother and housewife, she literally dragged grassroots Kentucky into the mansion's parlors and big dining room as she unapologetically transferred the social environment from Rosedale in Carter County to Frankfort. She said she had a fondness for fresh milk and kept two jersey milk cows penned at night behind the mansion. By day the animals grazed the lawn out front, greatly reducing

the cost of mowing the demesne. By her own count she kept 140 chickens in a henhouse. She mothered seven children, two daughters and five sons. The youngest daughter was ten years old when the Fields arrived in Frankfort in December 1923. Years later she told a *Louisville Courier-Journal* magazine writer that she did not "go much for the social life that is customary among the First Families of Kentucky." She disliked the formal affairs that took place in the mansion and elsewhere. She said, "I had to attend a good many formal receptions and dinners but beyond that I didn't take much part. I simply did not enjoy the social life, and with children growing up I had plenty to do without that." She doubtless did not shout a cry of jubilee when William stood in My Old Kentucky Home in Bardstown and lavishly welcomed Queen Marie of Romania and her son Prince Nicholas to the commonwealth. It must be said that Mrs. Fields was physically unable to engage in many social events. She underwent two surgical operations and suffered ill health much of the time she was in Frankfort.[55]

Following World War I there seems to have been no detailed inventory of the furnishings and contents of the governor's mansion. With the change in tenants every four years, additions to and losses from the furnishings went unrecorded. Too, there appear to be no records differentiating private from public furnishings. When the W.J. Fields family moved into the mansion its contents were valued for insurance purposes at $5,000, a modest figure for post–World War I values. Undoubtedly much of the mansion's furnishings were worn, cracked, chipped, or missing. At a meeting of the Sinking Fund Commission, Emma Guy Cromwell, the secretary of state, was appointed to confer with Mrs. Fields "as to any furnishings that may be wanted at the Executive Mansion." The two women were given leeway to purchase any furnishings they deemed necessary.[56]

In its meeting on March 17, 1925, the Sinking Fund commissioners received a resolution from the Kentucky Conference of the Daughters of the Revolution that the state purchase three or four of the John J. Audubon Bird Prints, then in the Henderson Public Library. The ladies suggested that these should be framed and hung in the governor's mansion. The prints were to be removed from the Elephant Edition of the Audubon collection. Their proposal met with short shrift by the commissioners, and immediately following a reading of the resolution there was a motion to adjourn.[57]

A sensitive issue which dated back into the immediate post–Civil War days was the use of convict trusties

The mansion ballroom, circa 1925. (FCS)

as servants in the mansion. Almost no record of this practice seems to have been made. The Sinking Fund commissioners in their meeting on September 3, 1925, approved this practice, requiring only that the number of necessary trusties be clearly stated in writing, and in time for the warden to make selections. Some of the mansion trusties won the confidence and friendship of the governors and their families and were pardoned to become respectable citizens.[58]

Near the close of the Fields administration, the contents of the mansion were insured for $10,000.[59] This represented either a considerable addition, or, more likely, an insurance adjustment. The most significant

change in the physical structure of the mansion was the fact that the superintendent of public buildings was instructed by the Sinking Fund Commission to have screens installed over all the doors and windows, and to make various repairs and replace the roof.[60]

Hardly had the last roofing nail been driven before it was time for William J. and Dora Fields to move back to Carter County. The record is unclear as to what happened to their chickens and the milk cows. Before they departed they turned the mansion over to the incoming Flem and Susie Steele Sampson with a flourish of grace.

The Democratic party had been split during the 1927 gubernatorial campaign over prohibition, racetrack

121

Governor Flem D. Sampson displaying his pride and joy, the Kentucky license plate of 1929, which told the public wherever a Kentucky automobile went that Kentucky was for progress. (KHS)

betting, taxes in general, and internal improvements. Measured by many criteria, "Honest Bill" had been a respectable governor, but the times were out of joint for him. The ghost of Stanley-Black corruption still lingered in the mansion.

That year the Republicans again resorted to their political heartland and nominated Court of Appeals judge Flem D. Sampson (1875–1967) of Barbourville as their candidate for governor. The press portrayed Judge Sampson as a "self-made man in every respect." His parents, Joseph and Emoline Kellum, had ten children, and Flem Sampson was said to have worked as a callow child to earn enough money to purchase his school textbooks at Union College and Valparaiso Law School. He practiced law in Barbourville and was elected to a judgeship on the Court of Appeals bench.[61]

Before William J. and Dora Fields departed Frankfort,

they indulged in a final hurrah in a lavish reception on December 2, 1927. Five hundred guests gathered in the mansion to bid the unusual couple goodbye, and to greet the incoming Flem D. and Susie Steele Sampson and their three daughters. That night the mansion was once more aglitter with bright lights and stylishly gowned women. The halls were banked with baskets of long stemmed white and lavender chrysanthemums. The state reception rooms were abloom with roses and ferns, and the ballroom was smothered with chrysanthemums and ferns. Red roses decorated the dining room, and the table held bowls and dishes filled with white mints, salted almonds, and pecans.[62]

In the receiving line stood Governor and Dora Fields, Flem D. and Susie Sampson, and their daughter Mrs. J.J. Martin. Flanking them was a collection of judges and politicians ad infinitum. There was that

Governor Flem D. Sampson, 1927–1931. (KHS)

An orchestra played throughout the inaugural reception and during the "lunch," when guests were served chicken sandwiches, frozen fruit salad, pies, nuts, and coffee. Maybe the chicken came from Mrs. Fields' flock of mansion hens. The mansion glowed with the promise that Flem Sampson would lead Kentucky into a bright and progressive future, a fact he would assert on an oversized automobile license plate which said in bold lettering "Kentucky for Progress."[64]

Whatever may have been the lumpy experience of "Honest Bill" Fields as governor of Kentucky, his family departed from the mansion and Frankfort with a flash of style. Before he vacated the governor's desk he pardoned a generous number of inmates at the state's medieval penitentiary. Almost with the same flourish of the pen he commissioned a comparable number of Kentucky Colonels, two of whom were Frankfort ministers. In return for his good work, grateful friends and state officials presented the couple a silver service, and the state banking commissioner, A.S. Phillips, presented Fields with a fancy alligator skin handbag.[65]

In response to the public generosity, Dora Fields loaned the Kentucky Historical Society an antique bear trap. Her Irish ancestor, she said, had brought the trap to America prior to the American Revolution. It had been passed down from one McDavid generation to another until there were no bears left in Carter County to trap. "Honest Bill" Fields went back to Grayson in Carter County to face an uncertain future as a lawyer and politician who would attempt unsuccessfully to reclaim his congressional seat.

In December 1927, the governorship and mansion were securely in the hands of the Republicans Flem and Susie Sampson. The inauguration of Governor Sampson was turned into a major social and political event,[66] and they had already planned a reception and inaugural ball. Nowhere in the mansion after that date were there to be seen "Honest Bill's" prohibition placards and the anti-liquor artifacts. No 9:00 P.M. curfew dampened the women's rollicking party. Even Governor Sampson's young grandson, Richard Gerrish, was caught up in the excitement and informed his parents he would attend the inauguration and the great ball.[67]

In the inauguration of Governor Sampson the Republicans introduced a tradition-breaking innovation. Pathe News cameramen came to Frankfort and made a visual recording of the event. When completed, the film was rushed to Cincinnati for development and later was run in the Capitol Theater in Frankfort. The film, said the *State Journal,* would be stored in the state

night no 9:00 P.M. curfew but also no liquid cheer. Mrs. Fields stood in the reception line wearing a velvet gown trimmed with rhinestones. She carried, said a reporter, a corsage of pink roses and lavender sweet peas. Mrs. Sampson wore a black transparent velvet gown trimmed with gold lace. She wore pearls and held a corsage bouquet of roses and lily-of-the-valley. Feminine guests wore the latest fashion creations including transparent velvets, coral crepe romaine, georgette, taffetas, and pink satin. Special guests for the occasion were Congressman Virgil Chapman and his wife, and Mrs. W.H. (Mary) Flannery, the first woman to serve in the Kentucky General Assembly. A native of Carter County, and a graduate of the University of Kentucky, Mrs. Flannery was an active supporter of the creation of the Morehead and Murray State Normal Teachers Colleges.[63]

Susie Steele Sampson, wife of Governor Flem Sampson. (FCS)

archives, a then non-existent institution. It would be available to Kentuckians for all time to come to savor the triumphant moment.[68]

The Sampsons' baggage was carried into the mansion in December 1927 just as that of the Fields was being carried out. The grand reception to follow was greeted by a veritable hailstorm of social journalism hyperbole. A reporter for the *State Journal* asserted that "Never before in the history of the New Capitol has there been such a brilliant gathering within its marble walls as assembled there for the inaugural ball and reception." Both the mansion and the capitol swarmed with "beautiful women attired in gorgeous gowns." As the *State Journal* reporter wrote, "The very latest in fashion's decree was worn by smartly gowned women at the Inaugural and Reception Ball. Velvets, georgettes, and taffetas of pale pink and very pale leaf green, lame and satin, are the outstanding materials for evening frocks, judging by those seen at the ball . . . were the in-styles." The heavily beaded and "transparent" style of the Fields era was gradually fading into antiquity.[69]

No woman in the reception line was more gorgeously dressed than Mrs. J.J. Martin, Governor Sampson's daughter. She was robed in a colonial white satin bodice aglitter with pearls and rhinestones. Her hoop skirt, very bouffant, was made of tiny ruffles of tulle. Thus the Sampson reception promised a new sunburst of social affairs in the mansion in what proved to be but a short moment of near Kentucky affluence.[70]

Underneath the glitter and excitement of the Sampson inaugural party lurked a somewhat grim under-lay of reality. Furnishings in the mansion, in almost traditional fashion, were soiled and worn, so much so that not even lavish bowls of red rosebuds and white and lavender chrysanthemums could entirely conceal the fact. Indicative of this was the fact that Governor Sampson told the Sinking Fund commissioners that the mansion's sewer system emitted an unpleasant stench. In a meeting of the Sinking Fund Commission, Emma Guy Cromwell, state treasurer, and Ella Lewis, secretary of state, were asked to assist Mrs. Sampson in the refurbishing of the walls and furnishings of the ballroom and dining rooms. In November 1929, they informed the Sinking Fund commissioners that Connell-Sudduth of Lexington would restore the rooms at a cost of $1,480.50. The commissioners approved the bid, but made clear that the company would have to await its pay until the General Assembly would appropriate the money. The company was assured its bill would draw interest.[71]

But soon neither elaborate social events nor the

The age of the automobile traffic jam about the governor's mansion and the capitol arrived during the Sampson administration. (KHS)

wear and tear of daily use of the mansion could obscure the fact that the Sampson head lay uneasily on the executive pillow; a vengeful Democratic General Assembly stripped him of much of his executive powers in what were called "ripper" acts.

Troubles were compounded during the Sampson occupation of the mansion when the governor became embroiled in a bizarre textbook scheme in which locally written texts would be bound in a single volume to be used throughout most of a child's public school years. This idea was literally laughed out of court, in part because of the convoluted language and grammar which appeared in one or two sections. Also, there was

The family dining room, circa 1930. (FCS)

labor unrest in the coalfields, especially in the eastern section. One of the most serious thorns embedded in the gubernatorial foot, however, was the dispute that arose over the use of the area about the falls on the Cumberland River. Sampson proposed the construction of a hydro-electric generating plant at the falls, but in 1928 Thomas Coleman DuPont contributed $230,000 to purchase 2,200 acres of land for a state park. These and other issues, many of them bitterly partisan in nature, deepened the shadow of unrest on the Sampsons during their years in the governor's mansion.[72]

Structurally, much of the governing process in Kentucky was gripped in the political mores of the nineteenth century. For this and reasons of partisan myopia, there occurred a sharp contrast between the mode of departure of the Sampsons from the mansion in December 1931 and their arrival there four years earlier. The Kentucky revenue system was so archaic that only severely limited funds were made available for repair and refurbishing the mansion. By the latter year

the Great Depression had generated a creeping sociological and fiscal paralysis in Kentucky, and the ill fortunes of the Hoover presidential administration had spread to the Kentucky governor's mansion.[73]

In 1931 the Democrats reclaimed the governor's mansion, but the arrival of the circuit judge from Madisonville created less ruffling of crinolines, georgettes, and velvets than had been the case in 1927. Ruby Laffoon brought to the mansion less color and less bowing to the latest styles than had his immediate predecessors. Meanwhile, the Sampsons went home to settle down in the tranquil environment atop a knoll overlooking the town of Barbourville. There they found isolation from the critical editorials of the *Lexington Herald* and the *Louisville Courier-Journal*, and time to mourn for their daughter Helen, who had died the year before.[74]

The mansion itself seemed indifferent to the political labels of its tenants; it still needed constant repair and refurnishing.

CHAPTER 10

A House Gripped in Depression and Politics

P olitical and economic times were out of joint in
Kentucky in 1931. That year Democrats fiercely
determined to retake the governor's seat in
Frankfort. Few other events in Kentucky's political history were so charged with cross currents of factionalism
as the Democrat convention meeting in Lexington's
Woodland Park that May. Factional leaders and aspi-
rants worked at several levels, both in the auditorium
and downtown in the Phoenix Hotel.[1]

Amidst passionate charges of duplicity and numerous
bruised egos, Judge Ruby Laffoon (1869–1941) of
Madisonville emerged as the gubernatorial nominee,
and newcomer Albert Benjamin Chandler of Versailles
was nominated as the candidate for lieutenant governor.[2] The slate had been moulded in a cauldron of
party in-fighting and compromises, and likely only a
small contingent of insiders knew how the candidates
were actually chosen.

Laffoon and Chandler conducted a vigorous campaign.
Judge Laffoon made many a courthouse square and
country picnic ring with his bullhorn-tone speeches, in
which he mixed political and biblical quotations. Later,
when his moment of victory arrived and the governor-
elect was to spin his inaugural web of promises for the
ensuing four years, Governor Laffoon responded in a
vigorous campaign stump manner. He waved an olive
branch of harmony and peace in his party's ranks, and
promised to set right the misdeeds of partisan "ripperism."[3]

Governor and Mary Nisbet Laffoon represented the
way of life in a Kentucky county seat town.[4] The governor's roots, except for a brief interval when he studied
law at Washington and Lee University, were deeply

Governor Ruby Laffoon, 1931–1935. (KHS)

embedded in Hopkins County. The Laffoons had married in 1894, and by 1931 their three daughters were
married and had homes of their own.[5] When the past-
middle-age couple arrived in Frankfort to take up residence in the "Beaux Arts Castle," they moved into a

127

Mary Nesbit Laffoon in her official photograph made in the governor's mansion in 1933. (FCS)

residence which had an elegant facade and an aging interior, and which cried out for major renovation. Unfortunately, Kentucky's fiscal coffer was not only empty, it was filled with unpaid warranty debts.[6]

Only perhaps Governors John Adair, Thomas Elliott Bramlette, and J.C.W. Beckham had faced so clouded a political and fiscal future as did Laffoon. In 1931 he and his wife moved into a mansion during an unsettled moment in both state and national history. At the capitol the Democratic party was torn by factionalism, and the Great Depression was rapidly tightening its grip on the state's economy. The governor's placating inaugural speech proved to be no more than an eloquent oratorical gesture. Both governor and legislators were faced with the evils of past irresponsible acts of "ripperism" and its hovering ghost over the present.[7]

In that fleeting historical moment when a horde of shouting partisans had lined the parade route on Tues-

day, December 6, 1931, no one could have foretold with certainty the opening of the wide chasm of economic despair which would soon grip Kentucky. In time, the state treasurer's ledger would record the grim fact that the commonwealth's revenue structure was as archaic as Abraham Lincoln's birth cabin in Hodgenville.[8] A shortage of revenue would all but halt the effective operation of state government, and the maintenance of the governor's mansion was far down on the list of needs.

In February 1932, and almost before the Laffoons were settled in the mansion, they permitted the ladies of the Frankfort Garden Club to use it to hold a dress-up reception on George Washington's birthday. The ladies staged a glittering social gathering just before the Great Depression precluded such affairs. Assembled that evening in the ballroom were representatives of Kentucky business, political, and social affairs. The ladies came dressed in current high-style garments, and were generously adorned with jewels and furs. The masculine contingent was clothed in "named brand" suiting purchased from Lexington, Louisville, and Cincinnati haberdasheries.[9] Except for this party interlude, social life in the mansion in the future would be on a more modest scale, differing little from that lived in conventional middle-class Kentucky homes.

By necessity of the times, and by the tangled skein of politics, the governor's mansion became the eye of the storm. No doubt most of the strategies of the Laffoon administration were hatched there rather than across the way in the capitol. This was especially true in the planned thwarting of the powers of the mountain political boss Allie Young, master of the Senate,[10] and the rising power of the Ben Johnson-Dan Talbott-"Happy" Chandler troika. Both of these power centers loomed on the Laffoon political horizon. No doubt much political scheming and maneuvering took place in the mansion, and almost certainly outbursts of embittered wrath echoed within the walls of the governor's office-library during the many stormy sessions that took place there.

Obviously the published record portrays Governor Laffoon as being a complex personality. His moods were said to range from expressions of warm human kindness and good humor to outbursts of Vesuvian wrath. Publicly he expressed himself in an old-style Kentucky oratory delivered in a mode of campaign stump speaking. Privately, however, his language was said to be as "salty" as a country smokehouse meat trough. Reflecting this fact was an account by James W. Martin, a University

Governor Ruby Laffoon receiving the Melvin Taylor party at the governors mansion. Left to right, G.R. Reed, James Garrett, Melvin A. Taylor, Mrs. James Garrett, and the governor. (KHS)

of Kentucky professor and tax consultant. He and an associate were invited to a luncheon with Governor Laffoon in the mansion. They arrived ahead of the governor and stood talking to his young grandson when they saw three men turn up the walkway. Martin asked the child who the men were. The boy took a close look and replied, "One of them is grandpa, I don't know who those other two sons of bitches are."[11]

The Great Depression created several crises for Governor Laffoon, none more troubling than the complex banking situation in the state. In a moment of monetary panic, Governor Laffoon in March 1933 proclaimed a banking holiday as a means to find a solution to potential widespread banking failures. The proclamation provoked resistance from bankers whose institutions were more fiscally stable than many of the state-chartered banks, and they ignored the proclamation. Governor Laffoon then issued a second proclamation,

this time just before President Roosevelt proclaimed a national banking holiday.[12]

Though the bank holiday aroused both anxiety and anger, the rage was relatively mild compared with that stirred by the attempt to raise revenue in the midst of the depression, when the governor initiated a tax on retail sales. Several of the southern states had instituted this tax. In Kentucky however, it was a ready-made political issue for the Chandler-Talbott faction of the Democratic party, one that would likely heighten the tempo of life in the governor's mansion.[13]

Like Flem D. Sampson before him, Governor Laffoon had too little political peace of mind to become deeply concerned with the creeping paralysis of the mansion. He clearly had ample reason to empathize with Marie Antoinette and the troubled political moments she had had in her own Petit Trianon.

In the midst of the most biting moments of the Great

\The ballroom of the governor's mansion decorated for the wedding of the Laffoons' friend Suzanne Shackleford in 1933. (FCS)

Depression there appeared in Frankfort three so-called armies of protesters. They came to protest the lack of aid to the unemployed, to express concern about tobacco sales, and just to protest generally. Encamping on the mansion and capitol grounds, they aroused anxiety for the safety of the residents and state officials. Units of the Kentucky militia were called into action, with instructions to feed, bed down, and get the uninvited visitors on the road home as quickly as possible.[14]

Amidst the comings and goings of protesters there came those homegrown characters who traveled the political and philosophical roads to nowhere, fervently seeking election to office. In a sense these feral bullocks flung their dignity and ambition upon the altar of Kentucky politics with no hopes of greater rewards than gorging themselves on campaign barbecue and whimsical notices by the press. Such a self-anointed, sacrificial altar calf was the eloquent, perennial gadfly "Walking" Munn Wilson, a Hopkins County native. In the dim past he and Ruby Laffoon had been classmates in the Old Baugh one-room school. He also claimed a somewhat pale blood kinship linkage with the governor. However, he disclaimed being a "dyed in the wool" supporter.[15] Disagreeing with "Cousin Ruby," Munn picketed the governor's office, sitting beside its entry waving a placard protesting everything in general and

Musicians in the mansion ballroom for the Shackleford wedding. (FCS)

nothing in particular. It was said that at noon Governor Laffoon would leave his office to have lunch in the mansion. He would take Munn with him, and after lunch the governor would return to the capitol, and Munn to his placard.

During the Great Depression and Kentucky's revenue shortfall, only the most elementary patchwork could be performed on the mansion. The house was livable, and like every governor since James Garrard, the Laffoons had to tolerate the inefficiencies of their home.

In the face of the reduction of revenue, the banking crisis, and the generally blighting effects of the Great Depression, Governor Laffoon surely had to draw on deep human resources. The ghost which stalked both the mansion and the capitol, however, was the Chandler threat. In that age of "no holds barred" politics, chicanery and maneuvering were an accepted norm. Happy Chandler, a confirmed political opportunist, had the support of a cabal of managers and maneuverers who helped to usher in a new age of colorful, if not dramatic, "new politics" and personalities.

As lieutenant governor, Happy Chandler had been

"ripped" of most of his prerogatives in the Senate. He was left with little if anything to do but build future political fences.[16] Ingeniously he used the time to season a political persona. Frequently the capitol halls rang with his singing "Danny Boy," "There's Pie in the Sky," and "My Old Kentucky Home" to tourists and straggling citizens or potential supporters.[17]

The magic moment for setting the Chandler political career arrived in 1935, when Governor Laffoon and his chosen successor, Thomas Rhea, went to Washington to explain to President Roosevelt why Kentucky did not hold a primary presidential election, and no doubt to seek New Deal funds. Almost at the very moment their train crossed the Big Sandy River and they were across the state border, Acting Governor Chandler called a special meeting of the General Assembly to consider a gubernatorial nominating primary for both parties.[18] Governor Laffoon and Thomas Rhea rushed home to undo the political damage, but the Chandler action was upheld by the Court of Appeals on constitutional grounds.[19] Laffoon and Rhea then compounded their problem by securing authorization for two primaries.

They won the first and lost the second; Happy Chandler won the Democratic gubernatorial nomination.[20]

Late in December 1935, the Laffoon family responded to the constitutional decree of succession, packed up their possessions, and returned to the more hospitable environment of Madisonville. On their way home, Governor Laffoon's writing hand must have tingled with cramps, as during the closing hours of his administration he showered the penitentiary with pardons and commutations of sentences, and saturated the nation with colonel commissions. He euphemistically labeled the outriders "staff aides."[21] Despite whatever Governor Laffoon felt he might have accomplished as governor, through no fault of his own he left the state mired in debt, in fiscal disarray, and in economic depression. Similarly, he certainly left the mansion no better off than he had found it. He assuredly was aware that the era between his nomination in the raucous Woodland Park Auditorium and his bidding farewell to the mansion staff had been a troubled one. One thing was permanently tangible, though: he left behind six tightly packed cartons of pardons and colonel commissions.[22]

Humanely or politically, Governor Laffoon set at liberty a veritable flock of rapists, murderers, robbers, storehouse breakers, and horse thieves. Perhaps some of those pardoned had served as trusties in the mansion. Among the murderers set free was Curtiss (Curt) Jett, who was serving a life sentence for the 1903 murder of J.B. Marcum, the Breathitt County prosecuting attorney. At the same time, Laffoon pardoned two other Breathitt County convicts who were serving life sentences for their notorious acts in the Hargis-Cockrell Feud. To even things out Governor Laffoon commissioned Beach Jett a Kentucky Colonel.[23]

Kentucky Colonel commissions flowed out of the Laffoon office as briskly as the flood tide in the Kentucky River at the rear of the mansion. He honored the high and the low, among them William Randolph Hearst Jr., Fred G. Olsen, Oliver Hazard Perry, and Paul Topefert. Almost at the final tick of the executive clock, Governor Laffoon mustered into service twenty-eight doughty yeomen of Stamford, Connecticut. They were joined by a hundred or more aides of the rank of colonel in New York. The governor covered his western flanks with a hundred or more aides in Chicago.[24] Before his pen was left dry on the desk, Governor Laffoon commanded more colonels than did all the generals in the United States Army from 1775 to 1865.

Not all of Governor Laffoon's concerns, however, had been with the issue of an over-crowded hellhole of a

Governor Albert Benjamin Chandler, 1935–1939, 1955–1959. (KHS)

penitentiary. There were the matters of death sentences. In the mass of records was the warrant for the execution of Sam Magee, who had been sentenced to death by the McCracken County circuit court. The governor signed the execution warrant on March 27, 1933.[25] The case added to the governor's troubled conscience by the public turmoil it created. Few gubernatorial candidates who became governor, perhaps, had stopped to think that this question of prisoner executions might face them.[26]

The 1935 gubernatorial primary election against the Laffoon choice, Thomas Rhea, and then the full election brought about many changes in the mansion and in state government.[27] "The People," as Happy Chandler fondly dubbed them, by their exercise of the ballot, had ushered in a new if not a strident age of politics and governmental operation. The lively incoming family set a new tone of living in the mansion. The two Chandler boys, Ben and Dan, roamed the mansion, capitol, and neighboring ground at will, and the two

Mildred Watkins Chandler posing for her formal portrait in the parlor, circa 1936. The artist is Howard Chandler Christy of New York. (Mimi Lewis family collection)

daughters, Marcella and Mimi, helped bring a burst of youthful spirit to the house as well.[28]

In 1925 Albert Benjamin Chandler (1898–1991) had married Mildred Watkins, a Virginian teacher at the Margaret Hall School in Versailles. She became one of the most energetic hostesses to live in the mansion. She must also have been one of the most patient and tolerant. She often stood by and heard her governor-husband tell guffawing audiences that when they got married he took Mildred to a place she had never been, the kitchen. He said she was his secretary of war, and in time she became known statewide as "Mama."[29] What-

ever might have been said in jest, Mildred Chandler brought verve to family and social life in the mansion.

In an oral taped interview, Ben Chandler Jr. gave an insight from a boy's perspective into life in the mansion. He was fascinated by the comings and goings of politicians, state officials, special guests, and the household staff. He enjoyed some intimacy with the latter, from the patrol officer-driver to the cooks in the basement kitchen. The trusties (convict servants) intrigued him and won his affection. He even hinted that he came to know something of their dalliances in the coed dormitory out back of the mansion.[30]

Ben and Dan Chandler with their friends seated on the steps to the mansion in 1939. (Ben Chandler family collection)

The nooks and crannies of the mansion invited boyish exploration. He mentioned a locked closet which piqued his curiosity. He assumed that was the place where the records of convicts sentenced to die were kept.[31] Outside the mansion the Chandler boys roamed the neighborhood and played with the local children as freely as if they were on a farm in Woodford County. The self-designated protectress of the mansion grounds, neighbor Mrs. Margaret Dawson, said in an interview with Jack Brammer of the *Lexington-Herald Leader* that once Ben Chandler had hit her daughter in a childish squabble, and she had told Ann, "If Mr. Chandler smacked her, she should smack him right back. She later got him down on the ground, kicked him, and got the best of him. She listened well." Mrs. Dawson seems to have been a lady with sharp eyes and tongue. She told Jack Brammer, "Now, those Chandler boys could be ruffians."[32]

By no means did the Chandler boys create all the excitement, despite what Mrs. Dawson might say. For instance, there occurred one incident in the house which perhaps not even Gilbert and Sullivan could have imagined. Catherine Conner of Bardstown was active in social and political affairs in Washington during the New Deal days. In the round of social gatherings she formed an acquaintance with the minister of the Dominican Republic, Andres Postoriza. In the course of affairs he told Mrs. Conner that the notorious dictator Generalissimo Rafael Leonidas Trujillo Molina was interested in horse breeding and would like to visit Kentucky. Mrs. Conner informed U.S. Secretary of State Cordell Hull of the fact, and he approved extending an invitation for a visit on the grounds that the United States in case of war did not want the Dominican Republic to become a German submarine base.

In her autobiography, *From My Old Kentucky Home to the White House,* Mrs. Conner has written that late in 1939 she arranged for the Dominican Generalissimo to visit central Kentucky. She persuaded Frazer Lebus of Cynthiana to entertain him and his party at lunch in his home. She also persuaded Mildred Chandler to have him as a guest in the governor's mansion while Governor Chandler was away in Chicago.

The Trujillo party arrived in Louisville, but it was far larger than Mrs. Conner had anticipated. There was a small brigade of bodyguards, too many to be accommodated by the travel arrangements Mrs. Conner had made. There followed a mad scramble to commandeer enough cars and pickup trucks to make the trip to Cynthiana, and then to the mansion in Frankfort. That evening when the Trujillo cavalcade reached the mansion, a garrulous neighbor dropped in for a casual visit. In the course of conversation, this neighbor told the suspicious visitors that members of the household staff were convicted murderers. Thus suspicions ran high. Mrs. Conner wrote that the servants were just as suspicious of the guests as the guests were of them. After a somewhat strained evening, Generalissimo Trujillo bedded down promptly at 11:00 P.M. in the guest bedroom. His security entourage occupied other rooms and the hallway of the second floor. Around 2:00 A.M. an automobile horn began blowing out in front of the mansion (in his taped interview Ben Chandler said he thought it was a gun shot or a firecracker). Draped in dressing gowns and barefoot, Mildred Chandler and Catharine Conner came down from their third-story bedroom to investigate the noise. They stepped around and over the guardsmen asleep on the hall floor and went out to the capitol drive to find a boy leaning on his car horn. He had just been jilted by his girlfriend and had gotten drunk to ease his heartbreak. There followed a spicy exchange between Mildred Chandler and the intoxicated boy. In the round she had a capitol guardsman arrest him.

The noise soon awakened the Generalissimo and his guards, and in the melee which followed, the drunken lad sobered up enough to realize his predicament and flee into outer darkness, no doubt with a firm resolve never to blow an automobile horn in front of the governor's mansion again. Suddenly Generalissimo Trujillo lost interest in Kentucky horse breeding and the governor's mansion, and cut his visit two days short of schedule. Fortunately, however, he did not grant haven to German submarines.[33]

As hostess of the governor's mansion, Mildred Chandler faced challenges of a more substantive nature than the entertainment of an unpopular Caribbean dictator. There was the ever-present lack of funds to make a full renovation of the house, or to fully adapt it to the needs of a large family. Just as past governors and their families had done, the Chandlers made temporary repairs and did limited refurbishing of the interior and furnishings.

In January 1937, the governor's mansion became a crisis center during one of the most serious disasters in Kentucky history. Twenty inches of rain had fallen during the latter part of the month, raising the Kentucky River flood level to 47.2 feet and threatening devastation to bordering towns and large areas of the state's most productive farmlands. At Frankfort the Kentucky River rose well above its banks, and floodwaters backed up the creeks and low-lying areas, turning the old capitol and old mansion grounds into rapidly shrinking islands. The waters poured into the penitentiary compound, threatening the lives of 2,900 prisoners. Governor Chandler entered the penitentiary by canoe to assure the prisoners that they would be removed and taken to a place well away from the flood. At the foot of a cliff to the rear of the new mansion the floodwaters threatened to drown the power and heating plant. From Ashland to Paducah, Kentucky towns along the Ohio River were flooded as well, and none of them was more threatened than Louisville.[34]

No one in Kentucky, not even the weathermen, could predict when the torrential rains would cease or how much damage the flood waters would wreak on the state.[35] This calamitous blow on top of the Great Depression made an enormous social and economic impact. Even had there been a will in the General Assembly to authorize a full-scale renovation of the governor's mansion, there was no prospect of having enough money to pay the bill.[36]

Just when the Great Depression had begun to let up and Kentuckians in the devastated flood plains were digging out of the mud, there loomed on the international horizon the threat of a second world war. There also came an abrupt and unexpected change of tenants in the mansion. United States Senator Marvel Mills Logan died on October 3, 1939, and on the 9th at precisely 10:30 A.M., A.B. Chandler resigned the governorship and Lieutenant Governor Keen Johnson, then in the midst of a campaign to become governor, was sworn into the office. Johnson then appointed ex-Governor Chandler to fill out Senator Logan's term.[37] No doubt Governor Chandler looked forward to the future race for United States Senator. Before he departed the governor's office he commissioned two or three brigades of "well wishing" colonels.[38]

That morning the Chandler family was busily preparing to leave on the evening train for Washington. Life in the mansion had moved at a fast and merry clip for the Chandlers. There had been considerable entertaining of guests, official and private, including the fiasco

The mansion's basement kitchen before and after the 1936 renovation. (FCS)

The state dining room before the Chandler restoration. (FCS)

Governor A.B. Chandler greeting guests in the state dining room in 1936. (FCS)

The laundry room in the new mansion in 1935. (FCS)

The basement gymnasium and playroom during the Chandler administration, circa 1936. (FCS)

The governor's reception room soon after the Chandler renovation, circa 1936. (FCS)

of the Generalissimo's strange visit. The young family members had added spice to life in the mansion and its surrounding neighborhood, and of course there had been the traditional processions of politicians, favor seekers, Derby breakfast guests, and official receptions.

In their last moments in the governor's mansion, the Chandler family placed the ultimate strain on the house's wiring system. Every light in the place—from the basement to the third floor—was aglow. In the excitement at leaving the mansion, it is doubtful that either the governor or members of his family anticipated that four gubernatorial elections later they would return to Frankfort.[39]

Governor Keen (1896–1970) and Eunice Nichols Johnson, along with their daughter, Judith, moved into the mansion on the departure of the Chandler family. Judith was just beginning high school at Frankfort High, which was within walking distance of the mansion. Eunice Johnson, a Missouri native, was a hospitable hostess. She arrived in the mansion in the midst of her husband's campaign for election to the governorship in his own right. As was the case for so many of the preceding hostesses, there was too little money available to do much to improve the house. The state was in debt, and Governor Johnson was a frugal man. They held the traditional receptions for members of the General Assembly,

Governor Keen Johnson, 1939–1943. (KHS)

members of the Court of Appeals, and other officials. And in time the Johnsons entertained the governors and first ladies of Tennessee and Missouri. They had been classmates of the latter in college. In the midst of war, the Derby breakfasts became rather modest affairs attended by a select number of invited guests.[40]

The Johnson family lived in the mansion by much the same routine they had lived in Richmond. Eunice Johnson had Frankfort bridge club friends, and on occasion invited her Richmond friends to come as guests and spend a couple of days playing bridge. Judith, like all the mansion's neighboring children, walked back and forth to school, except in bad weather when she rode in the governor's car. She said her friends came and went in the mansion as casually as they did in other homes along the street. There were neither formalities at the entrance door nor paranoiac concern about the safety of the governor and members of his family.[41]

During World War II both Eunice and Judith Johnson participated in war aid activities. They knitted

sweaters, rolled bandages, and participated in other projects.[42] Then there were those tense moments when Governor Johnson received word of fatal battlefield casualties. In an expression of sympathy for families, and as a gesture of respect for the fallen, Governor Johnson issued posthumous colonel commissions.[43] At the same time, and on the dark side of the commonwealth's official coin, was the soul-searching matter of the execution of prisoners who had been condemned by the courts to die. Specifically there was the case of Otis Peter, a murderer convicted and given the death sentence by the Fayette County Circuit Court on August 21, 1942. Judith Johnson said that for a week there was an emotional tenseness in the governor's mansion when her father had to decide whether or not to grant a stay of execution. She said her mother instructed her not to ask her father any questions. If she wanted to know something she should ask her mother. Governor Johnson had to be concerned with two other death sentence cases, but the courts calmed his emotions by re-opening the cases for review.[44]

It was not until 1943 that Governor Johnson had a driver-patrol aide. In that year Dan Gray, a state police patrolman, was assigned the position with a salary of $1,800 a year.[45] Gray patrolled the mansion and capitol grounds and drove the governor's car. In a taped interview, Judith Johnson recalled that the doors of the mansion may never have been locked in the daytime, even during the stressful years of the war.

The commonwealth was deeply mired in warranty indebtedness during the 1940s, and Governor Johnson was committed to relieving the commonwealth of this burden. With no funds available to make even the most moderate renovations, the house stood in peril. This was eloquently demonstrated when a battery of *Life* magazine reporters and cameramen came to gather material for a story. When they turned on the klieg lights and cameras, they blew out every fuse in the house.[46] Thus in 1943 the governor's mansion was in no better or safer internal condition than it had been in a decade or more before. Doubtless a strict inspection by the state fire marshal would have caused its closure to human occupancy.

Governor Johnson followed the practices of his predecessors when he met with advisers, members of the General Assembly, budget makers, and others at breakfasts, luncheons, or special sessions in the mansion. He also entertained Democratic committees to plan campaign strategies or to discuss other partisan issues. However, Judith said he lacked enthusiasm for following the

Eunice and Judith Johnson in the drawing room in 1939. (FCS)

The mansion in 1939 at the beginning of the Keen Johnson administration. (FCS)

Laffoon-Chandler practice of granting colonel commissions wholesale, even though his executive journal reflects the fact that he did make numerous appointments.[47] The journal also reflects the fact that he attempted to reduce some of Kentucky's social and fiscal problem by issuing an unusually large number of commutations and pardons of penitentiary convicts. On the advice of the Kentucky Parole Board he either commuted or pardoned outright nearly a thousand prisoners, among them members of the mansion's trusty staff.[48]

The general election in 1943 brought new tenants to the governor's mansion. Simeon Willis (1879–1965), a Republican, was a congenial, Lincolnesque type of lawyer. He had defeated a somewhat colorless Democrat, Lyter Donaldson of Carrollton. In time of war stringency Governor Willis brought to the office broad experiences as a practicing attorney, and as a judge on the Kentucky Court of Appeals bench. He was largely a self-trained attorney who was seasoned in the earthy practice of his profession by riding the eastern court circuits of Kentucky. As a corporation attorney he had

gained a scholarly reputation by revising and rewriting *Thornton on the Law of Oil and Gas*.[49] Intellectually, he had an interest in the history of Kentucky.

In 1925 Simeon Willis had married Ida Lee Millis, a deputy Boyd County clerk. They became the parents of a daughter, Sara (Sally) Lesley, who in time was to live for a brief period with her husband, Henry Meigs, in the mansion. In 1943, however, when Governor and Ida Lee Willis moved into the mansion, Sally was a student at Sarah Lawrence College in New York.[50] Her parents were well oriented in Frankfort; they had resided there when Judge Willis was a member of the Court of Appeals. On their return to the town Ida Lee became an energetic hostess of the mansion. She had a passionate love of flowers, and Sally said she wanted them placed fresh daily in every room in the house. For this reason she was instrumental in having a greenhouse constructed on the back lot of the mansion grounds.[51]

Like their predecessors, the Willis family tolerated many of the mansion's decrepit features. Sally described the deterioration of the wallpaper and curtains, saying

Governor Simeon S. Willis, 1943–1947. (KHS)

Popular *Louisville Courier-Journal* columnists Allan Trout and Joe Creason were welcomed guests in the mansion. Their iconoclastic colleague, Howard Henderson, however, was not included on any guest list. Howard was the author of a critical—if not scurrilous—column about the Willis administration. Ida Lee and Sally sought to keep the piece out of the governor's sight, but a patrolman, perhaps Nat Britton, showed him the column. The governor took it to his bedroom, and Sally and Ida found the governor sound asleep with the article lying across his chest.[54]

Governor Willis did achieve some administrative victories during the war years and immediately after the return of peace. He made advancements in rectifying Kentucky's archaic revenue system, in improving public education, and in managing natural resources. He was also able to make a slight breach in the state's racial barrier by appointing a black citizen to the Kentucky Board of Education.

Governor Willis's relationship with Democratic legislators, however, might have been as traumatic as those of Sampson and Laffoon had it not been for the fact the Democrats were involved in an internal factional division. Whatever the pressures generated by war, the restoration of peace, and the ascerbations of partisan Kentucky politics, there was an unbreakable connection between the governor's mansion and the capitol.[55]

In the face of war-troubled times there occurred a romantic interlude in the mansion during the Willis occupancy. Their daughter, Sally, was a student when she met Air Force Captain Henry Meigs III in New York City. After a short courtship, marriage soon followed. The wedding of Sally to Captain Henry Meigs took place in the Frankfort Episcopal Church of the Ascension, not in the mansion as legend had it. Sally invited a full cadre of her eastern girlfriends to be attendants in her wedding. They arrived by train in Frankfort and in the flurry and excitement of greetings they forgot they had brought the wedding cake with them. It went on for a brief visit to Louisville.[56]

The wedding of Sally Willis and Henry Meigs caused a stir of excitement in the mansion. Patrolman Nat Britton said he made five trips to Louisville in one day to pick up clothing and guests, and to run other errands. The excitement was short-lived. The young married couple went directly from the spacious Frankfort Petit Trianon to cramped living in a military camp in northern Michigan. There Henry and Sally shared close quarters with other officer couples.[57]

When the war ended, Sally and Henry Meigs returned

that bits of the fabrics were literally dropping to the floors. Her family found the house rather stark and bare when they entered it on the night of the inaugural ball. It had been left, no doubt as was the custom, with the thought that the incoming family would furnish and arrange it to suit their taste.[52]

Ida Lee Willis was a hospitable but strong-willed hostess. In one instance she had to resolve an annoying social problem concerning the trusty household staff. Male and female members of the staff were housed in a coed barracks; men in one wing and women in the other, with the state police patrolman housed between them. Rumors indicated that there was a congenial inter-relationship between the wings of the barracks. To quiet the rumor, the women's sleeping quarters were moved to the basement of the mansion. Whatever element of truth the rumor contained, some of the trusties won the Willis family's affection. One of the women became a virtual mother confessor to Sally, and eventually was pardoned by Governor Willis and went west to join her family.[53]

The first floor hallway of the governor's mansion, circa 1945. (FCS)

Sara Lesley Willis descending the grand stairway on her way to be married to Captain Henry Meigs III in the Frankfort Episcopal Church on December 30, 1944. (FCS, Meigs family collection)

The ball in the mansion following the marriage of Sally and Captain Henry Meigs. (FCS, Meigs family collection)

Ida Lee Willis in her first lady's photograph, 1943. (KHS)

to Frankfort to live in the rooms on the third floor of the mansion. Henry entered the University of Kentucky, and Sally was pregnant. Following a difficult birth in a Lexington hospital, Simeon Willis Meigs was born. In a short time the baby, accompanied by a nurse, moved to the mansion, but Sally remained for an extended stay in the hospital.[58]

In a taped interview Sally Meigs described some of the problems of the house, including worn-out draperies that fell apart at the first touch. The chronic woes of the facilities required both patience and ingenuity. Her husband, Henry, became an in-house handyman who could coax the electric and plumbing systems back into action, and Sally said his work equaled that of the capitol building's caretakers. He should have received hazard pay. When the family saw a man sitting on the mansion's patio with a gun across his lap, Henry Meigs went out to see what he had in mind. The man said he wanted to see the governor, but thankfully he seems to

have wanted only to pay a courtesy call rather than to generate another page of Kentucky violence.[59]

During her four years as hostess of the mansion, Ida Lee Willis became deeply involved with official receptions, with the Derby breakfast, with house and political guests, and in later years with the Kentucky Heritage Commission. In fact, she was so occupied that Sally had difficulty telling her mother she was getting married. The mansion patrolman-driver-family friend Nat Britton said that on one occasion he drove Mrs. Willis to Louisville and let her out of the car near the Brown Hotel. She instructed him to wait there for her return. When Mrs. Willis came back to the car Britton was asleep. She had to beat on the car window to awaken him. She told Britton she was embarrassed at having to do so in such a public place. After some extended scolding Captain Britton stopped the car and explained he had driven too many miles without sleeping.[60]

Like some of the other wives of governors, Ida Lee

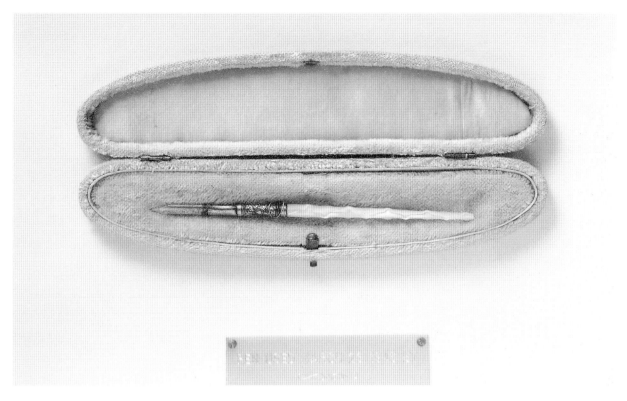

The pen Governor Willis used on March 23, 1946, to sign the bill to renovate the old governor's mansion. (KHS, FCS)

Willis was unable to oversee the renovation of the mansion and to improve its surroundings, so her family made the necessary limited adjustments to keep the house livable. Mrs. Willis's later interests extended well outside of the mansion, with her concern about Kentucky's landmark architectural and institutional heritage. She aroused an appreciation in Kentuckians for the landmarks of their cultural past. Her memory is brightened annually by the awarding of the "Ida Lee Willis Medallion" to individuals and institutions that have made significant contributions in the field of preserving Kentucky's heritage.

At the cessation of World War II, and the ending of the Willis administration, Kentucky entered a new political era. Willis had for the most part escaped the trauma of Sampson and Laffoon, largely because the Democrats, as usual, were at loggerheads within their ranks. Nevertheless, the gubernatorial election in 1947 returned a Democrat to occupy the palace. That year a dynamic political personality-leader became governor. Earle Clements was to make a deep imprint on the pages of Kentucky political history, and upon the mansion.

In the traditional grooves of their immediate predecessors in the mansion, Simeon and Ida Lee Willis no doubt departed with paradoxical sentiments. Externally the house stood as firmly as they had found it, but like an aging figure, its internal clock was advancing. That day of their departure in December 1947, the couple took with them mixed memories of moments of joy when their daughter came home to be married, when she and her husband came back to live, and when their grandson was brought to the mansion from a maternity hospital.

Ida Lee Willis, energetic mansion hostess and active Frankfort social figure that she was, welcomed Earle and Sara Blue Clements to the mansion with the hospitable gesture of a baked Kentucky ham and a cake. That last day, Governor Willis must have inwardly reviewed his years in the house. He and his family had resided there in the bitter years of war and in the stirring times of returning peace. Internally, these had been years troubled by partisan deadlocks over fiscal matters. An all but unbridgeable philosophical chasm had existed between the governor and Democrat legislators. Nevertheless the tide of time and history swept unrelentingly over Kentucky, a force which neither governor nor legislator could stem.

CHAPTER 11

An Aged House Teetering on the Brink of a New Age

K entucky at mid-twentieth century experienced a discernible contrast between an out-going Republican governor and an incoming Democratic one. The post–World War II times, politics, and Kentucky economy cried out for vigorous leadership. For three decades the commonwealth, in many respects, had floundered in the shifting sands of depressed finances and partisan and factional defeatism. Few comparative national statistical scales did not list Kentucky in a low position.[1] One of the few things which enjoyed favorable national ranking was the handsome governor's mansion. Its impressive facade, however, concealed an interior in sore need of complete renovation.[2]

The governor's election in 1947 brought a new and vigorous personality to the office, and to the mansion. But the circuitous path leading there had been somewhat arduous. The son of a Union County farmer-politician, Earle Clements (1896–1985) grew up in two worlds, one on the land, the other in the Union County courthouse. In the early years of World War I, he was enrolled as a student in the College of Agriculture at the University of Kentucky. There he perhaps became better known as a football player than a scientist. He was drafted into the army as a private and later discharged as a captain. After World War I, Earle Clements served an extended apprenticeship in local and national politics. He was a county clerk, a sheriff, and judge in Union County, and he served a term as a United States congressman.[3]

Sara Blue Clements, a quiet-mannered and handsome lady, was a social and temperamental counterbalance to her energetically charged husband. Paul Hughes, a writer on the *Louisville Courier-Journal Magazine*, wrote that Sara was able to smooth over the rough edges of her husband's direct actions.[4] Bess, their fourteen-year-

Governor Earle C. Clements, 1947–1950. (KHS)

old daughter, like Judith Johnson and Sally Meigs, adapted quietly to life in the mansion and Frankfort.

Before the inauguration of incoming Governor Clements, Ida Lee Willis and Sally Meigs graciously invited Mrs. Clements and her daughter to visit the mansion. As they were shown through the house, Mrs.

Earle C. and Sara Blue Clements entertaining guests in the family dining room, circa 1950. Radio station WFKY is recording. (FCS)

Willis indicated the personal properties which they would remove, such as the ballroom furniture that Mrs. Willis had purchased from Mrs. John G. South, who had used it when her husband was the ambassador at the United States embassy in Lisbon, Portugal.[5] Meanwhile, Mrs. Clements made notes of the things they would have to bring from Morganfield.

Sara Blue Clements was told that earlier the Chandler family had spent $15,000 on repairs of the wiring and plumbing. The record is devoid of specific changes that the Clementses might have made. In Morganfield the Clementses left a new and comfortable home to which they had devoted much care in planning and constructing.[6]

The move into the governor's mansion somewhat disrupted Bess's childhood friendships and associations. In June 1948, the Clementses entertained fourteen of their daughter's Morganfield schoolmates in a combination dance and slumber party. This company of boys and girls was brought to Frankfort in a chartered bus. In the evening, after dinner on the lawn, they danced in the ballroom, and at bedtime they were bedded down, the girls on the second floor, and the boys on the third.[7]

Most of the time Bess no doubt was the apple of her father's eye, but there was at least one moment in which she was threatened with a loss of status. In an oral interview, Captain Nat Britton said he was teaching Bess to drive when she rammed the governor's car into a

Governor Lawrence W. Wetherby, 1950–1955. (KHS)

Symbolically, the mansion's need for full-scale renovation in 1947 reflected the fiscal and general economic condition of the commonwealth. Nationally, Kentucky still ranked low in the cardinal areas of public support. Many Kentuckians, half in jest, half in lamentation, were uttering the defeatist cliché, "Thank God for Mississippi and Arkansas!" At war's end the time had been right for the election of a hard-handed governor who could wield enough executive power to quell the senseless partisan-factional negativism which in past administrations had shoved the commonwealth deeper into the abyss of social and economic failure. The governor's mansion in December 1947 stood, with its sinking floors, shabby ceilings, and cracking walls, as a fair symbol of what had happened in the state during the past quarter of a century. The time had arrived for the governor and General Assembly to make the choice of renovating the house or, possibly, building a new one.[10] Financially, Kentucky was not in a sound enough fiscal condition to meet this challenge.

At heart Earle Clements held a fast bond to the land, and to the rural way of life. He seems to have had few recreational interests, despite his athletic past. He spent only a limited amount of time with his wife and daughter in the private quarters of the mansion. Outside he devoted time to the beautification of the capitol and mansion grounds, negotiating the $10,750 purchase of lots in the northwest quadrant of the mansion grounds. Ever the farmer, Governor Clements converted some of the new grounds into a vegetable and flower garden, and no doubt dirtied his hands there whenever possible. As gardener, Clements followed the earthy precedent set by Dora McDavid Fields.[11]

Earle Clements also followed the Stanley-Chandler tradition, cutting short his gubernatorial term to run for—and win—a United States senatorship. He resigned the office of governor on November 27, 1950,[12] and Lieutenant Governor Lawrence (1908–1994) and Helen Dwyer Wetherby were in the house in time to celebrate Christmas. Luckily for Kentucky, Earle Clements left a far more definable mark upon the commonwealth than on the governor's mansion. He had begun the modernization of Kentucky's public school system, removed salary limitations of public officials from the constitution, initiated the expansion and improvement of farm-to-market roads, and stirred change in other areas of state government. Unfortunately, he did little to refurbish the mansion.[13]

Although Clements and Wetherby had worked together harmoniously, there was a wide chasm of dif-

stone wall and damaged the front end. Captain Britton prevailed upon a Frankfort garage man to treat the repair of the car as a matter of emergency and to make almost instant repairs. This was done, and the car was returned to the mansion before Governor Clements came home. He perhaps never knew the car had been damaged.[8]

In the social area, the Clements held the traditional receptions for members of the Kentucky General Assembly, state officials, and members of the court. Otherwise their life in the mansion was generally in keeping with the way they had lived in Morganfield.

Earle Clements, perhaps as much or more than any other governor, made the mansion a working adjunct to the governor's office in the capitol. In the mansion he met with advisers, staff personnel, budget planners, and Democrat politicians. Both Robert Bell and Edward Farris said in oral interviews that frequently Governor Clements and his staff worked in the mansion until the late evening hours.[9]

Helen Dwyer Wetherby in her inaugural photograph, November 1950. (KHS)

ference in their personalities, and in that of their wives. Socially the two families marched to the beat of different drums.[14]

Helen Wetherby was an energetic hostess of the mansion. She devoted considerable time to the supervision of the household staff, to refurbishing the interior of the mansion, and to formal social affairs. Like some of the former hostesses, she gave close attention to the arranging of fresh flowers daily in the various rooms, including the ladies' lounge. In turn, she worked at making the public house a family home for her three children. Her aesthetic taste in decor and furniture favored American-Victorian antiques. Like Ida Lee Willis, she rummaged through the mansion's attic and the state surplus properties storage warehouses for "retired" furniture. In refurbishing the public rooms Helen Wetherby depended upon the advice and assistance of Louisville friend Ruby Vissman. Together they chose paint tints, wallpaper patterns, and fabrics. Workmen from the state's public building authority made limited repairs to the walls, ceilings, and facilities, modifying some of the plumbing fixtures and the electrical wiring. Some of the interior work damaged walls and trim, which then had to be repaired.

During the five-year Wetherby administration (1950–1955) the state spent $91,070.10 on interior refurbishing of the house and its surrounding grounds.[15] Possibly a piano had sat in the ballroom ever since the opening of the house in 1914. Some past governor's wife had had the instrument painted a bright "Kentucky blue," and upon the advice of Mrs. Vissman, Helen Wetherby had the instrument covered with a marbleized paper, an act which was said to have improved its tone. This, however, may have been the only piano in the history of the instrument to sound forth from beneath a marbleized camouflage. In keeping with the history of furnishing the governor's mansions since 1798, the furniture in the public rooms of the house was a bastard mixture of American, English, French, and other styles. An artist gave color to some of the rooms by painting designs on the wood panels.[16]

The governor's and guest rooms on the second floor were trimmed in gray and apricot shades. The twin beds in the governor's room were of Heppelwhite style, spread with Martha Washington coverlets. The walls of this room, and the governor's study-library, were adorned with hunting, fishing, and athletic prints and photographs. These reflected rather faithfully the recreational interests of the Wetherby family members, who regularly attended University of Kentucky athletic events.

There was a close association, if not friendship, between Lawrence Wetherby and Paul Bryant, football coach at the University of Kentucky, a friendship which cooled off just before Bryant accepted a head coaching position at the Texas Agricultural and Mechanical University.[17] During the Wetherbys' tenancy their oldest daughter, Suzanne, went to New York to pursue a career as a fashion designer. Lawrence Jr. and his wife, like Henry and Sally Meigs, occupied the house's third-floor apartment while Lawrence attended classes at the University of Kentucky Law School. Barbara, the younger daughter, attended high school in Frankfort.

Ed Farris, Wetherby's chief of staff, in a taped interview said the governor was a diligent worker and dedicated public servant. This was an era when the state, nation, and world were caught up in the vortex of social change.[18] Lawrence Wetherby made a far less dramatic approach in meeting his challenges than had Earle Clements and A.B. Chandler. Fortunately, Kentucky in the decade of the 1950s experienced an improvement in both its domestic and fiscal economy. Nevertheless, there were pressing demands for the modernization of state government, the highway system, and public education. During his tenure, Governor Wetherby placed all public employees under the Social Security umbrella, and the Rural Electrification Authority spread its network of power lines across the geographical face of Kentucky, bringing electrical current to the humblest dwelling in the remotest corners of the land. This, as much as anything in Kentucky's domestic history, revolutionized the traditional way of rural life.[19]

The Clements administration had set a precedent in its farm-to-market road plan. In the Wetherby era, however, the public roads program shifted to the building of multi-lane limited-access highway arteries. Kentucky sat squarely across three of the new roads. Lawrence Wetherby supported the construction of a limited-access road between Louisville and Elizabethtown, and advocated charging a toll for its use. In the 1955 gubernatorial campaign, when former Governor Chandler campaigned for re-election to the office, he ridiculed the Louisville-Elizabethtown limited-access road as a grand boondoggle, saying, "When you could find and get on it, you couldn't get off." He said it started "nowhere and ended nowhere," and advocated lining the road with bleachers for spectators to sit and watch Barney Oldfield automobile races in continuous contests. He also claimed that construction of a rest station at the mid-point of the road robbed little businessmen of the opportunity to "milk" the tourists. History and the United States Transportation Authority defied the campaign bombast.[20]

On May 17, 1954, the United States Supreme Court rendered its monumental social decision in *Brown* v *Board of Education*. This far-reaching decision called for a quick and positive response from Kentucky. Governor Wetherby, in a terse statement, said Kentucky would obey the decision and the law. Historically this proved to be a sane voice speaking out in a moment—and in a region (the South)—in which sentiments were all but hysterical with anger.[21] There is no record of where or when Governor Wetherby reached his decision. It may have been in the stillness of his mansion bedroom, in his capitol office, or as the presiding officer of the Southern Governors' Association that the governor formed his decision. Certainly a good number of complex subjects were discussed in the work sessions which the governor held in the mansion.[22]

On the calmer domestic front, Helen Wetherby was an active hostess of the mansion. She no doubt played some part in her husband's day-to-day official routine, as a sharing recipient of the inflow of at least 30,000 letters a year from constituents. Many of these in some way involved the mansion, were addressed to Mrs. Wetherby, and usually sought favors.[23] Groups and organizations requested use of the public rooms of the mansion in which to hold meetings and social affairs, while the curious sought descriptions of the routine of daily life in the mansion. Then there were the charity solicitors who sought articles associated with the mansion or first family to be sold at fundraising auctions. Among the items solicited were neckties which Lawrence Wetherby had worn. If Governor Wetherby had granted all such requests he would have had to have spent an inordinate amount of time tying and untying neckties. Then there were the emotional letters from supplicants asking Helen Wetherby to intercede with the governor to grant paroles and pardons, or to favor individuals to be appointed to state jobs.[24]

Helen Wetherby solved the gift problem by purchasing certain objects by the gross and having them stored in the mansion so that when a request came for something "which had been in the mansion," she could make a ready response. There also flowed into the mansion a stream of invitations to attend local festivals and religious services, to speak to all sorts of organizations, and to attend luncheons and dinners.[25]

Hosts of Kentuckians have seemed to look upon the governor and his wife as *in loco parentis*. Both received letters from persons bowed down with personal problems, problems with family and neighbors, and with "sharpers" of one art or another. In one case, an "artist" offered to paint—for a price—the road from Jerusalem to Jericho to grace the governor's bedroom. He might have made a stronger pitch had he proposed painting the road from Louisville to Elizabethtown.

One Christian County entrepreneur wrote Governor Wetherby indicating he would make the heart-wringing sacrifice of selling him an inch-wide river mussel pearl for the bargain basement price of $249,000. He in turn would agree to contribute $100,000 to a child welfare agency and to old age assistance. The pearl merchant, however, was completely vague as to how he would spend the remaining $149,000. On a much more modest monetary scale, an Eastern Kentucky citizen wanted the governor to tell him how deep a grave should be on the upper side of the slope. The governor could make only a vague response because his correspondent forgot to tell him the degree of the incline.[26]

Doubtless Lawrence and Helen Wetherby lay awake at night under their Martha Washington bedspreads cogitating answers to constituents' letters, especially the one from a furious citizen who wrote from the geographically insulative cover of Evansville, Indiana. She sought gubernatorial intervention in ridding her unidentified Kentucky community of what must have been Kentucky's most universal villain. The culprit, she said, had raped two young girls, robbed two defenseless boys, choked a baby so vigorously that it still could not talk at five years of age, had beaten his wife and children with a hot skillet, stolen chickens, and had a brother in the Eddyville Penitentiary. Speaking for Governor Wetherby, Ed Farris suggested that she might seek relief at the hands of a grand jury, but his advice was floated on thin air; his letter was returned marked "the correspondent has changed addresses."[27]

More to the point, the gubernatorial mind was disturbed by the campaign for the governorship in 1955. This campaign was to be singled out in the history books for the careful—more accurately, careless—use of facts. In one of the rowdiest gubernatorial campaigns in Kentucky politics, ex-Governor A.B. Chandler, seeking reelection to the governorship, hurled barbs and ridicule at the non-candidates, Clements and Wetherby, labeling them "Clementine" and "Wetherbine." He charged outgoing Wetherby with some form of waste of money in connection with the penitentiary at LaGrange, and with other indiscretions, including the Louisville to Elizabethtown toll road. When members of the press

Corporal George Bernard and Barbara Wetherby Perry on the main staircase of the governor's mansion following their marriage ceremony in the Frankfort Church of the Good Shepherd. (FCS)

Helen, Barbara, and Governor Lawrence Wetherby at the mansion reception for Barbara and Corporal George Bernard Perry, August 27, 1954. (FCS)

confronted Chandler with a charge of falsifying facts, he admitted he had done so, but the people, he said, liked to hear what he had to say, fact or no fact. Few gubernatorial campaigns received a greater volume of press notices than that of Chandler versus Bert Combs in the Democratic primary.[28]

While Helen Wetherby was an active hostess and certainly left her mark on the house (and on some religious and social institutions in Frankfort), the record is remarkably quiet as to whether or not the Wetherbys stood with a country ham and cake in hand to welcome the return of the Chandler family to the mansion. Too many hard things had been said in the gubernatorial campaign that year. Lawrence Wetherby never got around to following Governor Chandler's suggestion that the Louisville-Elizabethtown Highway be lined with bleachers for spectators to watch automobile races.

When Governor Chandler and his family returned to live in the mansion in 1955, the daughters were grown and Mrs. Dawson's "naughty Chandler boys" were enrolled as students at the University of Kentucky. In Frankfort, the new inhabitants found that age and use had taken a toll on the house, which had sheltered thirteen different gubernatorial families since its dedication in 1914. It was said that the plaster in every room needed some degree of repair, and the walls and trim needed a new coat of paint. The rugs and carpets were said to be threadbare, and the furniture of mixed design and age might well have been labeled "A rare vintage surplus property storage collection." This despite the fact that Helen Wetherby and Ruby Vissman had completely replaced Ida Lee Willis's mixed collection of Kentucky-American antiques, and had the decor adapted to this style.[29]

Mildred Chandler returned to the governor's mansion with far more experience and sophistication than she had possessed in 1935. At the outset she negotiated a contract with the well-known Jeanette Marks, an interior decorator and antiques dealer. She was given virtual carte blanche to refurbish the decor and furnishings of the mansion, and her itemized bill reflected the extent of the renovation. Mrs. Marks supplied an impressive yardage of costly fabrics and carpeting. Mildred Chandler's bedroom was carpeted wall-to-wall, and the governor's bedroom was completely redecorated, leaving no sign that his predecessor had occupied the room. The bed was draped, enclosed, and covered with silk fabrics at an approximate cost of $1,000. Even rooms on the first floor were redecorated. Had ex-Governor Wetherby only seen the Marks bill.[30]

Governor A.B. and Mildred Watkins Chandler at the time of Chandler's second inauguration as governor in 1955. (FCS)

Every component of the Marks contract bore the phrase, "with Mrs Chandler's approval." The contract was signed by some unidentifiable person. Of all the thousands of signed Kentucky public documents, perhaps no signature was more undecipherable than this one. The Chandler administration spent $260,692.97 on the refurbishing and refurnishing of the two mansions.[31]

Mildred Chandler was praised by the press as a gracious hostess, and in his oral interview Captain Nat Britton said she was both loved and feared by the mansion's staff. He said that occasionally she would come down to the basement and dine with staff members, and then play poker with them. He also said that one time, when Mrs. Chandler became ill, the family and household staff held a prayer vigil on the second floor for her recovery.[32]

The issue of removing racial barriers from public classrooms and institutions hung heavily over the heads of Kentucky's mid-century governors. Like Governors

The Chandler family in December 1955. (KDLA)

A Chandler-Watkins family dinner in the mansion's state dining room in 1957. (Chandler family collection)

Governor Bert Combs, 1959–1963. (KHS)

Clements and Wetherby, Governor Chandler had to face the desegregation of the public schools and colleges. He acted promptly and took stern actions to quell the resistance of schools in the villages of Clay and Sturgis, and to bring them into compliance with the law as defined in the *Brown* decision. It was a public issue that surely invaded the governor's mansion, but it was just one issue. The second four years of the Chandler occupancy of the house were distinguished both by problems of state and by rather extensive social activities. Thankfully, by the time they left the house, it was in much better condition than they found it.

There was a marked contrast between the Chandler occupancy of the mansion and that of the incoming Combs administration in 1959. In the primaries Bert Combs (1911–1991) had been opposed by Chandler-backed Harry Lee Waterfield, a Calloway County farmer, newspaper publisher, and the lieutenant governor. Combs won in the heated Democrat primary, and then handily defeated the Republican nominee John

Robsion Jr.[33] Even a casual reading of the contemporary newspaper reports of the campaign reveals that there was little or no inclination to hold a welcoming party at the front entrance of the mansion. The General Assembly, however, took note of the upcoming transition by requesting that the mansion committee bring about an exchange of tenants.[34]

Measured by several personal criteria, Bert T. Combs was an interesting and somewhat unusual political figure in Kentucky history. He was born and grew up in a strong natural environment in the remote "Beech Creek" area of mountainous Clay County. He was enrolled and passed through a series of private and public schools, and attended Cumberland College. After graduating from the University of Kentucky Law School, he entered the practice of law in Eastern Kentucky. Combs later served as a judge of a circuit court and as a member of the Kentucky Court of Appeals. He married Mabel Hall in 1937, and they became the parents of two children, daughter Lois and son Tommy.[35]

Combs was the fourth governor to come from the Appalachian Highlands, a fact which no doubt gained him favor with a considerable segment of the Kentucky voters. On his inauguration day in December 1959, approximately a hundred thousand supporters gathered in Frankfort. A *Louisville Courier-Journal* reporter said it took three hours for the parade to pass a given point. Of far more significance, however, was the feeling that distinct change was on its way in Kentucky gubernatorial politics. The Chandler era was ending, never again to be revived. On inauguration day Bert Combs brought new management to state affairs, and he opened the new period from the inaugural podium. The reporter from the *Louisville Courier-Journal*'s Frankfort bureau wrote that Governor Chandler's spirit in passing on the gubernatorial mantle was "Defiant. His Administration, he declared had been good. His record was clean. 'There has not been during my time here,' he said, 'a single dishonorable act.' He then qualified his remark by saying, 'With my knowledge.'"

Governor Combs promised reform and progress. He said, "By reform I mean the elevation of moral and political tones of government . . . an attitude of mind which views every problem from the viewpoint of scrupulous honesty, decency, and ethics." The acidity of the gubernatorial campaign was still virulent, even into the moment of the official succession of office.[36]

When Bert and Mabel Combs and their two children, Lois and Tommy, moved into the mansion, the governor ordered that a detailed inventory be made of the

Standing, from left to right, Former Governors Keen Johnson, Earle Clements, and Lawrence Wetherby. Seated, Lieutenant Governor Wilson Wyatt and Governor Bert Combs. (From Harrison and Klotter, *A New History of Kentucky*, 1997; Edward T. Breathitt Jr. family collection)

household furnishings. This involved even counting the washcloths stored in the linen cabinets. He seems to have been the first governor to require that a record be made of every item purchased for use in the house. The inventory report included entries for items as minuscule as shoe polish and a box of Rebecca Ruth bourbon candy.[37] The itemized purchases of china, glassware, and table silver not only included the fact of purchase but reflected the Combs family's lifestyle and mode of entertainment. Listed in the inventory was an appreciable number of ashtrays—it was an era of free smoking of cigars and cigarettes in the mansion, and of petty thievery by souvenir collectors.[38]

Over time the governor's mansion had become an important link in the administrative process of government. By a process of political osmosis it became a centralizing social, semi-cultural, and political institution. By tradition the first floor, since 1914, was largely regarded as being in the public domain. Here citizens' groups, special guests invited on ceremonial occasions, and even private citizens came for tours while visiting the capitol and other Frankfort attractions.

Among the hordes that came to the mansion were the ubiquitous souvenir hunters who looked upon any small item lying around loose as free for the taking. Beginning with the Combs administration, the pilferers

158

Mabel Hall Combs in 1959, shortly after her husband's inauguration. (University of Kentucky Special Collections [UKSC] and FCS)

were baited with napkins, paper hand towels, and matchbooks bearing the state seal. Many a visitor went away, so it has been said, with two napkins bearing the impressive Kentucky state seal, one for its intended purpose, and the other to be kept as a remembrance of having visited the mansion.

As for the mansion itself, engineers and the Kentucky fire marshal declared it a firetrap. A report prepared largely by the fire marshal in 1960 recommended a complete overhauling of the electrical wiring, the closing of fireplaces, and the installation of fire doors and smoke detectors. At the same time the director of state properties employed the Louisville architectural firm of Harters and Henry to make a thorough examination of the mansion's basic structure and its time-worn facilities. This company submitted a report in July 1960, fundamentally confirming the fire marshal's

report. The company recommended that the building undergo a major renovation, once again emphasizing danger from fire.[39]

Contained in the architects' report was the observation that the multiple coats of paint which had been smeared on the interior walls over the years should be scraped off down to the bare surface, and that substantial rearrangements needed to be made in the stairways, doors, and service facilities. The architects also called attention to a serious oversight in the original Weber plan. They suggested that there should be installed on the first floor, "*Men's and women's toilets, and a new cloak room. These to be located in the original porch area.*" At the moment there was only one small lavatory and limited coat space. Guests attending gatherings on the first floor had to go upstairs to a bedroom to leave their wraps, or to use a toilet or lavatory.

Late in the evening of December 8, 1959, when the newly inaugurated Governor Bert T. Combs, his wife, their children, and a gaggle of kinfolk left the Grand Ball to take up their residence in the governor's mansion, they could have hardly imagined the problems which would involve the house during their tenure. Within the next four years there would arise issues about awarding repair contracts, charges of nepotism, and the employment of convict trusties as household servants.

At the outset Governor Combs appointed an oversight committee of Frankfort residents to examine and report on the condition of the mansion, its structure, furnishings, and decor. Mrs. William Fairleigh headed the committee and in time reported the mansion was in "deplorable condition."[40] This despite the fact Governor Chandler had spent an impressive amount of money on repairs and refurbishing. The oversight committee recommended that the owner of the Covered Wagon Shop in Danville be commissioned to refurbish the interior of the house. The building's equipment and structure, however, needed major architectural and engineering attention.[41]

Repeatedly the Kentucky fire marshal warned of the danger of fire and possible human tragedy. Twenty-nine invitations were sent to prospective contractors seeking bids to make the repairs. Only one contractor submitted a bid, the Stivers Brothers Company of Frankfort. They agreed to do the work for $37,800, and the state accepted the non-union company's bid.[42]

During the "dog days" of August 1961, the editor of the AFL-CIO *Kentucky Labor News*, finding himself short of anything to print, wrote a protest story against the use of non-union labor to work on state property.

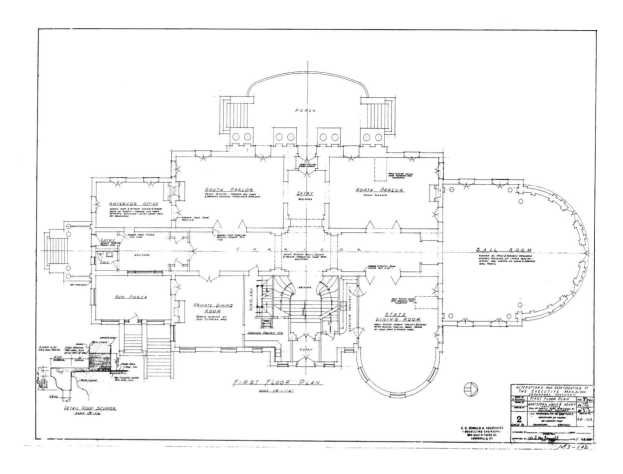

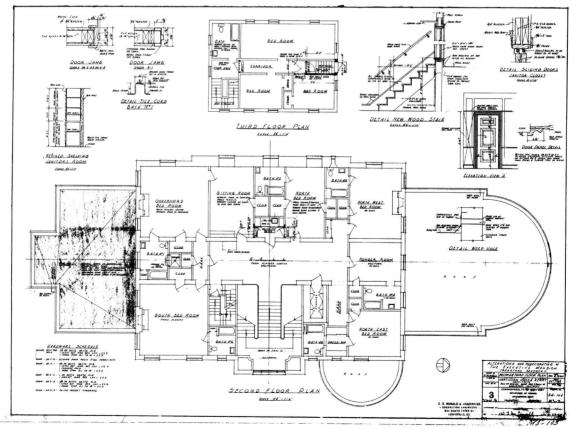

First and second floor plans for the 1960 renovation. (FCS, Engineering Department)

The resulting tempest caused Governor Combs to effect an amicable revocation of the contract with the Stivers Brothers on the grounds he did not wish his abode to be encircled by a picket line. Finally, some of the work was done by the state engineers.[43]

One of the oversight committee's recommendations was the employment of a housekeeper, and Mrs. Hazel Savage, wife of an assistant attorney general and a sister of Mabel Combs, was employed with the title "senior cook." Mrs. Combs was concerned about the safety of the couple's two children when she had to be absent from the mansion with Governor Combs. News reporters were quick to point out that, besides Mrs. Savage, five other members of the widely extended Combs family were on the state payroll. Some of them the governor said he did not know, but he gave instructions that if his kinsmen did not perform their duties effectively they should be fired.[44] In this instance it would have taxed even an ingenious genealogist with broad knowledge of Eastern Kentucky kinships to determine who was not a distant Combs cousin.

When the editor of the *Kentucky Labor News* had a second go at the mansion, he opened a veritable Pandora's box by raising the question of using convict trusties as household staff members. The issue was soon taken up by the public press. The ubiquitous Cy Ramsey of the Frankfort Associated Press bureau stirred the cauldron even more with a story bearing the headline, "Convict Workers at the Mansion Usually Are Killers."[45] At the moment eight men and women worked on the residential household staff. *The Kentucky Labor News* editor took the high ground, saying that "guests of Kentucky from over the world visit our residence. It is degrading for us to parade our prison labor before those who expect to see a better variety of hospitality. The use of prisoners at the Mansion is as undignified as slavery and has no place in this state in 1962."[46]

This article provoked a somewhat emotional discussion of the trusty issue. The editor of the *Lexington Herald* admitted he had little or no knowledge of the use of convicts to staff the governor's household, but he believed the practice had outlived its time. He wrote, "A change should be made regardless of whether murderers, pickpockets, or chicken thieves are used at the Mansion." In response to the upheaval, Governor Combs said he merely followed the custom of using prisoners in the mansion and that the practice is a tradition in the South.[47] In truth, the use of prisoners as household servants in the governor's mansion actually grew out of the freeing of slaves at the end of the Civil War.

Governor Bert T. Combs admires a new bicycle with his son Tommy. (UKSC)

The publicity given the subject of trusty household servants in the governor's mansion led to the preparation of an enlightening analysis of the economic and social realities of the practice. The steward of the LaGrange Penitentiary explained that first-time passion murderers were selected as having the greatest prospect of making dependable servants. Robbers, embezzlers, sex offenders, and common smoke and henhouse thieves were off the list. For a prisoner who had the good fortune to be selected a mansion servant, there was almost a certain promise of a parole or pardon.[48]

Feeding the trusty household staff was the responsibility of the LaGrange Penitentiary steward. The lists of meats, vegetables, fruits, and staple groceries are fascinating historical documents; however, they may be misleading in their use. The penitentiary steward reported that from 1949 through 1964, supplies to the mansion averaged $96 a month, or $3.35 per meal. Everything was grist to the gubernatorial campaigners. Louie B. Nunn in September 1963 told a campaign audience in Lancaster that during fifteen weeks in

The Combs family sits down to dinner in the family dining room, circa 1963. (UKSC)

1961 Governor Bert Combs was feeding friends and mansion visitors from the public trough. He had secured photostatic copies of requisitions for food supplies for the mansion. The requisition was for 390 T-bone steaks, 125 cube steaks, 213 frying chickens, and 150 hens.[49] Nunn apparently overlooked or ignored the fruit and vegetable orders.

E.E. Senn, the steward of LaGrange Penitentiary, disputed the political contentions. He wrote, "This factor alone [being a mansion trusty] I believe has served as a strong incentive for regular inmates at the reformatory to attempt to procure assignments here by good behavior and as an incentive to maintain duty here by appropriate conduct when assigned."[50]

Knowing the trivialities uttered in gubernatorial campaigns, Governor Combs attempted to avert accusations of purchasing irregularities by requiring the preservation of even the most minimal receipts for furniture purchased, and for everyday purchases of goods for mansion use.[51] It is likely that no other governor except Christopher Greenup was more meticulous. The Combs papers even include receipts for country ham and clothes pins.

Ever a man of plain Jeffersonian democracy, Governor Combs dealt with a matter of confusion which had lingered unsolved from the days of James Garrard. Without delusions of grandeur he mandated in an executive memorandum that the title of the executive residence should be brought closer to earth. He observed, "The trend is away from the antebellum word 'mansion.' The homes of most public officials are known as residences. The building/ Kentucky's mansion/ can hardly be classed as a mansion by modern standards." This was an attempt to clarify a title and to give a more realistic

Governor Bert Combs's floral clock, a permanent feature of the capitol grounds today. (FCS)

status to the house. There prevailed the ancient confusion as to whether the residence should be called a "palace," a "mansion," or a "residence."[52]

Coming from a rural agrarian background, centered at the head of a Clay County creek valley, Bert Combs had a love of the land and the soil. Like Nettie Pitzer Black, Dora Fields, and Earle Clements, he maintained a hands-on interest in the capitol and mansion grounds and in gardening. During his years living in the mansion he acquired some notoriety as a gardener, and, perhaps, as a poultryman (his cousin Mason Combs said he owned at least one rooster to awaken him every morning). Combs tended a garden on the plot used by Earle Clements and furnished vegetables for the mansion kitchen.[53]

Governor Combs's fascination with Kentucky's natural beauty led him to be influential in persuading state and federal highway engineers to plant trees along the medians of the new limited-access roads. His joy, however, was the designing and construction of the floral clock on a site alongside the Executive Office Building. This novel project stirred an appreciable amount of comment, some of it derisive. A Combs contemporary said that on occasions ex-Governor Chandler stood beside the clock and told visitors that it was "Two petunias past Jimson weed." He ridiculed the erection of the clock as a shameful waste of public funds. As when Chandler made political capital of the Louisville-Elizabethtown toll road, however, the floral clock in time disproved its critics. It was said that on occasion Combs went out to the floral clock and made presents of his vegetables to visitors.[54]

Flowers have ever been a part of the mansion tradition. In an oral interview, Gwenneth Cullen said that as a friend of Bert and Mabel Combs, she visited the

Bert T. Combs entertaining members of the Kentucky General Assembly at breakfast in the governor's mansion. (UKSC)

mansion on several public occasions. She felt the flower arrangements could be improved, and made this known to Governor Combs. He invited her to take over the task of arranging flowers on the public first floor, including the two parlors, the ballroom, and the state dining room. Apparently the servant staff just cut the flowers and stuck them into water-filled vases.[55]

On March 24, 1961, the service division of the Department of Finance listed the non-trusty members of the mansion household staff as Colleen Porter, administrative assistant, Hazel Savage, senior house-keeper, and Roberta Hogan and Frances Beam, cooks. A year later there were listed eleven nameless trusties who performed varied services, for which each was paid five dollars a month.[56]

Governor Combs made as much or maybe more use of the mansion as an administrative adjunct than any of his predecessors. The dining tables in both the state and family dining rooms were often turned into work stations for the discussion of pending legislation, the state budget, public policy, and, always, politics. In this era the line between the capitol and the mansion was a thin if not invisible one.[57]

Though the governor's mansion at the end of the Combs administration sorely needed a complete reno-vation after a half-century of occupancy, the state itself

The Kentucky governor's mansion in 1963. Its interior would be extensively renovated the next year. (FCS)

had experienced progress in the fields of education, transportation, and conservation of resources.[58] The gubernatorial campaign which followed was in many respects a rowdy, transitional one. Ex-Governor A.B. Chandler undertook to become the first governor to be thrice elected to the office, but times had changed. No longer was it possible to attract more than dyed-in-the-wool supporters to the courthouse hustings. Radio and television had taken their place. Edward T. (Ned) Breathitt Jr., a rising young Democrat, fell heir to the Combs mantle. Educational improvement was a principal issue in the state, and Breathitt had received a strong teacher and educational leadership vote.[59]

Edward Thompson Breathitt Jr. (1924–) of Hopkinsville bore a surname imprinted deeply in Kentucky political history. A distant kinsman, John Breathitt, had served an abbreviated term as governor, 1832–1834. His grandfather, James Breathitt Sr., served as attorney general, 1907–1911, and his uncle James Breathitt Jr. served as lieutenant governor, 1927–1931. Edward T. Breathitt had served a term in the House of Representatives, as commissioner of personnel, and as a member of the Kentucky Public Service Commission.[60]

When Ned and Frances Holleman Breathitt arrived in Frankfort for the inauguration in 1963, they were unready to take up full-time residence in the mansion,

Governor Edward T. Breathitt, 1963–1967. (KHS)

because their four children (Mary Fran, Linda, Susan, and Edward III) were in school in Hopkinsville. Despite the delay in moving to Frankfort, the Breathitts were cordially welcomed to the mansion by Bert and Mabel Combs. Following the precedent set by Christopher Greenup, it was necessary to make some internal arrangements to accommodate their children and the household staff.[61]

The Breathitts brought a cook and houseman from Hopkinsville, but perhaps celebrating his advancement to the staff of the governor's mansion may have been too heady an experience for the houseman. He went into Frankfort on his first weekend, landed in jail for drunkenness, and was sent home. Mrs. Breathitt, as had other governors' wives, had reservations about using penitentiary trusties with young children in the house. Nevertheless, trusties were employed, and the Breathitt family developed affection for some of them. At the conclusion of his administration, Governor Breathitt assembled the trusty household staff in the state dining room and pardoned or commuted their sentences.[62]

Racial desegregation continued to inflame the South, and in Kentucky it came to a head especially over public school issues in Louisville. At one time blacks under the leadership of Dr. Martin Luther King Jr. threatened to hold a sit-down across the racetrack at Churchill Downs to disrupt the running of the Kentucky Derby. Governor Breathitt, in a personal conference with Dr. King, staved off what might have been a most unhappy incident.[63]

News received by way of the LaGrange Penitentiary reached Frankfort that the governor was a possible target of hired killers because of his stand in preventing the placement of slot machines across the state. Because of this news, Governor Breathitt, apparently over his objection, was accompanied by guards back and forth from the mansion to his capitol office. Not until the would-be assassins were apprehended and arrested in a Frankfort motel did the traditional feeling of security return to the capitol-mansion grounds.[64]

Sometime in the vague past a governor invited some of his friends to have a Derby Day breakfast with him. Over the years, as administrations came and departed, and politicians, horsemen, and an ever-growing horde of private citizens swelled the Derby breakfast list, the event became a gubernatorial campaign or circus tent affair. Inevitably there would come to the Derby Day breakfasts gate crashers. None of these free-loading guests, however, was more skilled in the act than George Jessel. Well past his time as a singer, he may have won as much fame as a gate crasher. He gained some international fame by not only crashing the governor's Derby party, but by crashing the gates of Churchill Downs as well. Somehow he even made his way into the winner's circle and was pictured with the governor and the derby winners. When he was finally barred from the Churchill track he protested that his inalienable personal rights had been denied him under the guarantee of some unspecified constitutional amendment.[65]

For the Breathitt family the mansion was a seven-day-a-week home. Unlike some past governors' families, they seem to have made few weekend returns to their private home. The four Breathitt children lived in the mansion during some of the formative years of their lives, and that ubiquitous mansion watcher, Margaret Dawson, told Jack Brammer of the *Lexington Herald-Leader* that during "slow summer days, 1963–67, young Edward Breathitt would come over and spend idle time in the workshop with her husband. The boy felt so grown up watching Jim work and we enjoyed his company."[66] Later Edward Breathitt III would become a talented sculptor.

Susan and Edward Breathitt III roasting marshmallows in a governor's mansion fireplace in December 1966. (KHS, Breathitt album)

Frances Holleman Breathitt and her three daughters, Susan, Linda, and Mary Fran, dressed for wintertime adventure. They are standing on the mansion's front steps, circa 1964–1965. (KHS, Breathitt album)

Governor Edward T. Breathitt Jr. and Secretary of Commerce Luther Hodges, the former governor of North Carolina, in the ballroom in July of 1964. (KHS, Breathitt album)

During the Breathitt administration changes were made in the domestic management of the mansion. On March 6, 1964, because of electrical and plumbing problems, a leaking roof, and worn-out floors, the Kentucky General Assembly enacted an emergency law pertaining to mansion expenditures. The law reiterated the fact that both the new and old governor's mansions were possessions of the commonwealth, and that they should be maintained and operated, "in such a fashion which will reflect favorably on the reputation of the Commonwealth for gracious hospitality." While the law was couched more in the form of a resolution than that of a formal statutory instrument, responsibility for management of the mansions was placed in the hands of the Department of Finance.

The Department of Finance was mandated to purchase food and related items for the mansions. Also, the department was to approve the costs of the governor's out-of-state travels and to have oversight of the domestic service personnel. The law authorized, "A reasonable amount [of money] shall be deducted from

the salary of the Governor for the consumption by the Governor and his family of such food and supplies."[67] The emergency action became operable the moment the governor signed the bill.

Edward Thompson Breathitt Jr. and his family departed the mansion after four years of excitement on one hand, and a successful adaptation of an intimate family life in a public house on the other. In December the Breathitts left behind in Frankfort a mansion still in need of major renovation, but a state government experiencing progressive changes in nearly every area except modernizing an ancient and time-worn constitution. In 1967 Kentucky was in one of its rare moments of some degree of general prosperity, but ironically so.

Once again the pendulum of political fortune swung in favor of the Republican party when Louie Nunn of Barren County defeated Henry Ward, the Democratic candidate. The governor and his wife, Beula Cornelius Aspley Nunn, brought to the mansion a colorful, distinctive pair of personalities.

The new governor's mansion in the snow. (FCS)

The governor's mansion in 1964, before the trees were cut to make way for the formal garden. (FCS)

CHAPTER 12

Mansion or Heritage Museum?

L ike some ancient Cretan wandering through the labyrinths of the famous Minoan maze, Louie B. Nunn made his way through the more complex one of partisan Kentucky politics to become governor. He had opposed Edward Thompson Breathitt Jr. in 1963 and lost the election by a narrow margin. But following in the tradition of William O. Bradley, Augustus E. Willson, Edwin P. Morrow, Flem D. Sampson, and Simeon Willis, in 1967 Nunn caught the Democrats in another of their divisive moments and won the day.[1]

Nunn was born on March 8, 1924, in the village of Park in Barren County, and grew up in a strong political environment. His father, Walter H. Nunn, was a farmer and storekeeper, and a confirmed Republican.[2] Louie spent his boyhood on his father's farm and working in the family's country store. He attended the Park country school and studied for a time to become a businessman at Bowling Green Business University. His education, however, was interrupted by three years in the United States Army infantry during World War II. After the war he attended the University of Cincinnati, and in 1950 he graduated from the University of Louisville Law School.

In Barren County and Glasgow, Nunn served a local public service apprenticeship as chairman of the local Christian Church board of trustees, as a member of the Rotary Club and Chamber of Commerce, and as a county judge. In the latter position he underwent preliminary political seasoning for the governorship. He also managed statewide campaigns for John Sherman Cooper and Richard Nixon.[3]

Like the Republican William O. Bradley, Louie B. Nunn was a vigorous campaigner who understood well the mind of the rural Kentucky voter. He was a master at telling rich Kentucky anecdotes, and at communi-

Governor Louie B. Nunn, 1967–1971. (KHS)

cating with courthouse rally audiences. On his inauguration day, *The Glasgow Republican* honored him by publishing an elaborate biographical-historical inaugural souvenir which gave a generous amount of background historical information.[4] At that cardinal moment on December 12, 1967, when Nunn took the oath of office, just across the way the mansion stood in its chronic need of major repair and refurbishing. During the past four years Governor Breathitt and his family had lived in the house in the manner of a family homestead. In those years there had been a serious shrinkage of funds, and little more could be done than keep the doors open and household facilities functioning.[5] Everything in the house reflected the passage of time and the tramping feet of fifty-six years. In a light moment, Governor Nunn said that the only thing he and his family found in the mansion was a well-worn telephone directory.[6]

Eight years before Louie and Beula C. Aspley Nunn and their children, Jennie Lou and Robert Steven, arrived in Frankfort, Mildred Chandler had made surface improvements in the furnishings and decor of the mansion, but by 1967 the house stood in need of major renovation of both the building and its furnishings.[7] Beyond this, Beula Nunn, in a public address in Ohio, expressed the feeling that the furnishings in the house did not reflect the legacy of Kentucky. She described the decrepit condition of the mansion when she and her family moved into it in 1967. She said the roof leaked, and perhaps no one could say how many coats of paint had been applied to the woodwork and some of the furniture. Convict laborers undertook the tedious task of scraping away the rings of paint down to the bare face of the wood surface. A fresh color scheme was adopted, and a wallpaper pattern selected. The floors were covered wall-to-wall in a golden-hued carpet, but not with shag rugs as a reporter said. The windows were trimmed with long, flowing valances, and a section of Governor McCreary's fine study was turned into a library.[8]

In the process of making the changes, Beula Nunn enlisted the cooperation of the Kentucky Mansion Trustees or Oversight Committee. At the same time she began a tireless hunt for eighteenth- and nineteenth-century native Kentucky pieces of antique furniture and other indigenous materials. She sought to borrow, beg, or accept such items as gifts.[9]

Speaking in Hamilton, Ohio, to an audience of ex-Kentuckians who called themselves O'Tucks, Beula Nunn said that when Louie Nunn learned that he had been elected governor he had a conversation with her, saying that he would run the capitol and the state government, and she could run the mansion. She said he told her she had to stay out of the capitol. In her search for pieces of period furniture, however, she went across the way to rummage in an almost forgotten storage room in the capitol basement. She said the room had not been unlocked for years, and after an intensive search a custodian was finally able to find a key. The dark room was piled high with discarded pieces of furniture and

Beula Nunn in 1967, when she became first lady of Kentucky. (KHS)

the screens that had been removed from the capitol's windows when the building was air-conditioned. While rescuing some pieces of furniture, she instructed the custodian to haul the antiquated screens off to the Frankfort city dump. The latter request stirred up a tempest. When she returned to the mansion, every phone in the house was ringing. The governor was on one asking what she had been doing in the capitol ordering the discard of surplus state property? Beula implied to her O'Tuck audience that there was some pillow talk that night about her raid.[10]

Beula Nunn was a highly motivated woman who had a background in the insurance and real estate businesses. She was diligent in her pursuit for furniture, paintings, watercolors, and other historically related materials. One of the items she found in a public storage place was a bedstead, said to have belonged to Governor Isaac Shelby. It was reported to have been either given or loaned to the Kentucky Historical Society, and was stored with the Society's other historical artifacts. The bed was placed in a second story mansion room named the Isaac Shelby room.[11] In time the removal of the bed from storage was to create some emotional reaction between the Historical Society's director, General William Buster, and Beula Nunn.

The Shelby bed was described as a four-poster with carved pineapple capitals. The bed seems to have had a mixed history, if not some contradictions. In the 1971 inventory made by Larry Perkins, it was listed as having been obtained from Josie Colton of Harrodsburg. A second bed involved in the dispute, one which was presented to the Historical Society by Mrs. James McNeilly of Omaha, Nebraska, was said to have been some governor's bed used in the old mansion.[12]

Whatever the facts were, the beds were released from the Historical Society's storage by Finance Commissioner Russell McClure. When he had left office and the bed controversy was still going on, he wrote his successor in reply to a memorandum from General Buster: "There should be no great mystery about three items. I, as Secretary for Finance . . . released these items and have a signed receipt for items for use by the Kentucky Mansion Preservation Foundation. This, in my opinion, is much superior to storage. Mrs. Nunn and I will be happy to discuss this matter with you if you wish."[13] Mrs. Nunn branded the whole matter, "Just as political as it can be. If they want to make a political issue out of it, I'll take 'em on." Under the headline "Bedlam," Livingston Taylor of the *Louisville Courier-Journal* wrote, "Confusion reigns over disposition of some famous furniture."[14]

Beula was instrumental in the 1969 creation of the Kentucky Mansions Preservation Foundation, Inc., of which she was president.[15] This organization, as in connection with the bed issue, was created to be the recipient of gifts to the mansion and the two other historic houses (White Hall and the Mary Todd Lincoln house) which Beula Nunn espoused. Loans and gifts were made to the foundation from several historic homes. For instance, one of the pianos in the mansion came from Winton Place, homestead of the famous Robert Peter family in Fayette County.[16]

A donated chandelier was erroneously said to have come from White Hall, the home of Cassius M. Clay. Actually it came from Brutus J. Clay's home. When he was United States Minister to Switzerland he had acquired and shipped the chandelier home to hang in his house, Lynwood, in Madison County. Dr. John Floyd, a Clay-Marstellar son-in-law, wrote Beula Nunn that he thought the chandelier was of eighteenth-century origin, and that it might have hung in the palace at Versailles. It had been bought in Paris by an American dentist, but for some reason he had never shipped it to the United States. Later, Dr. Floyd said, it had been shipped to Kentucky and stored along with some of Cassius M. Clay's property on the Marstellar farm, where Beula Nunn found it.[17]

Among the Kentucky materials collected by the Kentucky Mansions Preservation Foundation were large watercolors by Paul Sawyier. These hung in the upstairs hall of the mansion. There was also a Robert Burns Wilson painting, along with numerous others, including several Ray Harm bird prints.[18]

Strangely, in the history of the two governor's mansions there appear no mention of books. Frequently the office in the old mansion was referred to as "the library," but this seems to have been a purely euphemistic designation. The inventory of the contents of the mansion in 1960 lists two sets of bookends. Wanting a more formal library, Louie and Beula Nunn converted James B. McCreary's office space into an attractive depository of Kentucky authors' writings, and books about the state. A Cincinnati newspaper wrote in 1969 that they had blocked out a window in the renovation, a statement Governor Nunn adamantly denied.[19]

Ten years previously Mildred Chandler had spent considerable amounts of time, energy, and money in refurbishing the mansion. In keeping somewhat with this precedent, Beula Nunn set out to accomplish what Dr. John Floyd called "The Kentuckianization" of the house. The main guest room on the second floor was furnished with rosewood love seats, a table, and two chairs which were said to be precise copies of the furniture that Abraham and Mary Lincoln had moved in 1860 from their Springfield home to the White House. It was in this room that the Nunns lodged Richard and Pat Nixon. Other bedrooms, including that of the governor, were refurnished in a mixed American-French decor.[20]

Downstairs the walls of the parlors, ballroom, and state dining room were scraped bare of their paint and were papered. Some of the furniture in these rooms came from the famous Jefferson County Hurstbourne Manor.[21] Possibly the only genuinely indigenous Kentucky presence in the first floor parlors were the mantels and their wood facings. When workers removed heavy layers of paint, they discovered that the wood facings were of virgin highland poplar, Kentucky's state tree. When the transformation was finished, the *Lexington Herald* published a series of photographic panels elegantly portraying Beula Nunn's handiwork.[22] These showed off the dining room, parlors, library, hall, and guest rooms.

The refurbished mansion was ready to receive at a grand scale luncheon the wives of Republican governors meeting in conference. Governor Nunn went all out to welcome his fellow governors. As a gesture of hospitality he presented the group with a thoroughbred horse, an act that stirred a reverberation. In what might have been both protest and an attempt to grab public attention, the Poor Peoples' Alliance of Kentucky presented the governor a mule. In the presence of his colleagues, Governor Nunn accepted the "Poor Peoples' Mule" in a gracious tongue-in-cheek reply. Whatever the members of the Poor Peoples' Alliance and their mule thought of it is not a matter of record.[23] Several of the visitors told Governor Nunn that his residence was superior to their abodes.

Fifteen-year-old Steve Nunn had fond memories of the mansion, including being taught to box by one of the trusties, and the great parties, complete with good hamburgers. "[President Richard] Nixon came and spent the night once in 1969. I can remember eating breakfast with the president and then following him and mother around as she showed him the place."[24]

In May 1969, the governor's mansion was in the best interior decorative condition since its opening in 1914. More than the decor had been changed. Philosophically there bubbled up the issue of what image of Kentucky the house should convey. The process, including both mansions and grounds, cost the commonwealth $276,088.54, almost $200,000 more than the new mansion had cost to build.[25]

For Governor Nunn's inauguration in December 1967, some unidentified historian published a description of the mansion couched in romantic terms. Realistically, however, he or she observed that operating the mansion cost a good deal of money. At that date there was budgeted $80,994 for its general operation. There was appended to this document a notation that in the course of past years, governors and their wives had made improvements and even additions to the mansion's furnishings at their own cost. The author seems to have based his or her assumption "of exceptional beauty" in December 1967 upon the fresh decor in the ballroom furnished with a cane and mahogany suite. This was the furniture that Ida Lee Willis had purchased from Christine Bradley South. It had adorned the United States embassy in Portugal when Mrs. South's husband was ambassador to that country. Unfortunately, this description of the mansion's furnishing is at a variance with the Oversight Committee's report.[26]

Like most of their predecessors, the Nunns were family oriented. Following a strenuous day and evening of inaugural celebration the Nunns returned to the mansion to experience four years of excitement, some of it tumultuous, and to enjoy as much domestic calm as they could snatch away from the public. The first Sunday after the inauguration the family prepared to attend church. Governor Nunn was ready before his family and was seated in one of the parlors waiting for them. There appeared a tall and awkward trusty waiter bearing a tray filled with every kind of fruit juice to be had in Frankfort. The man, a convicted first-time passion murderer, perhaps had never handled anything more delicate than a shovel handle. Every glass on the tray was tinkling. The man bowed to the governor, tilted the tray, and spilled the contents on his head. It required most of the household staff to clean up the new Kentucky chief executive after his ceremonious baptism, and the overly polite field hand was returned to the "Box," as prisoners called the LaGrange Penitentiary. Jennie Lou Nunn made a plea in behalf of the trusty, and he was brought back to the mansion, but this time to serve in a more compatible environment. After that, almost as a morning ritual, he was on hand to bow to the governor on his way to the capitol office.[27]

As was customary with past governors and their families, there developed bonds of affection with many of the prisoner-household staff. There was one especially who won Governor Nunn's affection, named Jesse. On one occasion Governor Nunn had to have some dental work done, and the dentist placed wiring on his teeth. Nunn took Jesse into an upstairs room, locked the door, and then into the bathroom and locked it. He showed Jesse the wires and told him he was wired so he could hear and know everything that went on, and the precise time of its happening. An incident of some kind did occur, and by chance the Governor knew what had happened and the time of the incident. Thereafter the "wired governor" was a person to be respected and obeyed.[28]

Two trusties once made a break for freedom, and the mansion patrol undertook to halt them by firing shots over their heads, but the absconders fled into the brush unscathed. This scene occurred with all the household staff of trusties looking on. Governor Nunn instructed the patrolmen that in the future they were to shoot to kill; there were, he said, no more attempts to escape.[29]

The state paid the working trusty staff the lowest possible wage. None of them was able to accumulate much if any money. At Christmas time Governor Nunn personally gave each servant twenty-five dollars and had them driven into Frankfort to purchase presents for their families. Governor Nunn even took trusty Jesse on hunting and camping trips. Following gubernatorial custom, Governor Nunn either pardoned or paroled the trusty household staff at the conclusion of his administration.[30]

Unlike many of his predecessors, however, Governor Nunn said he did not transact any gubernatorial business in the mansion. He was of the opinion that the first floor rooms were essentially in the public domain, but that the rest of the house was a family home. He felt that transactions carried on in the governor's office in the capitol bore a strong imprint of authority.

On the very eve of the departure of Louie and Beula Nunn from the mansion, the newly appointed state curator, Larry Perkins, made a full inventory of the residence's contents. Contrary to gossipy rumors, he listed no "shag rugs" or other such plebeian furnishings. Strangely, however, one can examine the listings in the inventory without getting even a hint of the "Kentuckianization" of the house. No doubt much of the antique Kentucky furniture and other indigenous materials were on loan or were private gifts to the Kentucky Mansions Preservation Foundation. Whatever the truth, there is inherent in the inventory listings a strong French and English influence. The inventory listed a French rosewood piano, a chest and chairs of Panamanian origins, various pieces of mahogany furniture, including the chairs in the family dining room, a Wurlitzer organ, a French inlaid chest of drawers, French mirrors, and Heppelwhite pieces. The listing included a cherry nightstand and a square walnut table. Maybe these cherry and walnut pieces were of Kentucky origin.[31]

Far more significant in 1971 than the image and decor of the governor's mansion was the fact that the course of Kentucky partisan politics was never a direct or consistent one. Four years before, and in true Kentucky gubernatorial form, voters had sent to Frankfort a split party governor-lieutenant governor administration. Louie B. and Beula Nunn occupied the governor's mansion on the west bank of the Kentucky River, and Wendell Hampton and Jean Neel Ford lived in the old mansion on the eastern bank. Politically, however, more than a river separated the governor and lieutenant governor.[32]

Wendell H. Ford, in 1967, had been advancing rapidly up the ladder of Kentucky politics. A native of agriculturally prosperous Daviess County, and the son of Ernest M. and Irene Schenk Ford, he, like many former Kentucky governors, grew up in a pervasive

Governor Wendell H. Ford, 1971–1974. (KHS)

rural-agrarian environment. His father was a farmer-politician who served a term in the Kentucky Senate. The son's educational background practically paralleled that of Earl Clements and Louie B. Nunn. He graduated from the Daviess County High School, attended briefly the University of Kentucky, served as a sergeant in the United States Army, and at the end of World War II enrolled in courses in the Maryland School of Insurance. Later he was president of the Junior Chamber of Commerce. In the latter position he developed a keen insight and gathered experience in the field of public relations.[33]

Perhaps no Kentucky governor was more family oriented than Wendell H. Ford (1924–).[34] He married Jean Neel in 1943, and they became the parents of one daughter, Shirley, and a son, Steven.[35] Jean was an active mother and housewife with a taste for a well-ordered and decorated house. In public life she and her lieutenant governor husband had been the second couple to occupy the restored old governor's mansion. There she gained a concept of being hostess and manager of a public executive mansion.

In 1967 the house on High and Clinton Streets bore only a general resemblance to the one James and Elizabeth Mountjoy Garrard came to occupy in 1798. Some of the overall exterior features on the house had either been modified or removed, and the interior was so greatly changed that "Cold Water" Preston Leslie might have had difficulty locating the water pitcher. A considerable amount of the materials used in renovating the house had come from outside sources. For the Fords, moving into the old mansion had not been an unpleasant experience. None of the creeping ailments of the past afflicted the old mansion in 1967.[36]

For Wendell and Jean Ford it might be said that a long political career began at the High Street entrance to the rehabilitated old mansion. In an interview with Shanna Columbus of *The Kentucky State Employee* magazine, Jean Ford said that when she married Wendell in 1943 she had no dream of becoming a governor's wife and shouldering the responsibilities for a public mansion.[37] The record is vague as to the life of a lieutenant governor and his family in the "second mansion." Too, the matter of bi-party association between Governor Nunn's and Lieutenant Governor Ford's families during the years 1967–1971 is also blurred.

The record exists and is clear as to the differences in the sense of purpose and the style of internal decor between Beula Nunn and Jean Ford. The differences in time were to receive attention from state officials and the public press.[38] Shanna Columbus quoted Jean Ford as saying that "Being the lieutenant governor's wife, especially his being of a different party from that of the Governor, has helped prepare me for my new role [as hostess] of the governor's mansion."[39]

Later, when the Fords moved across the Kentucky River to occupy the new mansion in 1971, Jean Ford had developed both a philosophy and an idea as to the kind of house in which she and her family wanted to live. Awaiting the Fords in the new abode were two maids, a butler, three cooks, and eleven general household servants. Internally the mansion reflected a mixed decor of Kentucky, British, and French origins. Most of all it appeared to be a quasi-museum.

During the more recent years of the mansion's history there had crept in a subtlety of elevated aesthetic taste, and evidence of the more active role of governors' wives to leave their mark upon the house. In this era there arose a fundamental question as to the central mission of the mansion. Was it to be an active part of the political scene in Frankfort, primarily a residence of a public servant, or a "people's" house-museum? To date no one

Jean Neel Ford, first lady from 1971 through 1974. (FCS)

had clearly defined the purpose or enunciated a central policy regarding its administration.[40] Historically the basic assumption had been that the mansion was a residence provided governors by statute law which required them to live in Frankfort.[41]

There prevailed the assumption that the General Assembly had the final control over the mansion. Periodically a legislative committee inspected the house and made a summary report on its condition. None of the reports, however, showed much concern with the interior decor or usage practices, and rarely did anyone make a searching inventory of the public properties in the house. Both the assumption and the practice were that each family would make changes and adjustments to suit its needs and tastes. Little if any thought seems to have been given as to what image the mansion should present beyond those of dignity and hospitality.[42]

When Ida Lee Willis became hostess of the mansion in 1943 she seemed to wish to leave her mark upon the house and its legacy. She had a deep interest in both interior decor and architectural styles, and later Helen Wetherby followed somewhat her precedent, but perhaps with a more definite domestic touch. The changes Helen Wetherby made in the mansion were less comprehensive and more adjusted to practical purposes. Mildred Chandler and Beula Cornelius Aspley Nunn sought to effect a deeper influence, aesthetically and historically, on the mansion. They seemed to think of the mansion in terms of perpetuity of purpose and style. Beula Nunn, especially, sought to insure perpetuity in these areas by injecting the idea of creating a reflection of a Kentucky tradition.

Thus a destiny for the mansion had been set, and it was furnished and decorated when Wendell and Jean Ford moved into it in December 1971. At the outset Jean Ford expressed her objectives for the mansion. She told Shanna Columbus that she and Governor Ford had an understanding. He was "to run the office and I to run the home." She added, "and I think it's important that he [Governor Ford] has a relaxing comfortable home to come to when he finishes working at the capitol. I'd like for people to feel that the Executive Mansion is the governor's residence . . . not a museum."[43]

In this statement were embedded the seeds of controversy. Acting directly, and apparently oblivious to the state's cumbersome procedures of purchasing, she engaged Cornelius E. Hubbuch, a Louisville interior designer and furniture dealer, to change the decor of the first floor chambers. Hubbuch, in conformity to the pseudo-French Beaux Arts architectural design of the building, proposed the undoing of Beula Nunn's pattern of decor and reversing her philosophy of the purposes of the house.[44] Among the numerous changes which he proposed was steaming the paper off the walls, concealing the cracks in the plaster beneath a gossamer fabric covering, and painting them once again, removing what he called the "store grade" gold wall-to-wall carpeting, sanding and refinishing the parquet flooring, and returning the Aubusson rugs used by a former hostess. Hubbuch also advised the purchase and installation of a style of furniture compatible with that of the mansion.

The private employment of Cornelius E. Hubbuch appears to have caused some concern on the part of Donald E. Bradshaw, Commissioner of Finance. He wrote Governor Ford in September 1972 a tactful but inquiring letter concerning the transaction. He said in essence that on examining the agreement with

Hubbuch his staff had concluded that because of a shortage of time before purchases had to be made for the redecoration of the public areas of the mansion, some kind of compromise could be made in the bidding procedure. However, he said, "We would like to suggest for your consideration that furniture and furnishings, draperies, window coverings, carpeting, and possibly the upholstering of large groups of items be bid where there is sufficient time to do so. Possibly your upstairs apartment in the Mansion and your office fall into this category."[45]

Bradshaw did suggest that most former governors had purchased furniture and interior decorating materials through professional decorators without seeking bids. He assured Governor Ford that "our interest is making sure you do not get criticized or at least in making a case for your doing it the way you want to." He said some way would have to be found for making satisfactory compromises with Governor and Mrs. Ford, and with Mr. Hubbuch.[46]

A more fundamental question arose in the summer of 1972 as to whether the state should spend an appreciable amount of money renovating the structure and facilities of the mansion, or abandon it altogether. Finance Commissioner Bradshaw favored abandonment on the grounds that the building was worn out. He wrote, "The older it gets, the more maintenance and redecorating it requires. It takes a tremendous beating from the thousands of visitors who come through each year." Because of this wear and tear the building had to be refurbished every four years. Bradshaw favored the building or purchase of a mansion well away from the capitol, an idea that was opposed by the surviving and present governors. Clearly Donald Bradshaw was convinced that the mansion should be a gubernatorial residence and not a public museum. He skirted the issue of the different feminine tastes of succeeding governors' wives, or the public use of the house.[47]

In the heat of the mid-summer sun in Frankfort in 1972, Donald Bradshaw must have shared heartily his immediate predecessor's frustration. Albert Christian, Commissioner of Finance in the Nunn administration, wrote in a moment of utter confusion that "For sometime the Commissioner of Finance has been confused, amazed, disheartened by the frequent and unorganized efforts in the pursuit and acquiring, maintaining, and operating mansions. . . ."[48]

After the gubernatorial inauguration on December 12, 1971, the fate of Larry S. Perkins and the office of state curator was sealed. There was a sharp reversal in concepts of what the governor's mansion should be between Beula Nunn and Jean Ford. This fact quickly came into public view. While campaigning for her husband in the United States senatorial race in 1971, Beula Nunn told a partisan coffee klatch of supporters that she had just been handed a newspaper clipping out of Covington saying that Mrs. Ford was refurbishing the mansion. Beula was reported as saying that Jean Ford was, "Redoing the Mansion in French provincial style." She told the gathering that she was concerned about the fate of the fine antiques and paintings and prints that she had collected and which were now being removed. She urged the audience to "Tell the governor what's on their minds, tell him they would like the Governor's Mansion to be an historic house."[49]

The office of state curator and its first director, Larry S. Perkins, experienced what, perhaps, was the shortest interval of activity in Kentucky bureaucratic history.[50] On December 23, 1971, Governor Ford issued an executive order abolishing the office of state curator on the grounds that the General Assembly had made no appropriation of funds for its support.[51] It must be said that during his exceedingly short term in office Larry S. Perkins proved to be a man of action. His detailed inventory of December 6, 1971, appears to justify Cornelius Hubbuch's proposal to refurnish the mansion's first floor in the original Beaux Arts style.[52]

In the midst of the controversy over the style and purposes of the mansion, a brief survey was made to determine what neighboring states did with their executive houses. It was found that in Ohio the management and furnishing of the governor's mansion was left up to the governor's wife. In West Virginia the general assembly appointed a governor's mansion executive committee of six *ex officio* members, including the governor, an interior decorator who was a member of the American Institute of Interior Designers, and a building contractor. This committee exercised an oversight function, making recommendations as to what refurbishing or changes might be made. Apparently Tennessee had no policy. The wife of Governor Winfield Dunn visited Frankfort around 1970 and adopted the Kentucky Mansions Preservation Foundation plan.[53]

No matter how much discussion and conflict of views occurred over the interior provenance of the mansion, the house as an efficiently functioning structure remained unchanged. Behind the scenes, and out of public sight, it was threatened with the ills of aging, potential for a fiery holocaust, and other deficiencies.[54]

When Wendell and Jean Ford had arrived in Frankfort

in 1967 to live in the refurbished old governor's mansion, they brought with them a daughter, Shirley, and a son, Steven. Shirley was almost ready to enter college, and Steven was enrolled as a student at the Frankfort High School. There he had a successful career as an athlete, a student, and a participant in school social affairs. For him both the old and new mansions were prestigious bases from which to launch his school career. The Fords, however, had to move out of the old mansion and live in a much smaller house near the Kentucky River when the old mansion's kitchen floor was once again torn up and workmen were busy making the house livable.[55]

When Wendell Ford was elected governor in 1971 and like James B. McCreary in 1914, made the move across the river to the new mansion, he and Jean were well oriented in the ways of Frankfort and the political mores of the capital. His father had served as both a legislator and a public official, and as a young boy, Wendell had served briefly as a page in the General Assembly. Jean Ford came to the new mansion with established social and domestic relations in Frankfort.[56]

In the move to the new mansion, Shirley was away in college and Steven, like the Chandler sons and Edward Breathitt III, resided on the third floor of the mansion. As a high school student, and later as a student at the University of Kentucky, he entertained his friends at mansion parties. On one occasion members of a party danced on the back patio in their sock feet, leaving behind a fuzzy lint coating to shine in the next morning's sun. On at least one occasion the band played so loudly that protesting neighbors called the mansion to say the noise had awakened the cows on the farm across the Kentucky River.[57]

During his tenure as governor, Wendell Ford gained the reputation of operating a tightly controlled administration. Senator Charles Freeman of Harrodsburg wrote that "The Governor has had more control over the legislature than any I have ever attended." During the years 1971–1974 some major changes were made in Kentucky government and administrative organization. The governor's mansion at times became a virtual center of political action. Among the integral changes made in the mansion, the library nook, which Beula Nunn had created, was reconverted to its original purpose as an office for the governor. There, and in the big room in the basement, Wendell Ford conferred with constituents, state officials, and politicians. In the larger basement room the circles of papers and documentary materials indicated that it was a center of budget

Five Democratic governors. Left to right, Edward T. Breathitt, Bert T. Combs, Wendell H. Ford, Lawrence Wetherby, and Albert B. Chandler. (KHS, Breathitt album)

making, the reconstruction of the state government, and other administrative gatherings. No doubt it was both in the mansion's governor's office and the basement "war room" that discussion of the coal severance tax, the management of leveling mountain tops by strip mining, the environment, the Kentucky Horse Park, and the state merit system were discussed.[58]

Like governors' families before them, the Fords lived in the mansion with a sense of security. Governor Ford walked the short distance to his capitol office with little or no fear. On one occasion, however, he was confronted by a strange man who seemed to be persistent. The

governor sought the mansion's state police patrolman. The man explained that he wanted to touch Governor Ford and ex-Governor Louie Nunn and turn them into pillars of salt. When the man was searched, the police found he was carrying a substantial amount of cash in the bosom of his shirt. Both Ford and Nunn escaped the plight of Lot's wife, perhaps because neither looked back. More realistically, they were threatened only by a wandering soul whose addled mind conceived more magic power than his crumpled old fingers could produce.[59]

Across the Kentucky River in the restored old mansion, Julian and Charlann Carroll waited to move into

The governor's mansion in early spring 1972, when it was listed on the National Register of Historic Places. (FCS)

the new mansion. They had spent three active social and political years in the old one, and undoubtedly had heard stories about James Garrard, Thomas "Stonehammer" Metcalfe, Robert Letcher, and Simon Bolivar Buckner at the old site, and about James B. McCreary, John Dixon Black, and William Jason Fields in connection with the new one. Like most of them, Julian Carroll had a rural-agrarian background. He had elevated his position in the acquisition of liberal arts and law degrees.[60]

Elected lieutenant governor as a running mate of Wendell Ford, Carroll was placed in line for the governorship. As a resident of the old mansion and lieutenant governor, he presided, *ex officio*, over the Kentucky Senate. He had reached this position by the time he was forty years of age.

When the Carroll family of five had moved into the original governor's mansion, that pile of "sticks and stones" had been scraped bare of its ancient afflictions. No longer were floors propped up with timbers or buckled from wear and moisture. The scars of the fires the house had suffered were erased. Not even Simon Bolivar Buckner with his vaunted wealth and elite young wife ever saw the house in such handsome condition. Builders had removed the detracting built-on appendages, remodeled the entry way, and provided the rooms with an interior decorative finish they had never known before.[61]

In the expensively restored palace, the Carrolls found themselves well situated to be hospitable hosts. They entertained somewhat extensively "for political purposes," as Governor Carroll later said in a taped interview. In a more social vein they invited guests who were non-political and talented in several cultural areas. Jesse Stuart, Kentucky's poet laureate, came and read his poetry and Homer Ledford, a musical instrument-maker and dulcimer player, entertained at a lieutenant governor's mansion party.[62]

Kentucky politics in 1974 ran its traditional course of changing events and personalities. On March 23, 1974, Wendell H. Ford announced his candidacy for election to the United States Senate. He ran in opposition to the sitting Republican Marlow Cook and won. Cook graciously withdrew from the office and allowed Ford to be sworn in ahead of time so that he would gain in seniority.[63] Thus ended the issue of the decor and purpose of the governor's mansion so far as the interiors were concerned. However, it did not put off the inevitable Armageddon for the house. That lay immediately ahead.

Ford, like Stanley, Chandler, and Clements, resigned the governorship and abandoned the new mansion to his one-time lieutenant governor. The adjective "new" when applied to the governor's mansion on Capitol Drive was little more than a euphemism. In their transfer across the river, the Carrolls and their three children, Kenneth, Patricia, and Bradley, ironically advanced up the political ladder but moved down in safety and condition of their residence.

The years in which the Carroll family occupied the new governor's mansion were mixed with some degree of prosperity and grievous human tragedy. The Kentucky economy as a whole was promising, but the state government was still handicapped by an archaic revenue system. But Julian (1931–) and Charlann Harting Carroll were gregarious people, and they continued to entertain groups and guests in the mansion. They held receptions, Derby breakfasts, and numerous other gatherings.[64]

It may be that no preceding governor had ever made greater official work use of the mansion than did Governor Carroll. He utilized a basement lounge or "war room" for extended discussions of governmental problems and procedures for budget-making, formulation of legislative programs, and political strategies. An attendant present in one budget planning session said that after the governor had already recommended projects

Governor Julian Morton Carroll, 1974–1979. (KHS)

in excess of $20 million over the funds in hand, and then still proposed a new one, saying it was "a good project," a time- and patience-worn old Department of Finance official retorted, "Governor, good projects exist *ad infinitum!*"

During the Carroll occupancy there flowed into the mansion a plethora of horrendous news. First was that of the Scotia Mine disaster in March 1976. This tragedy brought into broad public focus the failures of state and federal governments to strictly enforce vital mine safety rules.[65] Just as horrendous was the burning of the Beverly Hills Supper Club in Southgate on the evening of May 28, 1977, when more than 2,000 people were crammed into the Zebra Room, and 165 of them perished in the flames and smoke. When news of this tragedy reached Frankfort, Governor Carroll was dressed in his pajamas and was ready for bed. He quickly dressed and went to Southgate.[66] Added to the flaming calamities was the costly damage caused by the severe winter of 1977–1978 to the Kentucky economy.[67] The mansion's spate of morbidity was finally broken by the birth of a daughter to Julian and Charlann Carroll.

Charlann Carroll posing in her inaugural gown on the grand staircase in 1974 when Julian Carroll succeeded Wendell Ford to the governorship. (KHS)

Not since the birth of Eleanor Beckham on August 16, 1901, in the old mansion had a governor's child been born in the mansion (Simeon Willis Meigs, a grandson of Governor Willis, had been taken to the mansion directly from a hospital nursery; in 1922 Benny Lee Waddle Hay, a niece of Mrs. Morrow, was born in an upstairs bedroom). Ellyn Carroll quickly became "The apple of her father's eye." Gwenneth Cullen, in a taped interview, said she was the prettiest child she had ever seen. Governor Carroll, she said, was quick to present the

infant to mansion visitors. On a special occasion a group of young women from the Caribbean were being entertained in the mansion, and Governor Carroll brought down his infant daughter to show her off. Gwenneth Cullen said one of the young women asked whose child it was, and the governor replied emphatically that she was his.[68]

Though verging on being uninhabitable, during the Carroll administration the mansion continued to serve as a center for numerous public assemblies and gather-

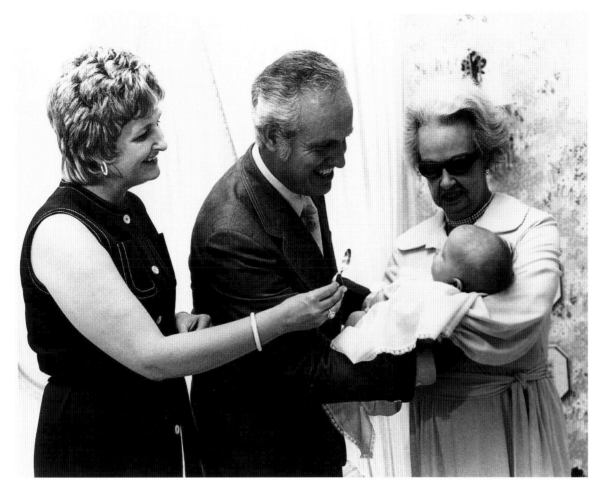

Charlann and Julian Carroll with baby Elly greet Eleanor Beckham, the first child born to a governor in the old mansion. Ms. Beckham presented one of her silver spoons to Elly. (KDLA)

ings, ranging from the Boy Scouts to nature preservationists. The first floor parlors were favorite meeting places for the Daughters of the American Revolution, social planning groups, and public receptions. Periodically there were the special events visitors, such as members of the General Assembly, the Court of Appeals, or Derby breakfast guests.[69]

Derby time brought its bevy of celebrities, including Bob Hope and other Hollywood personalities. Special guests included Governor James B. Edwards of South Carolina, a Republican, and Governor Carroll's first cousin.[70]

On top of the tragic news of the Scotia Mine, the Beverly Hills Supper Club fire, and the harsh winter damages, political problems caused anxiety in the governor's mansion. Like Governor Ruby Laffoon, Julian Carroll was victimized by his lieutenant governor. During his

absence from the state, Lieutenant Governor Thelma Stovall called the General Assembly into special session to enact a tax-cutting law. The resulting "House Bill 44" would eventually exact a harsh toll on the financial capabilities of the state, and clouded the record of the Carroll administration. No effective plan could be devised in the mansion's basement "war room" to offset the damage.[71]

Added to the disruption of peace of mind in the mansion was the bitter controversy which raged over the damming of the Red River. There arose a hot conflict between conservationists and the United States Corps of Engineers. Ostensibly the dam across the river would create a reservoir of water for Lexington and neighboring towns, but it would also flood the great Red River Gorge and destroy much of the beauty of the region. Governor Carroll closeted himself on the mansion's third floor and spent a day and night analyzing the data

The Library of Kentuckiana as it appeared at the end of the Julian Carroll governorship in November 1979, just prior to the major renovation during the John Young Brown administration. (FCS)

The mansion's family dining room during the last months of the Carroll administration. (FCS)

relating to this project before making the decision to halt the project.[72]

During their occupancy of the mansion, the Carrolls made only minor changes within the house. A full basement was dug under the ballroom, giving more space to the enlarged security department and providing room for more service facilities and housing for twelve female trusties.

When John Young Brown Jr. was elected governor in November 1979, Governor and Mrs. Carroll volunteered to vacate the mansion at an early date so Brown and his family could move into the house and be partially settled by inauguration day. As it turned out, this courteous gesture was almost meaningless. That long impending day of decision had arrived in the form of an order from the Kentucky fire marshal. The commonwealth finally had to face the question of whether the state should build a new governor's mansion, or completely renovate the present one. The Brown family hardly had time to unpack their clothes before they had to move back to their Cave Hill residence near Lexington to spend most of the next four years. The mansion had been declared off limits for overnight human occupancy.[73]

The drawing room or first lady's parlor as it appeared in March 1980 during the Carroll administration. (FCS)

The governor's reception room as it appeared in November 1979, the closing month of the Carroll administration. (FCS)

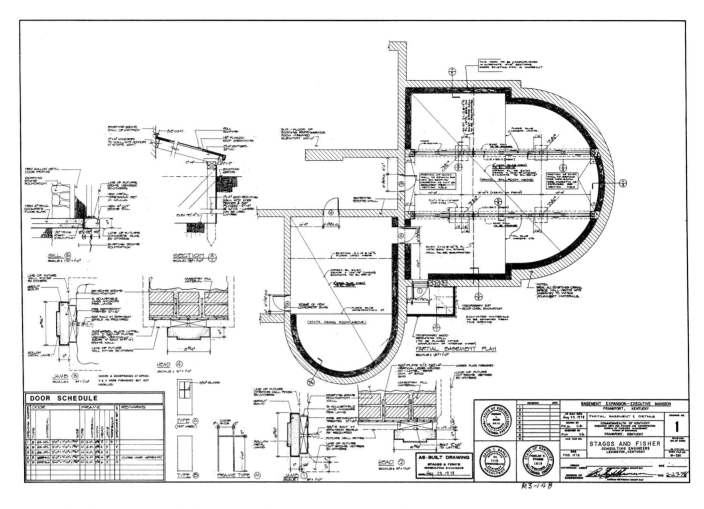

A 1978 plan for expansion of the mansion's basement to accommodate more office and storage space. The expansion area is on the north side under the ballroom and state dining room. (FCS, Engineering Department)

PART III

A Symbol of Dignity

The state dining room appointed for guests early in the John Y. Brown administration. Note the needlepoint captain's chair to the right. (FCS)

CHAPTER 13

Kentucky's Petit Trianon

Eighteen of Kentucky's governors and their families, in four- or five-year intervals, occupied the new mansion between 1914 and 1979. Some left more discernible marks on it than others. They all, however, made domestic demands on the building, the furnishings, and the facilities. Well before 1980, the electrical wiring and the plumbing-drainage system deficiencies far exceeded the safety codes. Physically the basic structure of Bowling Green stone was as sound as when the foundations and walls were laid, but the interior bore the deep wrinkles of age and use. In some of the rooms, the parquet flooring had been sanded and polished so many times that it was almost paper thin. Walls, ceilings, and interior adornments had been painted over and over, and they were out of style and beyond identity. Furniture, carpets, rugs, and fabrics were soiled and worn, and much of the china and silverware broken and scarred. Little or none of the interior decor harmonized with the early twentieth-century Beaux Arts architectural and interior decorative styles. Perhaps the most definitive description that can be offered is that internally the mansion was as eclectic as the Kentucky governorship itself. On that glorious January evening in 1914 when James Bennett McCreary's chosen guests flaunted their jewels and high fashion gowns and then tramped over a muddy walkway going home, the electrical and sewer systems were already inadequate.[1] From time to time in the coming years the main wiring, breaker boxes, wall outlets, and fixtures were out of code. To save the state money the government even allowed surface water and sewage to flow away from the mansion in a common conduit, much to the irritation of Frankfort city officials.

The deterioration of the mansion's electrical and plumbing systems had plagued every occupant of the house since 1914. No one, however, fully realized how

Governor John Young Brown Jr., 1979–1983. (KHS)

badly deteriorated they were. Within a month of moving his family into the mansion in 1979, Governor John Young Brown Jr. (1933–) ordered an inspection of the wiring system.[2] In response John R. Groves Jr. and John Johnson, on March 1, 1980, made a "walk through" examination of the electrical system. In their preliminary report they indicated they had found outmoded

The family dining room in March 1980, before renovation, featuring a Kentucky poplar mantel and paneling. (FCS)

fuse boxes, circuit breakers, and crumbling wire insulation. Outlets were worn and hazardous, and some were no longer even usable. So deficient was the wiring system that Groves said, "If this was a privately owned or privately operated structure, this office [the Department of Buildings and Construction] would have no alternative other than to give the operator 30 to 60 days to rewire the structure."[3] Groves declared that the wiring made the structure a virtual firetrap. In a supplementary comment, the secretary of the Department of Finance, George Adkins, wrote Governor Brown, saying, "I was told that if this was a public meeting place, that the entire facility would be condemned because of the hazards that exist."[4]

Immediately after receiving the Groves and Adkins communications, Governor Brown decided to move his family out of the mansion. Groves was reported as saying that "based upon our inspection of the electrical wiring . . . it is our determination that the use of the mansion for overnight purposes or to accommodate group meetings shall be discontinued until corrections have been made."

John and Phyllis George Brown moved back to their home, Cave Hill, near Lexington. In making the transfer, the Department of Finance drafted one of the most fascinating domestic documents in Kentucky gubernatorial history, cloaking it under the bureaucratic title, "Governor's Official Residence Expenditure Analysis."

Visitors review drawings of proposed mansion renovations in October 1981. (FCS)

This document sets out in greater detail than any previous one the precise condition of the gubernatorial residence and its general maintenance problems.

Cave Hill was officially designated as the temporary executive mansion, and the Department of Finance categorized the amount of support and services the commonwealth would render. A list of materials to be furnished was included. The state would pay the governor's grocery bill and the expenses for entertaining official guests. However, state employees in service at Cave Hill would be required to reimburse the state for their meals. Generous travel allowances were made for both the governor and employees at the temporary mansion. The state would pay for public—but not private—phone bills. It would purchase no furniture for the residence. Nor would it pay for improvements.[5]

Certainly no one had any realistic notion of how much it would cost to renovate the mansion. In March 1980, the Department of Finance estimated that it would cost $125,500 to inspect and test the utilities system in the house. Engineers estimated that the cost of a general renovation would probably be $1.5 million. The estimated cost for replacing the electrical system alone exceeded by $50,000 the cost of the original 1914 construction.[6]

Faced with the proposition of either abandoning the mansion as a residence and constructing a new one for the governors, or instead attempting to renovate the old one, the Kentucky General Assembly enacted House Bill 914 in March 1980 creating a Governor's Mansion Commission to be responsible to the Department of Finance. This six-member body was to have policy oversight of the renovation of the governor's mansion. Extra-officially, Phyllis George Brown, the governor's wife, however, was to exert a strong influence on the extent of the renovation and the making of day-to-day decisions. Her name is mentioned more often in the official records than that of even the governor.

Phyllis George Brown, Texas-born and a former Miss America, was an imaginative and energetic force in the renovation of the mansion. She had expressed a clear concept of what she hoped the governor's mansion would become, advancing the idea that it should be as fine as the original French Petit Trianon, and the way was cleared for the realization of her dream when the Kentucky fire marshal ordered the mansion closed to overnight occupancy.

To enable the renovation and restoration of the mansion to its adapted Beaux Arts style, Phyllis George Brown conceived a plan to solicit private funds to pay the cost of internal decorations and furnishing. On May 14, 1980, she used the Governor's Office and press facilities to announce the organization of the "Save the Mansion" group that would solicit and manage private gifts. She told the newspaper press that William Barrow Floyd, Kentucky's curator of public properties, would direct the drive. She said he would coordinate staff activities of the forthcoming campaign and would serve as the chief consultant of the renovation of the mansion's interior.[7]

At the outset of the renovation both Governor Brown and Secretary Adkins expected Kentucky to receive a substantial sum from the federal revenue sharing fund, as much as perhaps $70 million. Of this sum they planned to expend $1.7 million on the mansion. By May 1980, however, President Jimmy Carter had mandated a halt on dispensing the revenue sharing funds. This left Kentucky with a substantial financial shortfall.[8]

The withholding of federal revenue sharing funds placed the renovation of the governor's mansion in a state of uncertainty and seemed to indicate little more could be done for the mansion than once more doing necessary patchwork on the electrical and sewer systems. Momentarily a full-scale renovation of the mansion was placed in jeopardy. Nothing in the official documents indicates that state officials were willing to do more. That would have to come from the first lady and her Save the Mansion organization.[9]

From the outset, Phyllis George Brown had the support of William B. Floyd, Mrs. Frank Metts, Steve Wilson, Henry and Sally Meigs, and a substantial number of state officials. Floyd indicated that since his taste and experience enabled him only to deal with early American furniture and interior styles, that William Seale of Alexandria, Virginia, should be invited to become a consultant.[10] Persuasively, Phyllis George Brown said, "No one wants to see the Mansion continue to deteriorate the way it has done the last twenty years." She expressed a strong ambition to refurbish it with the fine furnishings that would tie it to Kentucky and the state's past. At the same time, however, the mansion should reflect a quasi-romantic French image. She said to Kentuckians that, "We can have one of the most beautiful mansions in the world right here in Kentucky. There is no reason why the Kentucky Mansion can't rival the White House or the newly remodeled State Department reception room in Washington."[11]

Floyd was placed in charge of the interior renovations, and the rest of the magical transformation would be accomplished by the state's engineers and public property managers, who were given responsibility for the renovation of the physical structure and its facilities. In an undated news release, Governor Brown said Floyd was nationally recognized as a historical preservationist, especially in the field of early America.[12]

When William Seale came to Frankfort to make a preliminary survey of the mansion's interior and its current furnishings, he was asked to work within the existing building's structure, as there were no plans to modify its original plan.[13] Seale filed his survey report on June 11, 1980; it contained several intriguing observations. He proposed renovating of the mansion by creating its interior in the context of the first decade of the twentieth century, recognizing that it had to serve the dual purpose of being a gubernatorial residence and a public house. He indicated the Kentucky mansion was a derivative, not a true copy, of the French Trianon in Versailles. It stood in close harmony, he said, with the neo-classical mode of the new Kentucky capitol. That building, he said, contained features of French architectural style. Seale compared the Kentucky Beaux Arts derivative mansion with a precise copy of the Petit Trianon which had been constructed in California, and described the latter as a "vulgar copy cat."

The Kentucky mansion was described as "eclectic, and in proper setting with its place and purpose." To gather a more certain understanding of the Beaux Arts architectural style and its implications in the governor's

William Seale, historical consultant, and the mansion's curator, Jason Fenwick, collaborate on final plans for the renovation. (FCS)

mansion, John and Phyllis George Brown visited Versailles, France, to study the original Petit Trianon, inside and out. No doubt they placed more emphasis on the interior and furnishings than upon the basic structure of the building itself.

Seale reported further that essentially the Kentucky governor's mansion was a historical building and should be treated as such. It should not be subjected to an "exact restoration. It is vital," he said, "that this is a living house, and not frozen in time." Seale observed that public buildings like the mansion were at once historical and as new as the current date. He complimented both the Kentucky mansion and its previous tenants. Over the years its occupants had treated it consistently well and with considerable respect. It had never been brutalized, as was true with most public buildings. Historically, Seale said, neither the old mansion nor the new had been frozen in time. As to the

new mansion, Seale wrote, "The house has been redecorated over and over again, often in a sad attempt to make it into something it is not. Let it be itself! A new world will open up."[14]

William Seale, the purist, looked not to the opening of a contemporary world, or an American provincial one for that matter, but to the opening decade of the twentieth century with its strong seventeenth-century tastes and adaptations. That was an era of an American architectural renaissance. Within this context there was a paradoxically sharp contrast between the romantic French continental era and the realistic one of provincial Kentucky. Unfortunately, in no area was this fact more obvious than Kentucky's fiscal capability of embarking upon a costly Beaux Arts adventure. The renovation of the mansion raised several fundamental questions and involved the making of complex decisions. From the perspective of faithfully creating the house in

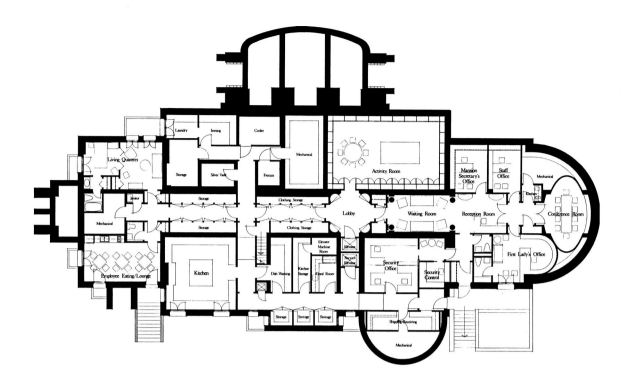

Basement Plan

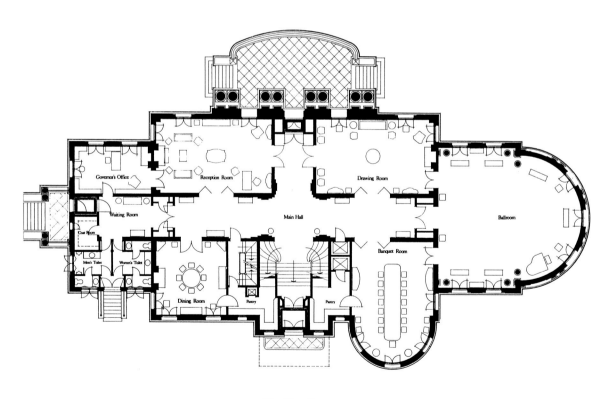

First Floor Plan

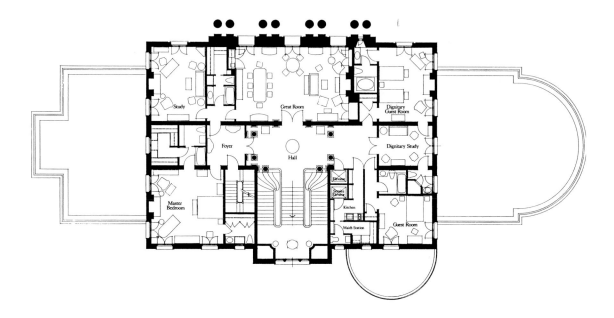

Second Floor Plan

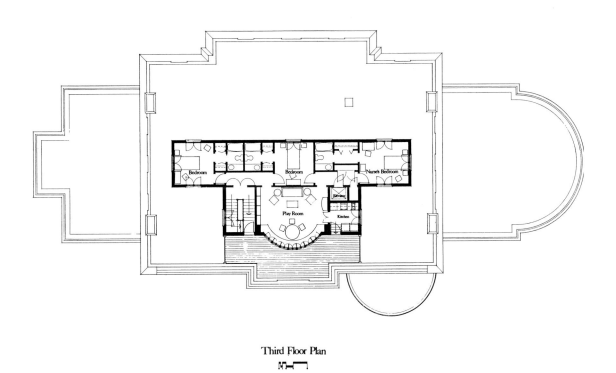

Third Floor Plan

Floor plans of the mansion in 1981. (FCS)

Construction view of the mansion basement during renovation. (FCS)

Walls between a second floor bedroom and sitting room were removed to create the second floor great room where modern first families relax. (FCS)

Excavation on the southeast corner of the mansion. A conduit tunnel containing wiring, heating, and water pipes connects the mansion with the capitol power plant. (FCS)

its original style, a basic decision to determine the scope of renovation had to be made at the outset. The choices were either to adhere to Augustus E. Willson's observation that the mansion should be in keeping with the lifestyles of men usually elected governors of Kentucky, or to adopt a newer concept of an imperial governorship, justified by the contention that the governor's mansion in Frankfort should be a tangible symbol of excellence in cultural and artistic achievement and a physical documentation of the commonwealth's heritage.[15]

Aware that the rooms of the Petit Trianon in Versailles were overstuffed with furnishings, Seale warned that the rooms in this house should be more sparsely furnished. Over the years, governors and their families added little if anything to the mansion which might be called a state collection. Not even the curator of public properties had done this. Seale recommended that no furnishings manufactured after 1930 should be placed in the house. Decorations of the rooms, he said, "should

follow the ideas of the early 20th century toward French type decoration, without necessarily including all French furniture. All must be harmonious, in keeping with the ideas of the time. I would not make the rooms too full, and certainly strive not to make them too cozy, with groupings and coffee tables around the fire."[16]

Seale's report on the mansion set a dream as to what the house might become in its full renovation, after being drawn into a stylistic whole. He justified the French concept of both the capitol and the mansion by saying they represented the American architectural view prior to World War I. He said, "A Petit Trianon made good sense with the neo-classical theme of the Capitol, and the French sources in its architecture, as well as, more deliberately, the [Louis XIII] Reception Room."[17]

Given virtually carte blanche to redesign the interior of the mansion, William Seale had to fit a seventeenth-century style of decor and furnishings inside the sturdy walls of native Kentucky Bowling Green stone.

The mansion became a construction zone, complete with a "Danger—Keep Out!" sign on the south door. (FCS)

His report went far beyond what any Kentucky official or legislator could have originally conceived. It obviously appealed to Phyllis George Brown.[18]

At some stage of planning the renovation, the engineers or the superintendent of public buildings and properties unearthed an original, undated copy of the Weber-Adkins perspective of the mansion. Strangely, in the preliminary planning, the commission mandated by the General Assembly in 1980 seems never to have been called into consultation. In fact, as General William Buster later observed, no chairman had been designated.[19]

Because of the dual sources of financing the renovation, management of the project functioned at two dif-ferent levels. The part of the project that was financed by the state was under the control of the secretary of the Finance Cabinet, and the part financed by the Save the Mansion group was under their control. On April 3, 1980, George L. Adkins expressed concern about the loss of federal funds in relation to the renovation of the mansion. He suggested that the house be placed in line with other projected public buildings. He informed the governor that, "By not condemning the mansion, the facility will still be available for use on an as needed basis until determination of renovation programming can be made."[20]

At that date no one in state government had a firm

Governor and Mrs. Brown take a break after a hard day of mansion renovation. (FCS)

notion of what the renovation of the mansion might ultimately cost. Adkins's letter seems to suggest that the building might be converted to other uses, and certainly that he and the engineers had not sensed the full extent of how much work was needed. Surely Gilbert Ellis, the Kentucky fire marshal, had no inkling of the cost when he ordered the house vacated for overnight use.[21]

It was not until October 22, 1981, that even a tentative cost for renovating the building was estimated. Channeling the solid stone walls to relocate the interior wiring and reconstructing of the drainage and sewer systems were estimated at somewhere in the neighborhood of $175,000, and the quote for the full renovation

of the interior came to $1,762,000. There was no estimate of the cost of redesigning the driveway and the creation of a formal garden. By January 1982, the general estimate to renovate the building would be at least $2.9 million.[22] The actual cost of the full renovation of the building and grounds was at least $3.5 million.

By the latter date Phyllis George Brown was almost completely in charge of the project. Her goal seems to have been to move her family back into the mansion before Derby Day in 1982. Ralph Graves of the office of the Secretary of the Finance and Administration Cabinet, however, wrote Mrs. Brown that the contractor would be only about a third finished with his work by

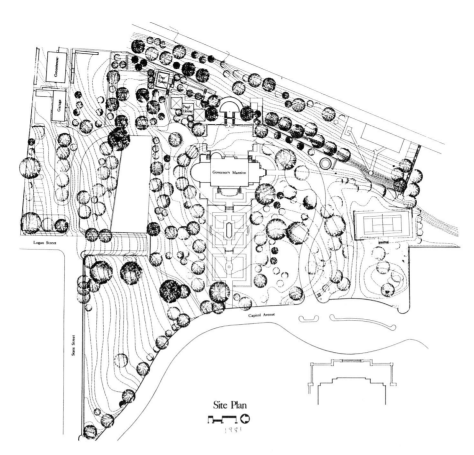

The site plan for the renovated mansion, complete with formal garden. (FCS)

then. He told Phyllis, "Realizing how anxious you must be to get back into the mansion, we will do everything possible to meet the October 1982 date suggested by Steve." The driveway would be unfinished, said Graves, and the grounds would be muddy and littered with construction equipment, and before she scheduled a visitation to the mansion she should be informed about the condition of the grounds. The weather and contractor machines would be a consideration.[23]

No part of the governor's mansion restoration caused so much emotional reaction as that of reshaping and converting the area at the front of the mansion into a formal garden. In January 1914, the area about the mansion had been raw and largely treeless. Several gestures were made to cover it with trees and shrubbery, and eventually Mrs. J.D. Black had planted some trees, with the result that there were in 1980 a dozen or so fairly large cherry, oak, and tulip poplar varieties. Many of the trees had suffered from disease, storm damage, and lack of care. Strangely there does not seem to have

been much if any public reaction to renovating the mansion in a style foreign to the Kentucky scene and tradition, but cutting trees stirred up a storm of protest.[24]

The Kentucky General Assembly showed only a casual concern with the mansion problem, apparently assuming that it had divested itself of responsibility when it created the special six-member commission. In turn the commission was all but inactive. It was not until September 18, 1982, that it held its first meeting. Members of the initial commission were General Dillman Rash of Louisville, Cornelia Cooper of Somerset, General William Buster of Midway, Dr. B.B. Baughman of Frankfort, and Jason Fenwick. General Buster, director of the Kentucky Historical Society, was chosen temporary chairman. He explained that the reason the commission had held no meetings was the fact that no chairman had been appointed.[25]

Ironically the mansion commission was formed basically to have oversight over the renovation of the governor's mansion, but actually it had little if any part in

A 1982 aerial view of the mansion under construction, showing a footprint for the formal gardens, before plantings were installed. (FCS)

the restoration. It did become involved in the controversy surrounding the creation of a formal garden. When this issue arose, Clayton Farmer, a spokesman for the state engineering division, said that his office, with the approval of the Browns, had decided to resurrect the plans made for a garden in 1912.

Once word of the plans for creating a garden seeped to the public, there arose an emotional reaction. Mrs. Robert Cullen, a Frankfort gardener, said the idea of the garden was to create "A pseudo French Hollywood type." Mrs. James Dawson, a neighbor to the mansion, complained about the cost of the projected garden and sought a restraining order from Franklin County Circuit Court Judge Squire Williams, barring state workmen from cutting trees on the front lawn of the mansion.[26] In turn, Judge Williams issued a restraining order informing Governor Brown that no trees on the mansion grounds were to be cut until he could arrive at an ultimate decision in the matter. In the meantime, a suit was filed in the Franklin Court by two Frankfort women and John Gray, the latter president of the Historic Frankfort group, asking a stay of plans for creating a garden of the early twentieth-century type. In the moment of contention, Clayton Farmer estimated that a garden in harmony with the mansion's Beaux Arts style would cost from $30,000 to $40,000. In addition it would cost at least $4,000 each to remove the trees from the site.[27]

Judge Williams dissolved the Frankfort plaintiffs' suit on September 1, 1982. A spokesman for the plaintiffs was reported as having said "He felt a major purpose of the suit had been accomplished by having the matter discussed openly before the commission." There was plenty of discussion, and emotions ran high.[28] Some of the critics of the garden plan suggested the state should be true to its image and the mansion lawn should be sown in bluegrass. A.N. Mackie, a mansion neighbor, said the idea of a formal garden with a fountain in its midst might have been proper in 1914, but in 1982 "it's an anachronism. It might have been nice in 1914, but [many people] would rather have bluegrass." A nameless "gentleman" asked, "Have you given any consideration to the possibility that some future governor may want to throw a lawn party with some shade trees?" He evidently meant a party under shade trees.[29] A second woman neighbor objected to the installation of a fountain in the garden because children would play in it. She complained that it was already impossible to keep them off of Bert Combs's controversial floral clock. There was a shrill but ill-informed plaint that some of

the trees being threatened were historic, antedating the construction of the mansion, but Clayton Farmer produced photographs indicating the grounds were bare in 1914. Perhaps the complaining lady had never heard of Mrs. J.D. Black's tree-planting activity.[30]

Once the court dissolved the restraining order, Farmer, the Commonwealth's facilities manager, lost no time in having the trees cut down. Almost in the twinkling of an eye the lawn gave the appearance of being the scene of a major storm disaster.[31] It is doubtful that many issues, if in fact any, in Kentucky history, except those bearing dim landmark blazes, aroused more intense emotions or spilled more printer's ink. In this case the cutting of the seven trees (they eventually cut down a total of thirteen) became almost as dire an incident as shooting a mountain man's favorite squirrel dog.

When the trees were removed, and the mansion gave the appearance of standing amidst a backwoods clearing, a rather massive excavation was made between the building's pediment and Capitol Avenue. Landscape planner Don Fleming described the garden plan, with annual flowers bordering the walkways, enclosed within rows of junipers and boxwood hedging. The walks would be interspersed with small plots of lawn, centered by a fountain and reflecting pool. The central walkway would be constructed on three levels between the pediment of the mansion and Capitol Avenue, necessitating the relocation of the driveway.[32] The plan for the garden was irreversibly set, and the battle of the trees, like so many emotional outbursts of the kind, passed into historical oblivion. The planned formal garden was to be a sharp contrast with the mansion's riparian location, and with the capitol grounds.

For the better part of three years, state fiscal officials, engineers, and four individual contractors participated in the mansion's renovation. The four contractors were the Bill G. Tucker Construction Company of Lexington for mechanical and electrical alterations, the Niemeir Company of Louisville for foundation and conduit demolition and excavation work, the Barmore Company of Louisville to do internal structural work, and William Seale as the consultant and general overseer in the creation and installation of the interior finishes and furnishings.[33]

The renovation was accomplished at four or five specific stages or levels, each stage requiring time and skill. While there was not an appreciable amount of invasion of the inner structure of the house, some walls, ceilings, moldings, and floors did have to be restored or replaced. Once the basic structural work was finished

The portrait of First Lady Phyllis George Brown installed in the newly decorated first lady's parlor, where the portrait of each first lady is traditionally displayed. (FCS)

The governor's reception room adjacent to the mansion's ballroom is decorated in commonwealth blue and gold. The painting at the left is *Dahlias in a Vase* by Joseph Henry Sharp. (FCS)

there remained the interior painting, trim, and furnishings. Outside there was the task of tree removal, excavation, design, and creation of the formal garden. Around the mansion the soil had to once again be stabilized after the contractors had removed their heavy equipment.

Several ill winds blew during the years of renovating the mansion. First was the loss of the federal revenue sharing funds, which caused a drastic restriction on public construction. Then there was the unanticipated need for replacing room ceilings and moldings, parquet floors, and the channeling of solid stone walls to accommodate utility lines. A major structural and financial

crisis occurred when four tons of plaster crashed through the ceilings of two floors, causing $150,000 damage, almost twice the cost of the original construction of the building.[34] All of these caused delays in completing the renovation.

Running through the official inter-office correspondence is a thread of anxiousness on the part of the Browns. Phyllis George Brown seems to have dreamed of entertaining Derby Eve celebrity guests in the mansion, and both of them seemed to look forward to Derby breakfasts. Ralph Graves wrote Phyllis on January 18, 1982, that construction clutter in and around the man-

Faux painting to resemble marble was a popular Beaux arts decorative technique, as seen on the governor's reception room mantel. The marble-based candelabra were donated to the mansion by Sally Willis Meigs. (FCS)

sion would not be conducive to opening the building to guests for entertaining or viewing. Outside the grounds were deep in mud and littered with heavy construction machines.[35]

After all the delays, work was far enough along in February 1983 to extend invitations to the General Assembly to view the renovated building at 10:00 A.M. on the second day of March.[36] A second viewing of the renovation occurred on March 19, 1983, when special contributing guests were invited to a reception. The occasion, in fact, was a fund-raising event, costing each guest $192. It was the fourth wedding anniversary of the Browns, and the fiftieth of the Save the Children organization which shared in the collected funds.[37] This reception, however, contrasted decidedly with that of January 21, 1914. This time there was no glittering receiving line of fashionably dressed ladies, or flashy men. This day, said Beverly Fortune of the *Lexington Herald-Leader,* Phyllis George Brown, several state employees, and private volunteer helpers worked diligently for more than twelve hours to prepare the mansion for the reception. At 6:15 P.M., Phyllis boarded the governor's much-publicized helicopter and swirled off to Cave Hill to wash her hair, dress, and be back in the mansion in a little over an hour. The original plan called for Robert Redford, the movie actor, to be a celebrity guest, but at the last hour he became involved in an actors' labor dispute and canceled his visit.[38]

Guests that evening were reported as enthusiastic in their praise of the renovation. Kathy Kelly of Louisville told a reporter, "It really needed a face lift . . . Phyllis has excellent taste. I'm glad she could bring these changes about." George Prewitt, who was described by an interviewer as living in a historic Lexington neighborhood, said the restored mansion was well worth whatever they spent on it. "It has been preserved for our children."[39]

Not everybody offered flattering remarks about the mansion. An editorial writer for the *Lexington Herald-Leader* wrote, "The $2,500,000 of tax money that went into the project has brought the public no more than a small glimpse of the comfortable little home they are providing Gov. and Mrs. John Y. Brown Jr. That small glimpse encompasses the first floor of the Mansion."[40] Another critic was mansion neighbor Margaret A. Dawson. Still angered over cutting the trees on the front lawn, Mrs. Dawson viewed the collection of fees for viewing the mansion's interior to be an affront to tax-paying citizens. She said, "After all the people of Kentucky own the building, at least nominally."

Margaret Dawson's name did not appear on the list of the 155 guests who attended the reception.[41]

Neighbors notwithstanding, it was certainly a successful evening. The 155 select guests left behind cash and commitments amounting to $20,000, to be divided between the Save the Mansion and Save the Children funds. Another reception, this time a grand ball, was held in the mansion on April 15, 1983, in the honor of Save the Mansion subscribers and the fund's staff. This fancy dress affair also proved to be a good money raiser.[42]

In late April 1983, on the eve of re-opening the governor's mansion, the Save the Mansion support group found itself approximately $100,000 in debt. The managers of the volunteer fund drive elected to conduct a nine-day showcase visitation of the mansion during the fortnight, April 17–25. A scale of fees was set: $10 for viewing the ground floor public section of the mansion. Groups of more than ten would be charged $8 each, and school bus loads of children would be charged a flat fee of $50.[43]

During the showcase interval, only the public ground floor section, the second floor family quarters, and the basement would be open. (Visitation to the family quarters and basement would cost a higher fee.) But charging to view "The People's House" stirred a tempest almost as intense as the one that rose over cutting down the trees. Eugene Stuart of Prospect, a member of the Kentucky House of Representatives's joint committee on state government, sought an attorney general's opinion on the legality of collecting fees to visit the governor's mansion. He said he had no objection to placing a basket in a highly visible spot soliciting voluntary contributions, but with profound insight into the human psyche he admitted that some people would make contributions while others would not.[44]

Other critics of the showcase fee plan also called the attorney general's office to protest the charges. Attorney General Steve Beshear responded by filing a petition for the issuance of another restraining order by Judge Williams. After hearing arguments, Judge Williams dismissed the suit and lifted his restraining order.[45]

Attorney General Beshear immediately appealed the case to the Kentucky Court of Appeals on the grounds "That we continue to believe the governor's mansion is the people's house, and that the taxpayers whose money has paid for the construction and maintenance cannot legally be charged a fee for touring their own house."[46]

A three-member panel of the Court of Appeals met in Louisville to hear the fee collection appeal. They upheld Judge Williams's decision. As usual the mist of

The first floor sun parlor was the room most dramatically changed during the renovation. Formerly the governor's office/library, the sun-filled room, decorated with antique wicker and chintz, became a casual meeting room for first families. (FCS)

Kentucky politics cast a veil over the fee collection controversy. Governor John Young Brown Jr. was quoted by Anne Pardue of the *Louisville Courier-Journal* as saying Steve Beshear's opinion was silly, and he labeled it a political ploy to bolster the attorney general's campaign to be nominated the Democratic candidate for lieutenant governor in the May primary elections.[47]

Cleared of the Frankfort emotional firestorm, and the wrangling in court, the nine-day showcase event began on the morning of April 17, 1983. A long line of willing, fee-paying citizens lined up before "their house" to pay

$10 to view its interior. The most audible complaint heard that day was that "the people" had to wait so long in line.[48] Over the nine-day period, between 14,000 and 16,000 people were said to have gone through the mansion. Some were so excited by its appearance that they chose to pay the additional fee to visit the upstairs area.[49]

The process of renovating the governor's mansion had been a long and time-consuming undertaking. No one in May 1980 could have predicted with certainty the expenditure of time and capital funds which would be required to accomplish so complete an overhaul of

Kentucky poplar is featured in the paneling and mantel of the first floor family dining room. The working fireplace adds warmth to family meals and small meetings. (FCS)

The mansion's grand ballroom ready for company. The table is appointed with the mansion's official Lenox china bearing the state seal, and a custom-designed silk tablecloth. (FCS)

The second floor great room was constructed during the renovation by combining a bedroom and sitting room. Providing the most spectacular view of the mansion formal gardens and capitol dome, this private family room includes a wet bar, dining area, entertainment center, and seating area surrounding the fireplace. (FCS)

the sixty-six-year-old structure. There, however, was one cheering note, for the basic structure of the building was as sound as the day it was built.

In April of 1983 Clayton Farmer said it had cost $708,000 just to replace the electrical and sewer systems. Overall, Farmer later estimated the cost of the renovation would be at least $3.5 million. He explained further, "We haven't exceeded what the legislators allowed us to spend."[50] Farmer's statement of the cost may have been more a presumption than a precise statement of fact. Several variable statements of the costs of reno-

vating the mansion were published. Perhaps no one, including the Department of Finance and the Kentucky state auditor, could say precisely the cost. The Save the Mansion organization alone had raised over $1 million, and the showcase yielded a considerable sum of money.

When the mansion was finally ready for reoccupation by Governor Brown and his family in April 1983, it far exceeded in grandeur the concept enunciated by former Governor Augustus Willson that the mansion furnished future governors should not be so elaborate as to put it beyond the capabilities to occupy and main-

Shades of blue decorate the second floor north guest room. (FCS)

tain it. Both the house and the furnishings he said should be the best obtainable, but at the same time suited to the lifestyles of the men usually elected to the Kentucky governorship.[51] Perhaps John Y. and Phyllis George Brown never read Governor Willson's message to the General Assembly. The restored mansion in 1983 no doubt far exceeded the usual democratic lifestyles of any past governor of the commonwealth.

Ed Ryan of the *Louisville Courier-Journal* quoted Governor Brown as saying, "I had nothing to do with it but I'm thrilled with it. I don't think there will be a more beautiful mansion [in the country]. I regret having to go out of office. I'm looking forward to living here.

It makes Cave Hill look like a guest house."[52] He told Ryan that Phyllis had worked harder in renovating the mansion than he had worked at being governor of the commonwealth.

No doubt the renovated mansion sited on the first rim of the Kentucky River Palisades would have pleased both Louis XVI and Marie Antoinette. Within the context of the plainer lifestyles and homesteads all across the commonwealth, the mansion in Frankfort was a masterful achievement in the mode of the Beaux Arts and of Kentucky politics and fiscal resources. The governor's mansion after 1983 took on the living dimension of an imperial governorship. There was a

During the Brown administration, a second floor bedroom decorated with red silk and French furniture was a guest room. During the Collins administration, it became daughter Marla's bedroom. (FCS)

far distance between the old days when the citizenry tramped in and out of the ancient palace on Clinton and High Streets and the fine new high-style mansion atop the Palisades.

In eloquent outpouring of pride and rhetoric, William Seale viewed his interior handiwork and uttered the eloquent benediction that "Phyllis George Brown's dream for Kentucky's premier house succeeded. . . . The house is now a model official residence, blending harmoniously the functions of private life in a setting delightful to the eyes and symbolic of the state's conti-

nuity of spirit through a rich flavoring of history."[53]

By this time the governor's family had grown with the birth of a son, Lincoln Tyler George, born June 17, 1980. Lincoln would be followed by Pamela Ashley, born in November 1983.[54]

On a far more mundane note, Phyllis George Brown told an Associated Press reporter that she and her family hoped to move back into the mansion on April 27, 1983, but before then they had "a lot of things to do here. We need to get sheets, towels, silverware, and all those things that make it a home."

Lincoln Brown taking a spin on his birthday tricycle in the ballroom on his third birthday, June 17, 1983. (FCS)

There was indeed a lot to be done before Phyllis George Brown's dreams of an elegant governor's mansion—and a Derby Day breakfast—could be brought into full reality. Time and destiny crowded in upon her. That moment when the crimson clad trumpeter would sound his clarion call for the running of the Kentucky Derby, May 5, 1983, was close at hand. Not only did the mansion have to be finished, polished, and displayed in all its imperial Beaux Arts glory, the entire surrounding physical domain of the commonwealth had to be drawn into service. The formal garden, the capitol, and the executive annex had to be turned into stations of high drama. On Derby Day eve the mansion was once again in its history, to become the scene of a grand ball and the next day be the center of the grandest Derby Day breakfast of all time.[55]

The logistics of arranging for the Derby Day ball and breakfast must have been fifty times greater than those of preparing Isaac Shelby's army militiamen to go away and participate in the great Battle of the Thames in the War of 1812. On the site of the Annex parking lot an 85 x 220-foot tent was raised, and on the ledge behind the mansion one measuring 60 x 120 feet went up to shelter the V.I.P. guests. Both tents were festooned with banners, balloons, and flags. Tables were covered with pastel cloths, and some heavy kitchen equipment was in place. Arrangements were made to serve 400 people in the V.I.P. tent, and only God knew how many in the Governor's tent. Approximately 8,000 invitations were sent forth.[56]

The pantry for the day was stocked with 100 country hams, 8,000 pre-cracked eggs, 150 pounds of country sausage, a generous supply of sausage patties, 8,000 biscuits, 30 bushels of apples and as many more of fresh fruits, 100 gallons of fruit juices, and 30 pounds of grits. The spokesman for the occasion told a reporter, "a small amount of grits goes a long way." All of this for yeomen guests in the big tent, who were each served a slice of ham, a pattie of sausage, scrambled eggs laced with green and red peppers and onion, a hot biscuit, and a sip of fruit juice.[57]

Across the way in the V.I.P. tent, the menu read like something directly out of the choicest restaurant, plus the more common ham, sausage, scrambled eggs, sticky buns, a variety of breads, and Derby Pie. Cooks were brought in from the state parks service kitchens, and the servers, waiters, and others were state office and Frankfort volunteers. That morning the rich and seductive aroma of frying Kentucky country ham permeated the runways of legislators, clerks, and lobbyists, killing for a moment the earthy stench of tobacco smoke. Trucks and drivers stood ready at a moment's call to hustle supply orders to the tents. Roving facilitators were equipped with newly introduced walkie-talkie phones and, like colonels in a field command, sent orders to all troop divisions.[58]

The *hoi polloi* line for the Governor's Derby Breakfast began assembling before 7:30 A.M. Soon the line had grown to such a great length that Martin Booe of the *State Journal* wrote, "nobody was quite sure where it began or ended." The wavering line snaked around the capitol to Shelby Street and back on itself somewhere near the Executive Annex Building. There was said to be at least an hour and a half wait between servings. Along the way Al Hirt, Tom T. Hall, Merle Travis, Kenny Price, the Louisville Jug Band, and the Deep

The bedroom in the mansion's master suite. (FCS)

South Cloggers from Jackson sang, danced, and played the day away. There was an array of clowns, stilts-walkers, riders of antique bicycles, and jugglers on hand to do their things. Mixed in with them were Kentucky folk craftsmen peddling their primitive wares. Karen Burham of Country Crafts Cabin was there with an exhibit, and nobody knew how many freelance hawkers and traders were on hand.[59]

The breakfast line was a godsend to the politicians on hand, some of them no doubt staring longingly into the front entrance of the mansion, and with great expectations. They passed out cards, free pencils, buttons, and hearty handshakes with prodigal generosity.

The air was filled with helium-inflated balloons, and just outside the governor's office floated a huge crimson formation of balloons. A 20 x 30-foot Kentucky flower basket quilt designed by Mrs. Melzie Wilson of Louisville and quilted by women from across the state was mounted inside the great tent.[60]

At 7:30 A.M. the flaps of the Governor's breakfast tent were pulled back and the guests moved in. When the crowd was seated there pealed forth an *a capella* rendition of Stephen Collins Foster's lilting-haunting tribute to an Uncle Tom of yesteryear, *My Old Kentucky Home, Goodnight.* There was a moment of indecision in the tent when half the audience rose to

The governor's second floor master suite study provides a private office for the governor and first lady. The two arm-chairs beside the fireplace were designed and needlepointed under the direction of Jean Ford, and have been treasured and used in many rooms of the house. (FCS)

its feet while the other half remained seated.[61]

Both the setting and menu were different in the V.I.P. tent. Their breakfast began at 10:30 A.M. Many of the invited guests that morning had attended the Beaux Arts ball the night before. Ex-President Jimmy and Rosalynn Carter headed the list, which included five governors and their wives, among them Bill and Hillary Clinton from Arkansas. A boardroom full of industrial nabobs, such as Armand Hammer, Ralph Davidson, chairman of Time-Life's board, Marvin Traub, chairman of the board of Bloomingdales, and David

Mahoney, chairman of the board of Avis, and others also attended. There was a generous representation from the world of sports and a veritable herd of radio, television, and Hollywood personalities. Martin Booe reported the comic opera incident when ex-President Carter was being greeted by well wishers. He said Carter "patiently endured the crowd's enthusiasm, even as one woman lunged at him, threw her arms around his neck and kissed him." "My, my," the former president quipped in good, shy, Georgia country boy fashion.[62]

That day it was said that Frankfort and the capitol

Olivia Newton-John visited Governor Collins's family during the 1986 Derby celebration. Pictured from left to right are Margaret Lane, Ms. Newton-John, and Dana Green. (FCS)

grounds literally crawled with Secret Service security guards. Some guests were said to have strolled about the grounds and in the formal mansion garden hoping to catch a glimpse of a celebrity, but they were rewarded with nary a shadow.[63]

The Derby party spirit raged on. That Saturday evening following the running of the great race in Louisville there was the traditional dinner party back in the governor's mansion in Frankfort. Surely late on Sunday afternoon, after the last guest had drifted away, and as public employees were folding the tents and raking up the debris left by the Saturday stampede, Phyllis George Brown must have paused to watch the lazy May sun sink behind the horizon of the western Kentucky Palisades with the realization that two big dreams had come to realization. The mansion stood in regal glory behind its formal garden, its rebirth brought about by the expenditure of a prodigious amount of talent and

energy by many Kentuckians—to say nothing of an impressive amount of money. The 1983 Derby breakfast had more than made up for those three lean years when it was held in the less regal setting of the Horse Park in Lexington.[64] Phyllis must have taken some deep satisfaction in the fact Kentuckians had not made such a social-pageantry splash even in the reception and entertainment of the revered Marquis de Lafayette. Later that month the Kentucky Heritage Commission laid its hand of blessing on the mansion restoration by presenting its highest award, the Ida Lee Willis Award for Historic Preservation, to Phyllis George Brown and the Save the Mansion, Inc., consortium.[65] Before the year was over, however, John Y. Brown would undergo quadruple bypass heart surgery and remain seriously ill for several weeks. According to Mary Tachau, "Brown emerged from his brush with death with his usual optimistic determination."[66]

CHAPTER 14

A New Breed of Tenants

The Kentucky governor's mansion in December 1983 stood in fully restored, if not imperial, glory. The mob of Derby breakfast guests was gone, the tents were hauled away, and the helium-filled balloons had drifted off to be snagged on mountainside redbud bushes. A gubernatorial administration which had promised so firmly to run state government like a business approached its end. In this moment, however, the business was in a state of coma caused by that ancient and insidious cancerous fiscal ailment called "a shortfall of revenue." Early in the spring of 1983, six faithful Democrats sought to gain possession of the keys to the governor's mansion by gaining the nomination to be the Democrat nominee for governor. No doubt they were all in Frankfort that May morning and worked the Derby breakfast line.[1] In a lackluster primary campaign the Democrats added a new chapter to Kentucky political history by electing, by a narrow margin, a woman candidate. Martha Layne Collins (1936–) sought the nomination from the office of lieutenant governor. She was a native of Bagdad, a village in outlying eastern Shelby County. Collins was not exactly a political novice when she entered the primary, having cut her political teeth as a worker in the campaign to elect Wendell Ford governor. She then was elected clerk of the Kentucky Court, and lieutenant governor on the John Young Brown ticket in 1979.[2]

A photograph pasted on the cover of the first volume of her executive journal easily documents the fact that she was the most handsome of all the Kentucky governors.[3] She came to office with good background training in the domestic sciences, and with extensive experience in the Kentucky public schoolroom. Having graduated from the University of Kentucky, she taught in the Louisville public schools while her husband,

Governor Martha Layne Collins, 1983–1987. (KHS)

William Collins, studied dentistry at the University of Louisville. When he located a dental practice in Versailles, Martha Layne taught in the schools of that town.[4]

Martha Layne Collins was a well-disciplined person who gave strict attention to details and organization. In an interview with Mary Branham of the *Georgetown*

News and Times, Governor Collins gave an insight into her personality when she said, "I'm the type person, if you say it can't be done, I'll show you."[5] First she had to show that she could defeat Harvey Sloane, ex-mayor of Louisville, in the Democratic primary, and then the popular Republican congressman Harold Rogers in the general election.[6] At the same time she had to be a mother to her son Stephen and her daughter Marla, and a wife to her dentist husband Bill.

A distinctively new chapter in the state's history opened when Martha Layne Collins became the commonwealth's first female governor. She perhaps was the first school teacher ever to hold the office, and she was certainly the first person to be both the host and hostess of the state and of the governor's mansion, making her husband, Dr. Bill Collins, the first governor's spouse to be in the anomalous position of living in the mansion but ineligible to have a portrait hung in the mansion gallery of first ladies.[7] When Governor Collins moved her family across the Kentucky River from the old mansion, she came with a seasoning of experience at being hostess and an official at the same time.

Late in December 1983, Governor Collins, her husband Bill, and their children moved into the new mansion to become its first four-year tenants after the major renovation and refurbishing. During the inaugural ceremony on December 13, 1983, Governor Collins said she knew the state and she knew its people, and that while every governor makes decisions, a good governor must have the knowledge and experience to make the right decisions.[8] She could at that moment hardly have visualized what lay ahead for her in both the mansion and the capitol. In January 1984, when she presented her first message to the General Assembly, she clearly outlined the challenges the commonwealth faced, and the decisions which would have to be made.[9]

The considerable volume of Collins administration papers now in the Kentucky State Archives reveals the fact that no other governor, except General Simon Bolivar Buckner, gave so much attention to details. As hostess in the mansion, with a trained eye for housekeeping details, she all but made a ritual of a daily inspection of the housekeeping, flower arrangements, and other matters.[10] Thus during the Collins administration the mansion was a prime site for discussions of public issues, gatherings endeavoring to find solutions to Kentucky's economic problems, and for general public use. In that first message to the General Assembly Governor Collins said, "We have . . . heard the people of Kentucky speak clearly. They want a better future for

our state." She said her budget proposal contained a demand for a degree "of educational accountability we should never have abandoned."[11] This was the nub for the future Kentucky Education Reform Act.

The new governor was well aware of the unsatisfactory standing of Kentucky in nearly every national statistical table, and she recognized a leading cause for the state's lack of consistent budget projection and fiscal management. She emphasized in her first executive message that the General Assembly could not cancel maintenance appropriations or use special accumulated funds and "one time monies" to finance emergencies. Succinctly she told legislators, "The patchwork methods and the news that another $100 million shortfall was imminent meant that further cuts could not be made without reducing the services to our people."[12] This situation made the image projected by the mansion's extravagant 1983 Derby breakfast a great incongruity.

Another penny-wise effort Martha Layne Collins encouraged was actually instituted by the General Assembly at the instigation of Governor Edward T. Breathitt.[13] She organized a chart for every meal served in the mansion and its cost. Jolene Greenwell, executive director of the Office of Historic Properties at the time, gave a graphic description of the task of keeping this record complete and up to date. The policy was adopted to halt abuses which had arisen in the past of furnishing staff and hangers-on with free meals. Even the kitchen staff was required to record the meals they consumed.[14]

Never had a governor of Kentucky come into office with a better organized plan of governmental operation than Martha Layne Collins. On December 30, 1983, she presented an extensive executive order which was a virtual reorganization of the internal operation of the state's administrative branch of government.[15] At that time the mansion stood ready to be used as an almost magic auxiliary to the planning and promotion of future social and economic programs.

A segment of Kentucky's economic future was held in the delicate balance of human decision at an important moment in 1985. For some time it had been known that the Toyota Automobile Manufacturing Company of Japan was in search of an American location to produce its Camry model automobile. Governor Martha Layne Collins, Secretary of Commerce Carroll Knicely, and others were engaged in enticing the Toyota officials to locate their Camry plant in Kentucky, even to the point of visiting Japan.[16] Later she told Eugenia Potter, editor of *Kentucky Women* that "Competition was fierce

The portrait of Kentucky's first woman governor, Martha Layne Collins, is seen as it appeared in the first lady's parlor. (FCS)

Executive Mansion
November 14, 1985

Mint Juleps

Sushi   Sashimi
Southern fried peg legs
Crabmeat stuffed pea pods
Kentucky country ham on biscuits

Chicken Bouillon Julienne
Kentucky Bibb Lettuce Salad
Poppyseed dressing
Tournedos 'a la Beef au Bernaise Sauce
Executive Potatoes
Vegetable Medley
Commonwealth Corn Pudding
Bluegrass Baked Alaska

Pouilly-Fuisse
Chateau Lartigue
Champagne Freixenet Cordon Negro

The menu for one of the most important dinners held at the executive mansion. The guests were officials of the Toyota Motor Manufacturing Company. (Lane collection)

among the nation's governors to land the plant and I was determined to get them to choose Kentucky."[17] One of the enticements which she offered was to give a full-scale elegant dinner for the Japanese Toyota officials. Over the scope of almost two centuries Kentucky governors and their wives had entertained at dinners and levees in the mansions. These ranged in style from Robert Letcher's roasted pig's head frolic to the formal post-dedication banquet given by James B. McCreary to Beula Nunn's dinner for the Republican governors. All of the earlier banquets and dinners challenged the skill and ingenuity of the mansion's kitchen and household staffs. None, however, was more challenging or

charged with more mystery than the one Martha Layne Collins held for the Toyota officials on the evening of November 14, 1985.[18]

The top Toyota officials were in the United States to make their final decision, based upon inspection findings. Despite the advice of businessmen and cabinet officials who suggested a business luncheon, Governor Collins planned a dinner menu and entertainment to appeal to oriental tastes, and belatedly, a fireworks finale. Over it all there hovered an air of secrecy and speculation about the expected guests. Aside from the food and entertainment, waiters had to be trained in the art of serving a formal meal to people of another culture—including drilling them in the act of passing hot cloths to guests before the beginning of the meal.[19]

The "hot cloth" act challenged both the laundry staff and the waiters. The "dry run" cloths (new white terry face cloths) were heated in the basement in the vegetable steamer, and the first batch upset the chef because his equipment had become permeated with the fragrance of Downy fabric softener. Finally the cloths were served heated without the softener.[20]

The Japanese visitors were coming to Frankfort from Nashville by bus, but the Tennesseans delayed the departure by more than an hour, increasing both the strain and anticipation of the mansion staff. Also, a phone call came from the governor to the governor's office staff at 4:30 P.M. requesting that arrangements be made for a fireworks demonstration. At that late hour, in Frankfort, it seemed impossible to find a fireworks company who could prepare a display on such short notice. Jolene Greenwell found such a man in Louisville whom she called "Johnnie." While Johnnie was setting his explosives, said Greenwell in a taped interview, she and Crit Luallen, the commissioner of arts, were behind the Capitol Annex digging a safety pit for him to hover in while he touched off the "bombs."[21]

Catering to the Japanese fondness for Stephen Collins Foster songs, the Bardstown Stephen Foster Singers were asked to come to the mansion to sing for the guests. They arrived and were escorted to the third floor of the mansion to dress and wait for the dramatic moment.[22] Governor Collins had made careful plans for the dinner with the assumption, she told a reporter, that it would end by 9:00 P.M. and the fireworks would be touched off, but the plan was completely thrown into disarray.[23]

Governor Collins and some of her staff knew that the Japanese had a fondness for bourbon whiskey. When the bus finally arrived and the guests were ushered into the mansion and offered drinks, to a man they asked for Wild Turkey, a bourbon distilled just up the Kentucky River in Anderson County.[24] Wild Turkey and traditional Japanese sushi represented the international flavor of the evening to come.

Once the Toyota guests were seated at the dining tables, the ritual of passing the hot cloths was performed flawlessly by waiters who had never heard of the practice. Then there was the grand procession of waiters serving Bibb lettuce salads, Kentucky beef, and other dishes prepared by Executive Chef Vincent Ashby and his staff. The *pièce de résistance* of the dinner, however, was a sparkling baked Alaska dessert. A parade of ten waiters entered the darkened ballroom, each bearing atop a silver tray a bread loaf-sized baked Alaska studded with sparklers. The effect was electrical. While the guests cheered, Mansion Director Beverly Greenwell and Margaret Lane quaked with fear that the sparklers would touch off the smoke detectors and break up the party in pandemonium.[25]

Perhaps Governor Collins and the Americans present at the dinner had not fully recognized that the Japanese were nocturnal in their social moments. When champagne bottles were popped open, a spate of toasts was offered, and toasting continued to extend the length of the dinner. Jolene Greenwell said that she, Bob Stewart, Crit Luallen, and others were seated in the mansion basement at typewriters drafting toasts for the Kentucky guests, and they could tell how effective their handiwork was by the volume of cheers that followed.[26]

The banquet and toasting dragged on far beyond Governor Collins's schedule. She had planned for the dinner to be over and the other parts of the program finished by 9:00 P.M., but it was now after 11:00 P.M. and the fireworks still hadn't been exploded. Jolene Greenwell said the Bardstown Singers waited, waited, and waited on the third floor of the mansion. Meanwhile, "Johnnie," the fireworks man, sat in his safety pit and waited the call for action. There is some inconsistency in the statements as to the approximate time the banquet was over and the guests moved out onto the mansion's portico to hear the Bardstown Singers render *My Old Kentucky Home* and other Foster songs. Then came the fireworks.[27] Governor Collins told a reporter later, "The fireworks went with great resounding noise . . . absolutely beautiful in the dark sky . . . all over Frankfort children screamed and people leapt out of bed. Some said they thought the town was being bombed."[28] The citizens of the town had gone to bed that night with the secure feeling that they faced no greater threat to their peace and security than a meeting of the Kentucky legislature.[29]

It is safe to suggest that the banquet was highly successful. It was to have repercussions on Kentucky life and economy far beyond the memory of the hot cloths, blazing baked Alaska, and the thunderous fireworks. Even in the year 2002, the social and economic effects have not fully been fathomed.[30]

The Commonwealth of Kentucky issued a certificate of incorporation to Toyota Motor Kentucky, Inc., on January 23, 1986.[31] Later Governor Martha Layne Collins and Dr. Shoichio, president of the Toyota Automobile Manufacturing Company, signed an agreement in which the Commonwealth of Kentucky would make available to the company $147 million in incentives in the form of site acquisition and preparation, construction of roads, selection and training of workers, and other services. In turn Toyota Motors Kentucky promised to build 200,000 cars a year, to spend $800 million on constructing a plant, and to employ at least 3,000 laborers.[32]

When news of the Kentucky-Toyota agreement was published, a veritable hailstorm of letters was unleashed, pro and con—the handwritten anonymous notes on scraps of paper, the lengthy and wrath-filled ones on several pages of ruled school tablet paper, and the more sophisticated ones typed and on printed letterheads. The tightly packed storage box containing all these letters is now part of the Kentucky Archives.[33] There also came a two-page letter written in bold hand addressed to "Dear Collins." The writer said, "You don't deserve Honorable in front of your name." Perhaps Governor Collins never saw this letter.[34] The office routing sheet indicates it was filed without comment. Then there was the masterpiece of scorn addressed to "Dear Mrs. Collins, I am writing this letter of complaint. I am sick of the way you are running our state. I think you are a discrase [sic] to our wonderful state!

"I hope how soon you are out of office where you can do no more damage. A VERY MAD CITIZEN."[35]

There also was that jocular cartoonist who distributed his self-admired artistic offering. The drawing showed a new model TOYLET for 1988 as produced by Toyota and Martha Layne Collins. With adolescent humor, the machine was advertised as a single holer, but two could be purchased optionally, as could all of the other accoutrements. This document also slithered into the Toyota file without official routing or comment.[36]

Then there came the sensitive letters from veterans who had served in the Pacific during World War II, all of which were treated with dignity and concern. There also came pleas from hopeful men and women who sought the governor's aid in securing jobs. For instance, one letter arrived just before Christmas 1985 from Ronnie Collins, one of the hundreds of Appalachian highlanders who had emigrated to Hamilton, Ohio. He said he needed a job and was very hard worker. "All Collins," he said, "are hard workers." He said he was raised poor but honest.[37] In essence that was what the Toyota agreement was about. The overwhelming mass of the correspondence was positive and in favor of the Toyota agreement. Governor Collins's strongest support, however, came when both houses of the Kentucky General Assembly unanimously adopted resolutions listing the budgeted expenditures involved in the $147 million incentive commitment.[38]

Governor Collins may have seen only a few of the Toyota letters, as notations on the file routing slips indicate that some of the letters were answered by Carroll Knicely, Secretary of Commerce, but almost none by the governor.[39] She did answer, personally, a letter from Betty Steven Marcum of Florence, a doting grandmother. Mrs. Marcum had sent the governor a letter about the Toyota deal written by her granddaughter. In her reply Governor Collins explained what she conceived would be the benefits derived from the Toyota enterprise, and she welcomed the receipt of any other ideas which Mrs. Marcum and her granddaughter might wish to send.[40]

The climax of the big dinner in the mansion in November 1985 did not come with the dying notes of the Stephen Foster songs and the fizzling of "Johnnie's" last firecracker. No, it came a decade later, on October 8, 1998, when Toyota Motors U.S.A. celebrated its tenth anniversary, with ex-Governor Collins as the honored guest at the Georgetown plant and at an elaborate banquet in Lexington. Charles Haywood, in an analytical article in the *Lexington Herald-Leader,* said that Kentucky had garnered $1.5 billion from the incentive investments it made in 1985.[41]

Many other issues confronted Kentucky during the Collins administration. Discussion of these matters flowed in and out of the mansion. None was more challenging than that of improving the quality of the public schools. To help promote the matter, Governor Collins formed a coalition of former governors, legislators, business leaders, civic groups, educators, sports enthusiasts, and media personnel. This consortium worked out of the mansion and the governor's office to spread information about the needs of public education

in Kentucky, garnering $3 million to support improvements.[42] The campaign, no doubt, grew out of the emphasis in Governor Collins' first budget message to the General Assembly on January 1984. In that message she told legislators that "The budget I propose . . . is an investment we must make."[43] This was a subject that in time would virtually turn the governor's mansion into a public forum–bill drafting center, culminating in 1990 with the enactment of the ponderous House Bill 940, or the Kentucky Education Reform Act.[44]

In searching through Governor Collins's papers detailing her campaign for improving education, attracting outside industries, and operating the mansion, one wonders how she had time to make speeches. One of her virtues was brevity in addressing the public. Usually she went directly to the point, said her piece, and sat down. She seldom if ever resorted to the use of traditional Kentucky jocularity or frivolity. There was one notable exception. Just barely settled down in the mansion and the governor's office, she gave a toast to the Kentucky Colonels at their May 1984 banquet in Louisville. Her toast must surely be a memorable bit of Kentucky literary fantasy. No doubt lifting a mint-stuffed silver julep cup, she said, "I give you a man dedicated to the good things of life, to the gentle, the heartfelt things. To good living, and to the kindly rites with which it is surrounded. In all the clash of a pleasant world he holds firm to his ideal . . . a gracious existence in the country of content 'where slower clocks strike happier hours.' He stands on a tall columned veranda, a hospitable glass in his hand, and he looks over the good and fertile earth, over rippling fields, over meadows of ripening bluegrass. The rounded note of a horn floats through the flagrant stillness. Afar, the shining flanks of a thoroughbred catch the bright sun. . . . Here he stands, then, in the finest sense, an epicure, a patriot, a man. Gentleman, I give you the Kentucky Colonel."[45] Surely, from somewhere in Valhalla, Augustus Owsley Stanley and Congressman Virgil Chapman doffed their broad brimmed confederate gray hats, swished their snow white frock coats, and said to each other, "The woman Governor has trumped us." Her Kentucky Colonel, however, was as difficult to present in the flesh as the location of John Swift's legendary silver mine. One can only wonder who sat at a basement room typewriter and pecked out this bit of dreamy-eyed Kentucky "doggery."

Life in the governor's mansion between 1983 and 1987 was never devoid of excitement of one tempo or another. Dr. Bill Collins, Kentucky's "First Spouse," and

The Collins piano in the mansion's ballroom. (FCS)

a cadre of "friends" joined forces to create and present the governor with a special gift. For the first time since 1914, the mansion ballroom was without a piano, as John Young and Phyllis George Brown had taken theirs back to Cave Hill when they left the mansion in December 1983. Dr. Collins turned to William Daniel (Billy) Wilson, a Lexington music teacher and owner

of Klareveda Musik, to help locate a piano maker who would create a special instrument. The objective was "to symbolically incorporate the attributes of our Governor, of the Commonwealth in a piano cabinet complimenting the Executive Mansion Ballroom and the decor."[46]

To fulfill this mission Billy and Molly Wilson went

to Germany, where they visited the Bluther Piano Fabrik in Leipzig. Later it was said they visited a maker in West Berlin.[47] Wherever the place, Wilson negotiated that the case of the instrument would be fabricated from walnut wood cut from a tree near Governor Collins's Versailles home. The trim would be made of Indian satinwood, and the overall design of the case was to be of a curvature shape. A floating panel was to bear Molly Costich's renditions of the Kentucky cardinal, a sprig of goldenrod, and the Great Seal of the Commonwealth. The crest of the Collins family was to be placed on a separate panel.[48]

Later Billy Wilson testified that Dr. Collins had presented him a check in the amount of $35,312, signed "DLJ." Wilson later said in court he did not know the signor (Donaldson, Lufken, and Jenrette, of a New York bond underwriting house). When the time came to present the piano to Governor Collins, Wilson said Dr. Collins indicated it was a gift from family members and friends. The presentation ceremony took place in the mansion's ballroom with fifty to a hundred guests present.[49]

When Governor Collins's term of office ended in December 1987, she and her family moved to a house in the Griffin Gate subdivision in Lexington, and the piano was moved there with their other furnishings. But there arose a question as to who owned the instrument, the state or Governor Collins. Cathy Conroy, spokeswoman for Donaldson, Lufken, and Jenrette, said it was gift from the bond underwriting company to the State of Kentucky.[50] In Frankfort, Jolene Greenwell, executive director of Historic Properties, said the piano was never listed among the public properties in the mansion.[51] Later Billy Wilson testified that in 1988 ex-Governor Collins called him and said that she wanted to have the piano removed from her living room. She said that "she felt bad it was just sitting and no one was playing it and that it should be utilized by good musicians." She told Wilson she had decided to present it to the University of Louisville's School of Music. Dr. Donald Swain, president of the university, said Larry Hayes, a trustee and a former secretary of the Collins Cabinet, had asked the university to accept the instrument.[52]

On February 12, 1986, Governor Collins was standing before a bank of open microphones with President Ronald Reagan when she was asked by a reporter about a tanning bed that had been purchased for the governor's mansion. She dodged the question by saying, "I think ODM, I think agriculture, I think trade agreements are

a little more important"[53] She possibly did not know precisely about the purchase of the tanning bed. A Wolfe System tanning bed had, in fact, been purchased in the summer of 1985 by the mansion's hostess-director, Beverly T. Greenwell, a cousin of the governor.[54]

Later Greenwell said she thought the idea was a good one and that she had placed the order through the Department of Parks, and it drifted through the bureaucratic slough of four or five other departments and a half dozen hands, with Lowell Clark, head of the Governor's Cabinet Office of Management Services, saying that he could not remember who asked him to purchase the bed.[55]

This incident was ready-made for exploitation by the press and media. Reporters sought and received comments from legislators, citizens "on the streets," and anyone else who wished to express an opinion on the subject. In the meantime the tanning bed apparently was sent to the morgue of gubernatorial gifts.[56] Don Lathem, manager of the general property branch of the Finance Cabinet, told reporters he would advertise the sale of the tanning bed to the highest bidder in the major daily newspapers.[57] A group of senators, headed by Michael Moloney of Fayette County, won the bid at $3,500.[58] Governor Collins said she was glad to have the tanning bed issue behind her, saying "Some people have had a lot of fun with this issue."[59] She sent a note to Gordon Duke to be transmitted to the successful bidders, saying, "Buyer beware. Overexposure to this equipment will cause severe burns. Good luck." The governor sent along, free of charge, a can of Solarcane.[60] True to Governor Collins's description, a lot of people did have fun out of the issue. For instance, Roger L. Guffy published in the *Lexington Herald-Leader* a bit of synthetic medieval doggerel entitled "A Grim but Tan Fairy Tale." He wrote, in part, "But all was not lost. A cadre of knights and other knaves led by Sir Lance-the-Lot came forth to console her. 'There, there, good Queen Mitha. We shall go out and drum up the money to buy the bed for you at an exorbitant price and we will give it back to you. That will show these plebes and remind them of their place.'"[61]

No doubt because Martha Layne Collins was Kentucky's first woman governor, she had an unusually high public profile. At moments she may have even prayed fervently that she be delivered from the embrace of "friends" and given enough leisure time to gain back her color by exposure to God's sun.

Similarly, Dr. Bill Collins's position as the gubernatorial spouse also made him the focus of press attention, often causing his governor wife some concern. Governor Collins, demonstrably at times, seemed to be disturbed by the attention the press paid her husband. Like her predecessors, she had to deal with reporters about the multiplicity of public matters, but she also had to be attentive to press coverage of her family and the mansion. Dr. Bill Collins was at best in an anomalous position, and many of his actions were open to public scrutiny. None, however, became more entangled in state affairs than the organization of Collins Investments, which had the arterial potential of soliciting and awarding state bonding contracts and commissions.[62]

A reflection of Governor Collins's sensitivity on this subject occurred on June 18, 1986, when she and a group of state officials were ready to depart Frankfort in the much-publicized Sikorsky helicopter for the remote Pulaski-Russell counties corner to dedicate the agricultural center near Jabez.[63] A *Louisville Courier-Journal* reporter asked about an investigation of Collins Investments, and in a subsequent article Mark R. Chellgren wrote that Governor Collins had replied, "There's no investigations. OK? That's a bad word."[64] This question was provoked apparently by a *Courier-Journal* statement that forty-five of the ninety-eight limited partners of Collins Investments had received state contracts or appointments to boards and commissions. The governor informed the reporters that later she would answer questions about what had happened in Kentucky since May that year.

She did hold a press conference on December 11, 1986, in which she discussed her achievements during the past three years. She assured reporters that she was going to work until "the last day I walk out of here." She said her three main thrusts as governor were education, bringing the Toyota plant to Kentucky along with other industries, and the creation of 2,000 new jobs, and $250 million in new capital.[65] Admittedly this was an integral part of the history of the governorship, but it was also a part of the associative history of the mansion.

For Governor Collins, a devoted mother, one of the happiest moments was the wedding of her son to Mary Diane Spalding of New Haven. At the time Stephen was an entering student in the University of Kentucky Law School, and Diane was a teacher. This was the first marriage of a governor's child to be performed in the new mansion.

A thousand guests were invited to attend the Collins-Spalding wedding. The front facade and portico of the mansion were decorated with floral groupings, the for-

From left to right, Governor Martha Layne Collins, Dr. Bill Collins, daughter Marla, son Steve, and daughter-in-law Diane enjoying a rare private moment on the mansion's flagstone terrace with Riley, beloved Jinx's successor. (FCS)

mal garden was neatly trimmed and in full bloom, a reception tent was mounted behind the mansion, and the temperature approached ninety degrees. A paper-adorned aisle lined with bouquets of pink roses led from the capitol to the marriage altar. Just before 2:00 P.M. on June 16, 1984, the Lexington Philharmonic Quintet struck up Henry Purcell's *Trumpet Voluntary*. At that moment seven bridesmaids, along with Marla Collins and the maid of honor, marched along the aisle. They were met on the front terrace by eight groomsmen and Dr. Bill Collins, who acted as his son's best man. Stephen Collins joined his bride, who wore a flowing white gown and two-tiered veil, at the altar in front of the mansion's front entry steps. Governor Collins sat with her parents, Everett and Mary Hall, on the right

Steve and Diane Spalding Collins in the mansion's formal gardens after their marriage ceremony in June 1984. (FCS)

side of the main aisle, and the bride's mother, Josephine Spalding, sat on the opposite side. The Catholic marriage ceremony was abbreviated, much to the relief of the sweltering guests lined up on the west terrace of the garden. Among the special guests were Senator Wendell Ford, Congressman Larry Hopkins, ex-Governors A.B. Chandler and Louie B. Nunn, Louisville Mayor Harvey Sloane, and Terry McBrayer.[66]

Immediately after Stephen and Diane had exchanged wedding vows, the fountain below the terrace sprang into action. Then the couple walked down the central walkway in an impressive photographic setting. At the end of the ceremony, guests were invited to the reception tent. Jacqueline Duke said, "The guests lined up in a sweltering tent for sandwiches, tarts, and champagne."[67] Strangely, the *Louisville Courier-Journal* seems to have

A 1987 transition photo taken in the governor's reception room as retiring Governor Collins's family welcomed that of incoming Governor Wallace Wilkinson. Left to right, Glenn Wilkinson, Marla Collins, Dr. Bill Collins, Governor Collins, Governor-elect Wilkinson, Mrs. Wilkinson, Andrew Wilkinson, Diane Collins, and Steve Collins. (KHS)

taken no notice of the Collins wedding in its Kentucky edition, but did publish a photograph of the newly married couple along with a descriptive caption in its Indiana edition.[68]

On a lesser public scale was an emotional incident surrounding the Collins's dog, Jinx. Like many other governor's families, the Collins brought to the mansion a beloved dog. Jinx had some kind of psychological quirk causing her to dislike people wearing uniforms. One day in 1984, she pursued the mailman so furiously that she dropped dead with a heart attack. Her body was prepared by the Hall-Taylor Funeral Home staff, encased in a child's casket, and placed in the mansion's laundry room. Unfortunately, no one told the laundress

it was there, and when she came to work the next morning and found the casket she became somewhat emotional and refused to attend to her duties while the casket was in residence. The mansion staff finally arranged for a burial on the ledge out back of the mansion, during which they solemnly passed by the casket in the grave and dropped flowers on it.

After the burial, Margaret Lane, a member of the mansion's administrative team, realized that someone was forever digging in the area, and someday they would find the casket and set afloat one more legend about the governor's mansion. Bureaucratic procedures were begun to have a 5 x 6-inch plaque cast to mark the grave. It was to bear the inscription, "Jinx, Beloved dog of the

Governor Wallace G. Wilkinson, 1987–1991. (KHS)

Martha Wilkinson, first lady from 1987 until 1991. (FCS)

Collins Family, 1984." The files indicate an aluminum plate would cost $59.92, while a bronze one would cost $76.54. Margaret opted for the aluminum one, but it was never placed on the dog's grave.[69] At some future date a public archeologist performing a pre-construction dig may uncover the remains of Jinx and set in motion the spinning of another executive mystery.

Surely as the Collins administration ticked to an end on the afternoon of December 8, 1987, while her successor droned on with promises of things to be accomplished, Martha Layne Collins looked across the way to the mansion with mixed emotions. There she and members of her family had laid on a fresh patina of legends, and of errors and frustrations. She surely realized that the web of history is seamless, and that the unfolding of future events was but the pattern of the whole of events being printed indelibly upon the tapestry of passing time, and writ boldly in the imperishable chronicle of human actions.

The course of Kentucky gubernatorial politics took a right angle turn in both the primary and general elections in 1987. A new face came on the scene when Wallace Glenn Wilkinson (1941–), a Lexington bookstore owner, banker, farmer, coal operator, real estate dealer, and political novice with the backing of former Governor Albert B. Chandler entered the Democratic primary and defeated former Governor John Young Brown Jr. and Lieutenant Governor and former state Attorney General Stephen Beshear.[70]

Wilkinson had experienced phenomenal success in the college textbook field, in banking, and in real estate. He had begun his business career as a shoeshine boy and popcorn salesman in the rural Casey County seat of Liberty. In Lexington he had built a national school textbook enterprise up from a humble curbside stand hawking popular paperbacks.

In his race for the Kentucky governorship, Wallace Wilkinson established a new benchmark in spending.

In October that year he told a *Lexington Herald-Leader* reporter that his personal income in 1986 was $1.6 million after taxes, and that he had just signed a $3 million radio-television contract to publicize his campaign. In addition, he said, his supporters had raised an additional $6.5 million. Wilkinson would ultimately spend several times over the combined amount spent by Beshear and John Harper.[71]

True to traditional Kentucky political campaigning form, the 1987 campaign was peppered with personal innuendos, moanings over Kentucky's chronic fiscal malaise and cringingly low educational standards, and promotion of the legalization of a state-operated lottery as an instrument for painlessly raising educational revenue. In person, Wallace Wilkinson was a diligent campaigner; almost like the legendary Greek Aerial he was everywhere. During October, he dashed across the commonwealth, making five or six speeches a day, with some of the engagements being as far apart as Ashland and Paducah.[72] Fortunately, he was better equipped to travel than the mule-riding Owsley A. Stanley. He personally owned airplanes and a helicopter. Like Stanley and Morrow of old, Wilkinson established quick name and face recognition with Kentucky voters.

By self-description, Wallace G. Wilkinson sprang from a modest social and economic background in Casey County. His parents made their livelihoods as dealers in seasonal produce and modest merchandising. He was married to Martha Stafford, also of Casey County, a lady of both ambition and high energy. Together Martha and Wallace formed a close personal unity in marriage, business, and politics. They shared lofty ambitions. For Wallace Wilkinson, as for many of his gubernatorial predecessors, the path leading up to the portals of the governor's mansion was strewn with trials and tribulations. This he no doubt learned even before his campaign was underway.

A most cursory glance at the social and financial conditions in the commonwealth in 1987 appears gloomy at best. Kentucky was mired in debt, its revenue program was archaic, its educational standing was nearly the worst in the nation, and every public and social service shared the same tousled bed.[73]

In his mad dashes around the state in the closing weeks of the election campaign, Wallace Wilkinson surely must have perceived that Kentucky had too many courthouses and too many "Little Kingdoms" held in grip by too many tight political rings. There were too many poor roads wallowing prayerfully in mud and dust in supplication for a modern reincarnation. Thus

Wallace and Martha Wilkinson and their sons, Glenn and Andrew, arrived in the governor's mansion lugging ample baggage of promised reforms, quick riches for fortunate lottery players, and a sunny future for the commonwealth. Glenn and Andrew Wilkinson were at an impressionable age. Like governors' children before them, they were inevitably exposed to the public gaze, and criticism of the actions of their father.[74] In a post-governorship soul-searching, Wallace Wilkinson wrote in his book that for both himself and his family living in the governor's mansion was a learning experience, but he said he and Martha were too busily occupied with public matters to spend the necessary time with their sons.[75]

Like Ida Lee Willis, Charlann Carroll, and other first ladies in the past, Governor Martha Layne Collins invited her successor to visit the mansion prior to the inauguration to get themselves partially oriented to its general plan and decor. Since Governor Collins and her family were the first four-year occupants of the house following its full renovation, the mansion still sparkled with a rich glow of "newness." The Collins family had given the mansion dedicated care, leaving behind them little evidence of wear and tear, despite the fact that the public areas had experienced heavy visitations.

Years later in a taped interview, both Wallace and Martha Wilkinson were lavish in their praise of the internal beauty of the mansion's decor, and the fact that the entire house, inside and out, had been brought into conformity with its early twentieth-century Beaux Arts style and history. Wallace Wilkinson expressed appreciation for Phyllis George Brown's success in bringing the mansion's form and decor into harmony with its originally intended style.[76]

Few governors were ever so vocal in their expression of admiration for the mansion, or for its symbolic meaning to Kentuckians. When the Wilkinson family moved into the house, Wallace said in an interview that they almost had no need for change or repair, except the minor renewal of some wallpaper. The same was true with the outside grounds and the formal gardens.[77]

The Wilkinsons, however, did make changes and extensive purchases. During the first fiscal year of 1988 they were reported to have spent $40,000 on the mansion—at a time when the state was experiencing stringent fiscal shortages. They were reported to have spent $11,753 on silverware for the state dining room. Comparable sums were spent on new furniture, on refurbishing original pieces, on carpeting, and on the installation of new equipment, as well as $1,278 for video and stereo equipment. The picture framing bill was $1,100, and $1,220 was spent on water purification equipment.[78]

When Tom Loftus, a *Louisville Courier-Journal* reporter, inquired of Douglas Alexander, Wilkinson's press secretary, information about comparable costs with other administrations and their expenditures on the mansion, he was given no figures.[79] The Mansion Committee over the years has recorded little actual information about such expenditures and there is little if any material information on the subject in the Kentucky State Auditors' reports, and almost none in legislative records. (Apparently the mansion has been considered in large measure as being well outside the pale of the state's more mundane spending and accounting systems.) Whatever the cost in 1988, the state dining room and other areas of the mansion glowed brightly with the new china and silverware bearing the Kentucky state seal. This latter feature greatly impressed other state governors and their wives when they attended a governors convention in Frankfort.[80]

For a shoe-shining, popcorn-selling country boy, Wallace Wilkinson was highly perceptive of the mansion's furnishings. He said when he and his family moved in he quickly sensed something was missing. That "something" was the massive silver service from the decommissioned battleship *Kentucky*. When that ship was removed from service, the Department of the Navy had loaned the sixty-seven piece service to the commonwealth. At some time in the immediate past, possibly when the mansion was being refurbished, the fragile silver service had been transferred to the care of the Kentucky Historical Society, for display.[81]

Governor Wilkinson ordered that the Kentucky's silver service be returned to the mansion, an order that stirred a controversy. Robert Kinnaird, director of the Historical Society, refused to honor the governor's order. In turn, Governor Wilkinson instructed Adjutant General Michael Davidson to recover the service and return it to the mansion. General Davidson, in stiff military jargonese, ordered Mr. Kinnaird to have the silverware packed and ready. "I'm coming over for it, and I am prepared to come in a tank."[82] Regrettably for the folklorists, the silverware was returned across the Kentucky River in a more conventional cartage vehicle than a Sherman Tank. There it remained until it was returned to the Historical Society by Governor Brereton Jones, in preparation for its permanent display in the new Kentucky History Center. Either happily or unhappily, Kentucky history was denied the colorful anecdote of a

tank clanking up the east Frankfort Hill to the Kentucky Military Museum to snatch the long-forgotten battleship's serving silverware from the trembling hands of an embattled museum curator. Not even rugged old Governor Thomas Metcalfe and his legendary intoxicated crew of "brigands" could have dreamed up this Gilbert and Sullivan–style caper.

Shining through the mist of administrative and military bombast over silver plate was the more tangible fact that both Wallace and Martha Wilkinson, in after years, spoke in almost reverential tones of their residency in the governor's mansion. They followed tradition and opened the first floor areas to public access on Tuesdays and Thursdays. In his taped interview with Margaret Lane, Governor Wilkinson said that at other times he personally had admitted visitors to the mansion "to come in and look around."[83]

Few other governors used the mansion more heavily for administrative purposes than did Wallace Wilkinson. In fact, it became a functional adjunct to the governor's office in the capitol.[84] During his administration, a plethora of issues flowed into Frankfort, issues of public need which could not be left unconsidered. Among these were revision of the constitution, the creation of a more efficient revenue system, making plans for a lottery, the complete reorganization of the state's public school system, which had been declared unconstitutional by the Kentucky Supreme Court, and attracting to Kentucky both capital and industry to bolster a sagging economy.[85]

Governor John Young Brown Jr. had in large measure encouraged a surge of independence for the General Assembly members. This left future governors in a new administrative and political situation.[86]

In both an oral interview and his post-administrative book, Governor Wilkinson indicated that he utilized the mansion for one-on-one personal conversations, and for group discussion and the planning of a galaxy of public plans and issues. Like Governor Bert T. Combs before him, Wilkinson utilized the state dining room to productive advantage in dealing with legislators, and special interest groups gathered there for the discussion of public matters and even the planning of legislation and the resolution of issues. In fact, the mansion seems to have become a virtual forum and caucus site.[87]

Unlike most of his predecessors, Wallace Wilkinson seems to have made little or no use of the basement "war room" or gathering place. He said it lacked light and other qualities that help establish successful direct personal communications. The first and second floor

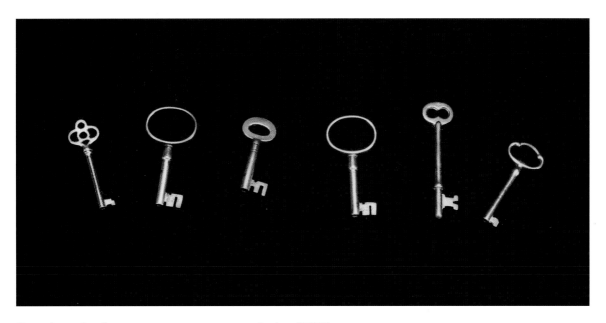

Brass keys for the many antique mansion locks. (FCS)

A modern executive place setting featuring Lenox china and antique sterling accessories. (FCS)

A spectacular epergne designed in 1900 for the battleship *Kentucky*. Complete with removable center sterling vase and candelabra, this showpiece resided in the mansion along with other items from the sixty-seven-piece collection for several administrations. (FCS)

rooms, including the special office space, were much more amenable places. It was in these areas of the public floor, for instance, that much of the analyzing and preparation of House Bill 940, the Kentucky Education Reform Act, was drafted. The public area of the mansion seems to have been highly adaptable to the Wilkinson style of administration.[88]

Living in the mansion for Wallace and Martha Wilkinson, however, surely provided many social adventures. In their taped interview with Margaret Lane they described a Halloween party in which they had draped the mansion in somber shades, turned the lights low, and produced a resident witch to startle, if not frighten, their youthful callers. They estimated that approximately 3,000 children came to the mansion dressed in every conceivable kind of costume. The governor and his wife stood out front passing out gifts of candy until 9:00 P.M. In the interview Wallace was almost ecstatic in describing the expression on the children's faces.[89] There also were the celebrations of at least two Christmases in

which the mansion was decorated inside and out and the holiday spirit ran high. At one of the Derby breakfasts Governor Wilkinson requested the presence of a state military drill team to give the occasion a formal military flavor.[90] The tone of their interview gave the house the aura of an imperial palace.

Wallace G. Wilkinson is the only Kentucky governor known to have produced a book. In his book, *You Can't Do That, Governor!* (one of the most reflective titles of any book relating to Kentucky), he reviewed his early life and experiences, and gave a somewhat disjointed explanation of the actions and events which colored his four-year occupation of the mansion and the governor's office. He seems to have become almost as much a messenger to historians of the future as to his contemporary friends and political foes. In a highly personal mode he wrote, as many other occupants of the governor's mansion and capitol office might have written, about the "fishbowl" and more private moments of life in "The People's House." Looking back, he wrote

The mansion grounds, draped with white after a February 1988 snowstorm. (FCS)

in a mixed note of sentimental nostalgia of his and Martha's disrupted relationship with their teenage sons, a situation created by the official and social demands of public office.[91] Life in an area of high-voltage public exposure created stresses and distractions from the press and from public eyes, a perpetual gaze which can be eloquently illustrated by what may be an apocryphal story: when a woman was caught peering through the mansion's window at the activities of the Wilkinson family, she justified her actions by declaring that she was a taxpayer and was privileged to see what was going on.

There was another kind of prying, that of newspaper and media reporters. Governor Wilkinson appeared in public action—and in the text of his book—to have regarded many reporters as the misbegotten sons of Ananias. He seems to have believed that many news media reporters were unfaithful minions of the fourth estate, and were as much entrenched in their interests and views as any hired lobbyist who padded the well-worn floor of "lobster alley" in the legislative office building and capitol. His administration, he wrote, could not have been an easier target.[92]

Despite stones and arrows from the press and media, Wilkinson wrote that the Kentucky governorship was "The best job in the world," but he tempered this superlative with the observation that "Some days you

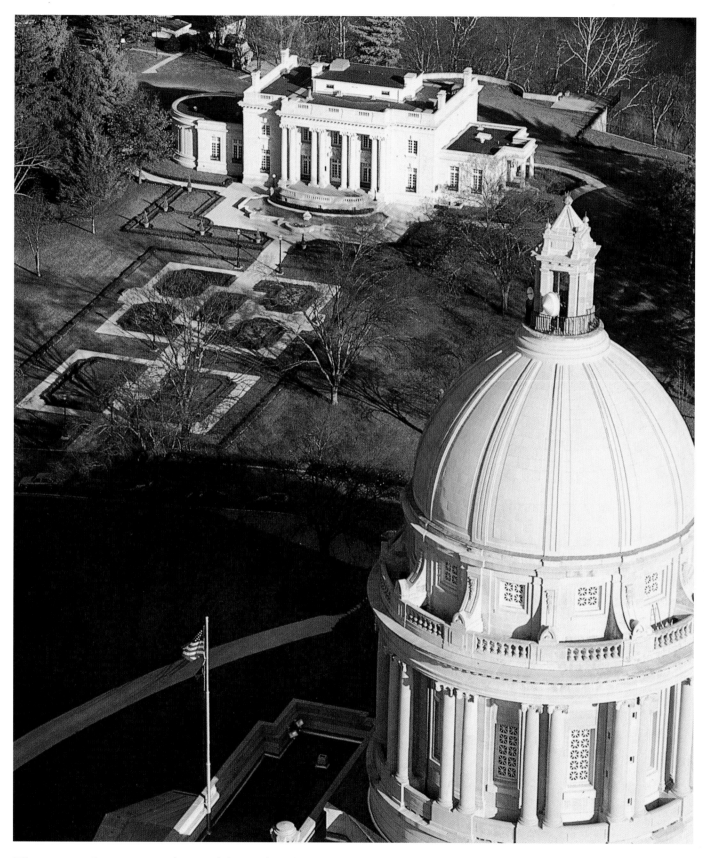

The governor's mansion and capitol dome. (FCS)

Governor Brereton Chandler Jones, 1991–1995. (KHS)

ought just stay in bed."[93] That certain unpredictability no doubt has for more than two centuries been one of the candles which has drawn the political "moths" to the flame of fame, of misguided hopes and ambitions, and, always, to the flickering torch of historical assessment, no matter how much fine china and silverware rested in the cupboard, or thick piled rugs lay beneath administrative treading feet.

The Kentucky gubernatorial election of 1987 had brought into office for governor and lieutenant governor disparate political personalities. Wallace Wilkinson, as indicated, was a self-made businessman, and his lieutenant governor, Brereton Jones (1939–), was a bluegrass tobacco and horse farmer. The latter grew up in West Virginia, was a Virginian by education, and was a former Republican member of the West Virginia General Assembly. In some measure his subsequent election to the Kentucky governorship renewed a historical-political legacy of Virginians holding high office in Kentucky.[94]

Following a modern precedent, the new Lieutenant Governor Jones and his family drove the short distance down the Leestown Pike to take up residency in the old governor's mansion on Clinton and High Streets. The old house had only recently, phoenix-like, shaken off the ashes of time, neglect, and decay to assume a new life of simple hospitality.[95] In the move, the Jones family entered into a distinctly new way of social and political life.

Brereton Jones was married to Elizabeth (Libby) Lloyd. In a way she was born and reared almost within the shadow of the capitol's dome. Her father, Dr. Arthur Y. Lloyd, had served as a professor of history and political science at Morehead State University, in various state public service offices, as Kentucky's Adjutant General, and as a member of the Kentucky Legislative Research Commission.[96] Thus his daughter, Libby, became first lady of the old mansion already well oriented in the ways of Frankfort social and political life.

It was from the old mansion that Brereton Jones cast his campaign for the governorship in 1991. In that year Kentucky still faced most of the challenges which prevailed in the era of the Wilkinson campaign, and Jones added a major emphasis on public health reforms. One reads his later executive messages wondering if he fully comprehended the depth of the state's fiscal deficiency. The gubernatorial campaign of 1991 set two possible historical records. The Republican candidate, Congressman Larry Hopkins of Lexington, ran an almost entirely negative campaign in which he attacked his Democrat opponent on two particular issues—Jones's borrowing $1 million and the continuation of welfare. Nevertheless, Jones's margin of victory was 245,000, which the *Lexington Herald-Leader* said was "the largest margin in modern history." The election also set a modern record of low voter participation. Only 44 percent of registered voters went to the polls.[97]

The interval between the election in November and the inauguration the second week of December was short. Margaret Lane, executive director of the old mansion, organized the Joneses' transfer to the new mansion, a transfer which perhaps was not the most pleasant to make because of philosophical and administrative differences between the two men.[98]

Nevertheless, Wallace Wilkinson, following tradition, left a note of welcome in the governor's office. Across the way, he and Martha left the governor's mansion in a condition comparable to that at the time of the Brown renovation.[99]

There had been remarkably little evident wear and

A Steinway grand piano, courtesy of the Gist Piano Company, is a focal point in the ballroom during the Jones administration. (FCS)

tear during the past eight years, despite the fact that visitations and public use of the mansion had increased since the renovation. Like most of the previous governors' families, Brereton and Libby Jones became full-time residents of the mansion, in sharp contrast to their occupancy of the old one. They moved in with their two young children, Lucy and Bret. Like the children of former governors, the Jones children had to make adjustments in their individual ways. Lucy, said her mother, found it more challenging than did her brother. Bret found living in the mansion an exciting adventure. He made friends with the state troopers and participated in many of their activities.[100]

Like many of the previous gubernatorial wives, Libby Jones became involved in numerous public activities. She was actively interested in the preservation of the

Kentucky land and environment, the preservation of historic buildings and landmarks, and in the routine ceremonial activities centered in the mansion. At the same time she was concerned with the lives and welfare of her two young children. On one occasion, when she was involved in a demanding schedule of conferences and public discussions, her daughter discovered a kitten that had become lodged in a mansion window well, starved and emaciated. Rearranging her official schedule, Libby remained in the mansion with Lucy, helping her administer to the needs of the kitten and to carry the animal to the veterinarian's office.

One of the most serious challenges that Libby Jones faced as the mansion's hostess was that of keeping household expenses at the lowest possible level. Brereton Jones came to the governorship when the

Governor Brereton Jones, daughter Lucy, son Bret, and first lady Libby Jones shown during their last holiday at the governor's mansion. (FCS)

commonwealth was bogged down by $400 million of debt, and as a result the cost of operating the mansion had to be reduced by a large percentage. This meant the employment of only a minimal household staff (no longer were penitentiary convicts employed as servants) and the curtailing of weekend mansion activities.[101] The custom of using convicts as household servants had been discontinued during the Brown administration.

Had there been a desire to make any changes in the decor of the mansion, there were insufficient funds to pay for them. This fact, however, did not limit the rather heavy usage of the public rooms and the inflow of state guests. Merv Griffin and Eva Gabor were among the latter who enlivened the mansion parties, and various arts and culture groups used the mansion to display their art and musical talents during regularly

scheduled Arts Evenings. Throughout the year there came an almost continuous procession of tens of thousands of school children and tourists from all over the world wanting to see where the governor lived. Following the tradition of most former governors, the Joneses observed regularly scheduled tour hours, during which guides from the office of Historic Properties greeted visitors and offered a view of the public first floor. The official mansion tour text was always at hand, printed in six languages.[102]

At a mansion birthday party for former First Lady Phyllis George Brown there was much hilarity stimulated by Griffin and Gabor. In the elegant interior environment which Phyllis George Brown had spent so freely to create, former Governor John Young Brown Jr. stood up and said Phyllis had made him a millionaire,

The mansion's elegant grand staircase is especially glittering when dressed in seasonal finery, and crowned by the family's great room holiday tree. (FCS)

and that before he married her he had been a *multi-millionaire*.[103]

Security was relaxed and unobtrusive during the Jones occupation of the mansion. In a taped interview Governor Jones said he felt free and unthreatened. Frequently at the end of his day at the capitol, he went alone to his Airdrie Stud farm to work with his horses. On one occasion he drove to Versailles to buy a pair of blue jeans at K-Mart. A stalwart yeoman approached him and asked if he were not the governor. When Governor Jones assured him he was, the man replied, "By-damn, I admire a governor who can be a normal guy!"[104] On another occasion, when a formal reception was in progress, a strange woman dressed informally in western-style clothing entered the reception hall. Governor Jones approached her and inquired who she was. She told him that she saw people coming into the mansion and followed them to look around. He invited her to make herself at home.[105]

During the Jones administration both the old and new mansions were used as planning centers. It was in the two houses that the governor formulated one of the most ambitious programs, that of improving the legal structure of public health administration. This was a far-reaching program which proposed to make revolutionary changes in the way Kentucky administered its health services. This effort met with only limited success, as Governor Jones said later in a retrospective interview, because too much was undertaken in too short a time.[106]

More positive were the plans initiated earlier by Governors Collins and Wilkinson to celebrate Kentucky's bicentennial year. Governor Collins's bicentennial commission held meetings in the governor's mansion on one or two occasions, and on the state's bicentennial date, June 1, 1992, the mansion became, along with the capitol, a center for major celebratory activities. It was on that day that the University Press of Kentucky

Culminating several years of planning, Kentucky's Bicentennial Commission gathered at the mansion in celebration of Kentucky's Statehood day on June 1, 1992. (FCS)

published and sold out of most of the first edition of the landmark *Kentucky Encyclopedia*, a fact which added substance to the reception in the mansion on the eve of Kentucky's bicentennial anniversary.[107]

Aside from the bicentennial celebration, plans were already underway, first in the old mansion, and then in the new, for the building of a modern history center. Libby Jones became deeply involved in the projection of the idea and in planning the center. She personally conducted legislative visit to view the Historical Society's ill-suited storage spaces in the discontinued Ancient Age Distillery barrel aging buildings and to acquaint them with the urgent need for more responsible care of the state's historical artifacts.[108] The visit, followed by light breakfasts in the state dining room, surely had a definite influence in the procurement of an appropriation to finance the construction of the

modern $30 million Kentucky History Center.

There were other strands of Kentucky social and political history running through the mansion and the governor's capitol office. In 1981, Governor John Young Brown Jr. sold an assortment of airplanes purchased by the Carroll administration and used the funds to buy a luxurious Sikorsky helicopter at a cost of $1.8 million. The helicopter was said to be the ultimate in aircraft safety. The purchase was made at a time when Kentucky's social services and educational system were suffering under a stifling fiscal stringency. Ed Ryan of the *Louisville Courier-Journal* peppered Governor Brown with taunts to sell the aircraft. In fact, he published a running count of the days that it remained unsold. The governor resisted the taunting and left the office, the mansion, and the helicopter behind.[109] Governor Wilkinson then used the machine, despite the fact he

The mansion ballroom awaiting a 1992 Derby celebration, complete with bronze equine sculptures and mint julep kits. (Lane collection)

had made a campaign promise to sell it and use his own helicopter. Finally, Brereton Jones fell heir to it and, like his predecessors, used the helicopter to collapse time and distance in his traveling about Kentucky. The *Courier-Journal* said, "The Governors valued the political mileage to be had from selling the aircraft as much as he or she valued the $1.9 million machine itself."[110]

The running ink battle over the Sikorsky and all its luxury appointments came to a sudden and fearful end in a Shelby County treetop at 11:45 A.M. on August 8, 1992. Governor Jones, three officials, and two pilots were headed for a speaking engagement at Fort Knox. Hardly out of sight of the National Guard airport in Frankfort, the craft dropped a tail rotor blade. Skillfully, if not miraculously, the ex-Vietnam pilots shut off the ignition and fuel, and landed the craft in a tree. The

wrecked craft fell to the ground, spilling its passengers. Fortunately Adjutant General Robert DeZarn was able to call the Frankfort air station on his cellular phone and report the faltering craft.[111]

When news of the helicopter disaster was relayed to the security officer at the mansion, Libby Jones was across the way in her capitol cubbyhole office. The mansion state trooper called and in a curt message said, "Mrs. Jones, I think you should return to the mansion." Back at the mansion, she heard the news of the helicopter crash, but there was no specific information as to the place of the accident. She set out with a mansion patrolman, driving along Interstate Highway 64 and Highway 60. Close to the village of Graefenburg, they spotted a Kentucky National Guard Black Hawk helicopter lowering in its flight. The patrolman crossed

The ill-fated Sikorsky after it crashed on August 8, 1992. (Kentucky State Police)

the highway median near the scene, and Libby Jones jumped from the car, climbed over a wire fence, and ran through the brush in high heel shoes.[112]

The scene which greeted Libby was graphically described to news reporters by Sam Dill, a bulldozer operator who was working nearby. He told reporters, "I walked down here and saw those five [*sic*] bodies sitting on this bank over here. I just couldn't believe it . . . to be quite honest with you, I didn't know it was the Governor, he kinder looked different lying there on the ground than when he does on the news." That was a prime understatement. Governor Jones suffered from severe neck and back pain and was forced to lie down, uncertain as to whether or not there were fractures. Several of his companions were more seriously injured. Both General DeZarn and one of the pilots had sus-

tained multiple bone fractures.[113] Press Secretary Bill Griffin, one of the helicopter's passengers, later expressed a bit of poetical wit about the experience:

Heli-Crash

We went up & we came down
And prayed away our fright
And proved two laws which are renown
God is great & Newton right.

The helicopter incident turned the governor's mansion into a convalescent retreat, and the house was flooded with flowers sent by sympathetic constituents. In a taped interview, Governor Jones said that in his convalescence he stopped feeling sorry for himself and adopted fresh perspectives on the office of governor.

243

A private terrace in the mansion's back yard surrounded by summer plantings. (FCS)

He, however, was to suffer a second serious accident which would give him more time to contemplate the trials and tribulations of being the chief executive of a state in time of local, national, and world changes.[114]

Airdrie Stud was close by the governor's mansion, and no doubt tugged at his heart. He wanted to be on his land, and in his stables. On one occasion while exercising what turned out to be a fractious horse, a saddle girt came loose and the governor was thrown to the ground and trampled. Thus there was even more convalescent time to contemplate the challenges of the governor's office, and how well he had met them.[115] He had reduced the state's indebtedness and created a surplus of funds. As for life in the mansion, the Jones family had come to feel comfortable with its routine, its ever changing affairs, and its ambience.

There came, however, that moment when its door would be opened to receive new tenants, a fact symbolized by the delivery at the rear entryway of another official hostess's clothing and personal belongings to be deposited in the second floor living quarters. The inevitable time had arrived for Brereton, Libby, and the Jones children to drive back up Old Frankfort Pike, over the road which they had traveled eight years before, this time with a full chapter of domestic and political history in their sentimental baggage. Behind them they left a mansion staff for whom they had great affection. In his taped interview it is difficult to tell which Governor Jones regretted leaving the most, the unfinished business of the governor's office or the heavenly lemon pies prepared in Executive Chef Ree Wilson's kitchen by the beloved sous chef, Fatemeh Salehi.[116]

The mansion's back lawn area has been redesigned many times, but this private flagstone terrace sheltered by shade trees has remained a favorite family refuge. (FCS)

CHAPTER 15

"Respect It, Revere It, Use It"

Electoral history in Kentucky came full circle in the twilight of the twentieth century. Paul Patton, a Pike County Democrat, like James Garrard two centuries earlier, held office astride a two-century dividing line. He had been elevated to the governorship at the end of roily primary and general election campaigns and came to the office in the moment when Kentucky voters approved an amendment to their constitution permitting a sitting governor to seek election to a second and consecutive term in office.[1] In this seminal era of constitutional change, the electoral contests for the offices of governor and lieutenant governor were heated. Amidst it all the old and new governor's mansions stood as complacent as the gentle summer current in the Kentucky River between them. In the Patton-Forgy contest, however, life in the lieutenant governor's mansion at times became as vigorous as a "high tide" fishnet in the river.[2]

By the very turns in electoral campaign history, the 1995 Kentucky governor's race will stand out in terms of strategy and voter complacency. In the May Democrat primary that year, Paul Patton jousted with a slate of five "wannabe" gubernatorial opponents. Even a casual analysis of the voting pattern in that election eloquently reflects the waywardness of Kentucky voters. Only 500,787 out of 1,424,592 registered Democrats went near the voting booths. By the same token, only 479,257 Republicans turned out to vote for Larry Forgy and Tom Handy.[3] Combined, only 44.4 percent of the voters had a hand in choosing a governor. Four years later, under the proviso of the amended succession article of the constitution, Paul Patton (1937–) in the Democrat primary of 1999 defeated four opponents, and in the general election in November defeated only token Republican opposition by 362,099 to 228,565

Governor Paul E. Patton, 1995–1999, 1999–2003. (KHS)

votes. That year the secretary of state reported there were 2,660,113 registered voters, but only 20 percent voted.[4] By that date Paul and Judi Patton were firmly established as tenants in the new mansion, where they would stay for a period of eight consecutive years, or twelve years in both houses.

There is no doubt that a basic time flaw exists in section 73 of the Executive Article of the Kentucky Constitution. This section was revised and ratified on November 2, 1992, and contains the provision that the in-coming governor and lieutenant governor be sworn into office on the fifth Tuesday after the general election. For an inexperienced governor coming into office after a vigorous campaign, the interval is too short for the organization of a basic framework for an administration.[5]

During the interval between the 1995 election and inauguration, Paul Patton made maximum use of the old mansion in organizing his administration. He said in a taped interview that he and his aides used every available space, even placing desks in closets and the pantry. So frantic was the effort to have in place heads of cabinets that when the list of choices was submitted to the governor-elect, he discovered it contained the names of several Republicans, including that of the wife of Larry Forgy's key manager.[6]

Looking back after six years in office, Governor Patton, with a mixture of amazement and humor, said that he had hardly been able to form even a skeleton administration before his inauguration. Despite the fact a lieutenant governor takes office at the same time, that official seems to learn little about the complexities of the office of governor.[7] The incoming governor takes the oath of office at midnight on the date of the administrative transition. The formal oath-taking in the inaugural ceremony is only pro forma in nature. Patton took the first oath in the old mansion, and the second one in the new.[8]

Three days before the end of his term, Governor Brereton Jones and his wife, Libby, offered to vacate the mansion so the Pattons could move in and get partially settled before the inaugural ceremony and ball. Literally, the Joneses were moving out the back service door and the Pattons were moving in the front.[9] In both cases the process was lightened by the Office of Historic Properties. As the Pattons moved into the mansion, they had the prospect of remaining there for eight years of consecutive occupancy. When James and Elizabeth Garrard had ridden up the Frankfort palisade hill on their return to their Bourbon County home, they had left behind a new state constitution and a one-term consecutive limit on the governorship. For two centuries this limiting constitutional barrier had remained in effect. Governor Paul Patton and Lieutenant Governor Stephen Henry were the first since 1800 to have an opportunity to remain in office for two full consecutive terms.[10]

Judi Patton, Kentucky's first lady from 1995 through 2003. (FCS)

Paul Patton, born in Lawrence County, a graduate of the School of Engineering at the University of Kentucky, a coal mine operator, and the judge executive of Pike County for ten years, brought to the office of lieutenant governor considerable knowledge of private business management and public local government. As lieutenant governor, he was actively engaged in attracting and developing new industries in the state.[11]

Judi Patton came to Frankfort with considerable social work and political experience. Her four-year residence in the old mansion had oriented her to many of the ways of state government, and to Frankfort and its community affairs. She is the mother of two children, and stepmother to her husband's children by his first marriage.[12]

The vita of Judi Conway Patton might well be one of the more extensive of Kentucky governor's wives. She has served as a special adviser to the governor's

Gallery of first ladies of the new executive mansion. The historic photograph collection was organized by Steve Collins, son of Governor Martha Layne Collins, and has become a popular item for visitors. Mildred Chandler is seen in 1935 and again in 1955, Martha Layne Collins was governor as well as first lady, and Judi Patton appears in successive terms of 1995 and 1999. (FCS)

office on the issue of child abuse and domestic violence services, combated breast cancer among women, and spearheaded conservation through backyard wildlife efforts. She has been active in the Appalachian Regional Health Care program, the Kentucky Country Music Hall of Fame, combating of the drug menace, in the expansion of statutory laws for the protection of abused children, and the expansion of the Kentucky Children's Advocacy Centers. Judi Patton has been the recipient of an extensive number of special awards, including ones from childcare organizations, from arts associations, and for her advocacy for assistance to women victims of sexual abuse. Specifically, she was awarded the Outstanding Leadership recognition by the commonwealth's attorneys' association, the Children First Award, and the Gold Medal Award from the Family Place in Louisville.[13]

The Pattons, like several of their predecessors, needed to move little more than their clothing and personal belongings into the mansion. They found the house in good condition with the exception of the minor repairs everlastingly associated with housekeeping. They shared with every governor and first lady since Augustus Owsley Stanley a deep-seated respect, even awe, of living in the house. But for Kentuckians there is ever-tugging at the heart a love of place. Paul and Judi Patton are not exceptions. They go back to their Pikeville home every weekend that they can, and throughout most of his allotted years in Frankfort, Governor Patton has had an almost paternal view toward his county. In an oral interview he said that one of his favorite spots to work is seated beneath an umbrella beside his Pike County swimming pool with a briefcase at his side, as his grandchildren splash in the water. In this case Governor Patton and his wife must be heavily indebted to former governor Bert Combs for the building of the Mountain (or Bert Combs) Highway from Winchester to Salyersville.[14]

Family members and invited guests have come and gone in the mansion. At least one visitor, however, was not pleased with it. The Patton's five-year-old grandchild told her grandmother that she did not like the place because it had no swimming pool.[15] Judi Patton might have taken the child out on the back patio and pointed down the cliff and told her that her grandfather had one of the longest swimming holes in Kentucky. In 1912, neither Governor James B. McCreary nor his Sinking Fund Committee even considered a swimming pool as a necessary household facility.

Perhaps the most distinguished visitors to spend time

in the mansion during the Patton occupancy were Vice President Al and Tipper Gore. They came accompanied by a corps of secret service men almost the size of Generalissimo Rafael Leónidas Trujillo Molina's army when he was a guest in the mansion during the Chandler administration. The mansion's security staff was small and almost invisible by comparison.[16]

Occasionally an individual wandered into the Patton mansion on public occasions as an unthreatening or unoffending visitor. Early in his residency in the mansion, Governor Patton went downstairs and saw a strange man walking about. He assumed he was a member of the household staff and engaged him in conversation, much to the consternation of the state police troopers. Even in an age when the security of public officials, schoolrooms, and commercial institutions is subject to violent and murderous attacks, there has been no act of threatened violence or invasion against the governor's mansion. The crowds that have passed through the public rooms of the house either as guests to public affairs or as tourists have been remarkably well behaved and civil.

Paul and Judi Patton have observed if not expanded the mansion's role as the people's house. Patterned after the Arts Evenings held by Governor Brereton and Libby Jones, the Evening at the Governor's Mansion program has met with great success. When David Hawpe, editor of the *Louisville Courier-Journal,* suggested to Governor Patton that the public areas of the mansion should be a place to showcase the arts, crafts, cultural, and literary talents of Kentucky, Governor Patton responded by opening the public areas, parlors, state dining room, and ballroom four times a year to artists, musicians, craftsmen, writers, and special groups of talented Kentuckians. Through an arrangement between Governor Patton and Virginia Fox, director of Kentucky Educational Television, the four talent affairs in the mansion are given wide publicity throughout the commonwealth. Thus far these occasions have seemed to fulfill David Hawpe's belief that the mansion could be used as a showplace for the latent talents of a host of Kentuckians.[17]

Historically, the mansion has been available to groups with social, public, and cultural interests. The ballroom especially has been the frequent scene of gatherings. For example, the Henry Clay Foundation has used the ballroom to solicit support for Ashland and to make its annual award of the Clay Medallion to an individual of state or national importance. There is a modest charge for use of the public rooms of the mansion, which recovers the costs associated with the events and pro-

Resplendent in all seasons, the mansion landscape is especially colorful when native Kentucky shrubs and trees, such as this pink flowering magnolia, bloom in spring. (FCS)

vides an endowment to purchase permanent improvements for the house. The Pattons have purchased a concert grand piano,[18] continuing the saga of the mansion and the piano since the days of James Garrard and Goodman's home-built instrument, and the specially built German instrument presented to Governor Martha Layne Collins.

Since that time in 1983 when the refurbished mansion was opened to visitors upon the payment of a modest fee, there have come on the appointed visitation days an almost continuous procession of school and tour busses dumping thousands of visitors into the public areas of the mansion. For the most part, the visitors have been orderly, if not awed by the elegant symbolic aura of the house.[19] But like every governor's family since 1798 and the occupation of the first mansion, the Pattons have had to deal with the matter of the compulsive souvenir grabbers. To meet this problem, trays filled with a piece of confection and wrapped in a miniature sheet of paper bearing a picture of the mansion are placed strategically about the public rooms, and dining room napkins and hand towels in the restroom bear an impressive imprint of the seal of the commonwealth.[20]

Like many hostesses of the mansion preceding her, Judi Patton is showered with correspondence bearing friendly greetings or requests for favors. There come the never-ending requests for something from the mansion to be auctioned in fundraising drives. She responds to these requests by sending a framed picture of the mansion. Inherent in these requests is actually an incipient desire to think of the mansion as a palace shrouded in a mist of romance. Almost annually the Derby Day breakfasts have documented this fact. In a taped interview, Governor Patton expressed the view that he enjoys these events in which Kentuckians and visitors from without the state are gathered in an open, neighborly occasion and the public rooms of the mansion are opened to visitation.[21]

For Judi Patton the post–Derby Day Monday, when the tents are still in place, has a far more human meaning. More or less without publicity she has invited women victims of cancer to come and spend a day in an uninhibited, friendly environment to exchange discussions of their experiences. Present on this post-Derby Monday are women who have been withdrawn and reluctant to reveal or discuss their experiences with cancer. For some of them the mansion ground gathering is, in fact, a "coming out" event. Some have been inspired to cast off their wigs revealing the temporary ravages of radiation therapy.[22]

As temporary tenants, previous governors used (or failed to use) the mansion as an auxiliary center of their administrations. Governor Patton said in an interview, like Louie B. Nunn before him, that he has made only limited use of the house for administrative or political purposes. There, however, was one major exception, the evolving issue of removing the Kentucky community college system from the control of the University of Kentucky. The questions that arose in this controversy, he said, threatened his administrative and political life with almost sudden death. He explained that at the outset he had not been deeply concerned about the administration and control of the community colleges, but advisors urged him to become involved. This drew him into a heated controversy with Dr. Charles Wethington, president of the University of Kentucky, and with some members of the institution's board of trustees.[23]

Once the community college controversy was highly publicized, the relationship between the two strong-willed and determined leaders became polarized. In time a discussion of the issue drifted into the mansion. Governor Patton invited a group of businessmen and citizen leaders to have breakfast with him in the ballroom. There he explained his position and invited discussion, and at the conclusion of the meeting the group gathered in the front entry to pose for a photograph. Doubtless the mansion breakfast and discussion had some appreciable impact on gathering support for the governor's position, and possibly on the salvation of his administration.[24] Few issues in Kentucky's long political, social, and cultural history generated such a heated controversy.

In a calmer time and less heated environment, Governor Patton, in an interview, said he practically does not involve the mansion in the administrative affairs of the state. He brings from his office in the evening a briefcase filled with papers to be read and, like every John Doe Kentuckian, eats his dinner, settles down in a favorite chair in the Great Room upstairs, reads the newspapers, watches television, and late in the evening gets to the papers in the briefcase.

The governor no longer has any direct responsibility for the upkeep and physical management of the mansion. That responsibility now rests in the hands of the Historic Properties Advisory Commission, the Division of Historic Properties, and the secretary of the Finance and Administration cabinet. At the mid-term of their second segment of mansion occupation, the Pattons have required no major refurbishing of the house or its furnishings.[25]

The state dining room is the scene of many official functions. The dining table, after the addition of several leaves, seats twenty-two guests. The sterling silver candlesticks against the wall at the back of the room belonged to Isaac Shelby's family, and the hundreds of halo lights adorning the bowed ceiling are original to the house. They were uncovered during the 1982 restoration. (FCS)

Originally installed in 1914, the hand-carved Kentucky poplar mantel in the family dining room is an example of expert Kentucky craftsmanship. (FCS)

The mansion's gardens of summer annual flowers greet hundreds of thousands of tourists each season, and provide a popular stop for photographers and their subjects. (FCS)

When Governor James Bennett McCreary and members of the Sinking Fund Commission labored over plans and construction details of the new governor's mansion in 1912, their minds were very much in the swimming hole and horse and buggy era. All the governor needed as far as they were concerned was a one-horse stable and a buggy shed. No one could have imagined Governor McCreary splashing around in a pool filled with city water. No one in Kentucky had even the remotest idea of need for an automobile parking lot. They still had their legs under them, and hitching places a-plenty.

Parking around the mansion and capitol grounds has become almost as much of a problem as getting rid of the anti-dueling oath. Space is severely limited about the mansion for more than family and security guard parking. The largely unused tennis court has been converted into a parking lot with a bank of green separating it from the side entrance of the mansion.

As spacious as the mansion and capitol grounds are, the area is constantly threatened by the creeping monster, automobiles and television station vans. The rear palisade cliff wall precludes mansion parking in that

The formal gardens in front of the mansion feature red tulips. (FCS)

area. Thus the residence stands somewhat, but gracefully so, isolated from a threat to its pleasant surroundings. There is no tennis court, and still no swimming pool to win the affection of the governor's space-age granddaughter.

In another segment of mansion history tradition, future governors and their families will come to live under its roof for longer spans of years and to spin out even more colorful incidents in a rarefied social and human environment. Who knows, there may come to one of the quarterly musical and literary evenings in the ballroom a rising genius who will give more substance to Kentucky history than some of the governors themselves. Already, a revision of the succession section of the state constitution has broken tradition, and opened the way to future variety in the way of life in

the governor's house. Potentially, as in the case of Paul and Judi Patton, some future governors and their families will come to live for so long a period of time in both the old and new mansions that they will lay permanent claim to them. In a more practical manner, the houses will not have to be refurbished every four years to placate the wishes of short-term tenants.

In an often repeated litany of sentiment and praise, governors and their wives have expressed emotional pride in having lived in the mansions, in having savored their mystique, and in having been so closely interwoven in this segment of Kentucky' political and social heritage. When Margaret Lane asked Governor Patton what advice he would offer future occupants of the mansion, he responded in the eloquent soliloquy, "Respect It, Revere It, Use It."[26]

Executive Chef Ree Wilson has served Kentucky chief executives for six administrations. Seen in the mansion's herb garden with his wife and mansion pastry chef, Judi Wilson. (FCS)

In 1993 the capitol rose garden provided beautiful specimens for Jane Alexander, landscape floral designer, to create massive flower bouquets for the mansion. (FCS)

On this crystal clear Kentucky spring day, a showcase of glorious mansion tulips adorns the formal gardens, hopefully (depending on Mother Nature's whims) lasting until Derby Day. (FCS)

The view from the mansion's second floor overlooking a dazzling spring display and the capitol dome. (FCS)

Monogrammed sterling silver serving spoons, dating to a past administration. (FCS)

A sterling silver demitasse tray featuring cups of silver and porcelain used during the Stanley administration (1915–1919). (FCS)

Even on a gray winter day, the executive mansion appears inviting, resplendent with its holiday trimmings. (FCS)

Because of its massive scale, the ballroom's live fir holiday tree is decorated with thousands of white lights and *pots* of red poinsettias. (FCS)

Notes

1. A Good and Convenient Dwelling House

1. *Kentucky Gazette*, Dec. 8, 29, 1826, March 26, April 20, June 20, 1827.

2. Littell, *Statute Laws of Kentucky*, 1: 32; *Journal of the Kentucky House of Representatives*, August 6, 1792, 22, 81 (hereafter *Kentucky House Journal*).

3. *Kentucky Gazette*, June 9, 1792.

4. Ibid.

5. Ibid.

6. Hubbard Taylor to James Madison, May 8, April 16, 1792, in *Papers of James Madison*, Hutcheson and Rachel, eds., 14: 218–19.

7. *Kentucky Gazette*, June 23, 1792.

8. There is little evidence that Isaac and Susannah Shelby were in Frankfort for any intervals of time between 1792 and 1796.

9. "Report of the Special Committee on the Subject of the Removal of the Seat of Government from the City of Frankfort," *Legislative Document No. 7*, 1867, 7–9; *Acts of the Kentucky General Assembly*, December 18, 1792, 27 (hereafter *Kentucky Acts*).

10. Ibid.

11. *Kentucky Acts* (1792), 27–28.

12. Marshall, *History of Kentucky*, 2: 6.

13. Elihu Barker, "Kentucky," Map 3 (1794–1795), and John Melish, "Kentucky," Map 5 (1806–1807), in Clark, *Historic Maps of Kentucky*, 68–70, 71–72.

14. John Bradford, "Notes on Kentucky," *Kentucky Gazette*, November 7, 14, 1828.

15. By general computation he had at his disposal about $1,500. *Kentucky Auditor's Report* (1792), 9.

16. *Kentucky Acts* (1795), 94.

17. Ibid. (1796), 7; *Kentucky Auditor's Report* (1792), 55.

18. *Frankfort TriWeekly Yeoman*, August 3, 1883; Darnell, *Filling in the Chinks*, 37.

19. "Susannah Hart Shelby," *Register of the Kentucky Historical Society* 1 (1903): 51 (hereafter *Register*).

20. Everman's *Governor James Garrard* is a full biography of Garrard. The colonel was a man of many parts, most of all a landed baron. See his extensive entries in Brookes-Smith, *Master Index*, 13, and the Kentucky Historical Society's *Index for Old Kentucky Surveys and Grants*, 60.

21. Jenny Chinn Morton, ed., "James Garrard, Governor," *Register* 1 (1903): 61. This account is surely in error. There was no wheeled vehicle in Kentucky prior to 1787 unless it was a crude homemade wagon. No doubt Elizabeth Garrard needed a coach because she was almost constantly pregnant. Everman, *Governor James Garrard*, 6.

22. Marshall, *History of Kentucky*, 2: 5–12.

23. *Frankfort TriWeekly Yeoman*, August 2, 1873; Everman, *Governor James Garrard*, 4–6.

24. *Kentucky Acts* (1795), 94; (1796), 7.

25. Ibid. (1796).

26. Ibid.

27. No documentary plan for the house exists. There may have been no more than a general drawing of the style of Virginian Georgian houses beginning to be erected in Kentucky towns and farmsteads at the time. *Kentucky Acts* (1796).

28. Evans, Documentary Data on the Old Mansion, vol. 3.

29. Thomas Metcalfe was born March 20, 1789. See William C. Mallalieu, "Thomas Metcalfe," *Dictionary of American Biography*, 12: 384, and Robert C. Cotterill, "Robert Letcher," *Dictionary of American Biography*, 11: 193.

30. Kentucky Acts (1796), 7.

31. John Bradford, "Notes on Kentucky," *Kentucky Gazette*, October 12, November 30, 1827, December 4, 1828.

32. Warfield, *The Kentucky Resolutions of 1798, passim*; John Bradford, "Notes on Kentucky," *Kentucky Gazette*, November 7, 1828; Sneed, *Decisions of the Court of Appeals of Kentucky, passim*; *Kentucky Acts* (1798–1806), *passim*.

33. Littell, *Statute Laws of Kentucky*, 1: 263.

34. James Garrard, "Message to the General Assembly," *Kentucky Acts* (1794), 253–64.

35. Ibid., 26.

36. James Garrard, Executive Journals, 1796–1804, KDLA; Littell, *Statute Laws of Kentucky*, 1: 357.

37. Everman, *Governor James Garrard*, 37–40; "The Mistresses of the Executive Mansion," *Louisville Courier-Journal*, March 24, 1901.

38. Everman, *Governor James Garrard*, 4–7.

39. Auditor's Journal, 1798–1900, gives a listing of palace expenditures. See also the unprocessed documents, "Treasurers Book, 1792–1799," Kentucky Department for Libraries and Archives, (hereafter KDLA) 107: 330–35. According to Property

Tax Rolls of Frankfort, 1797, KDLA, Garrard had a carriage and a wagon.

40. In December 1798, the General Assembly authorized a final payment for the palace of 1,389 pounds, and asked for public bids for a special service. *Kentucky Acts* (1798), 168. Thirty-one counties were created during Garrard's two terms as governor. Collins, *History of Kentucky*, 2: 26.

41. Brown, "An Address on the Occasion of the Century in the Town of Frankfort," October 6, 1886.

42. Darnell, *Filling in the Chinks*, 26.

43. "The Mistresses of the Executive Mansion," *Louisville Courier-Journal*, March 24, 1901. Many years later, another floor covering caused a stir when Governor A.B. Chandler accused Governor Lawrence Wetherby of paying $29,999 for a rug in the governor's office. Governor Chandler knowingly added a digit to the cost. Edward Farris pasted the bill on the office wall when Wetherby vacated the office to incoming Chandler.

44. Brown, "An Address on the Occasion of the Century in the Town of Frankfort," 48–49.

45. Darnell, *Filling in the Chinks*, 26.

46. Clark, ed., *Footloose in Jacksonian America*, 11, 17.

47. Collins, *History of Kentucky*, 2: 303–4; E. Merton Coulter, "Christopher Greenup," *Dictionary of American Biography*, 7: 589–90.

48. Cuming, *Sketches of a Tour to the Western Country through the States of Ohio and Kentucky*, 169–73.

2. Sheltering Kentucky's Warrior Governors

1. Hopkins, "Christopher Greenup," in Harrison, ed., *Kentucky's Governors, 1792–1985*, 11–14.

2. Cuming, *Sketches of a Tour to the Western Country through the States of Ohio and Kentucky*, 169–73.

3. Collins, *History of Kentucky*, 1: 25.

4. Connelley and Coulter, *History of Kentucky*, 1: 433–56; Clark, *Clark County*, 313–15.

5. Butler, *History of the Commonwealth of Kentucky*, 316–17; Collins, *History of Kentucky*, 1: 96; Alexander Leitch, "Aaron Burr," *Dictionary of American Biography*, 3: 313–14.

6. Samuel M. Wilson, "Charles Scott," *Dictionary of American Biography*, 16: 487; Collins, *History of Kentucky*, 1: 706–7.

7. Burnley, "Governor Charles Scott," *Register* 1 (1903): 11; Wilson, "Charles Scott," *Dictionary of American Biography*, 16: 487.

8. Burnley, "Governor Charles Scott," 12; Wilson, "Charles Scott," 16: 487.

9. Levine, *Lawyers and Lawmakers of Kentucky*, 581.

10. Harrison, ed., *Kentucky's Governors*, 14–17; Burnley, "Governor Charles Scott," 11–13.

11. Dawson, *Historical Narrative of the Civil and Military Services of Major General William Henry Harrison*, 273–77; *Frankfort Tri-Weekly Commonwealth*, July 1846; Collins, *History of Kentucky*, 1: 27.

12. Andrew Campbell to Governor Charles Scott, November 24, 1810, Charles Scott Papers, KDLA; J.M. White to Governor Charles Scott, April 15, 1809, Charles Scott Papers, KDLA.

13. The estate, Canewood, was established by Nathaniel Gist. See Clark, *Clark County, Kentucky*, 310–13. Also, Brookes-Smith, comp. *Master Index*, 75.

14. Brookes-Smith, comp., *Master Index*, 188.

15. Dawson, *Historical Narrative of the Civil and Military Services of General William Henry Harrison*, 273–77.

16. Ibid.

17. *Kentucky Gazette*, March 5, May 18, September 15, 1812.

18. Remini, *Henry Clay, Statesman for the Union*, 80–89.

19. Pratt, *Expansionist of 1812*, 40–61.

20. "The Governor's Mansion," *Register* 2 (1904): 35.

21. Dorman, "Gabriel Slaughter, 1767–1820, Governor of Kentucky 1816–1820"; Orlando Brown, "The Governors of Kentucky," *Register* 49: 215–24; Hopkins, "Gabriel Slaughter," in Lowell Harrison, ed., *Kentucky's Governors, 1782–1985*, 19–23.

22. *Kentucky Auditor's Report* (1812–1815).

23. Frankfort in 1812 had a population of approximately 1,100 (*Third Census of the United States*, 1810). In 1800 it was said to have had a population of 628 persons with 140 houses, 2 printeries, 1 bank, and 1 bookstore. The town was said to be improving, and building was taking place. Cramer, *Navigator*, 1919, 231.

24. Collins, *History of Kentucky*, 1: 27.

25. Ibid.

26. *Kentucky Gazette*, September 22, November 17, 1812; Collins, *History of Kentucky*, 2: 345.

27. *Kentucky Gazette*, March 7, July 28, September 1, 1812; Julius W. Pratt, "William Hull," *Dictionary of American Biography*, 9: 263–66; *Kentucky House Journal* (1814), 16.

28. Milo M. Quaife, "River Raisin Massacre," *Dictionary of American History*, 4: 2.

29. "Resolution," *Kentucky Acts* (1812), 109; *Kentucky Gazette*, August 3, 1813.

30. Clift, *Remember the Raisin*, 54–55; McAfee, *History of the Late War in the Western Country*, 219–56.

31. Collins, *History of Kentucky* 1: 27. "Isaac Shelby to Judges of the Court of Appeal," *Kentucky Gazette*, December 8, 1813.

32. *Kentucky Acts* (1813): 201.

33. *Kentucky House Journal*, (1813), 14–15; *Kentucky Gazette*, December 18, 1813.

34. *Kentucky Acts* (1812): 322.

35. It was a miracle that the governors and their families did not perish from dysentery and typhoid fever.

36. Kentucky Acts (1815), 522.

37. *Kentucky Senate Journal* (1816), "Report of the Lancaster Committee," 103–4, 152–55.

38. *Kentucky Acts* (1813): 2.

39. James F. Hopkins, "George Madison," in Lowell Harrison, ed., *Kentucky's Governors, 1792–1985*, 19–20; Collins, *History of Kentucky*, 1: 28.

40. *Kentucky Senate Journal* (1816), 153–55.

41. Ibid.

42. Ibid.

43. *Kentucky Acts* (1817), 167–68.

44. Consistently this mode of address appears in both the *Journals* of the Kentucky Senate and House of Representatives.

45. *Kentucky Senate Journal* (1815), 103–4; Clark, *A History of Kentucky*, 140–57.

46. *Kentucky Auditor's Report* (1818).

47. *Kentucky Acts* (1820), 27.

48. Adair, *Letters of Generals Adair and General Jackson, relative to the Charge of Cowardice made by the latter against Kentucky Troops at New Orleans.*

49. Ibid.

50. *Kentucky Acts* (1817–1819), 978–92.

51. Van Burkleo, "Green v. Biddle," in Kleber, ed., *The Kentucky Encyclopedia*, 390.

52. *Kentucky Acts* (1820), 272–73.

53. Clark, "*Blair v Williams*," in Kleber, *The Kentucky Encyclopedia*, 860.

54. Collins, *History of Kentucky*, 1: 31; *Kentucky Acts*, "Resolution" (1824), 213; *Kentucky Reporter*, November 8, 1824.

55. Bussey, "Joseph Desha," in Lowell Harrison, ed., *Kentucky's Governors, 1792–1985*, 20–28; Collins, *History of Kentucky*, 1: 131.

56. Johnson, *Famous Kentucky Tragedies and Trials*, 35–38.

57. Ibid.

58. *Argus of Western America*, January 15, 1825; *Niles Weekly Register*, July 30, 1824, 4: 330.

59. Johnson, *Famous Kentucky Tragedies and Trials*, 38–40; *Argus of Western America*, January 19, 1825; *Niles Weekly Register*, October 1, 1825, 14: 79.

60. Johnson, *Famous Kentucky Tragedies and Trials*, 40.

61. Joseph Desha, Executive Journal, KDLA, June 18, 1827, 4–11.

62. "Resolution," *Kentucky Acts* (1825), 242–79.

63. Ibid. (1824), 44–58.

64. John D. Wright Jr., "Horace Holley," in John Kleber, ed., *The Kentucky Encyclopedia*, 436.

65. Wright, *Transylvania: Tutor to the West*, 378–79.

66. Bamburg, ed., *The Confessions of Jereboam O. Beauchamp who was executed at Frankfort, Ky. On the 7th of July 1826, for the murder of Col Solomon P. Sharp*, 20.

67. Chivers, *Conrad and Eudora*; Simms, *The Kentucky Tragedy*; Warren, *World Enough and Time*; Levine, *Lawyers and Lawmakers of Kentucky*, 112–14.

68. "Resolution," *Kentucky Acts* (1824), 215–17.

69. Levasseur, *Lafayette in America in 1824–1825, or Journal of a Voyage to the United States*, 2: 101–84.

70. Ibid., 166–69.

71. Ibid.

72. Ibid.

73. Ibid.

74. Ibid.

75. Ibid.

76. Ibid.

77. Ibid.

78. Ibid.

79. *Blair v Williams*, 14 Kentucky (1823): 1–8; Sandra F. Burkelo, "Old Court–New Court Controversy," in John Kleber, ed., *The Kentucky Encyclopedia*, 693–94; Thomas Metcalfe, Executive Journal, Metcalfe Papers, KDLA, September 28, 1828.

80. Desha's papers, Governors Papers files, KDLA.

81. Joseph Desha, Executive Journal, KDLA, September 2, 1828, 34.

82. Ibid., September 2, 1828, 35.

83. *Frankfort Argus of Western America*, September 18, 1828; *Kentucky Reporter*, December 10, 1828.

84. Margaretta Brown to Orlando Brown, 1829, in Trabue, *Corner in Celebrities*, 1922.

85. General Lafayette visited Weisiger's Tavern and Liberty Hall, but not the capitol, which lay in ruins, or the governor's palace. Levasseur, *Lafayette in America in 1824–1825, or Journal of a Voyage to the United States*, 166–69.

3. A Mansion in the Maelstrom of Politics and Tragedy

1. The heated debate over the imported goods tariff, with a threat of nullification by South Carolina ("Resolution," *Kentucky Acts*, [1810], 282) and the Maysville Road Bill, and the presidential veto of said bill, all created a furor in Kentucky (*Louisville Daily Journal*, December 10, 1830). The question of Kentucky's free access to shipping and portage on the Mississippi River also became an issue. *Kentucky Acts* (1830), 284–300.

2. Thomas Metcalfe was an anomaly in Kentucky politics in that he was not strongly affiliated with the Adams-Clay party, and certainly not with the Jacksonians. His messages were clear and forthright. He created an editorial-legislative storm when he vetoed a resolution of a partisan Jacksonian legislature to have a cannon salute fired on January 8th. See *Frankfort Argus*, February 16, 1831; *Louisville Daily Journal*, December 10, 1830.

3. Collins, *History of Kentucky*, 2: 628.

4. W.C. Mallalieu, "Thomas Metcalfe," *Dictionary of American Biography*, 12: 584–85; "Governor Thomas E. Metcalfe," *Register* 55 (1957): 196–213.

5. *Kentucky Reporter*, April 28, 1827.

6. Ibid.

7. Ibid. September 3, 1828.

8. In spite of the political vitrol, rumors, and editorials of the times, both Joseph Desha and Thomas Metcalfe observed a certain degree of decorum. J.J. Marshall and J.J. Crittenden went to the governor's mansion to call on Governor Desha. Metcalfe presented a certificate that he had taken the oath of office. Ibid., September 10, 1828.

9. *Argus of Western America*, September 10, 1828.

10. "The Mistresses of the Kentucky Executive Mansion," *Louisville Courier-Journal*, March 24, 1901.

11. Ibid.

12. Thomas Metcalfe, Executive Journal and Blotter, KDLA, 1828–1830, *passim*.

13. Ibid.

14. Peers, *Report on the Status of Education in Kentucky to the Legislature and Governor in 1830 and 1831*, assorted tables; Collins, *History of Kentucky*, 1: 36, 2: 248–51; "Governor's Message to General Assembly," *Kentucky Senate Journal* (1830), 15.

15. Metcalfe, Executive Journal and Blotter, KDLA, 1828–1830, *passim*.

16. Ibid., December 2, 1828; *Kentucky Senate Journal* (1828): 15.

17. *Argus of Western America*, December 10, 1828; *Kentucky Acts* (1828), 229. Governor's Message, *Kentucky Senate Journal* (1828), 12.

18. J. Horley Nichols, "Maysville Veto," *Dictionary of American Biography*, 3: 362; "Governor's Message," *Kentucky Senate Journal* (1831) 9–10, (1832), 15.

19. After 1819, the number of steamboats on Kentucky streams increased phenomenally. Governor Metcalfe was alert to this fact. See "Governor's Message," *Kentucky Senate Journal* (1829), 10–11.

20. For the Lexington and Ohio Railroad charter, see *Kentucky Acts* (1830), 126–33.

21. "Governor's Message," *Kentucky Senate Journal* (1829), 115.

22. *Kentucky Acts* (1830), 272–80.

23. "Governor's Message," *Kentucky Senate Journal* (1829), 11–15.

24. "Governor's Message," *Kentucky Senate Journal* (1832), 11–13; *Kentucky House Journal* (1832), 145–50; "Resolution," *Kentucky Acts*, 1832, 301–16.

25. Slavery was a rising major incident in Kentucky history in the years between 1828 and 1832. See *Kentucky House Journal* (1828), 80, (1830), 173–75; *Kentucky Acts* (1830), 173–75, (1833), 258–61.

26. The law of 1802 provided for lashings on bare backs or hanging. Littell, *Statute Laws of Kentucky*, 3: 116–17.

27. Thomas Metcalfe, Executive Journal, KDLA, Dec. 8, 1829. In some way in the moral and political stirrings over the conditions in the penitentiary, the anti-slave importation discussion, and the general tone of society, the harsh penalties assessed against slaves were lessened. Blacks were sentenced to terms in the penitentiary sometime before 1842. In that year there were nine blacks and mulattoes out of 162 prisoners. Sneed, *A Report of the History and Code of Management of the Kentucky Penitentiary*, 273; *Kentucky House Journal* (1831), 213.

4. A House Grown Weary with Usage and Change

1. Collins, *History of Kentucky*, 2: 37.

2. John Breathitt, "Message to the Kentucky General Assembly," *Kentucky House Journal* (1833), 230.

3. John Breathitt, Executive Journal, 1832–1834, KDLA, 29.

4. Ibid.

5. Sneed, *A Report of the History and Code of Management of the Kentucky Penitentiary*, 193–94.

6. Breathitt, "Commencement of a Journal from Kentucky to the State of Pennsylvania, etc., March 25th, 1805," *Register* 52 (1954), 5–24.

7. *Kentucky Acts* (1834), 322; Collins, *History of Kentucky*, 1: 39.

8. Connelley and Coulter, *History of Kentucky*, 4: 1074; Levin, *Lawyers and Lawmakers of Kentucky*, Collins, *History of Kentucky*, 2: 437; *Kentucky House Journal* (1934), 323.

9. Morehead, "An Address in Commemoration of the First Settlement of Kentucky. Delivered at Boonesboro the 25th of May 1845," in Collins, *History of Kentucky*, 2: 602; Coleman, *A Bibliography of Kentucky History*, 434.

10. *Blair v Williams*, 14 Kentucky (1823): 34.

11. Kentucky Acts (1823): 476.

12. *Biographical Directory of the United States Congress, 1777–1989*.

13. Jennie Chinn Morton, "Governor James Clark," *Register* 2 (1904): 11–12.

14. The Clark family lived in a spacious georgian-type residence on a knoll amidst a broad lawn in Winchester. The house has been restored and is now a community center.

15. Evans, *Kentucky's First Ladies in Miniature*, item #14.

16. Train wrecks were so commonplace on the Lexington and Ohio Railroad that they hardly became news. The road was completed to Frankfort in January 1834, and a steam locomotive was introduced in 1833. See Clark, "The Lexington and Ohio Railroad—A Pioneer Venture," *Register* 31 (1932), 9–28.

17. Collins, *History of Kentucky*, 1: 40; Morton, "Governor James Clark," *Register* 2 (1904): 9–12.

18. *Kentucky Acts* (1873), 283; *Kentucky Senate Journal* (1872), 99–100.

19. Lewis County Court Order Book F, August 5, 1836, 233; Works Progress Administration, Writers' Project file, 1938, KDLA.

20. *Kentucky House Journal* (1837), 26.

21. Ibid.; Collins, *History of Kentucky* 1: 44.

22. There is no documentation as to how such a large family was bedded down in the governor's palace unless they had a trundle bed to be shoved under every upright one.

23. Gilliam, "Robert Letcher, Whig Governor of Kentucky," 6–26.

24. Adams, *Memoirs of John Quincy Adams*, 8: 336.

25. Margaret Robinson-Robertson-Johnson was the mother of the famous Justice George Robertson. Richard H. Collins wrote, "She was a woman of exemplary character, illustrating in practical life all the christian and social virtues." She died in the Letcher home in Frankfort on June 13, 1846, in her ninety-second year. Collins, *History of Kentucky*, 2: 687.

26. Inventory of furnishings in the mansion, 1840–1845, Robert Letcher Papers, KDLA.

27. Stuart Seely Sprague, "William Owsley, 1844–1848," in Lowell Harrison, ed., *Kentucky's Governors, 1792–1985*, 51–54.

28. William Owsley, "Message to the Kentucky General Assembly," *Kentucky House Journal* (1847), 40–43; Sneed, *A Report of the History and Code of Management of the Kentucky Penitentiary*, 336–42, 390–91.

29. *Kentucky Acts* (1845), 64; *Frankfort Yeoman*, September, 1847.

30. Some craftsmen sentenced to the penitentiary did credible woodworking.

31. Owsley Brown Frazier, statement to the author, December 2000.

32. There is no record of the Delia Ann Webster pardon in the Owsley's executive journal. If there is, it is highly veiled. I searched at least three times for it. See, Randolph Paul Runyon, *Delia Webster and the Underground Railroad*, 66–67.

33. William Owsley, Executive Journal, KDLA, December 31, 1847, 41.

34. Ibid.

35. During the past half century the governor's palace was patched up and propped up. Legislative inspection committees came and went, but the General Assembly often did little or nothing. During the Owsley administration it was not necessarily a warm, hospitable place. Governor Owsley was not a social man. W.C. Mallalieu, "William Owsley," *Dictionary of American Biography*, 14, 121–23.

5. "A Straggling Old Fashioned House"

1. Certificate of Election, John Jordan Crittenden Papers, KDLA; Collins, *History of Kentucky*, 1: 57.

2. E.M. Coulter, "John Jordan Crittenden," *Dictionary of American Biography*, 4: 546–49; Kirwan, *John Jordan Crittenden*, 6–14; Coleman, *The Life of John Jordan Crittenden*, 1: 13–18.

3. *Kentucky Acts* (1821), 267–68; Coleman, *The Life of John Jordan Crittenden*, 1: 55–56.

4. Coleman, *The Life of John Jordan Crittenden*, 1: 19.

5. Kirwan, *John Jordan Crittenden, The Struggle for the Union*, 64–65, 131.

6. Trabue, *Corner in Celebrities*, 42.

7. *Frankfort Commonwealth,* February 15, 1849.

8. *The Kentucky Yeoman,* March 8, 1849.

9. Prentice, *Louisville Daily Journal,* February 15, 1849.

10. Ragan, "John Jordan Crittenden, 1787–1863," 16–17; Kirwan, *John Jordan Crittenden, The Struggle for the Union,* 236–38.

11. He may have been a guest in the governor's mansion. The *Frankfort Commonwealth* of February 15, 1849, reported that after appearing before the General Assembly, "Thence he returned to the Mansion House in an open buggy with hat off, and acknowledging with deep and uneffected signs of gratitude the fervent greetings of the thousands. . . ."

12. *Report of the Debates and Proceedings of the Convention for the Revision of the Constitution of the State of Kentucky,* 1849, 5–11.

13. *Louisville Courier-Journal,* July 12, 1850.

14. Crittenden, Executive Journal, KDLA, July 30, 1850, 278; Kirwan, *John Jordan Crittenden,* 264; Coulter, "John Jordan Crittenden," 4: 546–49.

15. More than half the entries in the Owsley and Crittenden Executive Journals, KDLA, relate to the granting of remissions of petty fines, pardons, and the appointments to minor offices.

16. John Helm and his wife, Lucinda Barbour Hardin, did little if anything of note in their tenure of the mansion from July 1850 to September 1851.

17. Hamlett, *History of Education in Kentucky,* 41–78.

18. George Yater, "Bloody Monday," in John Kleber, ed., *The Kentucky Encyclopedia,* 88–89.

19. Stowe, *Uncle Tom's Cabin, or Life Among the Lowly;* Clark, "The Slavery Background of Foster's 'My Old Kentucky Home,'" *Filson Club History Quarterly* (1936), 4–17.

20. There is a discrepancy in the record as to the number of Helm children. See, Levin, ed., *Lawyers and Lawmakers of Kentucky,* 104.

21. "The Mistresses of the Executive Mansions," *Louisville Courier-Journal,* March 24, 1901.

22. Lazarus Powell had been a widower for four years before he was elected governor. His daughter, Mary Drake Metcalfe, served most of the Powell occupancy almost under duress. Levin, *Lawyers and Lawmakers of Kentucky,* 357–60.

23. *Biographical Directory of the United States Congress, 1777–1989,* 1029.

24. The mansion's interior was cosmetically refurbished in 1859. *Kentucky House Journal* (1859), Special Report, Documents 1–30.

25. Yater, "Bloody Monday," in John Kleber, ed., *The Kentucky Encyclopedia,* 88–89.

26. "Governor's Message," *Kentucky Senate Journal* (1855), 15.

27. *Frankfort Commonwealth,* August 31, 1859.

28. Ibid.

29. Ibid.

30. "Auditor's Report," Doc. 130, in *Kentucky House Journal* (1860), 946–58.

31. Ibid.

32. Ibid.

33. Ibid.

34. Mitlebeiler, "The Great Absconsion."

35. *Kentucky House Journal* (1860), Documents 1–30.

36. *Kentucky House Journal* (1859), 485, 786, (1859), 97.

37. Ibid., (1859), 485.

38. Ibid., 730; (1860), 97

39. Mary Homer to William Homer, October 26, 1859; "A

Traveler" to Beriah Magoffin, October 1859; Lawrence Thatcher to John Brown, October 22, 1860, all in Magoffin Papers, KDLA. These letters in the Magoffin file give every evidence of being originals.

40. Thatcher to Brown, October 22, 1860.

41. *Kentucky House Journal* (1861), 903.

42. *Kentucky Senate Journal* (1862), 203, 208.

43. Ibid., 199, 623–25.

44. Morton, "Governor James Robinson," *Register* 2 (1904), 61–62.

45. Ibid.

46. *Frankfort Tri-Weekly Commonwealth,* September 1862.

47. Charles Hinds, "Gov. Hawes Inaugurated Here During the Civil War in 1862," *State Journal,* September 10, 1962.

48. *Frankfort Tri-Weekly Commonwealth,* November 2, 1862.

6. Adopting a New Lifestyle in the Palace

1. Sprague, "Civil War," in John Kleber, *ed., The Kentucky Encyclopedia,* 192–94.

2. Harrison, "Thomas Elliott Bramlette," in John Kleber, ed., *The Kentucky Encyclopedia,* 112–13.

3. Ibid.

4. *Kentucky House Journal* (1865), 358; "Report of capitol location committee," *Kentucky House Journal,* February 7, 1865, 37. "Donald Price's resolution to remove the capitol to Lexington," *Kentucky House Journal,* February 16, 1871, 402.

5. *Kentucky Acts* (1864), 67.

6. This no doubt was a limited capacity plant installed inside the penitentiary walls to supply that institution in 1848–1849. William G. Sneed, *A Report of the History and Mode of Management of the Kentucky Penitentiary,* 449. Perhaps the governor's mansion was served from this plant. If it was, this was an early introduction of gas to Frankfort.

7. The Kentucky House of Representatives asked the Senate to initiate the act, but in the end it was defeated. *Kentucky Senate Journal* (1864), 397.

8. Harrison, "Thomas Elliott Bramlette," in John Kleber, ed., *The Kentucky Encyclopedia,* 112–13.

9. Dew, "Stephen Gano Burbridge," in John Kleber, ed., *The Kentucky Encyclopedia,* 142.

10. Ibid.

11. Ibid.

12. Bramlette papers, KDLA.

13. Ibid.

14. "Resolution on the Death of Daniel Clark," *Kentucky Acts* (February 28, 1872), 99–100.

15. Coulter, "John White Stevenson," *Dictionary of American Biography,* 17: 133–34; Owen, "John White Stevenson, 1812–1886," in Lowell Harrison, ed., *Kentucky's Governors, 1792–1985,* 814.

16. Morton, "Kentucky Governors," *Register* 2 (1904): 39; *Lexington Herald,* September 27, 1914.

17. *Kentucky House Journal* (1865), 358; "Report of Capitol Location Committee," *Kentucky House Journal,* February 7, 1865, 37.

18. Governor John White Stevenson, "Message to the Kentucky General Assembly," *Kentucky Senate Journal* (1869), 414–15.

19. The law provided space for the governor's office outside the mansion. *Kentucky Senate Journal* (1868), 13.

20. John White Stevenson, "Message to the Kentucky General Assembly," *Kentucky Senate Journal* (1869), 13.

21. Ibid., (1869), 19.

22. The issue of the permanence of the Kentucky capitol was a haunting one between 1864 and 1904. On December 4, 1864, the Senate adopted a resolution asking Kentucky towns to make bids for the location of the capitol. *Senate Journal,* December 4, 1864. See also *House Journal* (1967), page 1920; "Resolution 29," *Kentucky Acts* (1864), 155.

23. Governor Thomas Bramlette asked on January 7, 1868, that state office space be expanded. *Senate Journal* (1868), 13. The General Assembly appropriated $100,000 to construct a fireproof building. *Kentucky Acts* (1869) 1: 18–20.

24. Limited gas lights were installed in the mansion on February 16, 1868. *Auditor's Report,* 1869–1870, 35.

25. "Contingent Expenses," *Auditor's Report* for the Fiscal Year 1868, Document 17, KDLA, 19–20.

26. Ibid., 19.

27. Ibid., 12–13.

28. "Robber at Governor's House," *Frankfort Commonwealth,* September 7, 1870.

29. "Contingent Expenses," *Auditor's Report* for the Fiscal Year 1868, Document 17, KDLA, 19–20.

30. John W. Stevenson resigned the governorship on February 10, 1871. *Kentucky House Journal* (1871), 360.

31. Webb, "Preston Hopkins Leslie," in Harrison, ed., *Kentucky Governors,* 84–87; Morton, "Sketch and Picture of Governor Preston H. Leslie," *Register* 5 (1907): 13–16.

32. *Louisville Courier-Journal,* September 1, 1875.

33. "Report of the Special Committee on the Removal of the Seat of Government," *Legislative Document* no. 7 (1867), 3–17, January 17, 1870, 23.

34. *Kentucky Senate Journal* (1867), 474–75.

35. Ibid., (1870), 758–59, 761–62; (1873), 616; Preston Leslie, Executive Journal, March 12, 1871, 3; *Kentucky Acts* (1869), 18–19.

36. *Kentucky House Journal* (1873), 1145–1146.

37. *Louisville Courier-Journal,* September 1, 1875.

38. *Kentucky House Journal* (1871), 1081.

39. *Kentucky Senate Journal* (1877), 850.

40. Ibid. (1878), 852–53.

41. Ibid.

42. Ibid.

43. Ibid., 853.

44. Ibid.

45. Kentucky Federation of Women's Clubs, *Kentucky's First Ladies in Miniature,* sec. 28.

46. *Louisville Courier-Journal,* September 1, 1875.

47. Ibid.

48. Morton, "The Governor's Mansion," *Register* 2 (1904), 35–45.

49. James Bennett McCreary, "Message to the Kentucky General Assembly," *Kentucky House Journal* (January 1878), 35.

50. Inventory, Executive Mansion, August 27, 1879, Auditor's unprocessed documents, KDLA.

51. "Governor's Message to the Kentucky General Assembly," *Kentucky House Journal* (1878): 35; Robert Gunn Crawford, "A History of the Kentucky Penitentiary, 1865–1937," 24, 28, 122.

52. Crawford, "A History of the Kentucky Penitentiary, 1865–1937," Ph.D. diss., University of Kentucky (1955), 24–28.

53. "Governor Luke Blackburn's Message to the Kentucky General Assembly," *Kentucky Senate Journal* (1880), 39.

54. Crawford, "A History of the Kentucky Penitentiary, 1865–1937," 24–28, 102, 122.

55. Ibid.

56. "Mistresses of the Mansion," *Louisville Courier-Journal,* March 24, 1901.

57. Luke P. Blackburn, Executive Journal (1880), 134–44, statement for granting pardons, KDLA.

58. *Louisville Courier-Journal,* undated excerpt.

59. The initial document on this subject was Document 7, "Report of the Special Committee on the Subject of the Removal of the Seat of Government," *Kentucky Senate Journal* (1867), 4–17; *Kentucky Senate Journal* (1867), 476–77; "Mistresses of the Mansion," *Louisville Courier-Journal,* March 24, 1901.

60. *Lexington Daily Transcript,* September 5, 1883.

61. Ibid.

62. "A New Era," *Lexington Herald-Leader,* September 27, 1914.

63. Mitlebeiler, "The Great Absconsion," 335–47; *Kentucky Acts* (1888), 257.

64. Proctor Knott, "Governor's Message," *Kentucky House Journal* (1884), 11.

65. Stickles, *Simon Bolivar Buckner: Borderline Knight,* 323.

66. *Louisville Courier-Journal,* August 1, 1891; Stickles, *Simon Bolivar Buckner: Borderline Knight,* 343.

67. Morton, "Governor Simon Bolivar Buckner," *Register* 2 (1904), 23.

68. George C. Harris to Stella Harris, October 11, 1890, Vertical File, Kentucky Historical Society, Frankfort.

69. "The Roosevelt Visit," Mrs. George Clark, Essay, Vertical File, Kentucky Historical Society; Clark, ed., *Travels in the New South,* 1: 493; *Lexington Herald,* August 27, 1914.

70. Johnson, *History of Franklin County,* 219–21.

71. Ellison (Mounts) Hatfield, penciled confession, Buckner Papers, KDLA; "Buckner Message to the Kentucky General Assembly," *Kentucky House Journal* (1887), 62–66; (1889), 640–46.

72. Ibid.

73. Stickles, *Simon Bolivar Buckner: Borderline Knight,* 16–17.

74. *Louisville Courier-Journal,* September 2, 1891.

75. Ibid., June 11, 1891.

76. *Lexington Leader,* May 1, 1891.

77. *Louisville Courier-Journal,* September 2, 1891.

78. Ibid.

79. Ibid. May 8, 1895.

80. Ibid.

81. Ibid.

82. John Young Brown Jr. to Cassius M. Clay Jr., July 1, 1895, in Cassius M. Clay, Jr., Papers, Special Collections, King Library, University of Kentucky.

83. *Louisville Courier-Journal,* May 1, 1895.

84. *Kentucky Auditor's Report* (1895–1896), 18–28.

85. Simon Bolivar Buckner, "Message to the Kentucky General Assembly," December 3, 1889, in *Kentucky House Journal* (1889), 14–18; William O. Bradley, *Kentucky House Journal* (1896), 46–50; (1897), 13–16.

86. William O. Bradley, "Message to the Kentucky General Assembly," *Kentucky Senate Journal* (January 5, 1898), 35.

7. Mansion Tenants of a Fading Era

1. William O. Bradley, Certificate of Election, Executive Journal, KDLA, December 10, 1895, 1.

2. *Lexington Daily Leader,* November 7–8, March 7, 1895.

3. John Young Brown Jr. to Cassius M. Clay Jr., July 1, 1895, Cassius M. Clay Jr. Papers, Special Collections, King Library, University of Kentucky.

4. *Frankfort Argus of Western America,* December 26, 1895.

5. *Lexington Daily Leader,* December 10, 1895.

6. Ibid.; *Lexington Press Transcript,* December 11, 1895.

7. *Lexington Herald,* September 27, 1914.

8. Ibid.

9. "The Governor's Message," *Public Documents of Kentucky,* KDLA, 1861–1903, 3: 21.

10. *Kentucky Senate Journal* (1898), 35.

11. Ibid.

12. "Wives of Some of Kentucky's Governors to 1901," *Louisville Courier-Journal,* November 21, 1901.

13. *Lexington Daily Leader,* December 8, 1895.

14. This note runs throughout the W.O. Bradley executive journals.

15. Jillson, "Literary Haunts and Personalities of Old Frankfort," *Register* 39 (1941): 79–85.

16. Darnell, *Filling in the Chinks,* 49–50.

17. Ibid.

18. *Lexington Daily Leader,* February 10, 1899.

19. *Louisville Courier-Journal,* February 11, 1899.

20. Ibid., February 10, 1899.

21. Ibid.

22. Ibid.

23. Ibid.

24. Apparently Governor Bradley and his family returned to the repaired mansion sometime in August 1899. The Kentucky Auditor's Report indicates that repairs to the building cost less than the damages paid by the insurance companies. "Executive Mansion," *Auditor's Journal,* no. 62, 1899.

25. Minutes of the Sinking Fund, February 27, 1900, 394.

26. See Hughes, Schaefer, and Williams, *That Kentucky Campaign,* 201–13.

27. Clark, *Kentucky: Land of Contrast,* 207–29; Klotter, "Feuds in Appalachia," 290–318; Nall, *The Tobacco Night Riders of Kentucky and Tennessee, 1904–1909, passim.*

28. Clark, *Kentucky: Land of Contrast,* 207–29.

29. *Journal of Southern History* 5: 34–38; Clark, "The People, William Goebel, and the Kentucky Railroads," 32–48.

30. Klotter, *William Goebel: The Politics of Wrath,* 87.

31. *Lexington Herald,* February 26, 1898; *Kentucky House Journal* (1898); Clark, "The People, William Goebel, and the Kentucky Railroads," 38–42.

32. William O. Bradley, "Message to the Kentucky General Assembly," *Kentucky Senate* Journal (1898), 37.

33. Hughes, Schaefer, and Williams, *That Kentucky Campaign,* 146.

34. Ibid., 54–55; Klotter, "William Sylvester Taylor," in Lowell Harrison, ed., *Kentucky's Governors, 1792–1985,* 110–12.

35. *Louisville Courier-Journal,* January 31, 1900; Hughes, Schaefer, and Williams, *That Kentucky Campaign,* 124–34.

36. *Louisville Courier-Journal,* February 1, 1900.

37. Ibid.

38. *Louisville Courier-Journal,* August 14, 1953.

39. Governor Taylor was inaugurated December 12, 1900. The family occupied the mansion until May 20. See Hughes, Schaefer, and Williams, *That Kentucky Campaign,* 149; *Lexington Herald,* May 22, 1900. The United States Supreme Court rendered its 5–4 decision on May 21, 1900. *Lexington Daily Leader,* May 22, 1900; Clift, "Governor Taylor Took Refuge in Capitol," *State Journal,* March 23, 1969. The mansion was in poor physical condition when the Bradleys left it. There were still fire stains and propped-up floors.

40. *Lexington Herald,* May 22, 24, 1900; *State Journal,* May 23, 1900.

41. *Lexington Press Transcript,* May 22, 1900.

42. Clift, *Governors of Kentucky,* 110–11. *Louisville Courier-Journal,* November 12, 1900; Burckel, "J.C.W. Beckham," in Lowell Harrison, ed., *Kentucky's Governors, 1792–1985,* 115–18.

43. Hughes, Schaefer, and Williams, *That Kentucky Campaign,* 41–45.

44. William O. Bradley, Executive Journal, January 5, 1898, KDLA; *Louisville Courier-Journal,* November 25, 1900.

45. For sketch of Julia Tevis, see Clark, *History of Clark County, Kentucky,* 209–20. Julia Tevis, *Sixty Years in a Schoolroom, passim.*

46. Hughes, Schaefer, and Williams, *That Kentucky Campaign,* 16–42; Woodson, *The First New Dealer,* 157–58.

47. "Crowds," November 21, 1900; "Governor Beckham and His Bride," November 22, 1900; Annie Chambers Czapskl, "Observations by and about Mrs. Beckham," November 25, 1900; all in *Louisville Courier-Journal.*

48. Czapskl, "Observations by and about Mrs. Beckham," *Louisville Courier-Journal,* November 25, 1900.

49. Ibid.

50. Ibid., November 25, 1900.

51. Ibid. November 21, 1900.

52. Ibid. November 22, 1900.

53. Ibid. November 21, 1900.

54. Ibid. November 22, 1900.

55. Ibid. November 21, 1900.

56. Ibid., November 25, 1900.

57. Helen H. Evans, "Stories Resulting from Eleanor Raphael Beckham's visit to Old Governor's Mansion," in "Data from the Old Governor's Mansion," August 19–21, 1975."

58. Helen H. Evans, "Stories Resulting from Eleanor Raphael Beckham's visit to Old Governor's Mansion," in "Data from the Old Governor's Mansion," August 19–21, 1975."

59. Ibid.

60. Ibid.

61. *Lexington Daily Leader,* August 16, 1901; *Lexington Herald,* August 17, 1901.

62. *State Journal,* August 28, 1975.

63. *Kentucky Senate Journal* (1898), 35.

64. Evans, "Stories Resulting from Eleanor Raphael Beckham's Visit to Old Governor's Mansion," in "Data from the Old Governor's Mansion," August 15–21, 1975.

65. Ibid.

66. Beckham, "Governor Beckham's Message to the General Assembly," Executive Journal, KDLA, January 4–5, 1904, 12–28.

67. Harrison and Klotter, *A New History of Kentucky,* 279–80.

68. Ibid., 382–83.

69. J.C.W. Beckham, "Message to the Kentucky General

Assembly," *Kentucky House Journal* (January 5, 1904), 19.

70. "Authorization to Build New Capitol," *Kentucky Acts* (February 2, 1904), 6–9.

71. Ibid.

72. Ibid.

73. The records detailing the construction of the new capitol building are contained in the journals of the Sinking Fund Commission, 1904–1910, KDLA.

74. Harrison, ed., *Kentucky's Governors, 1792–1985*, 118–20.

75. Public Papers of Augustus Willson, KDLA.

76. Harrison, ed., *Kentucky's Governors, 1792–1985*, 18–23.

77. *Lexington Herald*, December 10, 1907; *Lexington Leader*, December 7, 1907.

78. Augustus E. Willson, "Message to the Kentucky General Assembly," *Kentucky House Journal* (January 28, 1908).

79. *Lexington Leader*, December 10, 1907.

80. The Official Papers of Augustus E. Willson, KDLA.

81. Augustus E. Willson, "Dedicatory Speech at the Dedication of New Capitol," Minutes of the Sinking Fund Commission, KDLA, January 4, 1910, 552–50.

82. *Louisville Courier-Journal*, November 1910; *State Journal*, November 1910; *Lexington Leader*, November 1910.

83. *Louisville Courier-Journal*, November 27, 1910.

84. *Lexington Leader*, November 27, 29, 1910; *State Journal*, November 27, 29, 1910.

85. Ibid.

86. Ibid.

87. Augustus E. Willson, "Message to the Kentucky General Assembly," *Kentucky House Journal* (January 8, 1908), 88–89.

88. Ibid.

89. Willson, "Explanatory Statement," Minutes of the Sinking Fund Commission, January 4, 1910, 552–59; McCreary's report to House of Representatives, January 6, 1914.

90. Ibid.

91. Ibid.

92. *Kentucky Acts* (February 7, 1912), 1–4.

93. Ibid.

94. "To Feed Crowd, Burgoo, Bread just 10 Cents," *State Journal*, December 4, 1911; Minutes of the Sinking Fund Commission, KDLA. During the years 1912–1914 the Sinking Fund Commission held frequent meetings, and discussed in detail the planning and building of the new governor's mansion.

95. Ibid.

96. *Kentucky House Journal* (March 10, 1914), 1007.

97. Governor James B. McCreary submitted a sales notice to the local *State Journal* saying an auction would be held October 12, 1914, for sale of the old mansion and public grounds. Clipping attached to minutes of the Sinking Fund, August 1914, 532; *Kentucky Acts*, 1914.

98. Minutes of the Sinking Fund Commission, February 1914, KDLA.

99. Whitaker interview, 1999.

100. Ellison, T. Kyle, "Kentucky State Reformatory," in John Kleber, ed., *The Kentucky Encyclopedia*, 514.

101. Allan Trout, "Trout's Trotline," *Louisville Courier Journal*, February 6, 1964.

102. Sanborn Map Company, January 1940, Kentucky Historical Society Collection.

103. Henderson, "Old Governor's Mansion," *Louisville Courier-Journal*, December 20, 1955.

104. Ibid.; Evans, Documentary Data on the Old Mansion, 3 volumes, KDLA, gives a full summary of the fortunes of the old mansion's decline and rebirth.

105. Harry Lee Waterfield was elected lieutenant governor in 1955, and he and Mrs. Waterfield moved into the renovated old governor's mansion as its first tenants in April 1956.

8. A Mansion to Match a Capitol

1. Augustus E. Willson, Executive Journal, KDLA, January 24, 1910, 20.

2. John White Stevenson, Executive Journal, KDLA; *Louisville Courier-Journal*, December 7, 1869.

3. *Kentucky Acts* (1912), 1–5.

4. Ibid., 1–2.

5. Minutes of the Sinking Fund Commission, KDLA, April 24, 1912, 497.

6. Nicholas C. Burkel, "James B. McCreary," in Lowell Harrison, ed., *Kentucky's Governors, 1792–1985*, 88–92.

7. Minutes of the Sinking Fund Commission, KDLA, February 22, 1912, 290.

8. Ibid.

9. Ibid., 322.

10. Ibid., March 12, 1912, 390, 399.

11. The Adkins family made this claim at the time of his death.

12. Minutes of the Sinking Fund Commission, KDLA, March 14, 1912, 400–402.

13. *Kentucky Acts* (1912), 3.

14. Deed, Franklin County Clerk's Office, Frankfort, March 26, 1912, Book 59, 300.

15. Minutes of the Sinking Fund Commission, KDLA, April 24, 1912, 407.

16. Ibid., May 7, 1912, 412.

17. Ibid., May 15, 1912, 415.

18. Ibid., June 19, 1912, 419.

19. Ibid.

20. Ibid., June 18, 1912, 420.

21. McCreary, Executive Journal, 1911–1914, KDLA.

22. Minutes of the Sinking Fund Commission, KDLA, June 29, 1912, 420.

23. Ibid., July 16, August 10, 1912, 422, 427.

24. "Original Plans for Mansion Lost," *State Journal*, July 17, 1966.

25. Minutes of the Sinking Fund Commission, KDLA, August 18, 1912, 24, 27, 420, 425.

26. Ibid., October 30, 1912, 427.

27. Ibid., July 16, 1912, 420.

28. Ibid., August 10, 1912, 428.

29. Ibid., April 9, 1913, 457.

30. Ibid.

31. Ibid.

32. Ibid., March 12, 1913, 458.

33. Ibid.

34. Ibid., January 9, 1914, 498.

35. Ibid., February 21, 1914, 482.

36. Ibid.

37. *Lexington Herald*, February 8, 1915.

38. *Kentucky House Journal* (1914), 83.

39. *Kentucky House Journal* (1914), 84.

40. Ibid., 78–79.

41. Minutes of the Sinking Fund Commission, KDLA, February 15, 1914, 50.

42. *Louisville Courier-Journal*, January 21, 1914.

43. Ibid.

44. *Louisville Courier-Journal*, January 21, 1914.

45. *State Journal*, January 21, 1914.

46. McCreary, "The Journal of My Soldier Life."

47. Weather report, *Lexington Herald*, January 20, 1914; *Louisville Courier-Journal*, January 20, 1914.

48. *State Journal*, January 21, 1914.

49. Ibid.

50. Ibid.

51. *Louisville Courier-Journal*, January 21, 1914.

52. Ibid.

53. Ibid.

54. *Lexington Herald*, January 21, 1914. The *Herald* reported that a suffrage leader from Nevada would be in Kentucky.

55. *State Journal*, January 21, 1914.

56. *Louisville Courier-Journal*, January 21, 1914; *State Journal*, January 21, 1914.

57. *Louisville Courier-Journal*, January 21, 1914.

58. Monahan, "The Louisiana Purchase Exposition," *Dictionary of American History*, 3: 307–8.

59. Clark, *The Greening of the South*, 117, 124.

60. *State Journal*, January 21, 1914.

61. Ibid.

62. Ibid.

63. Ibid.

64. Ibid., March 16, 1914.

65. *Louisville Courier-Journal*, March 12, 1914.

9. Riding a Mule into the Mansion

1. James Bennett McCreary, Executive Journal, KDLA, July 27, 1912, 423; ibid., June 6, 1913, 473; Flem D. Sampson, Executive Journal, KDLA, March 29, 30, 1928, 177, 190, November 15, 1929, 211.

2. The distance between the mansion and the rim of the Palisades is approximately two hundred feet

3. Beckham versus McCreary in the race for the U.S. Senate in 1914.

4. *Kentucky Treasurer's Report* (1914); James B. McCreary, "Message to the General Assembly," January 6, 1914, 23.

5. Paul Hughes, "Governor in Time of War, but Peace Is His Job Now," *Louisville Courier-Journal Magazine*, June 25, 1950. Also, *Lexington Herald*, May-November 1915.

6. "Augustus Owsley Stanley," *Biographical Directory of the United States Congress, 1774–1989*, 1861.

7. Jillson, *Edwin P. Morrow—Kentuckian*, 35.

8. Harrison, "Augustus Owsley Stanley," in John Kleber, ed., *The Kentucky Encyclopedia*, 847.

9. Hughes, "Governor in Time of War, but Peace Is His Job Now," *Louisville Courier- Journal Magazine*, June 25, 1950.

10. *Lexington Herald*, July 14, 1915.

11. Campaign materials, Stanley Papers, Special Collections, King Library, University of Kentucky, Lexington.

12. Jillson, *Edwin P. Morrow—Kentuckian*, 36–38.

13. Hughes, "Governor in Time of War, but Peace Is His Job Now," *Lousiville Courier- Journal Magazine*, June 25, 1950.

14. Ibid.

15. Ibid.

16. Jillson, *Edwin P. Morrow—Kentuckian*, 37–38.

17. Hughes, "Governor in Time of War, but Peace Is His Job Now," *Louisville Courier- Journal Magazine*, June 25, 1950.

18. Owsley and Sue Stanley's three sons were Augustus Owsley Jr., William Soaper, and Marion. Hughes, "Governor in Time of War, but Peace Is His Job Now," *Louisville Courier- Journal Magazine*, June 25, 1950.

19. Hughes, "Governor in Time of War, but Peace Is His Job Now," *Louisville Courier- Journal Magazine*, June 25, 1950.

20. Stanley, Executive Journal, KDLA, contains a hundred or so pages noting pardon actions. The official pages contain a large volume of petitions and correspondence relating to the subject.

21. Stanley, Executive Journal, KDLA, November 21, 1916, 351.

22. Ibid., 356–57.

23. Moonshine liquor was made in every section of Kentucky, but two areas were favorite ones for moonshining and bootlegging, the upper forks of the Kentucky River, and the land between the Cumberland and Tennessee Rivers at Golden Pond. The opening phrase, "The Governor this day granted a pardon . . . ," or "The Governor this Day honored the requisition of Governors" indicated the extent of the bootlegging problem. A specific example, "The Governors this day honored the requisition of the Governor of Georgia and issued this warrant for the arrest of Will Ewing charged in Polk County of said state." Executive Journal, KDLA, November 18, 1916, 356.

24. Most of the expenditures made on the mansion during the Stanley administration were for cleaning rugs and carpets, building a garage, and adding of an ice-making machine in the state power plant. Minutes of the Sinking Fund Commission, May 18, 1916, 579–91, July 7, 9, 1916, 580–81.

25. Ibid., July 7, 1916, 580.

26. *State Journal*, Inaugural Edition, October 11, 1918, quoting an interview with Mrs. James Dawson, a neighbor of the mansion.

27. Frances E. Beauchamp to A.O. Stanley, November 19, 1913, Stanley Papers; N. Miller to A.O. Stanley, undated, Special Collections, King Library, University of Kentucky. Also, *Louisville Times*, July 26, 1915.

28. Hughes, "Governor in Time of War, but Peace Is His Job Now," *Louisville Courier-Journal Magazine*, June 25, 1950.

29. *Cincinnati Enquirer*, May 18, 1918. The story of Stanley's regard for the governorship was told to the author in 1944 by Governor Keen Johnson, who was one of the group of governors.

30. *Louisville Courier-Journal*, May 9, 23, 1919.

31. *Kentucky Senate Journal*, 1916, 1918.

32. Kentucky State Treasurer's Report, 1919, KDLA, 32.

33. *Louisville Courier-Journal*, May 9, 1919.

34. "Governor's Message," *Kentucky House Journal* (1920), 18–19.

35. Edwin Morrow, Inaugural Address, *Louisville Courier-Journal*, December 9, 1919.

36. Ibid.

37. Ibid.

38. Black, Executive Journal, KDLA, December 1919, 68.

39. Kentucky Federation of Women's Clubs, *Kentucky's First Ladies in Miniature*.

40. In four-year intervals, as governors moved in and out, rugs and carpets were revealed as worn and shabby, and chinaware and furniture were found to be broken and worn. No one seems to have made records of what families brought with them or took away when they moved.

41. Trout, "It Takes a Heap of Money for the State to Keep Mansion at Below Par," *Louisville Courier-Journal*, February 6, 1964.

42. Morrow, Executive Journal, KDLA, December 9, 1919, 15.

43. The Will Lockett case especially attracted widespread public attention. Edwin P. Morrow, "Message to the Kentucky General Assembly," *Kentucky Senate Journal* (1920); Coleman, *Murder at the Courthouse*, 4–17, 21; *Lexington Herald*, February 8, 1920.

44. Jillson, *Edwin P. Morrow—Kentuckian*, 59–60.

45. Morrow, "Second Message to the Kentucky General Assembly," *Kentucky Senate Journal* 1 (1922), 23–24, 25–26.

46. Ibid., 16.

47. Morrow, Executive Journal, KDLA, 1922.

48. Morrow Inaugural Address, *Louisville Courier-Journal*, December 9, 1919; Morrow, "Message to Kentucky General Assembly," *Kentucky Senate Journal* (1920), 16.

49. Party Composition of the Senate of Kentucky, 1920.

50. Edwin P. Morrow, "Second Message to the Kentucky General Assembly," *Kentucky Senate Journal* (1922), 25–26; Jillson, *Edwin P. Morrow—Kentuckian*, 65–68.

51. "William Jason Fields," in *Biographical Directory of the United States Congress, 1771–1989*.

52. *Lexington Herald*, Sept. 3, 1923.

53. *Lexington Herald*, October 16, 1923; *Louisville Courier-Journal*, October 15, 1923.

54. Hughes, "William Jason Fields," in *Louisville Courier-Journal Magazine*, July 6, 1950.

55. Ibid.

56. Minutes of the Sinking Fund Commission, March 17, 1925, B2.

57. Ibid.

58. Ibid., September 3, 1925, 81.

59. Ibid., September 13, 1927, 112.

60. Ibid., February 2, 1927, 106.

61. *State Journal*, November 9, 1927.

62. Ibid., December 3, 1927.

63. Ibid., December 12, 1927.

64. Ibid., December 12, 1927. The Kentucky for Progress program also included *Kentucky Progress Magazine*, a publication of the Kentucky Progress Commission created by Flem D. Sampson. "The Present Job in Kentucky," *Kentucky Progress Magazine*, 1: 9.

65. Fields, Executive Journal, KDLA, December 13, 1927.

66. *State Journal*, December 14, 1927.

67. Ibid., November 29, 1927.

68. Ibid., December 14, 1927.

69. Ibid.

70. Ibid.

71. Minutes of the Sinking Fund Commission, July 1927, 212, 244.

72. *Kentucky House Journal* (1930), 88–96; *Kentucky Acts* (1930), 409–11.

73. *Kentucky House Journal* (1933), 382–83; *The Reports of the Efficiency Commission 1–2* (1924); *The Griffanhagen Report* (1919), 34, and (1924), 62–63; Sexton, "Flem D. Sampson";

Harrison, ed., *Kentucky's Governors, 1792–1985*, 135, 138; Clark, *A History of Kentucky*, 444–45, 459–60.

74. McKnight interview, 1999; Dungan interview, 1997.

10. A House Gripped in Depression and Politics

1. *Lexington Herald*, May 6–14, 1931; *Louisville Courier-Journal*, May 9–14, 1931.

2. *Lexington Herald*, May 12, 1931; *Louisville Courier-Journal*, May 12, 1931.

3. Ellis, "Ruby Laffoon, 1931–1935," in Lowell Harrison, ed., *Kentucky's Governors, 1792–1985*, 138–42.

4. "Governor Ruby Laffoon," *Register* 30 (1932), 22; Gipson, *Ruby Laffoon, Governor of Kentucky, 1931–1935*.

5. "Governor Ruby Laffoon," *Register* 30 (1932), 1–2.

6. Though Mrs. Sampson had redecorated the rooms, the electrical wiring, plumbing, and sewage problems persisted.

7. "Governor's Message," *Kentucky House Journal* (January 1932).

8. In 1932–1933 Kentucky collected in revenues $17,373.840.00, but spent $18,619,405.25 (*A Report of the Kentucky Efficiency Commission*, 12). Governor Laffoon told legislators, "The deficit will be greatly increased over what it will be for the ensuing period from July 1, 1932" ("Governor's Message," *Kentucky House Journal*, March 23, 1932).

9. "George Washington Birthday Party," *State Journal*, February 23, 1932.

10. Clara Keyes, "Albert W. Young," in John Kleber, ed., *The Kentucky Encyclopedia*, 972.

11. Martin interview, 2000.

12. Laffoon's second banking proclamation, issued before Roosevelt's banking holiday, was declared on February 27, 1933. Laffoon Official File, 1933, KDLA.

13. Morrison, "Ruby Laffoon," in John Kleber, ed., *The Kentucky Encyclopedia*, 529.

14. "Guards on Duty at Mansion," *Louisville Courier-Journal*, May 17, 1934.

15. Trout, "Walking Munn Wilson, 83, Political Vagabond Dies," *Courier-Journal*, March 4, 1956.

16. Harrison, "Albert Benjamin Chandler," in John Kleber, ed., *The Kentucky Encyclopedia*, 179.

17. The author witnessed and heard a performance of this type in the Kentucky state capitol in 1933.

18. Harrison, "Albert Benjamin Chandler," in John Kleber, ed., *The Kentucky Encyclopedia*, 179.

19. "Ruby Laffoon," in Harrison, ed., *Kentucky's Governors, 1792–1985*, 141.

20. Roland, "Albert Benjamin Chandler," in Lowell Harrison, ed., *Kentucky's Governors, 1792–1985*, 144.

21. The extensive pardon grants are contained in the file of Governor Ruby Laffoon's collected papers, KDLA.

22. Ibid., Cartons 1–6 (1931–1935).

23. Laffoon, Executive Journal, KDLA, 1935, 102.

24. Ibid.

25. Laffoon Papers, KDLA.

26. This was a dark and haunting matter that was never mentioned in gubernatorial campaigning, and perhaps was not fully considered beforehand by incoming governors.

27. Roland, "Albert Benjamin Chandler," 143–44. Perhaps no

other Kentucky governor used family references and humor as freely as did Governor Chandler. His references to his wife and family became good copy for reporters, and appealed to the public. Governor Chandler enlisted the expert services of Professor James W. Martin and his academic associates in the modernization of Kentucky's fiscal and governmental system in the reorganization act of 1936. Roland, "Albert Benjamin Chandler," 144–45.

28. The Chandler family moved into the mansion in late December. It included two daughters, Marcella and Mimi, and two sons, Ben and Dan.

29. The intimate correspondence of the Chandler courtship and marriage are contained in the Chandler collected papers, King Library, University of Kentucky.

30. Ben Chandler Jr. interview, 1997.

31. Ibid.

32. Brammer, "Good Neighbors," *Lexington Herald-Leader*, April 2, 1985.

33. Catherine Connor, *From My Old Kentucky Home to the White House*, 109–20; Ben Chandler interview, 1997.

34. *State Journal*, January 20, 1937–February 28, 1937; "Flood of 1937," in John Kleber, ed., *The Kentucky Encyclopedia*, 327–28.

35. *Lexington Herald*, February 20, 1937.

36. Ibid.

37. Governor A.B. Chandler, "Message to the Kentucky General Assembly," *Kentucky House Journal* (1939), 37.

38. A.B. Chandler, Executive Journal, KDLA, October 9, 1939, 580.

39. Roland, "Albert Benjamin Chandler," in Harrison, ed., *Kentucky's Governors, 1792–1985*, 148–49.

40. Johnson interview, 2000.

41. Ibid.

42. Ibid.

43. Keen Johnson, Executive Journal, KDLA, December 2, 1942, 514.

44. Johnson interview, 2000. Governor Johnson faced the horrendous decision in the execution of Otis Peters, August 14, 1942. Keen Johnson, Executive Journal, KDLA, 1942, 155. There was a stay of execution for Robert H. Andrews, December 29, 1942, (Keen Johnson, Executive Journal, KDLA, 1942, 553).

45. Johnson interview, 2000.

46. Ibid.

47. Keen Johnson, Executive Journal, KDLA, 1943, 489.

48. Ibid. The executive journal reflects an astonishing number of pardons and conditional pardons. These, however, resulted from recommendations made to the governor by the Kentucky Board of Pardons. These pardons reflected a change of social, economic, and administrative attitudes toward extended terms of imprisonment, and the lack of state funds to maintain so great a prison population.

49. Klotter, "Simeon Willis, 1879–1965," in Lowell Harrison, ed., *Kentucky's Governors, 1792–1985*, 153–56.

50. Meigs interview, 1998.

51. Ibid.

52. Ibid.

53. Ibid.

54. Ibid.

55. Klotter, "Simeon Willis, 1879–1965," in Lowell Harrison, ed., *Kentucky's Governors, 1792–1985*, 153–56.

56. Meigs interview, 1998.

57. Ibid.

58. Ibid.

59. Ibid.

60. Britton interview, 1997.

11. An Aged House Teetering on the Brink of a New Age

1. Porter, "Weep No More Kentucky," in *Collier's Magazine*, March 30, 1946, 14–15, 57, 58, 59; Schacter, *Kentucky on the March*, 3–10; Beers, ed., *Kentucky, Designs for Its Future*, 177, 225; Butler, "What Is Really to Blame for High Illiteracy Rate," *Louisville Courier-Journal*, March 9, 1952; *Abstract of the Fifteenth United States Census*, 281.

2. "Report & Recommendations on the Governor's Mansion, Frankfort, Kentucky," July 29, 1960; Edward R. Ronald to W.T. McConnell, April 6, 1972; W.T. McConnell to Don Bradshaw, March 13, 1972, all in unprocessed records, KDLA.

3. "Earle C. Clements," in *Biographical Directory of the United States Congress, 1771–1989*, 792.

4. *Louisville Courier-Journal*, December 7, 1947.

5. Ibid.

6. Ibid., November 9, 1957.

7. Ibid., June 9, 1948.

8. Britton interview, 1997.

9. Bell interview, 1997; Farris interview, 1999.

10. Trout, "It Takes a Heap of Money for the State to Keep Mansions at Below Par," *Louisville Courier-Journal*, February 6, 1964.

11. In his three-year occupancy of the mansion, Clements spent $22,571.29 on repairs. The state, however, spent $337,778 repairing it. Trout, "It Takes a Heap of Money for the State to Keep Mansions at Below Par," *Louisville Courier-Journal*, February 6, 1964.

12. Syvertsen, "Earle Chester Clements and the Democratic Party," in Harrison, ed., *Kentucky's Governors, 1792–1985*, 160–61.

13. Clements, Executive Journal, December 9, 1947; Wetherby, Executive Journal, KDLA, December 19, 1947, 1; *Louisville Courier-Journal*, February 6, 1964.

14. Ransdell, "Christmas in State," *Louisville Courier-Journal*, December 20, 1952.

15. Trout, "It Takes a Heap of Money for the State to Keep Mansions at Below Par," *Louisville Courier-Journal*, February 6, 1964.

16. Ransdell, "Christmas in State," *Louisville Courier-Journal*, December 20, 1953.

17. "Minutes of a Joint Meeting of the Board of Directors of the Athletic Association and of the Board of Trustees," December 19, 1952, February 7, 1954, Athletic Association files, Special Collections, King Library, University of Kentucky.

18. Farris interview, 1999.

19. Kleber, ed., *The Public Papers of Governor Lawrence Wetherby*, Valedictory Address, December 13, 1959, 304–8; Clark, "Lighting the Soul of Kentucky," *Kentucky Living*, July 1998, 17–23.

20. *Louisville Times*, June 10, 1955; Lawrence Wetherby Newspaper Clippings, 15.

21. Kleber, ed., *The Public Papers of Governor Lawrence W. Wetherby, 1950–1955*, 102.

22. Farris interview, 1999.

23. Trout, "Tears and Chuckles Cascade into Wetherby's Daily Mail," *Louisville Courier-Journal*, October 10, 1952.

24. Ibid.

25. Ibid.

26. Ibid.

27. Ibid.

28. Lawrence Wetherby Newspaper Clippings, file no. 15.

29. Ransdell, "Christmas in State," *Louisville Courier-Journal*, December 20, 1953.

30. Contract, Commonwealth of Kentucky with Jeanette Marks, 1956, in Kentucky State Auditor Collection (unprocessed), KDLA.

31. Ibid.

32. Britton interview, 1997; Chandler interview, 1997.

33. Robinson, ed., *Public Papers of Governor Bert T. Combs, Biographical Sketch*, unnumbered pages.

34. "Inventory of Public Properties, Governor's Mansion," *Kentucky Acts* (December 9, 1959), in Kentucky State Auditor Collection (unprocessed), KDLA.

35. Robinson, *Public Papers of Governor Bert T. Combs, Biographical Sketch*, unnumbered pages.

36. "Editorial," *Louisville Courier-Journal*, December 9, 1959.

37. "Inventory of Public Properties, Governor's Mansion," *Kentucky Acts* (December 9, 1959), in Kentucky State Auditor Collection (unprocessed), KDLA.

38. Combs Papers, Box 96M57, Special Collection, King Library, University of Kentucky.

39. Report & Recommendations on the Governor's Mansion Frankfort, Kentucky, July 29, 1960, in Kentucky State Auditor Collection (unprocessed), KDLA.

40. Advisory Committee to Robert R. Martin, June 8, 1960, in Kentucky State Auditor Collection (unprocessed), KDLA.

41. Report on Mansion, August 18, 1960, in Combs File, loose papers, KDLA.

42. *Louisville Courier-Journal*, January 11, 1961; Combs Papers, Special Collections, King Library, University of Kentucky.

43. Ibid.

44. *Louisville Courier-Journal*, March 15, 1961; Combs Papers, Clippings file, Special Collections, King Library, University of Kentucky.

45. Associated Press report, Combs Papers, Clippings file, Special Collections, King Library, University of Kentucky.

46. van Curon, "Agree or Not, I Say What I Think," August 2, 1962, *Kentucky Labor News*, in *Louisville Courier-Journal*, August 8, 1962.

47. Ibid.

48. Senn to Governor Bert T. Combs, September 16, 1963, unprocessed collection, KDLA.

49. Kyle Vance, "Combs Says Prison T-Bones Only for Official Guests," *Louisville Courier-Journal*, September 18, 1963. Combs clipping file.

50. Senn to Governor Bert T. Combs, September 16, 1963, unprocessed collection, KDLA.

51. Combs Papers, Box 96M57, Special Collections, King Library, University of Kentucky.

52. Anne Pardue, "Repairs Start Next Month on Governor's Mansion," *Louisville Courier-Journal*, December 17, 1960.

53. Farris interview, 1999; Combs interview, 1996.

54. Ibid; Dotson interview, 1997.

55. Cullen interview, 1997.

56. "Monthly Consideration of Governor Combs," Report of Sgt. Lawrence Gay, Combs Papers, Special Collection, King Library, University of Kentucky.

57. During legislative sessions the state dining room became a breakfast-work room for Governor Combs and members of the General Assembly.

58. Robinson, ed., *The Public Papers of Governor Bert T. Combs*.

59. Harrison, "Edward Thompson Breathitt Jr.," in Kleber, ed., *The Kentucky Encyclopedia*, 114.

60. Kenneth E. Harrell, *The Public Papers of Governor Edward T. Breathitt, Jr., Biographic Sketch*, unnumbered pages.

61. Breathitt, taped interview, 1997. Edward Breathitt was one of the youngest men to become governor of Kentucky. He and Frances Holleman had four young children, three daughters and a son. Three of the children were still in elementary school, the fourth, Edward was four years old.

62. Ibid.

63. Harrell, "Derby Statement," unprocessed documents, May 4, 1969, 437–38, KDLA; Breathitt interview, 1997.

64. Livingston Taylor, "Four Ex-Governors recall Threats while in Office,," *Louisville Courier-Journal*, January 4, 1976.

65. Breathitt interview, 1997.

66. Brammer, "Good Neighbors," *Lexington Herald-Leader*, April 2, 1985.

67. *Kentucky Acts* (1964), 92–94.

12. Mansion or Heritage Museum?

1. "Certification of Election," November 1967, in Louie Nunn, Executive Journal, Secretary of State Archives, 1967, 1.

2. Sexton, ed., *The Public Papers of Governor Louie B. Nunn, 1967–1971*, 3–4; *Inaugural Souvenir*, biographic essay of Louie B. Nunn (1967): 3.

3. Ibid.

4. Ibid.

5. Edward T. Breathitt, Executive Journal, 1963–1967; Harrell, *The Public Papers of Governor Edward T. Breathitt, Jr., 1963–1967*, 55–65; "Message to the General Assembly, January 24, 1968," 37, Appendix I, 75.

6. Nunn interview, 2000.

7. Ann Bevins, "Mrs. Nunn Tells of a First Lady's Life," *Lexington Leader*, June 2, 1968; "On physical condition of the Mansion, in *Advisory Fire Protection Report, Governor's Mansion, Frankfort*, (1969); Heartstern, Louis, & Henry, "Rehabilitation of the Governor's Mansion," January 2, 1968; McDowell Builders, "Cost Estimate: Rehabilitation of the Governor's Mansion, Emergency Measure," undated; "Report," Mansion Committee, March 14, 1968, all in unprocessed documents, KDLA.

8. Taped speech to O'Tucks, Hamilton, Ohio, July 8, 1969; Stanley DeZarn to Beula Nunn, July 10, 1969, in Beula Nunn Scrap Book, Nunn Collection, Special Collections, King Library, University of Kentucky.

9. *Louisville Courier-Journal*, July 1, 13, 1969; Taped speech to O'Tucks, Hamilton, Ohio, July 8, 1969.

10. Taped speech to O'Tucks, Hamilton, Ohio, July 8, 1969.

11. Taylor, "Bedlam," *The Louisville Courier-Journal*, August 20, 1979.

12. Ibid.

13. Ibid.

14. Ibid. The Shelby bed is now back in the possession of the Kentucky Historical Society and was on display in March 2000 as a Kentucky treasure.

15. Though the Kentucky Mansions Preservation Foundation, Inc., indicates its formal incorporation in its name, neither the Kentucky Secretary of State archivist or the KDLA archivists have been able to find a record of the fact.

16. "The Governor's Mansion," *The Louisville Courier-Journal,* May 1, 1969.

17. Dr. John Floyd to Mrs. Beula Nunn, May 21, 1969, unprocessed documents, KDLA.

18. There were three inventories of the furnishings of the governor's mansion: Ruth Mason, Division of Engineering to Albert Christian, April 17, 1968; Inventory Governor's Residence, March 25–26, 1968, Larry S. Perkins, December 6, 1971; Charles E. Parish to James O. Roberts, April 5, 1972, all in KDLA, unprocessed documents.

19. *Lexington Herald,* May 1, 1969; Governor Nunn interview, 2000.

20. Pardue, "The Governor's Mansion, New Look, New Purpose," *Louisville Courier- Journal and Times Sunday Magazine,* July 13, 1969.

21. *Lexington Herald,* May 1, 1969.

22. Ibid.; *Louisville Courier-Journal,* July 13, 1969.

23. Governor Nunn interview, 2000.

24. Schwartz, "Growing Up with the Governor," *The Gazette,* 1990.

25. Jack C. Blanton to Albert Christian, January 8, 1969; "Total Expense, 1967–1970," in Commissioner of Finance File, KDLA.

26. Nunn inaugural program, 1967.

27. Governor Nunn interview, 2000.

28. Ibid.

29. Ibid.

30. Ibid.

31. Perkins Inventory, December 6, 1971, Unprocessed documents, KDLA.

32. There seems to be little documentary notation of any relationship between the two executive families.

33. Jones, ed., *The Public Papers of Wendell H. Ford, 1971– 1974,* 3–4.

34. Ibid.

35. Columbus, "Portrait of the First Lady," *The Kentucky State Employee* 3 (February 1972), 8.

36. Helen Evans, "A Brief Summary of the Old Governor's Mansion," in *New Tours of Official Property,* 1996; *Documentary Data on the Old Governor's Mansion,* 1.

37. Columbus, "Portrait of the First Lady," *The Kentucky State Employee* 3 (February 1972), 8.

38. *Lexington Herald,* May 1, 1969; Pardue, *Louisville Courier-Journal and Times Magazine,* July 13, 1969.

39. Columbus, "Portrait of the First Lady," *The Kentucky State Employee* 3 (February 1972), 8.

40. Perkins inventory, December 6, 1971.

41. *Kentucky Acts* (1796), 7. The terms "Mansion" and "Residence" appear throughout the official references to the house. The General Assembly recognized in an act that the mansion was to be used for broad public entertainment purposes, March 3, 1964, pages 92–94. An oversight committee was authorized April 3, 1980 (*Kentucky Acts,* 226–27).

42. *Kentucky Acts* (1796), 7; (1811), 104; (1820), 27; (1816), 153–54. Though the state law seemed to authorize a full oversight, the periodic inspections were summary in nature.

43. Columbus, "Portrait of the First Lady," *The Kentucky State Employee* 34 (February 1972); Pardue, presented a visual portrayal of the decor of the governor's mansion in "The Governor's Mansion, New Look, New Purpose," *The Louisville Courier-Journal,* July 13, 1969.

44. Pardue, "The Governor's Mansion, New Look, New Purpose," *The Louisville Courier-Journal,* July 13, 1969.

45. Donald E. Bradshaw to Governor Wendell H. Ford, September 19, 1972, KDLA, unsorted papers.

46. Ibid.

47. Ibid.

48. Albert Christian, "Statement Relative to Mansions, Shrines, and Historical Sites," September 18, 1968, Unsorted papers, KDLA.

49. Taped speech to the O'Tucks, Hamilton, Ohio, July 8, 1969.

50. The office of State Curator was created by legislative act, but not funded (*Kentucky Acts* [1970], 636–37). Larry Perkins was appointed November 15, 1971 (Nunn, Executive Journal, 602). He was dismissed December 20, 1971 (Donald E. Bradshaw to Larry S. Perkins, December 20, 1971); Ford, Executive Order 71–59, December 23, 1971, in Ford, Executive Journal, 1: 10; Larry S. Perkins to Ruby Neel Ford, December 10, 1971, in Ford unsorted papers, KDLA; Perkins inventory, December 6, 1971.

51. *Kentucky Acts* (1971), 636–37.

52. Perkins inventory, December 6, 1971.

53. Albert Christian, "Statement Relative to Mansions, Shrines, and Historical Sites," September 18, 1968, Unsorted papers, KDLA.

54. Cost estimate, Henderson, Lewis and Henry architects, August 2, 1960, E.R. Ronald and Associates, April 5, 1972, in "An Advisory Fire Prevention Report for Governor's Mansion," Frankfort, Kentucky, Unsorted papers, KDLA.

55. Jones, "Wendell Hampton Ford," in Harrison, ed., *Kentucky's Governors, 1792–1985,* 179–80.

56. "A Brief Summary of the Old Governor's Mansion History," General File of New Tours, in Evans, 1990.

57. Ford interview, 2000.

58. Jones, *The Public Papers of Governor Wendell H. Ford, 1791–1794,* 182.

59. "A Brief Summary of the Governor's Mansion History," General File, New Tours, KDLA, 1990.

60. Carroll interview, 1998.

61. Bell interview, 1997.

62. Ibid.

63. Jones, *Public Papers of Governor Wendell H. Ford, 1971– 1974;* Harrison, ed., *Kentucky's Governors, 1792–1985,* 182.

64. Carroll interview, 1998.

65. Sprague, "Julian Morton Carroll," in Harrison, ed., *Kentucky's Governors, 1792–1985,* 185–86.

66. Carroll interview, 1998.

67. Carroll interview, 1998; *Louisville Courier-Journal,* May 29, 1977; *Lexington Herald-Leader,* May 29, 1977. The temperature in Lexington averaged 17.8 degrees in January 1978, according to the 1999 *Weather Almanac,* 456.

68. Carroll interview, 1998; Cullen interview, 1997.

69. By 1988 the Derby Breakfast Festival had outgrown the

dining facilities of the governor's mansion and had been moved outside to tents.

70. James B. Edwards was elected Governor of South Carolina in 1974. He was the first Republican governor in that state in ninety-eight years. Edgar, *South Carolina, A History*, 548.

71. Sprague, "Julian Morton Carroll," in Harrison, ed., *Kentucky's Governors, 1792–1985*, 186.

72. This highly controversial issue was first introduced in 1968. Jones, *The Public Papers of Wendell H. Ford, 1971–1974*, 350–51.

73. George L. Adkins to John Brown Jr., March 25, 1980, in undated file copy, Ramsey, United Press, KDLA.

13. Kentucky's Petit Trianon

1. Repeatedly the statement was made that every governor since 1914 had patchwork repairs made on both the electrical and sewer systems.

2. *State Journal*, March 1, 1980.

3. John R. Groves Jr. to George L. Adkins, March 24, 1980, Official File, KDLA.

4. George L. Adkins to John Y. Brown Jr., March 25, 1980, Official File, KDLA.

5. George L. Adkins to Lt. William Adams, "Expenditures for Governors Mansion," March 19, 1980, Official File, KDLA.

6. "Project Cost Summary," Engineering File M-657, March 19, 1980, KDLA.

7. Press Release, Office of the Governor, May 14, 1980, Official File, KDLA.

8. "Project Cost Summary," Engineering File M-657, March 19, 1980, KDLA.

9. Adkins to Gov. John Y. Brown, "Mansion Renovation," April 3, 1980, Official File, KDLA; *State Journal*, May 10, 1980.

10. Seale, "Preface," *Kentucky's Governor's Mansion, A Restoration*, 9.

11. Press Release, Office of the Governor, May 23, 1980, official file, KDLA.

12. Ibid.

13. Seale, "Preface," *Kentucky's Governor's Mansion*, 10.

14. Seale, "Kentucky's Governor's Mansion, Consultation Report," July 1980.

15. Ibid., 4.

16. Ibid., 6.

17. Seale, "Preface," *Kentucky's Governor's Mansion*, 10.

18. Ibid.

19. *Kentucky Acts* (1980), 246–47.

20. George L. Adkins to John Y. Brown Jr., April 3, 1980, Official File, KDLA.

21. George L. Adkins to John Y. Brown Jr., "Governor's Mansion-Capital Grounds," May 5, 1980, Official File, KDLA.

22. "Summary of Costs Rehabilitation of the Governor's Mansion," January 1982, Official File, KDLA.

23. Ralph Ed Graves to Phyllis George Brown, January 18, 1982, Official File, KDLA.

24. *State Journal*, September 19, 1982; *Louisville Courier-Journal*, September 19, 1982; *Lexington Herald*, September 3, 1982.

25. Ibid.

26. *Lexington Herald*, September 3, 1982; *State Journal*, September 2, 1982.

27. *State Journal*, September 2, 1982; *Louisville Courier-Journal*, September 19, 1982.

28. *Louisville Courier-Journal*, September 2, 1982.

29. *State Journal*, September 19, 1982.

30. *Louisville Courier-Journal*, September 28, 1982.

31. Ibid.

32. *State Journal*, September 18, 1982.

33. Work order, August 7, 1981, Official File, KDLA; Niemeier Construction Company, November 30, 1981; W.P. Farris, "Mechanical/Electrical Renovation of Governor's Mansion," November 2, 1981, Official File, KDLA; *Kentucky Post*, January 1, 1983; *State Journal*, November 18, 1982.

34. *Lexington Herald*, August 6, 1982; *Louisville Courier-Journal*, August 6, 1982.

35. Ralph Ed Graves to Phyllis George Brown, January 18, 1982, Official File, KDLA.

36. Liz Dahl to Members of the General Assembly, January 1, 1982, Official File, KDLA.

37. *Lexington Herald-Leader*, March 20, 1983.

38. Beverly Fortune, *Lexington Herald-Leader*, March 20, 1983.

39. Ibid.

40. Ibid., April 21, 1983.

41. *Lexington Herald-Leader*, March 25, 1983.

42. Ibid., April 21, 1983.

43. Charging the $10 fee stirred a bitter controversy. *Louisville Courier-Journal*, April 9, 24, 1983; *Lexington Herald-Leader*, April 21, 1983.

44. Ibid.

45. Pardue, "Charging Fee at Mansion Isn't Legal Beshear Says," *Louisville Courier-Journal*, April 24, 1983.

46. Ibid.

47. *Louisville Courier-Journal*, April 22, 1983; *State Journal*, April 1983; *Lexington Herald-Leader*, April 21, 1983.

48. *Lexington Herald-Leader*, April 18, 1983.

49. Ibid.

50. Loftus, "Mansion Rebuilding Exceeds $3 Million," *Kentucky Post*, April 19, 1983.

51. Augustus E. Willson, "Message to the Kentucky General Assembly," in *Kentucky Senate Journal*, February 24, 1910.

52. Ryan, "No Place Like Home," *Louisville Courier-Journal*, May 6, 1983.

53. Seale, *The Kentucky Governor's Mansion*, 104.

54. Tachau, "John Y. Brown, Jr., 1979–1983," in Harrison, ed., *Kentucky's Governors, 1792–1985*, 192.

55. Malmer, "The Brunch Bunch," *State Journal*, May 6, 1983.

56. Malmer, "Derby Breakfast returns to Frankfort with Plenty of Changes, Exotic Foods, Notables," *State Journal*, May 4, 1983.

57. Booe, "They Came, They Saw, They Ate," *State Journal*, May 6, 1983.

58. Malmer, "The Brunch Bunch," *State Journal*, May 6, 1983.

59. Booe, *State Journal*, May 8, 1983.

60. Malmer, "The Brunch Bunch," *State Journal*, May 6, 1983.

61. Booe, *State Journal*, May 6, 1983; Wahlgren, *Lexington Herald-Leader*, May 7, 1983.

62. Booe, *State Journal*, May 6, 1983.

63. Sue Wahlgren, "Browns, Carter, Bush join 500 at Mansion," *Lexington-Herald- Leader*, May 7, 1983; Booe, *State Journal*, May 6, 1983.

64. Ibid.

65. Mastin, "Governor's Wife Wins Award for Preservation of

Mansion," *Lexington Herald-Leader,* May 25, 1983.

66. Tachau, "John Y. Brown, Jr., 1979–1983," in Harrison, ed., *Kentucky's Governors, 1792–1985,* 192.

14. A New Breed of Tenants

1. *Louisville Courier-Journal,* May 8, 1983; *State Journal,* May 8, 1983; *Lexington Herald-Leader,* May 7, 1983.

2. *Inauguration '83 Program, Governor Martha Layne Collins,* KDLA, 1.

3. Martha Layne Collins, Executive Journal, vol. 1, cover, Secretary of State Archival file, Frankfort.

4. *Inauguration '83 Program, Governor Martha Layne Collins,* KDLA; Collins Public Papers, 1983–87, KDLA.

5. *Georgetown News and Times,* December 12, 1985.

6. Official Kentucky Election Results, Primary & General Elections, (1983), Secretary of State Board of Elections File, Frankfort.

7. Gallery of First Lady Portraits, Sun Room, Governor's Mansion.

8. *Inauguration '83 Program, Governor Martha Layne Collins,* KDLA, 3.

9. "Budget Message to General Assembly," *Kentucky House Journal* (1984), 247.

10. Jolene Greenwell interview, 1998.

11. "Budget Message to General Assembly," *Kentucky House Journal* (1984), 247.

12. Ibid., 248.

13. *Kentucky Acts* (October 14, 1964), 292.

14. Greenwell interview, 1998.

15. Collins, Executive Journal, vol. 1 (1983), 27–47.

16. *Georgetown News and Times,* December 12, 1985.

17. Potter, ed., "Martha Layne Collins," in *Kentucky Women,* 44–45.

18. Lane, Memorandum describing preparations for the banquet, 2000; Greenwell interview, 1998; Potter, *Kentucky Women,* 44–45.

19. Greenwell interview, 1998; Lane memorandum, 2000.

20. Lane memorandum, 2000.

21. Greenwell interview, 1998.

22. Potter, *Kentucky Women,* 45.

23. Potter, *Kentucky Women,* 45.

24. Greenwell interview, 1998; Lane memorandum, 2000.

25. Lane memorandum, 2000.

26. Greenwell interview, 1998; Stewart interview, 1999.

27. Potter, *Kentucky Woman,* 45; Greenwell interview, 1998.

28. Potter, *Kentucky Woman,* 44–45.

29. *State Journal,* November 15, 1985.

30. Haywood, "State Reaping $1.5 billion from Incentives, Study Finds," *Lexington Herald-Leader,* October 9, 1998.

31. Certificate of Incorporation, 1986, Corporation Division, Kentucky Secretary of State Office, Frankfort.

32. *Lexington Herald-Leader,* October 9, 1998.

33. Collins, Toyota File, KDLA.

34. Mitch M. Connell to Gov. Martha L. Collins, May 8, 1986. The routing slip held notation C. Lanier, Er, Connel, Mitch M. "Negative remarks about the Toyota plant being in Georgetown, Ky" CC, File. Martha Layne Collins, Toyota File, KDLA.

35. Collins, Toyota File, KDLA.

36. Ibid.

37. Ronnie Collins to "Miss" Collins, December 10, 1985, Toyota File, KDLA.

38. *Kentucky Acts* (1986), 69–70.

39. It appears that Barbara Hadley-Smith might have been selective of the letters she took to the governor.

40. Collins, Toyota File, KDLA.

41. *Lexington Herald-Leader,* October 9, 1998.

42. Hamlett, *History of Education in Kentucky,* 195–221.

43. *Kentucky House Journal* (1984), 250–53.

44. Ibid., 252–53; Clark, "Education Reform Act of 1990," in John Kleber, ed., *The Kentucky Encyclopedia,* 287–88.

45. Martha Layne Collins, Speech File, KDLA, May 4, 1984. Governor Collins's speeches tightly fill an archival file box, KDLA.

46. Wilson, Klareveda Musik Folder, 1986, Lane collection.

47. Wilson, Klareveda Musik Folder, 1986. The Collins piano is a Bechstein built in West Berlin. *Lexington Herald-Leader,* September 14, 1993.

48. Wilson, Klareveda Musik Folder, 1986.

49. Ibid.; *Lexington Herald-Leader,* October 11, 1986.

50. *Lexington Herald-Leader,* March 14, 1986.

51. Ibid., October 7, 1988.

52. Ibid., September 14, 1993.

53. Ibid., February 20, 1986.

54. Ibid., February 20, 1986.

55. Ibid., February 14, 1986.

56. Edwards, "Warehouse Is Home for Governors' White Elephants," *Lexington Herald- Leader,* March 3, 1986.

57. Ibid.

58. Brammer, "Legislators Give up Green to Keep the Governor Tan," *Lexington Herald-Leader,* March 10, 1986.

59. Ibid.

60. Ibid.

61. Guffy, "The Queen's New Bed: A Grim but Tan Fairy Tale," *Lexington Herald-Leader,* March 31, 1986.

62. Certificate of Incorporation, Collins Investors, Inc., March 1, 1983, Corporate Division, Secretary of State, Frankfort.

63. Ostensibly the Agricultural Center at Jabez was established as a 4-H center. It has become a popular public meeting place.

64. Chellgren, "Question on Husband Gets Sharp Answers from Governor," *Louisville Courier-Journal,* June 18, 1986.

65. Taylor, "The Governor Expects her last Twelve Months to Build on Achievements of First 3 Years," *Louisville Courier-Journal,* December 12, 1986.

66. *Lexington Herald-Leader,* June 17, 1984; *Louisville Courier-Journal,* Indiana edition, June 17, 1984; *State Journal,* June 17, 1984.

67. Ibid.

68. *Louisville Courier-Journal,* Indiana edition, June 17, 1984.

69. Governor's mansion facsimile transaction sheet, November 11, 1995, from Nancy Cline to Sally Curtis Trophy Shop, Frankfort. Lane File, Versailles.

70. Official Kentucky Election Results, Primary & General Elections (1987), 36, Secretary of State Board of Elections File, Frankfort.

71. *Lexington Herald-Leader,* October 1987.

72. Wilkinson, *You Can't Do That, Governor!*, 28–29, 56.

73. Cross, "Wallace Glenn Wilkinson," in John Kleber, ed., *The Kentucky Encyclopedia*, 956.

74. Wilkinson interview, 1998.

75. Wilkinson, *You Can't Do That, Governor!*, 278–86.

76. Wilkinson interview, 1998.

77. Wilkinson interview, 1998.

78. Loftus, "Bills for Governor's Mansion Total More Than $40,000 under Wilkinson," *Louisville Courier-Journal*, November 27, 1988.

79. Ibid.

80. Wilkinson, *You Can't Do That, Governor!*, 383.

81. Memorandum from Kentucky Military History Museum to Governor's Mansion, regarding transfer of Battleship Silver Service, January 16, 1988.

82. Wilkinson, *You Can't Do That, Governor!*, 379–80.

83. Wilkinson interview, 1998.

84. Ibid.

85. Clark, "Education Reform Act of 1990," in John Kleber, ed., *The Kentucky Encyclopedia*, 287–88.

86. Wilkinson, *You Can't Do That, Governor!*, 270–75.

87. Wilkinson interview, 1998.

88. Ibid.

89. Ibid.

90. Wilkinson, *You Can't Do That, Governor!*, 367–68.

91. Ibid.

92. Ibid., 377.

93. Ibid.

94. Official Kentucky Election Results, Primary & General Elections, (1987), 57–60. Jones received 517,811, and Wallace Wilkinson, gubernatorial candidate, received 304,647; Register of Elections, Secretary of State, Frankfort.

95. Evans, *Documentary Data on the Old Governor's Mansion*, KDLA, Office of Historic Properties, Frankfort, 1974.

96. "Arthur Young Lloyd," in John Kleber, ed., *The Kentucky Encyclopedia*, 564–65.

97. *Lexington Herald-Leader*, November 10, 1991; Official Kentucky Elections Results, Primary & General Election, (1991), 4. Jones received 540,000 votes, and Larry Hopkins received 294,452.

98. Jones interview, 1998.

99. The Wilkinsons had spent $40,000 refurbishing the mansion. Loftus, "Bills for Governor's Mansion Total More Than $40,000 under Wilkinson," *Louisville Courier-Journal*, November 27, 1988.

100. Jones interview, 1998.

101. The last convicts served in the mansion during the Brown administration, 1979–1983.

102. Jones interview, 1998.

103. Ibid.

104. Ibid.

105. Ibid.

106. Ibid.

107. The editor and the three associate editors sat at a table in the old capitol and signed a good portion of the first printing for purchasers.

108. The abandoned warehouse's floors were smeared with a sticky, smelly mass from leaking soft drink and beer cans.

109. Barrett, "Four Governors Grew to Like Controversial Helicopter," *Louisville Courier-Journal*, August 19, 1992.

110. Ibid.

111. Ibid.

112. Jones interview, 1998.

113. *Louisville Courier-Journal*, August 19, 1992.

114. Jones interview, 1998.

115. Jones interview, 1998.

116. Ibid.

15. "Respect It, Revere It, Use It"

1. It was ratified on September 2, 1992. *Kentucky Revised Statues*, Supplementary, 1 (1992), 95, Section 7, 51.

2. Patton interview, 2001.

3. Official Primary and General Election Returns for 1995, November 7, 1995.

4. Ibid., November 2, 1999.

5. Kentucky Constitution, Section 73, *A Citizen's Guide to the Kentucky Constitution*, 184; *Kentucky Revised Statutes*, 1996, 1: 51., supplementary section, 51.

6. Patton interview, 2001.

7. Kentucky Constitution, Sections 82–84. This despite the fact the lieutenant governor served as president of the Senate until April 2, 1992, and the adoption of the succession amendment.

8. Patton interview, 2001.

9. Ibid.

10. *Kentucky Revised Statutes*, November 5, 1995, 1: 51, supplementary section. Sections 70–71 of the Constitution were revised with the adoption of the succession amendment.

11. Biographical sketches of Paul Patton appear in *Who's Who in America*, 1999–2000 ed. (Alabama-Montana ed.), 851; *The Almanac of American Politics*, 2000, 666–67.

12. Harrod, "Biography of Judi Conway Patton," website entry. This is a full listing of Judi Patton's public service background. http://www.state.ky.us/agencies/gov/firstlady/

13. Ibid.

14. Patton interview, 2000.

15. Ibid.

16. Patton interview, 2000; Lyons interview, 2000.

17. Ibid.

18. Lyons interview, 2000.

19. Patton interview, 2001.

20. Lyons interview, 2000.

21. Patton interview, 2001.

22. Harrod, "Biography of Judi Conway Patton," website entry, http://www.state.ky.us/agencies/gov/firstlady/biography.htm

23. Patton interview, 2001.

24. Ibid.

25. Ibid.

26. Ibid.

Bibliography

Kentucky State Documents

Abstract of the Fifteenth United States Census, 1800–1990. Washington, D.C.

Acts of the Kentucky General Assembly, 1792–1990.

Bush, Charlie, ed., *A Citizen's Guide to the Kentucky Constitution*. Frankfort, 1987.

Compilation of Governors' Messages to the General Assembly, Assembled with historical notations, Files, Kentucky Historical Society.

Contract, "Commonwealth of Kentucky with Jeanette Marks, 1956." Unprocessed papers. Kentucky Department for Libraries and Archives, Frankfort, 1956.

Decisions of the Court of Appeals of Kentucky. Kentucky, 1919.

Edward R. Ronald to W.T. McConnell, April 6, 1972. Unprocessed records, KDLA

Executive Journals, Kentucky Governors, 1792–1967. Kentucky Department for Libraries and Archives, 1967–1990.

Governors' Papers Files, 1792–1994. Kentucky Department for Libraries and Archives.

The Griffanhagen Report. Chicago, 1919.

Harrod, Kay, "Biography of Judi Conway Patton," website http://www.state.ky.us/agencies/gov/firstlady/

Hartsteen, Louis, and Henry, Engineers, "Condition of Mansion, Report and Recommendations on the Governor's Mansion, Frankfort, Kentucky," July 20, 1960, in Unprocessed documents, KDLA.

Journal of the Kentucky House of Representatives, 1792–1990.

Journal of the Kentucky Senate, 1792–1990.

Kentucky Auditors' Reports, Kentucky Department for Libraries and Archives.

Kentucky Revised Statutes, supplementary. Kentucky State Auditor Collection (unprocessed), Kentucky Department for Libraries and Archives.

W.T. McConnell to Don Bradshaw, March 13, 1972. Unprocessed records, KDLA.

Minutes of the Sinking Fund Commission, Kentucky Department for Libraries and Archives.

Official Primary and General Election Returns for 1995. November 7, 1995. Office of the Secretary of State, Frankfort.

Party Composition of the Senate of Kentucky, 1920.

Quadrilineal Primary and General Election Returns, Secretary of State Office, Frankfort, 1950–1999.

"Report and Recommendations on the Governor's Mansion, Frankfort, Kentucky," Unprocessed records, KDLA.

Report of the Special Committee on the Removal of the Seat of Government.Collected public documents, Legislative Document 7, KDLA.

Report of the Debates and Proceedings of the Convention for the Revision of Constitution of the State of Kentucky, Frankfort, 1891.

The Reports of the Efficiency Commission. Frankfort, 1924.

United States Department of the Interior National Register Listing, March 11, 1971, Kentucky Heritage Council.

Schacter, Harry. *Kentucky on the March*. Unprocessed records, KDLA.

Bibliography

Interviews

MARGARET LANE, INTERVIEWER

Robert D. Bell, August 27, 1997.
Edward Thompson Breathitt, December 9, 1997.
Nat Britton, July 1, 1997.
John Y. Brown Jr., May 1, 2001.
Julian Morton and Charlann Carroll, February 25, 1998.
Ben Chandler Jr., December 9, 1997.
Mason Combs, October 4, 1996.
Gwenneth Cullen, August 15, 1997.
Kenneth Dotson, December 9, 1997.
Peggy Dungan, Augustr 27, 1997.
Edward Farris, November 6, 1999.
Wendell and Jean Ford, June 6, 2000.
Phyllis George, May 11, 2001.
Jolene Greenwell, February 25, 1998.
Rose Gayle Waterfield Hardy, May 6, 2002.
Elizabeth Lloyd and Brereton Jones, December 10, 1997.
Mary Knight, May 12, 1995.
Mimi Chandler Lewis, November 19, 1997.

Rex Lyons, August 4, 2000.
Robert and Andrew McCreary, July 12, 1993.
Sally Willis Meigs, June 2, July 21, 1998.
Ben C. Moore, October 10, 1996.
Paul and Judi Patton, June 12, 2001.
Barry Peel, January 22, 1998.
Tootie Rabe, May 11, 1998.
Jouett Sheetinger, July 8, 1996.
Robert Smither, December 8, 1997.
Bob Stewart, October 3, 1999.
Billie Sue Whittaker, October 7, 1999.
Wallace and Martha Wilkinson, June 22, 1998.

THOMAS D. CLARK, INTERVIEWER

Martha Layne Collins, June 4, 2001.
Judith Johnson, June 20, 2000.
James W. Martin, October 18, 2000.
Louie B. Nunn, February 20, 2000.

Newspapers and Periodicals

Collier's Magazine, March 30, 1946.
Frankfort Argus of Western America, 1808–1840.
Frankfort Commonwealth, 1864–1867.
Frankfort Kentucky Yeoman, 1840–1882.
The Kentucky Gazette, 1996.
Kentucky Progress Magazine, 1925–1930.
The Kentucky State Employee, 1972.
Louisville Courier-Journal, 1868–1998.

Lexington Herald, 1875–1983.
Lexington Herald-Leader, 1983–1998.
Lexington Kentucky Gazette, 1792–1835.
Lexington Leader, 1888.
Lexington Observer and Reporter, 1832–1847.
Lexington Press Transcript, 1895–1904.
Lexington Weekly Transcript, 1879–1894.
State Journal, 1910–1998.

Clipping Files and Summaries

Combs Papers, Box 96M57, Special Collections, Margaret I. King Library, University of Kentucky, Lexington.
Evans, Helen. Documentary Data on the Old Governor's Mansion. 3 volumes, Division of Historic Properties, Frankfort.
Minutes of a Joint Meeting of the Board of Directors of the Athletics Association and of the Board of Trustees," December 19, 1952, February 7, 1954. Athletic Association files, University Archives, Special Collections, University of Kentucky, Lexington.

Nunn, Louie. Inaugural Program, 1967. Kentucky Department for Libraries and Archives.
Nunn, Louie, and Beula Nunn. Newspaper and miscellaneous documentary files. Special Collections, Margaret I. King Library, University of Kentucky, Lexington.
Nunn, Beula. Scrap Book. Nunn Collection, Special Collections, Margaret I. King Library, University of Kentucky, Lexington.
Wetherby, Lawrence. Newspaper clippings, 1950–1955. 15 volumes, Special Collections, Margaret I. King Library, University of Kentucky, Lexington.

Bibliography

General Works and Articles

Adair, John. Letters of Generals Adair and General Jackson, relative to the Charge of Cowardice made by the latter against Kentucky Troops at New Orleans. Frankfort, 1814.

Adams, Charles Francis. *The Works of John Quincy Adams*. Boston, 1850.

The Almanac of American Politics. 1972–2000.

Baird, Nancy Disher. *Luke Blackburn: Physician, Governor, Reformer*. Lexington, 1979.

Baird, Nancy Disher. "The Yellow Fever Plot." *Civil War Times Illustrated* 13 (November 1974): 66–23.

Bamberg, Robert D., ed., *The Confessions of Jereboam D. Beauchamp*, Philadelphia, 1966.

Barrett, "Four Governors Grew to Like Controversial Helicopter," *Louisville Courier-Journal*, August 19, 1992.

Baylor, Orval. *J.D. Talbott: Champion of Good Government, A Saga of Kentucky Politics from 1900 to 1942*. Louisville, 1942.

Beasley, Paul W. "The Life and Times of Isaac Shelby, 1750–1826." Ph.D. diss., University of Kentucky, 1968.

Beauchamp, Jereboam O. *The Confessions of Jereboam O. Beauchamp, Who was executed at Frankfort, Ky. on the 7th of July 1826, for the Murder of Col. Solomon P. Sharp*. Bloomfield, Kentucky, 1826.

Beers, Howard, ed. Kentucky Designs for Her Future. Lexington, 1944.

Bevins, Ann. "Mrs. Nunn Tells of a First Lady's Life." *Lexington Leader*, June 2, 1968.

Biographical Directory of the United States Congress, 1771–1989. Washington, D.C., 1989.

Biographical Encyclopedia of Kentucky of the Dead and Living Men of the Nineteenth Century. Cincinnati, 1878.

Booe, Martin. "They Came, They Saw, They Ate." *State Journal*, May 6, 1983.

Brammer, Jack. "Good Neighbors." *Lexington Herald-Leader*, April 2, 1985.

———. "Legislators Give up Green to Keep the Governor Tan." *Lexington Herald-Leader*, March 4, 1986.

Breathitt, John. "Commencement of a Journal from Kentucky to the State of Pennsylvania, etc." Frankfort, 1833.

Brookes-Smith, Joan E., ed. *Master Index: Virginia Surveys and Grants, 1774–1791*. Frankfort, 1976.

Brown, John Mason. "An Address on the Occasion of the Century in the Town of Frankfort." Frankfort: Kentucky Historical Society, October 6, 1886.

Burnely, Pattie. "Biographical Sketch of General, Afterwards Governor Charles Scott." *Register of the Kentucky Historical Society* 1 (1901): 30–31.

Butler, Wendell. "What Is Really to Blame for High Illiteracy Rate." *Louisville Courier-Journal*, March 9, 1952.

Chellgren, Mark. "Question on Husband Gets Sharp Answers from Governor." *Louisville Courier-Journal*, June 18, 1986.

Clark, Thomas D. *Clark County, Kentucky*. Winchester, 1995.

———. "Education Reform Act of 1990." In John Kleber, ed., *The Kentucky Encyclopedia*, Lexington, 1992.

———. *The Greening of the South*. Lexington, 1984.

———. *Historic Maps of Kentucky*. Lexington, 1979.

———. *A History of Kentucky*. New York, 1937.

———. *Kentucky: Land of Contrast*. New York, 1968.

———. "The Lexington and Ohio Railroad—A Pioneer Venture," *Register of the Kentucky Historical Society* 31 (1933) 9–28.

———. "Lighting the Soul of Kentucky." *Kentucky Living*, July 1998, 17–23.

———. "The People, William Goebel, and the Kentucky Railroads." *Journal of Southern History* 5 (February 1934): 34–48.

———. "The Slavery Background of Foster's 'My Old Kentucky Home.'" *Filson Club History Quarterly* 10 (1936): 3–17.

———, ed. *Footloose in Jacksonian America*. Frankfort, 1989.

———, ed. *Travels in the Old South*. Vols. 1–3. Oklahoma, 1956.

Clift, G. Glenn. *Governors of Kentucky, 1792–1942*. Cynthiana, 1947.

———. *Remember the Raisin*. Frankfort, 1959.

Coleman, Mrs. Chapman. *Life of John Jordan Crittenden*. Philadelphia, 1871.

Coleman, J. Winston. *A Bibliography of Kentucky History*. Lexington, 1949.

———. *Death at the Courthouse*. Lexington, 1952.

Collins, Richard H. *History of Kentucky*. Vols. 1–2. Covington, 1874.

Columbus, Shanna. "Portrait of the First Lady." *The*

Kentucky State Employee 3 (February 1972): 8.

Connelley, William E., and E. Merton Coulter. *A History of Kentucky.* 2 vols. Chicago, 1922.

Conner, Katherine. *From My Old Kentucky Home to the White House.* Lexington, 1999.

Cramer, Zadock. *Navigator.* Pittsburgh, n.d.

Crawford, Robert Gunn. "A History of the Kentucky Penitentiary, 1865–1937." Ph.D. diss., University of Kentucky, 1955.

Cross, Al. "Wallace Glenn Wilkinson." In John Kleber, ed., *The Kentucky Encyclopedia,* Lexington, 1992.

Cuming, Fortesqué. *Sketches of a Tour to the Western Country, Through the States of Ohio and Kentucky.* Pittsburgh, 1810.

Dawson, Morris. *Historical Narrative of the Civil and Military Services of Major General William Henry Harrison.* Cincinnati, 1826.

Darnell, Emma Jett. *Filling in the Chinks.* Frankfort, 1966.

Dictionary of American Biography. 21 vols. New York, 1944.

Dorman, John Frederick. "Gabriel Slaughter, 1767–1820, Governor of Kentucky 1816–1820." *Filson Club History Quarterly* 40 (1960): 338–56.

Edgar, Walter B. *South Carolina, A History.* Columbia, S.C., 1998.

Edwards, Don. "Frankfort Warehouse Is Home for Governors' White Elephants." *Lexington Herald-Leader,* March 3, 1986.

Ellis, William E. "Ruby Laffoon, 1931–1935." In Lowell Harrison, ed., *Kentucky's Governors, 1792–1985.* Lexington, 1985.

Evans, Helen. *Kentucky's First Ladies in Miniature.* Louisville: Kentucky Federation of Women's Clubs, 1972.

Everman, H.E. *Governor James Garrard.* Paris, Kentucky, 1981.

Faragher, John Mack. *Daniel Boone: The Life and Legend of an American Pioneer.* New York, 1992.

"George Washington Birthday Party." *State Journal,* February 1932.

Gilliam, Will D., Jr. "Robert Letcher, Whig Governor of Kentucky." *Filson Club History Quarterly* 24 (1950): 6–26.

Gipson, Vernon. *Ruby Laffoon, Governor of Kentucky, 1931–1935.* Hartford, Kentucky, 1978.

Grace, Nancy. "State's First Daughter Has Her First House Party." *Louisville Courier-Journal,* June 19, 1948.

Guffey, Roger. "The Queen's New Bed: A Grim but Tan

Fairy Tale." *Lexington Herald-Leader,* March 31, 1986.

Hamlett, Barksdale. *History of Education in Kentucky.* Frankfort, 1914.

Hamilton, Holman. *Zachary Taylor, Soldier in the White House.* Indianapolis, 1951.

Harrell, Kenneth E., ed. *The Public Papers of Governor Edward T. Breathitt, Jr., 1963–1967.* Lexington, 1984.

Harrison, Lowell. "Cassius M. Clay and the True American." *Filson Club History Quarterly* 22 (1948): 30–49.

———. "John Young Brown, Jr." In John Kleber, ed., *The Kentucky Encyclopedia,* Lexington, 1992.

———, ed. *Kentucky's Governors, 1792–1985.* Lexington, 1985.

Harrison, Lowell, and James Klotter. *A New History of Kentucky.* Lexington, 1997.

Hargreaves, Mary M., Robert Seager, and Melba Porter Hay, eds. *The Papers of Henry Clay.* Lexington, vol. 7–10, 1981–1992.

Hughes, Paul. "Honest Bill Is Back Near Olive Hill Now" (feature article about Gov. William Fields), *Louisville Courier-Journal Magazine,* July 1950.

———. "The 'Ripper' Governor Sampson's Wounds Are Healing" (feature article about Gov. Flem Sampson), *Louisville Courier-Journal Magazine,* July 9, 1950.

———. "Life Has Been Good to the Boy Wonder" (feature article about Gov. A.B. Chandler), *Louisville Courier-Journal Magazine,* July 14, 1950.

———. "Head Lines Don't Tell the Story" (feature article about Gov. Keen Johnson), *Louisville Courier-Journal Magazine,* July 23, 1950.

———. "No Room for Rocking Under the Tree" (feature article about Gov. Simeon Willis), *Louisville Courier-Journal Magazine,* July 30, 1950.

Hughes, R.E., F.W. Schaeffer, and E.L. Williams. *That Kentucky Campaign; or the Law, the Ballot, and the People.* Cincinnati, 1900.

Hutcheson, William T., and William E. Rachal, eds. *Papers of James Madison.* Vol. 14. Chicago, 1962.

James, C.E. *A Short History of Franklin County, Kentucky.* Frankfort, 1881.

Jillson, Willard Rouse. *Edwin P. Morrow—Kentuckian.* Louisville, 1921.

———. "Literary Haunts and Personalities of Old Frankfort." *Register* 39 (1941): 79–85.

Johnson, L.F. *Famous Kentucky Tragedies and Trials.* Frankfort, 1916.

―――. *The History of Franklin County, Ky.* Frankfort, 1912.

Jones, W. Landis, ed. *The Public Papers of Governor Wendell H. Ford, 1971–1974.* Lexington, 1978.

Kentucky Historical Society, comp. *Index for Old Kentucky Surveys & Grants.* Frankfort, 1975.

Kentucky's New Capitol, pamphlet, 1912, 1933. Paul Sawyier Library.

Keyes, Clara. "Albert W. Young." In John Kleber, ed., *The Kentucky Encyclopedia,* Lexington, 1992.

Kirwan, Albert D. *John J. Crittenden: The Struggle for Union.* Lexington, 1962.

Kleber, John E., ed. *The Kentucky Encyclopedia.* Lexington, 1992.

―――, ed. *The Public Papers of Governor Lawrence W. Wetherby, 1950–1955.* Lexington, 1983.

Klotter, James C. "Feuds in Appalachia: An Overview." *Filson Club History Quarterly* 56 (April 1982): 290-317.

―――. *William Goebel: The Politics of Wrath.* Lexington, 1977.

―――. "William Sylvester Taylor." In Lowell Harrison, ed., *Kentucky's Governors, 1792–1985,* 110–12. Lexington, 1985

Klotter, James C., ed. *The Public Papers of Governor Simeon Willis, 1943–1947.* Lexington, 1988.

Kramer, Carl E. *Capital on the Kentucky: A Two Hundred Year History.* Frankfort, 1986.

Lawton, Helen. "Kentucky's New First Family." *Louisville Courier-Journal Magazine,* December 14, 1947.

Levasseur, Auguste. *Lafayette in America in 1824–1825, or Journal of a Voyage to the United States.* Philadelphia, 1829.

Levin, H. *Lawyers and Lawmakers of Kentucky.* Chicago, 1897.

Littel, William. *The Statute Laws of Kentucky,with Notes,* 5 vols, 1809–1819, Frankfort.

Loftus, Tom. "Bills for Governor's Mansion Total More Than $40,000 under Wilkinson." *Louisville Courier-Journal,* November 27, 1988.

Malmer, Victoria. "The Brunch Bunch." *State Journal,* May 4, 1983.

―――. "Derby Breakfast Returns to Frankfort with Plenty of Changes, Exotic Foods, Notables." *State Journal,* May 4, 1983.

Marshall, Humphrey. *History of Kentucky.* Frankfort, 1824.

Mastin, Bettye. "Governor's Wife Wins Award for Preservation of Mansion." *Lexington Herald-Leader,* May 25, 1983.

McAfee, Robert B. *History of the Late War in the Western Country.* Lexington, 1816.

McCreary, Maj. James Bennett, C.S.A. "The Journal of My Soldier Life." In *Filson Club History Quarterly* 33 (1935): 97–211.

The Mansion Saved. Frankfort, 1982.

Mitlebeiler, Emmett, "The Great Absconsion." *Filson Club History Quarterly* 27 (1953): 335–52.

Morton, Jennie Chinn. "Sketches of the Kentucky Governors." *Register of the Kentucky Historical Society.* Vols. 1–17, 1904–1919.

Nall, James O. *The Tobacco Night Riders of Kentucky and Tennessee, 1904–1909.* Louisville, 1939.

Noe, Kenneth. *Perryville: The Grand Havoc of Battle.* Lexington, 2001.

Nunn, Beula. Recorded speech to O'Tucks. Hamilton, Ohio, 1971.

Ogden, Frederic D., ed. *The Public Papers of Governor Keen Johnson, 1939–1943.* Lexington, 1982.

Owen, Tom. "John White Stevenson, 1812–1886." In Lowell Harrison, ed., *Kentucky's Governors, 1792–1985.* Lexington, 1985, 814.

Pardue, Anne. "Repairs Start Next Month on Governor's Mansion." *Louisville Courier-Journal,* December 17, 1960.

Peers, Benjamin O. *Report on the Status of Education in Kentucky to the Legislature and Governor in 1830 and 1831.* Frankfort, 1832.

Porter, Marion. "Weep No More Kentucky." In *Collier's Magazine,* March 30, 1946, 14–15, 57, 58, 59.

Potter, Eugenia, ed. *Kentucky Women: Two Centuries of Indomitable Spirit and Vision.* Big Tree Press, 1997.

Pratt, Julius, *Expansionists of 1812.* New York, 1925, 1949.

Ragan, Allan E. "John Jordan Crittenden, 1787–1863." *Filson Club History Quarterly* 18 (1944): 3–28.

Ramage, Thomas. "Augustus O. Stanley: Early Twentieth Century Kentucky Democrat." Ph.D diss., University of Kentucky, 1968.

Ransdell, Gail. "Christmas in State." *Louisville Courier-Journal Sunday Magazine,* December 20, 1963, 9–10.

―――. "The Governor's Mansion, New Look, New Purpose." *Louisville Courier-Journal,* July 13, 1969.

Remini, Robert V. *Henry Clay, Statesman for the Union.* New York, 1991.

Robinson, George W., ed. *Bert Combs the Politician: An Oral History.* Lexington, 1991.

―――, ed. *The Public Papers of Governor Bert T. Combs,*

1959–1963. Lexington, 1979.

Runyon, Randolph Paul. *Delia Webster and the Underground Railroad*. Lexington, 1996.

Ryan, Ed. "No Place Like Home," *Louisville Courier-Journal*, 1983.

Schacter, Harry W. *Kentucky on the March*. New York, 1949.

Schwartz, Christopher, "Growing Up with the Governor," *The Kentucky Gazette*, January 18, 1996.

Seale, William, et. al. *The Kentucky Governor's Mansion: A Restoration*. Louisville, 1984.

Sexton, Robert F. "Kentucky Politics and Society, 1919–1932." Ph.D. diss., University of Washington, 1970.

Sexton, Robert F., ed. *The Public Papers of Governor Louie B. Nunn, 1967–1971*. Lexington, 1975.

Shannon, J.B., and Ruth McGowan. *Presidential Politics in Kentucky, 1828–1928*. Lexington, 1948.

Simms, William Gilmore. *Beauchamp; or The Kentucky Tragedy*. Chicago, 1899.

A Sketch of the Life of General Thomas Metcalfe. n.d., n.p.

Sneed, William C. *A Report of the History and Mode of Management of the Kentucky Penitentiary from Its Origin in 1798 to March 1860*. Frankfort, 1860.

Sprague, Stuart. "William Owsley." In Lowell Harrison, ed., *Kentucky's Governors, 1792–1985*. Lexington, 1985.

Sprague, Stuart. "Julian Morton Carroll, 1974–1979." In Lowell Harrison, ed., *Kentucky's Governors, 1792–1985*. Lexington, 1985.

Steers, Edward, Jr. *Blood on the Moon: The Assassination of Abraham Lincoln*. Lexington, 2001.

Stickles, Arndt M. *The Critical Court Struggle in Kentucky, 1819–1829*. Bloomington, Indiana, 1929.

———. *Simon Bolivar Buckner: Borderline Knight*. Chapel Hill, 1940.

Stowe, Harriet Beecher. *Uncle Tom's Cabin, or Life Among the Lowly*. Boston, 1879, 1892.

Syvertsen, Thomas H. "Earle Chester Clements and the Democratic Party, 1920–50." Ph.D. diss., University of Kentucky, 1962.

Talbert, Charles Gano. *Benjamin Logan: Kentucky Frontiersman*. Lexington, 1962.

Tapp, Hambleton, and James C. Klotter. *Kentucky: Decades of Discord*. Frankfort, 1977.

Taylor, Livingston. "Bedlam." *Louisville Courier-Journal*, August 20, 1979.

———. "Four Ex-Governors Recall Threats While in Office." *Louisville Courier-Journal*, January 4, 1976.

———. "The Governor Expects Her Last Twelve Months to Build on Achievements of First 3 Years." *Louisville Courier-Journal*, December 12, 1986.

Tevis, Julia A. *Sixty Years in a Schoolroom*. Cincinnati, 1875.

Trabue, Alice Elizabeth. *Corner in Celebrities*, Frankfort, 1922.

Trout, Allan M. *Greetings from Old Kentucky*. Louisville, 1947.

———. "Tears and Chuckles Cascade into Wetherby's Daily Mail." *Louisville Courier-Journal*, October 10, 1952.

———. "Walking Munn Wilson, 83, Political Vagabond Dies," *Louisville Courier-Journal*, March 4, 1956.

Vance, Kyle. "Combs Says Prison T-Bones Only for Official Guests." *Louisville Courier-Journal*, September 18, 1963.

van Curon, S.E. "Agree of Not, I Say What I Think." *Kentucky Labor News*, August 2, 1962.

Wahlgren, Sue. "Browns, Carter, Bush Join 500 at Mansion." *Lexington Herald-Leader*, May 7, 1983.

Warren, Robert Penn. *World Enough and Time*. New York, 1950.

Who's Who in America, 1999–2000. Alabama-Montana edition.

Wilkinson, Wallace. *You Can't Do That, Governor!* Lexington, 1995.

Woodson, Uray. *The First New Dealer*. Louisville, 1939.

Wright, John D. *Transylvania: Tutor to the West*. Lexington, 1975.

Yater, George. "Bloody Monday." In John Kleber, ed., *Encyclopedia of Louisville*, Lexington, 2000.

Index

Numbers in italics indicate photographs.

Index

Index